PERGAMON INTERNA**TION**AL
of Science, Technology, Eng
The 1000-volume original paperba
industrial training and the
Publisher: Robert N

D0208911

The Ecological Transition:
Cultural Anthropology and Human Adaptation

Publisher's Notice to Educators

THE PERGAMON TEXTBOOK
INSPECTION COPY SERVICE

An inspection copy of any book published in the Pergamon International Library will gladly be sent without obligation for consideration for course adoption or recommendation. Copies may be retained for a period of 60 days from receipt and returned if not suitable. When a particular title is adopted or recommended for adoption for class use and the recommendation results in a sale of 12 or more copies, the inspection copy may be retained with our compliments. If after examination the lecturer decides that the book is not suitable for adoption but would like to retain it for his personal library, then our Educators' Discount of 10% is allowed on the invoiced price. The Publishers will be pleased to receive suggestions for revised editions and new titles to be published in this important International Library.

PERGAMON FRONTIERS OF ANTHROPOLOGY SERIES

EDITOR: Cyril S. Belshaw, *University of British Columbia, Canada*

The Ecological Transition:
Cultural Anthropology and Human Adaptation

JOHN W. BENNETT
Washington University at St. Louis

PERGAMON PRESS INC.

New York · Toronto · Oxford · Sydney · Frankfurt

U. K.	Pergamon Press Ltd., Headington Hill Hall, Oxford OX3 0BW, England
U. S. A.	Pergamon Press Inc., Maxwell House, Fairview Park, Elmsford, New York 10523, U.S.A.
CANADA	Pergamon of Canada Ltd., 207 Queen's Quay West, Toronto 1, Canada
AUSTRALIA	Pergamon Press (Aust.) Pty. Ltd., 19a Boundary Street, Rushcutters Bay, N.S.W. 2011, Australia
FRANCE	Pergamon Press SARL, 24 rue des Ecoles, 75240 Paris, Cedex 05, France
WEST GERMANY	Pergamon Press GmbH, 6242, Kronberg-Taunus Pferelstrasse 1, Frankfurt-am-Main, West Germany

Library of Congress Cataloging in Publication Data

Bennett, John William
  The ecological transition.

  Includes index.
    1. Human ecology. 2. Ethnology. 3. Social evolution. I. Title.
GF41.B46   301.31   74-30430
ISBN 0-08-017867-7
ISBN 0-08-017868-5 pbk.

Printed in Great Britain by A. Wheaton & Co., Exeter

Contents

The Author

John W. Bennett (Ph.D., University of Chicago) is Professor of Anthropology at Washington University, St. Louis, where he has served two terms as Chairman of the Department. He is a Senior Fellow of the Center for the Biology of Natural Systems and is a member of the Asian Studies Center of Washington University. Dr. Bennett's primary professional interests lie in three fields: the ecological and social aspects of agrarian development, the structure and changes of communal and sectarian societies, and the nature and change of modern Japanese society. This book represents his observations of ecological theory in anthropology, growing out of his work in all three fields.

Dr. Bennett's career in cultural anthropology has centered on the study of modern rather than tribal societies, and his theoretical views reflect this orientation. He has done field research in the United States, Canada, Japan, Israel, Taiwan, and India. He is a member of many professional societies in the fields of anthropology, sociology, economics, ecology, and Asian studies and has been President of the American Ethnological Society and the Society for Applied Anthropology, among others. He is a member of the Editorial Boards of the *Annual Review of Anthropology, Reviews in Anthropology, and the Encyclopedia Americana.* He has been a consultant to the Rockefeller Foundation, the National Institute of Mental Health, the National Science Foundation, the Canada Council, The U.S. Department of State, and has served on committees and research review panels in these and other organizations. He has published many articles in professional journals, is the senior author of two books on Japan, and the author of two books on his agrarian ecology research in Canada—one of them a treatise on the communal economics and social life of the Hutterian Brethren. He has taught at Ohio State University, the University of Puerto Rico, Waseda University, Japan, and the University of Oregon.

Acknowledgments

The first version of this book was a longish chapter, written in part at the urging of Morris Freilich, who had in mind a symposium of essays on problems of application and meaning in anthropology. The volume did not materialize due to no fault of Dr. Freilich's; believing the issues dealt with in my contribution deserved a fuller treatment, I continued to work on it, with this book—really a series of essays—as the result. I am indebted to Dr. Freilich for the urging and, later, for carefully reading early drafts.

The arguments and frame of reference have been influenced by the author's research in North American agricultural ecology—in particular, four studies: first, my continuing work in a 5,000-square mile region of Western Canada (Bennett, 1969); second, a continuing study of ecology and socioeconomic change in Hutterian Brethren colonies in Canada and the United States (Bennett, 1967C); third, a project on farm management strategies and social organization as they pertain to environmental pollution in the Illinois corn belt, sponsored by the Center for the Biology of Natural Systems at Washington University; fourth, a collation of data on environmental pollution in Japan, and the public and governmental response to it (Bennett & Levine, 1975). All of these research projects have dealt with the way human wants and social institutions structure the actions of men in coping with physical and socioeconomic environments.

Early versions received critical readings by Roy Rappaport and Andrew Vayda. Useful advice on key sections was obtained from Thayer Scudder, David Sills, John Eaton, Emilio Moran, Carl J. Bajema, E. L. Jones, Edward Montgomery, Edward Robbins, Mary Bufwack, and Jose Arrom. Needless to say, the responsibility for all statements and interpretations rests with the author.

The enormous quantity of available materials in the field of human ecology has required a careful strategy of citation. I have tried to exemplify key fields and styles of analysis and theory, but I have avoided any attempt at exhaustive documentation. Most references pertain to the early-1970's period when the project was conceived, but a partial up-dating was done in early 1974. I have no doubt that by the time this book is in print nearly every major citation will have been superseded.

Terry Yokota was my principal editorial assistant, and she, Susan Higgins, and Arline Wyner typed the manuscript. Diagrams were drafted by William Sawyer. Robert Franklin did the index.

I also thank all the publishers and authors for use of materials from the various publications cited (acknowledgments for figures are quoted in captions) and in particular the following:

Doubleday & Company, Inc. Garden City, for quotation from *Evolution and Human Behavior*, by Alexander Alland, Natural History Press, 1967.

Columbia University Press, New York, for material from *The Human Imperative*, by Alexander Alland, 1972.

University of Chicago Press, Chicago, for material from *The Human Condition*, by Hannah Arendt, 1968.

The American Anthropological Association for material from "Ecologic Relationships of Ethnic Groups in Swat, Northern Pakistan," by Frederik Barth, *American Anthropologist*, 1956, 58: 1079–1089.

Smithsonian Institution Press, Washington, D.C. for material from *Environmental Archeology and Cultural Systems in Hamilton Inlet, Labrador*, by William W. Fitzhugh. Smithsonian Contributions to Anthropology, Number 16, 1972.

The American Association for the Advancement of Science for material from "Feedbacks in Economic and Demographic Transition," by Harald Frederiksen, *Science*, 1969, 166: 837–847. Copyright 1969 by The American Association for the Advancement of Science.

The Bookhaven National Laboratory, Biology Department, Upton, N.Y. for material from "Stability in Ecological and Social Systems," in *Diversity and Stability in Ecological Systems*, by Crawford S. Holling. Report of Symposium held May 26–28, 1969.

National Museums of Canada, Ottawa, for material from "!Kung Bushman Subsistence: An Input-Output Analysis," by Richard B. Lee, in *Contributions to Anthropology: Ecological Essays*, Bulletin 230, Anthropological Series, No. 86, 1969, and Natural History Press,

New York for same material from A. Vayda (ed.), *Environment and Cultural Behavior*, 1969.

Duckworth, Ltd., London, for material from "Work Effort, Group Structure and Land-Use in Contemporary Hunter-Gatherers," by Richard B. Lee, in *Man, Settlement and Urbanism*, Peter J. Ucko, Ruth Tringham and G. W. Dimbleby, eds., 1972b.

MIT Press, Cambridge, Mass., for material from "Population Growth and the Beginnings of Sedentary Life among the !Kung Bushman," by Richard B. Lee, in Brian Spooner (ed.), *Population Growth*, 1972c.

Addison-Wesley Publishing Company, Reading, Mass., for material from *The Ecological Approach in Cultural Study*, by Robert McC. Netting, McCaleb Module, 1972.

John Wiley & Sons, Inc., New York, for material from *Environment, Power, and Society* by Howard T. Odum, 1971.

Ecology for material from "The Use and Abuse of Vegetational Concepts and Terms," by A. G. Tansley, *Ecology*, 16: 284–307.

Oceania for material from "Phases of the Process of War and Peace among the Marings of New Guinea," by Andrew P. Vayda, *Oceania*, 1971, 42: 1–24.

University of Washington Press, Seattle, for material from *The Mound Builders: Agricultural Practices, Environment, and Society in the Central Highlands of New Guinea* by Eric Waddell. Copyright 1972 by University of Washington Press.

McGraw Hill Book Company, New York for material from "Man and Culture" by Leslie A. White, in L. A. White, *The Evolution of Culture*, 1959b.

The New American Library, New York, for material from *The Aims of Education*, by Alfred North Whitehead, 1951.

Cambridge University Press, New York, for material from *Religion and the Transformation of Society: A Study in Social Change in Africa*, by Monica Wilson, 1971.

W. B. Saunders Co., Philadelphia for material from *Fundamentals of Ecology* by Eugene Odum, 1953, 1971.

It must be acknowledged that equality, which brings great benefits into the world, nevertheless suggests to men . . . some very dangerous propensities. It tends to isolate them from each other, to concentrate every man's attention upon himself; and it lays the soul open to an inordinate love of material gratification.

Alexis de Tocqueville, *Democracy in America*

Science is a river with two sources, the practical source and the theoretical source. The practical source is the desire to direct our actions to achieve predetermined ends . . . . The theoretical source is the desire to understand. I most emphatically state that I do not consider one source as in any sense nobler than the other, or intrinsically more interesting. I cannot see why it is nobler to strive to understand than to busy oneself with the right ordering of one's actions. Both have their bad sides; there are evil ends directing actions, and there are ignoble curiosities of the understanding.

Alfred North Whitehead

CHAPTER 1

Prologue: Images of Man and Nature

Anthropologists and their associates in geography have been studying relationships between humans and the physical environment for a very long time, and some of the history of that effort will be discussed later in the book. For most of this period, the topic was handled mainly in terms of description and classification: what kinds of cultures inhabited what kinds of environment? When explanation was desired, it took the form of attempts to measure the amount of influence a particular environment may have had in shaping particular cultural patterns. This task was approached from either an environmental bias, in which case the presence of considerable influence from Nature was assumed; or from a cultural bias, in which case environmental influence was assumed to be minimal, with humans in full control of Nature.

Only recently has the problem of relationships between humans and the physical environment broadened to include quite different questions. For one, the concept of environment has been extended beyond the physical into the social. That is, "other people" are seen as a milieu which influences human behavior and with which humans must cope; hence, the social environment must be given a weight equal to the physical in our ecological theory. For another, the question of causation or influence has become more complex, emphasizing the concept of *system*, in which both behavioral (or cultural) and environmental (either/or physical and social) factors are seen to be in a reciprocal process of interaction.

The use of the word *ecology* is recent in environmental studies in anthropology. This word, now almost done to death by its attachment to the environmental movement of our own time, originated in biology,

1

where it continues to connote the work done by researchers on plants and animals living in natural milieux. In anthropology, cultural-environmental research was not considered ecological until Julian Steward used the term "cultural ecology" in the late 1940s. However, there are many ecologies in anthropology, if we use the word as a general referent for studies of organism-environmental interrelations.

As we hope to show later, the "ecological" problems associated with the human species are very large in number and, at this juncture, probably impossible of synthesis in a general theory or subdiscipline. There is some question as to whether the term "ecology" should be used at all to describe these many interests and topics inside of anthropology and in other disciplines as well. The social sciences have a special problem here: since they include social phenomena as part of the environment with which humans cope, their central problem becomes one of distinguishing the relative influences or functions of social and physical environmental factors in human behavior and institutions. This problem, in one sense the central topic of anthropologist Julian Steward's cultural ecology, is not even close to some general solution, if indeed there is one.

At this time, two tasks need to be performed in this field of study. First, the work of cultural anthropologists on how social factors are implicated in human-Nature interrelationships or systems need to be reviewed, and its accomplishments assessed. This, in essence, is what I attempt to do in this book, although from a special point of view. The second task consists of a critique of some converging approaches in cultural anthropology, including cultural ecology, economic anthropology, social exchange, and behavioral adaptation. While this second task is not my major objective, it obtrudes, and many of the concepts and approaches discussed and proposed in the book are heading in this direction. I have no name for my approach: I call it simply "human adaptation," or "adaptive dynamics." Similarly, for want of a rubric for the many approaches concerned with culture-environment questions, I continue to use the term "ecology"— and, in the social context, "cultural ecology."

NATURE INTO CULTURE

The central thesis of this book is that the best case for the existence of something called cultural ecology can be made on the grounds of public policy. Research data that has significance for shaping environmental policies (mostly physical, but always including some social) can be obtained from something less than a comprehensive human ecological science or theory, which does not yet exist in any event. In formulating a policy-relevant cultural ecology, one also faces up to the need to bring anthropology as a discipline into somewhat closer contact with the historical present. This is necessary because of the "ecological transition"—the progressive incorporation of Nature into human frames of purpose and action—which is rapidly eliminating the cases of distinctive, isolated tribal adaptations to natural phenomena that have been a specialty of the anthropologists. The historical trend is now toward much larger systems, in which the behavior of tribal people or peasants toward natural resources is determined as much or more by social forces beyond their control as it is by internal concepts and needs. In its bare essence, our definition of cultural ecology is therefore a study of how and why humans use Nature, how they incorporate Nature into Society, and what they do to themselves, Nature, and Society in the process.[1]

This type of approach requires standards of measurement or effect. The fundamental criterion that I advocate for the assessment of impact by humans on Nature is *sustained yield*;* the basic value for man is *survival at a reasonable level of security*. These are very general criteria; over and beyond them are a host of other values, preferences, and means-end schema that characteristically conflict, and between which the citizen will be required to make choices, compromises, and trade-offs.

The term "adaptation," used frequently in this book, refers to my focus on strategic behavior as the key to a policy-oriented cultural ecology. The rational or purposive manipulation of the social and natural environments constitutes the human approach to Nature: the characteristics of this style of adaptation must, it seems to me, become the heart of any approach to human ecology that concerns itself with the question of what people want and how they go about getting it, and what effects this has on themselves and Nature. Adaptive behavior is viewed as multidimensional: what may be adaptive for one individual is maladaptive for another or for the group; what may be adaptive for humans may not be so for Nature. The effort to distinguish between these dimensions of adaptation is one of the tasks of an anthropological ecology concerned with policy.

My fundamental assumption is that the history of human-environment

*The term "sustained yield" refers to the state of the natural resource in use, not the product acquired by converting it. A term such as "constant supply" would be closer to the meaning of "sustained yield" in the resource context. A program of sustained yield in resource management can produce an increased yield of product, but not necessarily; it depends on the resource.

relationships, especially since the appearance of Homo sapiens,* has featured a growing absorption of the physical environment into the cognitively defined world of human events and actions—indeed, to the point where the argument seriously can be advanced that the concept "human ecology" is a myth, and that there is (or shortly will be) only, and simply, Human Society: people and their wants, and the means of satisfying them. Actually this idea has been clinging to the periphery of anthropological thought for many years. An example can be found in the old distinction between material and nonmaterial culture, which contained a proposal to the effect that water flowing over a dam becomes an item of material culture, since man is using the water as he uses any tool. Hence, humans are constantly engaged in seizing natural phenomena, converting them into cultural objects, and reinterpreting them with cultural ideas.

If Culture comes to embrace more and more of Nature, we are left with a dilemma: on the one hand, it becomes more difficult to work with theories that assume a permanent distinction between Nature and Culture—Humanity and Environment—Man-made and Natural environments. On the other hand, if Culture absorbs Nature, then what general theory of ecology shall we choose? The situation is responsible for considerable intellectual confusion: the merging of Nature and Culture might lead scientists to assume that a general ecology based on biological (plant-animal) ecology includes both, but I believe that the long-term trend will run in the other direction—toward a theory that assimilates Humans and Nature into a common social frame of reference.

The dualistic theories that opposed Humans to Nature led, in Western thought, to two contrasting conceptions: first, that Humanity, or Culture, is determined by Nature; and second, that as Humans developed natural resources, they became increasingly "independent" of Nature. These ideas were always subjected to criticism, but in the late 19th century, the second tended to predominate, since the majority of scholars found it

---

*The term "Homo sapiens" is used to refer to ourselves. Currently accepted hominid taxonomy makes a distinction between *Homo sapiens sapiens* (ourselves) and the other, no longer visible varieties, e.g., *Homo sapiens neanderthalensis*. The argument is more than a matter of taxonomy, if one takes the view that *Homo sapiens sapiens* is of quite recent origin, and the beginning of the exponential upswing in energy transformation dates from his emergence. Older *Homo sapiens* varieties would then have possessed behavioral incapacities or built-in controls over the behavior that has had such a severe environmental impact. However, the entire issue is still largely a matter of speculation by human paleontologists and I shall use "Homo sapiens" in this book, leaving the question of especially exploitative recent varieties for others to worry about.

difficult to conceive of a truly finite or limited environment: Kenneth Boulding's "space ship Earth" (1962).[2] Therefore, they went along with the Nature-exploiters of the age of industrialization who built a high-energy culture on the assumption that the benefits to Everyman, and especially to the profit-takers, were always greater than any possible costs. Anthropology, like other fields of study emerging in the 19th century, has been preoccupied chiefly with what people do for themselves, and not with what they do to Nature or to themselves in the process (Anderson, 1969; Shea and Emmons, 1972). Consequently, anthropologists, like other scholars, have spent most of their time refuting environmental determinism, rather than seriously examining the consequences of an anthropocentric ecological posture and theory.

The scientific fields concerned with human-environmental relations are in a transitional period marked by a struggle to evolve an adequate understanding of this long-neglected problem. The effort must proceed at both empirical and theoretical levels. At the time of writing, the most significant research undertakings are to be found in the natural sciences, where attention is given mainly to the polluting effects of human intervention and unrestricted transformation of resources. The social sciences are just beginning to show comparable interest. It is typical that while, among these social fields, anthropology has displayed more consistent concern through the years for human-environmental research, the majority of anthropological studies have been related to purely-intradisciplinary problems and have made little contribution to questions of policy.

THE ECOLOGICAL TRANSITION AND ITS IMAGERY

The title of this book, "the ecological transition," is to some extent a misnomer insofar as its substance is dealt with directly in only one chapter—Chapter 5. However, the idea pervades the book. By the "ecological transition" I mean, first, the development of an anthropocentric orientation toward the natural world that emerged in the Western Renaissance but has since characterized every civilization and nation. Although the substantive problems of this book concern a single scientific discipline—cultural anthropology—I try to visualize these problems and the problems of the discipline as artifacts of this historical transition.

In technological terms, the transition concerns the tendency to seek ever-larger quantities of energy in order to satisfy the demands of human existence, comfort, and wealth. The events associated with this transition are the topics of archeology insofar as one is concerned with the emergence of food-production, irrigation, fire and the wheel, improved tool-kits, and the technology of advanced architecture. The transition is the topic of historical study when we are concerned with armies, empires, and nations; it becomes the subject matter of economics when we consider industrialization and commerce. Each of these many events made its contribution to the transition, and to the increasing impact on Nature, but the process did not become overwhelming until the Industrial Revolution.

Sociologically, the transition is expressed by the increasing size of the social organ and the networks of communication associated with, and also causing, the ecological and technological changes. These social developments are always accompanied by another: the emergence of hierarchies of status that differentiate humans into those who have power and those who do not, or between those who have prestige (or standing) and those who lack it. While the rudiments of these differentiae are found in all human societies, however simple, they become a focus for chronic social unrest mainly in advanced stages of the transition.

Ecologically speaking, the transition is expressed in the growing incorporation of Nature into Culture and by the breakdown of local self-sufficiency—the ability of the local group to satisfy its needs with existing resources in a particular geographical range. Increasingly, as the transition proceeded, the local groups cultivated wants that could be satisfied only by resources at far distance, enlarging the "home range" indefinitely and subjecting Nature to intensified exploitation in order to acquire wealth for the implementation and enhancement of status. Thus, the transition is marked by the expansion of ecological impact resulting from the accumulation of substances and objects for social purposes unrelated to biological survival.

Philosophically, the transition concerns the replacement of certain images of humanity by others. Hannah Arendt, in her book *The Human Condition*, was concerned with some of these changes, and a modified version of her exposition can serve our purposes. The important concept is her use of the old term *Homo faber*, that personification of Homo sapiens that emphasizes the makings of things—"man the maker and fabricator, whose job it is to do violence to nature in order to build a permanent home for himself" (p. 304). The outstanding characteristics of *Homo faber* are listed by Arendt as follows:

> And, indeed, among the outstanding characteristics of the modern age from its beginning to our own time we find the typical attitudes of *homo faber*: his instrumental-

ization of the world, his confidence in tools and in the productivity of the maker of artificial objects; his trust in the all-comprehensive range of the means-end category, his conviction that every issue can be solved and every human motivation reduced to the principle of utility; his sovereignty, which regards everything given as material and thinks of the whole of nature as of "an immense fabric from which we can cut out whatever we want to resew it however we like"; his equation of intelligence with ingenuity, that is, his contempt for all thought which cannot be considered to be "the first step ... for the fabrication of artificial objects, particularly of tools to make tools, and to vary their fabrication indefinitely"; finally, his matter-of-course identification of fabrication with action. (pp. 305–306)

Of course, *Homo faber* has always been with us, since the term simply refers to an aspect of the human personality. This aspect can take on greater or lesser importance in particular times and cultures. We tend to view Oriental civilizations as keeping *Homo faber* in control and emphasizing another of Ms. Arendt's types—the *vita contemplativa*—as a more suitable cultural goal. The crucial development in the West, and in industrial societies generally, was not, according to Arendt, merely the dominance of *Homo faber* over other modes of the human personality, but rather the loss of standards of meaning concerning the nature of the objects produced. This loss came about as a result of a growing emphasis on instrumental rationality—on the process of fabrication itself. This shift to an emphasis on process over content detached men from the restraining ethics and philosophical meanings of civilization and defined the "what" in terms of objectives of power and mastery over Nature and over other men. Whereas the *vita activa*—the doing and performing (the political)—component was guided by the *vita contemplativa* in preindustrial culture (*vide* the image of the *samurai* writing poetry to define the meaning of his life), in modern culture the *vita activa* has lost these guiding restraints and is defined by the *Homo faber* instrumentalities. Hence, the increasing impact on Nature in the ecological transition.

Ms. Arendt's rather intricate and perhaps fanciful philosophical reconstruction is an oversimplification (or at least my rendition is such); but it is a useful one nonetheless, and it establishes the right mood. Anthropology, like other products of modern civilization, has undergone comparable changes in its basic imagery and conceptual foundations. One stream of thought in anthropology has tended to portray humanity as multipotential—both constructive and destructive, moral and amoral, traditional and innovative—which is of course nothing less than the truth, although just why the balance may tip one way or the other is another question. If the multipotentiality is viewed without choice or bias, then the resulting attitude is one of ethical neutrality—and certainly this has characterized anthropology (*via* cultural relativity) and the other social sciences for a long time.

But anthropology was never really content with this neutral stance; like other social sciences, it contained covert preferences or images. One, of course, was the concept of progress. This position, which implied that human proclivities worked more to the good than the bad whatever the context, saw the human adventure as a struggle upward toward the material conquest of Nature. As we shall point out later in the book, the emphasis in prehistory was on accomplishment and progress, not cultural decline or destructive impact on Nature as the price of advancement. Allied to the progress image was the liberal humanist version of humanity, which saw humans as essentially good, rational, and inclined to take the moderate course in the long run. The realization of human potential, whatever it may be, was seen as a generally desirable outcome of history.

These optimistic images have been considerably shaken by current events. The ethologists lean toward a pessimistic interpretation of the human potential, seeing man as a kind of rogue species with a bias toward the destructive that needs constant restraint. Radical cultural anthropologists are inclined to see progress in negative terms as equivalent to human exploitation by the powerful—the course of human history in its sociological context of status has been a very high price to pay for material conquest. The ecologists (though not as yet to any great extent in anthropology) see man as a despoiler of Nature and stupid to boot, since he ignores dangerous feedbacks that endanger his own survival. Obviously, these shifts in human imagery are leading to a reexamination of the theoretical basis of anthropology, and this book has been conceived in part as a modest contribution to that end. It is my conviction that only an injection of philosophy—a return to the consideration of value in things and in human actions—will do the job.

Many aspects of these images in anthropology can be seen in the history of culture concepts. The concept of the superorganic, which represented a kind of apex of the growing willingness of anthropologists to entertain notions of progress or at least humanity as the triumphant species—the climax of Nature's efforts to produce a conscious organism (or, in religious terms, divinity)—shaped anthropological theory for half a century and still influences our thinking about human qualities. The basic imagery was one of emergent evolution. The superorganic was conceived to be *above* the organic, which in turn was above the inorganic; and, since the superorganic was associated with just one species—Homo sapiens—it was a measure of his dominance and uniqueness.

Alfred Kroeber's 1917 article was the basic formulation of the superorganic idea, and Leslie White added his own special trimmings much later (1959B) to take account of the theoretical and empirical developments in anthropology since Kroeber's original statement. Both of these statements emphasize human uniqueness and dominance over the natural world: for example from White:

> The purpose and function of culture are to make life secure and enduring for the human species.... Tools are employed to exploit the resources of nature... the purpose of culture is to serve the needs of man.... In short, culture gives man the illusion of importance, omnipotence, and omniscience. These inner spiritual—or intraorganismal—needs of man are of course as real as those for food, shelter, and defense; in fact, they might be felt even more keenly. And these needs must be served if man is to succeed in the struggle of life. (pp. 8–9)

Of course White did not say that these functions were the only ones served by culture, and he acknowledges "illusions," but he does not face the problem of the human impact on the natural world, and the question of whether dominance over Nature and those "needs" for psychological omnipotence are in fact inevitable, uncontrollable, or universally desirable.

These themes have dominated the textbooks and theoretical works (including some of the writer's) for a long time. A contemporary version can be found in Yehudi Cohen's three-volume text reader (1968–70), which covers the entire field of anthropology and is devoted to the concept of adaptation as an organizing principle. Cohen makes adaptation synonymous with man's success in mastering Nature; for example, from his "Introduction" to Vol. II:

> ...focussing on the role of adaptation in man's attempts to construct his patterns of social relations and to free himself from the limitations of his habitats... when we say that a population is adapting we mean that it is altering its relationship to its habitat in order to make that habitat a more fit place to live.... The adaptation of man is accomplished principally by cultural means, through the harnessing of new sources of energy for productive ends.... (pp. 1–4)

Of course these statements are true, but they are only one-half of the truth, the other being the fact that men exploit and abuse environment for these same ends, and thereby create future problems for themselves and the environment.

Because I am working between theories and empirical reality, a number of paradoxical arguments appear in the book. Perhaps the most important

of these is the contrast between my concern for the excessive anthropocentrism of the anthropological theory tradition and my emphasis
on the fact that culture becomes the only important environment for
humanity, since to an increasing extent we take the natural environment
into our own cognitive and technological world. The contradiction is more
apparent than real. The incorporation of Nature may be unfortunate, but
it is an increasing—an exponential[3]—tendency. Therefore it has to be
inserted into our scientific and philosophical approaches to the problem. I
insist that the means for the control of human destructive actions must
be found in ourselves—in culture and behavior. To theorize that culture
controls man, or that culture controls environment, is not to solve
problems, only to disguise deterministic pessimism in scientific jargon. In
the last analysis, the human impact on the Earth will not be lessened, or
substantially modified toward sustained yield, until our fundamental
institutions are changed.

Another apparent contradiction concerns the emphasis in the essay on
the output function of human behavior; that is on *Homo faber*, man the
producer, or *over*producer, or what might seem to be a preference for
acquisitiveness, or "maximization" as general models for human behavior
and, on the other hand, my neglect of the obvious qualifications that such
arguments must have: namely, that people do not always seek to acquire
things, or maximize gain, but stop short for various reasons related to
built-in checks from cultural values and social relations, not to mention
genuine concern for the state of resources. Having offered data on how
and why certain farmers in North America choose to play it safe and live
more modestly rather than go for broke (Bennett, 1969, pp. 124–132,
214–217), I see no need to present any further qualifications for soundness
on this issue. Of course men do not always maximize according to
idealized economic extremes, and of course there are periods of relative
stability in Man-Nature relations, as well as cases of valuational checks
on greed and exploitation. But this book is preoccupied with the negative
cases: the consequences of the frequent failure to restrain such behavior,
and the evident fact that the thrust of human history, despite fluctuations
and long periods of stability, has been toward continually expanding—
exponential—use of resources and consumption, with relatively little
concern for the long-range consequences.[4] Hence I am chiefly (though not
exclusively) concerned with the output function: the transforming, producing, and consuming phases of human behavior. I think it is important
to do this also because anthropology has tended to dwell one-sidedly on
the cases of balance and symmetry between culture and resources. It is

time the other side of the coin were given some emphasis because here is where the policy problems are to be found.

While I express some criticisms of evolutionary conceptions of cultural development, I have to some extent relied on such interpretations in developing an approach to the problem of why Homo sapiens has exploited the physical environment to an increasing extent. It is perfectly evident that human impact on the environment increases with economic and technological scale—although there also are some well-known cases of massive impact under preindustrial and even tribal conditions. More specifically, my underlying view is in agreement with the position of Marshall Sahlins and others whose work suggests that small primary communities, relatively isolated from other societies, are likely to exhibit relatively stable, sustained-yield systems of resource utilization, sanctioned by the complex forms of reciprocity characteristic of social life in primary groups, and consuming all or most of the food they gather or produce with their own hands. Resources are, on the whole, owned or controlled collectively.

As population increased, and an expanding technology meant that more substance could be extracted from the environment, or dangers could be avoided more easily, a conceptual dichotomy developed: *Man* and *Nature.* This was an assymetrical, oppositional conception on the whole, with Nature the passive element and Man the active. The conception took various aesthetic forms—in some cases, such as that of Japan, Nature was seen as a source of beauty and truth; in other cases, as in the 19th-century United States, Nature was simply booty for the taking. However, the aesthetic components were really irrelevant to the process of exploitation, because once the passive-active oppositional mode developed, humans were free to exploit and use Nature however much they might love, admire, hate, or be indifferent toward it. There has been much confusion over this point: the presence of positive aesthetic attitudes toward Nature in some cultures has misled analysts into thinking that these cultures must therefore be conservationist.

The course of increasing environmental impact is taken when men begin to amass wealth, to differentially value product, to save and invest it, and to compete with each other for material and social prestige. Resources become economic goods and move toward private ownership. Exploitation of wants becomes a major strategy for those who seek power and wealth when industrialization causes society to become stratified into competitive socioeconomic classes. Corporate groups move into control of resources, and their needs set the pace of exploitation.

Extensive promises are eventually made to the "masses" to provide them with a higher standard of living, thus providing a materialistic version of equality. At the time of writing, there is no end in sight to this process, although spreading pollution and increasing materials shortages suggest the possibility of a slowdown.

But this evolutionary approach must not be allowed to obscure the fact that the behavioral propensities of Homo sapiens seem to be the same at all levels of development. The cases of simple food-gathering or agricultural peoples who remained for fairly long periods at a level of morally- or socially-sanctioned sustained yield are only pauses in the overall historical tendency toward exponential increases in environmental use and impact. This fact must always be remembered lest we commit the "ethnological fallacy" of locating desirable remedies for our own environmental ills in the specialized systems of tribal societies.

In technical language, this implies that cultural-ecological theories based on stability and predictability in human affairs are only one side of the coin and, likewise, that anthropological theories that idealize the "making"—Homo faber—aspects of human behavior and culture neglect the destructive side of these same processes. In the first case, I am critical of attempts to define cultural ecology in terms of the functioning of biological ecosystems, with particular emphasis on equilibrium—although I recognize that human ecology can exhibit such properties in special circumstances. In the second case, I am critical of the conventional theory of culture that has assumed that culture, as our prime adaptive mechanism, is designed exclusively to "serve man's needs" without considering the damage it does to humans and other species, and without regard for the responsibility humans have for the Earth and its creatures.

In some discussions of the contemporary ecological situation, there is a disposition to attribute environmental abuse to particular cultural values. For example, North American culture has been seen as the apotheosis of the Nature-destroyer[5]—the supreme example of a culture that has viewed Nature as a simple resource, as something to be immediately converted into "benefits." It is true that the processes described earlier have been especially acute among North Americans due to the open stratification system of their society: its tendency to reward effort with money and material goods and to allocate status by the demonstration of "success" or mastery over resources—patterns created by the recent frontier experience as well as by specific ideological (Lockean) elements. But, in more generalized terms, these North American patterns are versions of those common to developing or industrialized societies everywhere.

Despite a cultural heritage of Nature conservationism, Japan may be even more "American" than North America at the present moment; due to industrial growth, she is involved in a phase of mass culture and consumerism similar to that in the United States in the 1920s. At the highest level of cross-cultural generalization, we are dealing with the process of development; at a lower level, with the distinctive institutions of industrialism and/or capitalism; and at still more specific levels, with psychological elements characteristic of particular cultural styles.

If the methods of control emerging in primary group social milieux offer no realistic hope for exerting effective control over the present institutional processes, then there is a need to find other means. One theory of control rests on the assumption that a democratic society that encourages action by its citizens against unjust or dangerous phenomena will get the ecological situation under control through these means—that is, by public protest, publicity campaigns to stop the polluters and exploiters, and by the legislative or administrative measures these may stimulate. Undoubtedly, this process has its effects; it is already in motion and on some fronts the results are encouraging.

However, the pessimism that seems to emerge at several points in this book is based on the fact that the contemporary system of environmental use is so intimately tied to the entire institutional framework of modern society, and is buttressed by so many promises of well-being and gratification to the public, that long-range, effective controls probably cannot be expected from purely democratic means. I anticipate that some form of coercion other than the benevolent half-measures passed by representative bodies will be required. Such coercion could feed the drift toward an authoritarian bureaucracy, and of course *this* must be resisted. The future looks complex, to say the least: the presence of egalitarian and humanistic democrats in the ranks of the ecology movement generates contradictions, since many of their objectives probably can be met only with nondemocratic means.

I believe that an example of the contradictions resulting from these currents of thought is visible in Garrett Hardin's arguments concerning what he calls the "tragedy of the commons" (1968; 1972). Hardin is concerned about the recurrent social process involving the appropriation of resources by individuals for their own benefit, or, in general terms overloading the common resources of air, water, and soil. His original example was that of individual stockmen gradually adding animals to the herd grazing on a common pasture until the pasture is overgrazed and everyone suffers. Hardin proposes that benevolent forms of coercion must be developed to prevent this type of abuse. His emphasis on benevolence derives from his own humanistic preferences, as well as from his ecologistic imagery of natural species living in harmony. But humans are not always amenable to benevolence—force is often required to effect the change or to insure survival. Our attitude toward this may depend in the last analysis not on ethics, but on how urgent we perceive the problems to be.

However, it is probably a mistake to generalize about the problem of control. The contemporary environmental problem has many facets, some of them more amenable to change than others. The pollution issue, which is usually in the forefront, is probably on its way to some kind of partial solution. I believe that within a decade our air and water will be substantially cleaner, though by no means pristine. And, if the costs are passed on to the consumer, he may have to live more simply and forego his satisfactions.

But there will be many spheres where reforms will be exceedingly difficult because of the political entanglements of human wants and the benefits—political and monetary—to be derived from satisfying them. If incentives cannot be found to control population growth, the quality of life will change greatly and the landscape will be (already is) irrevocably altered to make many human uses of it impossible. And then there are the slow, hard-to-prove accumulations of damaging substances that can generate wasting diseases and injure the germ plasm. Natural resources will continue to diminish in supply, and the substitutes will be hard to find or turn out to be more dangerous than the original. The ecological problem is not unitary or simple; it is imbedded in all activities of human society as it has evolved up to now. The exponential increases that have become so alarming in recent decades are not new; they build on what has happened in the past: the accelerating consequences of humans trying to meet their needs and wants.

In a more Olympian mood, it is possible to say that an old era in world history is drawing to a close and a new one is beginning. The "old" represents that period of conquest of the Earth by the species Homo sapiens, a task that had to be done given his nature, and was accomplished without serious thought about the consequences to the Earth or to his fellow species. All the vicissitudes of human history up to now may be viewed as episodes on this journey. It is possible that in two or three generations these complicated, inspiring, and sordid events will no longer intrigue us because our attention will be riveted on something quite different: the refinement of social strategies so as to keep men off each other's backs and off the Earth's as well. We may look back on the past million years as one prolonged episode of juvenile enthusiasm and ambition, and we may wonder how man could have been so careless of his surroundings, so heedless of future dangers, so filthy in his ecological habits.

There are important research tasks for anthropology in this situation. The discipline's long historical perspective provides opportunities for research on sequences of culture-environment relations in the past that may illumine the present. The revived interest in the animal wellsprings of human behavior may help in outlining those proclivities of Homo sapiens that lead him to thoughtless and destructive habits. The cultural ecology of agrarian societies—a growing specialization in anthropology—needs only a twist or two toward relevant issues to turn it into a useful critique of economic development in the emerging countries. The coming changes in consumption patterns will require explorations of styles and standards, of new cultural interests and activities to serve as alternatives. The changes that must come in order to control polluting consequences of agriculture require detailed studies of how farming economy is tied up with competition, social prestige, and urbanized styles of life. Much work needs to be done on population.

These are important challenges, and anthropology will have to make a considerable effort to meet them. The profession is not particularly well-equipped to shift its intrascientific, descriptive, often precious and exotic interests toward research with clear policy implications—and yet something of this kind has to be done if the field is to survive as something more than an enthusiastic band of museum curators and liberal arts teachers, reciting the lessons of the past. Actually the traditional interests and activities of anthropology need not cease; it is simply that more work needs to be done on the contemporary world and its problems. The ecological crisis of our age—and I believe that it is a kind of crisis—is a mirror for our society, and it is a mirror for the anthropological discipline as well.

NOTES

[1]For an appeal to ecologists in the discipline of biology to turn toward more cogent and contemporary issues, see F. Fraser Darling, 1970, where he cites "the ecologist's apparent inability to make constructive proposals in the face of specific and urgent problems" (p. 7). For a survey of the spreading and conjunctive effects of environmental damage, see Goldman, 1970. All the social sciences have tended to neglect policy issues for intradisciplinary concerns.

[2]See Chisholm, 1913, for a statement of the problem created by the doctrine of man's increasing "independence" of Nature. He argued that Man's increasing use of natural resources was actually creating a growing *de*pendence as these resources become essential for supplying wants, which in turn become culturally defined as essential to survival or happiness. The pollution and environmental spoilage issue was perceived even earlier, in *Man and Nature: Or, Physical Geography as Modified by Human Action*, a book published in 1864 by the geographer G. P. Marsh. (For an account of Marsh's work, and that of other pioneers in the field of concern for the human impact on Nature, see Thomas (ed)., 1956 ("Introductory")).

[3]The exponential curve is shaped more or less like a reversed L; that is, the function—like the amount of energy made available by tools—begins with modest magnitudes and increases slowly (the bottom bar of the L), then, in a relatively short time, newly invented tools release large amounts of new energy, shown by the steeply rising vertical of the L. A number of graphable components of human history—but especially technology, energy, and the use of natural resources—follow these exponential curves ("exponential" refers to the fact that any increment of the curve is multiplied by itself in each similar unit of time—resulting in a very steep rise). (See Figs. 2A and 2B for examples, adapted from the originals in the September 1971 issue of *Scientific American*, devoted to a study of energy.) A curve that rises more or less exponentially and then levels off is called a sigmoid curve, and such curves are commonly found for certain episodes of technological history, when particular devices reach a peak of technical refinement (see Starr and Rudman, 1973).

[4]The preoccupation with stability and limited time spans has given rise in cultural ecology to a series of propositions, such as the following by Richard Beardsley (in his *Introduction* to a symposium, reprinted in Wagner and Mikesell, 1962, p. 395):

> However, the dynamics producing the various community types strongly suggest that although social organization may propel the culture in a certain direction, it can do so only within the limits set by the subsistence resources at its disposal. This is equivalent to saying that a certain population threshold is a prerequisite to the maintenance of certain socio-political structures, and that to cross this threshold a certain level of food production is essential.

There is considerable truth in this statement in the sense that it describes what in the long historical haul are momentary pauses, efficient causes, or necessary conditions of particular segments of change. However, every one of these "thresholds" is flexible, and every term in the equations is modifiable. Societies may strive to change their level of food production in order to move to a new level, either by intensifying farming, by conquering new farmers, or by starving part of their own population. This tendency to ignore the manifold possibilities and inherent dynamism of historical human ecology is an ethnological proclivity dating from the evolutionary preconceptions of the 18th and 19th centuries. It is being countered by the "new archeologists" who are studying the relationships of technology, resources, and macroinstitutions such as the state in prehistoric cultures.

[5]See, for example, the following: Huth, 1957; Dasmann, 1966; Glacken, 1966; Marx, 1970.

CHAPTER 2

Culture, Ecology, and Social Policy

Anthropology as a discipline has focused on peoples outside of the historical mainstream for so long that it is hard to establish a dialogue with the contemporary world and its issues. There are few links between anthropological knowledge and the critical ecological problems of the age. Such things as municipal power structures, automobiles and photochemical smog, the use of chemical fertilizers in order to "maximize" crop yields, benefit-cost computations, tax incentives vs. penalties for controlling environmental abuse, and many other things at the heart of the contemporary ecological situation are mainly outside the professional comprehension of anthropologists at this time. Perhaps anthropology as a field is not especially well-equipped to handle such matters, and perhaps its chief contributions to the environmental problem will lie in general theory and in intensive studies of human-environmental relations in special economic contexts, especially agricultural. However, even if the contribution should be a specialized one, anthropologists will need to revise their methods and their choices of research sites—they have been overly concerned with isolation and the notion that human-environmental relationships are studied more readily in "pure" contexts, free of the contaminating influences of high-energy technology. There is a curious parallel here to the plant-animal ecologists, many of whom still study "natural" ecosystems while ignoring the fact that human interventions have altered every environment on earth—indeed, that humans have been the major ecological force in Nature.[1]

As the tribal and peasant peoples of the world become part of new nations, they develop self-consciousness—"intentionality"—about their

17

own identity and culture, and they are no longer willing research subjects. Many anthropologists, unable to pursue their traditional activities, have had to turn to the contemporary world and its pattern of institutional development characteristic of industrial-urban-national entities. This has produced the term "complex society," the study of which is presently very much the thing among the younger practitioners in the field, although a few senior citizens (like the writer) have tried their hand more than once. It hardly need be pointed out that the semantics of the phrase imply that anthropologists see these societies as "more complex" than the societies they have familiarly dealt with for generations, although the precise meaning of "complexity" is by no means clear. In any case, along with this new interest goes an attempt to preserve anthropology as a distinct discipline, differing from sociology, economics, and other fields that emerged on the basis of the study of industrial national societies. Whether this can be done also is not clear at this time. Prolonged experience in research on complex societies by anthropologists will be required in order to determine how, or if, the battery of concepts and theories derived from the study of autonomous small communities can be applied to the larger entities.

SOCIETY AS ENVIRONMENT

At the heart of any attempt to deal with human ecology from the standpoint of social policy lies the question of whether society itself becomes an "environment" comparable to the natural environment. The equation is obvious in the contemporary ecological movement, where despoliation of the "human environment" becomes as critical an issue as pollution of the physical environment and resource exhaustion. But the issue has theoretical ramifications as well, largely because of the cognitive ability of the human mind to assimilate the properties of Nature into the domain of Culture. The companion mental process is the tendency to see other people as part of the environment with which people cope.

The issue is implicit in the conventional anthropological theory of social behavior, though the implications are not always recognized. For example, Alland (1972, p. 21) states that "man's major behavioral adaptation is culture," and that these cultural adaptations permit human groups to cope with varying environments more efficiently and speedily than genetic adaptation. This formulation adheres to what I have considered to be the "conservative" Culture-Environment dualism. But Alland notes in the next paragraph that "Man is born with a capacity to learn culture, not with culture" (p. 21); if this is the case, then immersion in a cultural milieu is necessary for the learning, and Culture thus becomes the Environment *sine qua non* for Man. With other species, an interplay of relatively specific genetic codes and physical-environmental factors produces behavior; with humans, the interplay is between some very generalized genetic factors, an important sociocultural milieu, and the physical world. Historically, as we noted earlier, this cultural milieu has become ever more important as *the* environment for humanity, and has correspondingly assimilated more and more of the physical environment.

Human-centeredness in anthropological thought is one of the causes of the emphasis on Culture as a distinctive human creation, which characterized anthropology from the late 19th century through the 1950s. As discussed in Chapter 1, Culture was visualized as a distinct level of reality, the "superorganic," thus putting humans, or at least human behavior, on a plane above the other species, the "organic." The difficulties for anthropology created by this philosophical position are well known: research on the behavioral continuities between humans and other animals was discouraged, and purely abstract or descriptive concepts such as culture were reified, treated as explanatory concepts, and anthropomorphized as having "forces" and "creating needs." The strong favorable emphasis on the *Homo faber* side of human behavior had its role to play in the tendency to ignore the state of Nature and the problem of human responsibility for the condition of Earth and its life. In other words, the philosophical substructure of traditional anthropology is part of the problem with which we are concerned in this book.

While I shall discuss the issues, I cannot really answer the questions of whether humanity or culture is best viewed as a component of a vast earthly ecology, whether it is uniquely outside of this frame, or whether it is one end of a scientific dualism. These are philosophical or even religious questions at root, and their scientific significance tends to be obscured by the complex and ambiguous rhetoric. My position in this book is relatively simple: by taking a stand on the social relevance of human ecology, I can say that people do exist in an environment that they use, but also must not abuse, and that part of this environment consists of other people. If this view is accepted, then the question of whether or not human ecology is to be understood as part of natural ecology becomes an empirical matter. When our analyses lead us in this direction, then we may accept its implications. We may also construct models of the social process that contain many features reminiscent of natural ecosystems, but we can, if we choose, remain agnostic on the question of whether this parallelism makes it necessary to view social systems *as* ecosystems.

SYSTEMS

This language echoes discussions in theoretical sociology and social anthropology on the nature of social systems. This discussion has been characterized by the development of competing definitions of systems in a search for the most generally applicable models, a rhetoric influenced by the strong tradition of systematic theory in sociology. However, whether a single model applicable to all social systems can be devised is not a question I care to deal with. The existing models developed by sociologists, with some anthropological collaboration have been described in a book by Walter Buckley (1967), which also advocates a particular one, based on "general systems" theory and methodology, as the most suitable and generally applicable. This model contains many features of the approaches developed in this book. However, *all* of the systems models described and criticized by Buckley contain useful elements for cultural ecology. The "process" or "adaptive" mode that he describes as most nearly approximating his own "general systems" approach is equally close to mine, since it is "loose" rather than strict, emphasizes changing events over fixed structure, and the constant human potential for the emergence of creative or innovative arrangements not determined by existing systemic processes. It is possible that "adaptational dynamics" as defined in this book (Chapters 8, 9) are a combination of Buckley's "general systems" and "adaptive-processes" models.

Model-building is a tricky operation, but perhaps its value for anthropology lies in its clarification of the limitations of the almost exclusive focus on tribal culture. Buckley contrasts his "general systems" and "adaptive-process" models with two others: the "mechanical" and the "organic." The "mechanical" involves the classic "equilibrium" approach derived from Pareto, which emphasizes the fixity of social components and the tendency to return to the original state of the system when moderate changes in their relationships occur. The social whole is compared to a machine and the social process to mechanical principles. The "organic" model is the origin of functionalism in both sociology and social anthropology, based on analogies to the cooperating (or in some versions, competing) organisms in a biological system. Like the mechanical model, however, the functionalist approach has emphasized order and equilibrium, or at least homeostasis (regular fluctuations, with maintenance of a constant average state of the system), over dynamic change and conflict. For many theorists, there is really no significant difference between the two approaches. The point is that for anthropology the isolated tribal communities that formed the largest body of professional data did conform rather well to aspects of both the mechanical and organic models, and this led to the tendency to view the relationships to Nature in terms of balance and stability.

It is not surprising, therefore, that with this conceptual and empirical heritage anthropologists have shown a disposition to experiment with concepts related to systems theory. All versions of systems theory are concerned with interdependence, regular processes, and predictability of outcomes, although different versions emphasize these more so than others. Ecosystem theory in biology places considerable emphasis on the stability and regularity aspects of systems phenomena. However, general systems theory and its offspring, systems analysis, are more open on this point and models of systems exist that acknowledge the greater dynamism and change of social systems as opposed to the mechanical and organic. The early phase of systems applications in anthropology emphasized ecosystem, but later applications have turned toward general systems theory in its several variants—energetics, communication, decision-making, games theory, and others.

The issue, of course, is not that stability and predictability are absent from human affairs, or from humanity-Nature relationships, but rather that their opposites, instability and innovative change, conferring low levels of predictability, are equally characteristic. The argument has familiar dimensions: it is similar to the standard critique of social-science functionalism: that the emphasis in functionalist theory on mechanical-organic systems models results in a neglect of the dynamic qualities of social life.[2]

Another critical element in systems approaches is the extent to which teleology is attributed to the system as a whole or purposes assigned to the human actors within it. There is nothing in general systems theory *per se* that requires the element of purpose; on the contrary, systems theory in essence is nothing more than a method for studying complex situations so that the largest possible number of interdependent factors can be included in the analysis. Typically, there are no assumptions about causes, directions of movement, or particular outcomes. This point is emphasized because human systems, in contrast to "natural" systems, frequently possess teleology and have conscious ideologies of causation. The question that should underlie the study of human systems is when and under what circumstances these teleological and causational elements characterize human systems and how important it may be to include them in the analysis.

The concept of system acquires special meaning when we consider the historic trend of absorption of Nature by Culture. I refer particularly to what I call *socionatural systems*: the increasingly complex cases of resources exploitation and economic handling that have endless ramifications in human institutions and the natural world. Some of these are discussed later: the sardine fisheries of the South American coast; automobile exhaust, photochemical smog and the economics of the automobile industry; the yellow fever epidemic of 18th-century Philadelphia; the Irish potato famine of the 19th century and its effects on politics, population, and agriculture. These are all examples of how human use of natural resources produced environmental and social dislocations on a very large scale and how economic and prestige investments prevented easy solutions. In all cases, the physical environmental components became inextricably fused with the institutional. Research on socionatural systems of this type must unravel the very many feedbacks before restraint (if that is what is required) can be exercised.

However, this book is not a treatise on systems theory and systems analysis. This has been done by others (for example, for sociology see Buckley 1967). Moreover, to work through all of the data produced by cultural ecologists in order to fit them to some sort of systems model would require many more pages and would be a task of questionable utility, since only part of this work has been done with systems models in mind—at least directly. The studies done under the aegis of Julian Steward's version of cultural ecology have a simulacrum of systems concepts insofar as reciprocal influence is sometimes acknowledged among the components, although the pure Stewardian model seemed (one cannot be sure) to emphasize linear causation from the technoeconomic "core" toward social forms. But most modern cultural ecologists have combined Stewardian ideas with Clifford Geertz' ecosystemicism (Geertz, 1963) and thus have been more respectful of interdependency. In any case, the systems model (if not the more specific concept of ecosystem) does, in general terms and in the opinion of this writer, make an important contribution to the classical cultural ecology approach, and one that should be utilized more often.

SOCIETY AS ENVIRONMENT (continued)

To return to the main topic: when we view human behavior and culture (broadly defined here as a body of past precedents for present behavior) as part of the milieu in which humans function, our concerns are practical, not philosophical. If culture is an environment for people because their own actions create problems and must be coped with, as people cope with weather, then the frame of reference includes human objectives, needs and wants, the ways people seek to fulfill or control these, the social strata in which these are configurated, and the environmental consequences of this process. Richard Adams (1970), an anthropologist interested in "complex societies" who has shown concern over the way culture concepts tend to direct attention away from social issues, has attempted to reconstruct concepts of political power along ecological lines—power, for him, is largely the attempt by humans to control their environments, which include the social as well as the natural.

As a matter of fact, the two views on the Culture-Nature problem we have been discussing really lead in quite different directions from the standpoint of concepts of social policy. If we assumed that sociocultural phenomena—generalized human behavior—are part of Nature and of natural ecology, then we assimilate humanity into the natural world and we tend to look for broad generalizations about human behavior as guided or channeled by forces and processes operating outside the sphere of conscious awareness or human will and purpose. "Men know not what they do"; that is, their actions are seen as component parts of larger configurations of natural events or as expressions of inner tendencies—a kind of revival of instinct theory. We also run the risk of slipping into the deterministic equations of the superorganicist approach to culture, only now we have moved down off the superorganic plane on to the organic. For certain theoretical purposes, this position can be defended, and knowledge may come of research guided by it. However, as a frame of reference it is also potentially misleading, since it tends to neglect the very relevant matters of human purposes and the relationships of ends and means.

If, on the other hand, we emphasize the second view of the problem and focus on the fact that people treat Nature much as they treat each other, we head straight toward an examination of human motives, needs, and desires—and the techniques for dealing with these, as they emerge between humans, and between Culture and Nature. It is this latter approach that leads us toward a policy-oriented cultural ecology, and toward adaptive behavior as a central topic and data source.

This position has an important procedural implication: it means that for the time being more or less separate versions of human ecology will continue to exist. Of course there must be philosophical and theoretical efforts to explore the possibilities of a grand general science of human ecology. But this is a long way off. We know little, and the very real problems of humanity's engagement with Nature force us to act. We shall continue to cultivate specialized branches—like the "cultural ecology" discussed in this book—but, at the same time, strive for more cross-disciplinary fertilization. The existing disciplinary specializations probably are not identical to the needed and desirable specializations: experimentation and new combinations are badly needed and will emerge in due course.

CULTURE AND ECOLOGY

As noted, this book deals with only one variety of the anthropological interest in Man-Environment relations[3]: *cultural* ecology. The term is relatively recent, deriving from the work of Julian Steward, who first used the term in 1937 (Steward, 1937) but whose empirical research in the 1950s established the groundwork. However, the long-range antecedents of cultural ecology consist of the results of several generations of ethnological work that Mary Douglas (1970) has called a "phenomenology" of the use of Nature by tribal man. These materials have not been subjected to a detailed analysis and synthesis, although there have been some oblique attempts.[4] The findings constituted the basis of the possibilistic theory of Man-Environment relations particularly associated with Franz Boas and his students (man uses what he wants in Nature, and this use, not Nature, modifies the direction of his culture). "Cultural ecology" goes further than this basically descriptive interest in the human use of particular resources, since it aims at theoretical explanations of feedback processes between culture, technology, and Nature, especially in agrarian settings. However, it should be noted that the key element of possibilism—the concept on voluntaristic *choice* of resources—was assumed but not explored by Boasian anthropologists. This is the basic ingredient of the adaptive approach sketched in this book.

Another familiar component of the "possibilistic" frame of reference in anthropological views of Culture and Nature is the notion that resources—environment—constitute both a facilitating and a limiting frame for human action. This book dwells on the first of these and neglects the second. Here again the choice is deliberate: by emphasizing the consequences of opportunity and expanding use of resources for the accomplishment of human ends (output), I am not implying that environment does not constitute a set of constraints as well. Of course it does and, paradoxically, if the present rate of use and spoilage continues unchecked, the ultimate state of man-made or man-despoiled Nature will feed back into the system and thus eventually limit opportunity and accomplishment (e.g., as in the dire predictions of Meadows et al., 1972). But that is another story, to be told at some future date. If we can exert some choice now, some control over the contemporary situation, perhaps we can avoid having to tell it. Again I resort to a long-range historical argument—an argument based on the familiar exponential curve of tool efficiency and energy release in the history of technology: the historical tendency has been toward discovery of new uses for new resources, despite fluctuation and exception, and it is that—and its consequences— which I emphasize in this book.

There are some important implications for anthropological method here. If one neglects human choice and need in favor of an abstract superorganicist conception of human relations with the environment, interest is displaced toward an evolutionary frame of reference. Culture, or human behavior generalized, is likely to be seen in a deterministic light: for example, the introduction of agriculture is considered to exert a strong push in the direction of sedentary life and nucleated settlement, wherever it occurs and on whatever cultural base; or, agricultural development, or "intensification," always results from increasing population density. While evolutionary generalizing has scientific value, the problem is to relate it clearly to the studies of small communities at particular times that constitute the largest part of the data of cultural anthropology and cultural ecology. The conventional approach is simply to cite the grand evolutionary generalization and then show how one's community may agree or disagree with the generalization. This procedure seems unsatisfactory, since it involves the comparison of what are essentially different kinds of data: broad temporal trends that average many detailed fluctuations, to specific information on one of these microcultural fluctuations. One way to introduce more coherence into the comparison of generalized processes with specific behavioral situations is to focus on action: when people want something and utilize particular means to get it, what consequences do these actions have for the social and natural environments over varying periods of time?

RELEVANCE AND POLICY

We define as socially relevant that cultural-ecological research that has implications for policies of human survival and environmental integrity—or, more specifically, survival at reasonable levels of security, implemented by a policy of sustained-yield utilization of natural resources. By "relevant" we mean any research that bears on these issues in any way—this includes research demonstrating that people are deprived of survival necessities, or that others live too well; it may include data on those who exert unreasonable demands on the physical environment and those who may underutilize resources.

Cultural anthropology has always produced research with some degree of social relevance for the simple reason that such research has concerned the needs and problems of a particular class of humanity: tribal and peasant peoples.[5] In this sense, all anthropological research also might be considered to have greater social relevance, or policy significance, than ecological studies of plant succession of host-predator relationships among animals. But even here it is necessary to qualify: since we tend to absorb Nature, such seemingly exotic topics can become crucial at some future date, as has already happened in the case of host-predator relationships among insects in our search for a "clean" substitute for chemical pesticides.

On the whole, however, ecological research by cultural anthropologists has had little relevance for human and environmental problems in the national industrial societies, the reasons for which can be listed: (1) Anthropologists have been concerned primarily with societies in the distant past, or in remote locations, where impact on the environment often, or usually, has been minimal. (2) Many if not most existing studies have treated the societies as isolates (whether they are or not) out of contact with larger institutional systems. Hence, in such cases, the study of the role of powerful forces external to these communities in molding their use and abuse of environment has not been considered. (3) The majority of cultural-ecological studies of living societies have been concerned with culture rather than ecology: subsistence systems are described, but the major emphasis is on their contribution to an explanation of sociocultural forms. (4) Few communities have been studied over sufficient periods of time to enable cultural anthropologists to determine the pattern of growth and change in resource use; hence there is a tendency to conceive of ecological relations as relatively stable and enduring.

A cultural ecology concerned with sustained yield and processes of resource utilization will need to explore problems of *power*. Humans take from Nature what they desire, and exert control over Nature *and* over society in the process. This means that political power and social stratification can be placed in an ecological frame of reference; ultimately, cultural ecology must investigate the question of how power is related to Nature *via* human actions.[6] (Concern for the power question need not be confined to studies of living peoples; on the contrary, archeological studies of developments such as Bronze Age irrigation and its relationships to stratification, statehood, and militarism are of growing importance for cultural ecology.)

A commitment to policy orientation in scientific endeavor of any kind requires an important qualification: while one can commit a scientific investigation to some relevant social objective, the conduct of the research itself must be guided by methodological rigor, a respect for factual data, and other factors indigenous to science. If social and ideological concerns are permitted to become criteria for scientific adequacy and payoff, the basis of scientific knowledge is undermined and the validity of findings becomes suspect.

Moreover, the scientific pursuit of truthful information is not always subject to "guidance" if the objectives are theoretical. That is, many abstract theoretical findings have at some later date formed the basis of important practical applications. An understanding of atmospheric and water pollution cannot be gained simply by a resolution to study them. Such understanding requires the help of theoretical knowledge of chemical and biochemical processes acquired in laboratory work. A certain freedom to carry on such work, free of pressing demands for topical relevance, must be granted to all sciences.

The situation may, of course, be different—or at least more complicated—for the sciences of man, where both data and methods are themselves implicated in the ongoing behavioral stream under study. That is, it is often difficult to know just what is "basic" or "theoretical" in these fields, since the frame of reference is human culture and its changing historical meanings and social interests. One answer to this is that since values form the core of human cognitive processes, they must also become the core of scientific research. However, it is one thing to recognize the pervasiveness of values and their relationship to meaning and significance and quite another to handle them as tools in scientific investigation. Therefore, one must be cautious in using topicality as a criterion of relevance.

As it may now be clear, I do not believe that there is a real issue with respect to values and scientific work. The formula that has proven inviting and yet so disturbing to the present generation—"science should be guided by values"—is an overly narrow construction of the issues. At least with respect to ecology, much could be accomplished by simply doing research on the environmental consequences of human activities and institutions (this can, of course, be guided by some value placed on environment or survival). Such research also would be guided by a certain element of objective skepticism: an understanding that people are not always good, that their means and ends need questioning. Values enter the picture most cogently once the consequences are known, since they must be judged. This judgment is a public matter, and contains debate and controversy that the scientist will or will not participate in as a matter of personal preference. The scientist always has to be cautious about getting into a position where he is required to determine policy, but he can (and should) provide information that will help make choices among available policies. A socially relevant science, then, is in my definition a policy-aware science. It is not, usually, an "applied" science, since in the applied, or "employed", context of service to large organizations one is not usually free to investigate consequences.

The contemporary dialogue on environmental problems often centers on the Malthusian question: will human population outrun the resources necessary for its survival?—are the increasing pressures on the environment traceable to the need to support a growing population at higher levels of living? Surely population pressure is not the only cause of environmental deterioration, since both increasing wants and technological innovation for its own sake play a large role in the process. But the Malthusian argument is not one that the anthropologist can dismiss, with his lengthy time perspective, because even its critics recognize that population cannot increase indefinitely. In the long run it will exert pressure on the finite resources of Earth, and every environmentalist is a neo-Malthusian in this sense.

The neo-Malthusian considers the exponential growth tendency to be evidence that things are out of control, and that built-in controls—or what the systems modelers call "negative feedback loops"[7]—arise out of human rationality and adaptability to get things under control before the catastrophe. This locates the check on the Malthusian or the exponential processes generally in a faith in man's psychological capacities. Since the two world-systems models mentioned in note 7 (the MIT *Limits to Growth* and the Sussex University *Models of Doom*) come to opposite conclusions—in the first, eventual disaster due to population increase and resources exhaustion and abuse; the other, a more gradual decline with reform and recovery—it would seem that computers and systems models cannot forecast the future. In the last analysis, the computer spews forth the exact amount of optimism or pessimism put into it.

But, more succinctly, the arguments associated with the Malthusian and environmental question, and discussed in this book, are as follows: (1) An emphasis on adaptive, means-end oriented behavior is essential for an ecological approach because it tells us how human ingenuity in utilizing natural substances and society for satisfying wants changes the world. (2) This same emphasis can, if construed optimistically, be used as an explanation of how men will check their impulses if they begin to abuse Nature and Society, forestalling catastrophe. (3) At present, environmental abuse and resources use, as well as world population and other things, appear to be on an exponential course. (4) This course is disastrous if one believes that humans will have difficulty controlling their behavior even if they have the capacity, because of the rigidity associated with increasingly large and complex institutions. (5) If one is more optimistic, then it is possible to find cases of exponential curves turning into sigmoid curves—i.e., leveling off—and other cases of seeming control over destructive actions (not including the obvious cases of low-energy tribal societies with their more or less built-in controls).

The optimists are of course right in one sense—things have not yet reached catastrophic proportions; we have some time left. But the pessimist, granting this, is inclined to say that we should make full use of this time in devising controls; in order to alert society to the need to do so, we may require "models of doom."

There is still another position: the Nature-fatalistic, which says that we are all part of Nature and hence we can really change nothing. Let things take their course; eventually through disaster pressure, the negative feedback loops will emerge to take care of the problems, and man starts over. This might also be called the "science fiction" model of the future. It may be true, and we may not be able to change the course of world processes, but certainly we can alter the time they take to work. We *do* have some choice in the matter, and this is why the adaptive behavior model is a vital one. As in the old ethnographic "possibilism" position on culture-environment relations, the "choice" factor is all-important; voluntarism may be an imperfect theory and a messy reality, but it is the only one we have, and we have to use it to find our way out of the suicide course.[8] It will not be easy; we may fail. The writer of this book is not quite as pessimistic as the doom-sayers, but he is not as optimistic as those who believe that things will turn out all right because humanity can be trusted. Both positions are extreme; the only sure thing is that we will have to work very hard to get out of the mess we have created.

RELEVANCE AND CULTURAL ECOLOGY

The perennial question for anthropology is how meaningful work on such large matters can be carried on with an existing conceptual apparatus that is polarized toward a description of microsocial entities on the one hand and, on the other, high-level, long-term evolutionary generalization. This, as I see it, creates the problem of cultural anthropology in a world of change and reform: can it find a way to transcend these overly particularized and overly generalized modes of presentation and deal with contemporary historical reality? Voluntarism is a critical factor here. While the anthropologists of the early years of the century had correctly spotted this important feature of the human involvement with Nature, they failed to realize what a powerful theoretical and practical tool it can become.

However, as anthropologists turn toward contemporary societies, they inevitably come to grips with policy issues. Cultural ecology as a whole is not a policy-oriented field, but in the past few years a number of important studies have taken bolder steps. The following are some examples:

Thayer Scudder and Elizabeth Colson went to Kenya to study Tongan culture, but arrived after a forced resettlement of the tribal groups. The human costs of this program, and the evident administrative blunders that had required payment of these costs, caught their attention. The resulting work (Scudder, 1968; Colson 1971; and other papers) on the Kariba Dam and its consequences provide us with the first major piece of anthropologically conceived research on relevant cultural ecological issues: human health and objectives, cultural integration, readaptation to changed conditions, and the needs for a more humane and scientific approach to resettlement.

Clifford Geertz took a historical approach: the cultural ecology of Java became for him a problem in the development of social and economic processes within a specific historical context—colonialism. His work (1963; 1965) shows how colonial regimes and international markets constrained growth, forcing peasant agriculture back into traditional channels—an "involution" of cultural-ecological process.

A third example is concerned with relationships between human subsistence regimes and environmental quality. Work by Harold Conklin (1963) and others in swidden agricultural regimes in the tropics shows how this technique, at optimum population levels and given a friable substrate, can produce a sustained-yield system, whereas forced development of more immediately productive agricultures may damage or exhaust the resource base.[9]

A fourth example may be found in the accumulating anthropological studies of the consequences of shifts to market and cash economy by tribal peoples. These changes are accompanied by cultural change, a consequence studied in the past by anthropologists who called it "acculturation," but the contemporary approach is inclined to see the process in ecological and economic terms, as exemplified by the studies of the Miskito Indians of Nicaragua by Neitschmann (1973) and others. In these studies the Indians, dependent on sea turtles for their protein, have been required by growing involvement in a cash economy to hunt the turtles and sell them to packing companies, thus depleting the supply and endangering the species, not to mention the Indians' livelihood.

The fifth example consists of examinations of strategies of environmental management as they evolve in social relations and then are projected onto the environment. Michael Moerman's studies of rice agriculture in Thailand (1968) were concerned with cultural conceptions of change, stability, and work as they impinge on the use of resources and the production of crops; and how the external society influences the conditions of production. In his approach, cultural ecology becomes a synthesis of human effort, available resources, and the bases for choice and decision in agrarian systems.

The writer's own preferences, as represented by his research on modern Great Plains agrarians (1967C; 1969) resemble both Scudder's and Moerman's. It is my conviction that a policy-oriented ecology will be achieved by focusing on strategic action, on the behavior of humans in dealing with Nature and society in order to achieve their objectives, on ways of controlling such behavior, and on the adaptive or maladaptive effects of the behavior on the natural and social environments. What do people want? How do they get it? What are the consequences?

To summarize the main points of this chapter:

As a long-range theoretical problem, there is no doubt that human ecology is continuous with the ecology of the natural world, and that, as a long-range process, the same mechanisms of control that operate in "Nature" will also operate for man. However, as a short-range problem, a theoretical commitment to such a naturalizing view of human ecology is not likely to furnish the explicit information and guidance we need to exert control over our own practices. For these purposes, we need specific information on how people behave in society, how they deal with what they conceive to be Nature, and the incentives available for modification of this behavior. The love of humanity, the love of Nature, or the scientific naturalizing of Homo sapiens is not enough.

It is necessary to see human behavior concerning the environment as part of a social system of feedbacks and processes resembling biological systems but composed of special human factors: means and ends, purposive actions, rational and irrational decisions, uncontrollable and controlled wants and desires, and natural substances becoming increasingly bound up in human concerns and contexts. If these aspects of cultural ecology are emphasized, the focus of the field will shift away from views of the relationships of technology, population, and environment as a static or balanced system characterizing small, relatively isolated groups, to concern for dynamic processes of resource use in complex socionatural systems—that is, the kinds of systems that characterize most of the world.

A degree of policy relevance in cultural-ecological research, therefore, can be achieved by studying the world, going out beyond the isolated, sheltered cases. At the same time, relevance is not necessarily achieved by fixing on purely topical issues. Relevance implies good theory; the two are not antithetical. Relevance also implies emphasis on the "middle range" of research and theory: something between the grand-scale evolutionary theorizing and the microscaled empirical community data, which have jointly characterized anthropological work for some time.

NOTES

[1] An exception to the rule is a group of historical ecologists in England, who are concerned with tracing the history of man's impact on natural environments in Europe and the British Isles (Tubbs, 1969).

[2] For some discussion and evaluation of systems theory applications in anthropology, see the following: Flannery, 1968; Harris, 1969; Kushner, 1970; Shack, 1971; Watson, LeBlanc, and Redman, 1971; Selby, 1972. Criticism of the functionalist position as overemphasizing order and control at the expense of the adaptive and dynamic aspects of social life is appropriate in the sense that it neglected the process of change and failed to build clearcut conceptions of change into its approach. However, control is a different issue entirely from the standpoint of policy: it is a simple necessity if we are to protect the physical and social environments from abuse. The brand of order and control visualized by the equilibrium-functionalist theorists is not necessarily the kind I am talking about in this book: for modern

society, these processes must be located in a rational milieu, not in some inherent or automatic working of the social process. (For critiques of functionalism in anthropology, see Nadel, 1951—the earliest; Collins, 1970—one of the latest.)

[3]For surveys of the content and methods of anthropological ecology, see the following: Y. Cohen, 1968–70, Vol. 1 (bio-ecology, evolution, and prehistoric human adaptations; Vol. II (cultural ecology: adaptations of living folk and tribal peoples). Baker and Weiner (1966) provide a review of adaptability studies in physical anthropology. Bresler's works (1966, 1968) include a number of bioanthropological items. *American Anthropologist* (1962) is a symposium of review papers on all facets of anthropological ecology of the period. Vayda (1969B) presents a collection of ecological studies done by anthropologists. Damas (1969) presents a similar collection for a later period. Abbott (1970) provides a useful historical review of ecological concepts in cultural anthropology. Netting (1972) provides the most recent brief review of the cultural ecology field, bringing Bates (1953), Helm (1962), Sahlins (1964), and Rappaport (1965) up to date. Frake (1962) presents another early review of cultural ecology. The symposium edited by Polgar (1972) reviews work by anthropologists on population. For a "reader" text that includes articles reflecting the point of view and topical coverage of the present book, I would recommend Michael Micklin's *Population, Environment, and Social Organization* (1973).

[4]As the writer found recently while assembling materials from anthropology relating to the use and development of water as a resource (Bennett, 1974). The older summaries with tangential relationships to ecology are by Forde (1934; 1937) and Lowie (1938).

[5]Nor should it be forgotten that the threat of industrial civilization and colonialism to the survival of tribal cultures and natural landscapes was one of the factors pushing anthropology toward a "salvage" approach to the study of human culture (Gruber, 1971). The notion of salvage—of saving these human and natural landscapes for posterity—also introduced an artificial conception of timelessness and changelessness into the data, since the object of the "collector" was a portrait for all time, and not an analysis of changing social and natural milieux. It is therefore ironic that the salvage approach, which has so impeded anthropology's efforts to broaden its intellectual and policy horizons, was conceived originally as an important, socially useful task. The irony is compounded by the fact that while the anthropologist often acted as protector and advocate of tribal cultures, nearly everywhere this role is now rejected by the "subjects" as paternalistic and demeaning.

[6]Cf. Adams, 1970, pp. 117ff. I think it is fair to point out that the discussion in this paragraph and elsewhere in the book concerning control and power in the ecological context were written before I had an opportunity to read Adams' interesting discussion. This is all the more curious since Adams, in his long Chapter 2—dealing with the anthropological approach to "complex societies," where his concept of power appears—takes issue with an older article of mine (Bennett, 1967B), although this same article leads him toward his own goal. In his critique, he faults the article for its qualification of the "social environment" issue. I say there that when farmers react to government bureaus that supply them with resources, the behavior resembles (but is not strictly the same as) reacting to the weather, since the bureaus consist of people, with whom one *inter*acts. Adams rejects this, saying that there is really no difference—sometimes the weather is more amenable than bureaus, sometimes bureaus more amenable than weather. I think Adams is assuming that once you create a concept of social enviroment, it can be treated as identical to natural environment. This is an intriguing idea, but it is necessary to see both the similarities and the differences. Of course, farmers or anyone else may cope with weather as they cope with bureaucrats, but they also have to work out quite different strategies for these two "environments" when the

occasion demands. With humans, you must engage in transactions and exchanges. (For contemporary discussions of the issues of control and power in a generalized ecological context, see Calder, 1971, and H. T. Odum, 1971.)

[7]For an example, see Marie Jahoda's chapter, "Postscript on Social Change," in Cole et al., *Models of Doom* (1973)—a critique of the Club of Rome-MIT reports, *The Limits to Growth* (Meadows et al., 1972). This interchange of "world systems modeling" experiments will be discussed later in the book.

[8]Leslie White has an interesting and well-known article (1948) entitled "Man's Control over Civilization: An Anthropocentric Illusion," in which he defends his position of cultural determinism, arguing that the hope of controlling and directing the course of culture is simply a hope, nothing more (although he defends our need to "exert ourselves while we live"). However, he states that the goals of the struggle are determined by culture, not by individuals. The fact that the ends are often desirable ones—like saving lives—simply means that often (but not always) cultural evolution works toward the good. The development of a "science of culture" is then mainly an effort toward adjusting man to culture, not *vice versa*: "We cannot control its course, but we can learn to predict it." This article cannot be dismissed out of hand, however much one might disagree with its message. White has a point: there *are* limits to man's ability to guide his destiny, or at least the possibility of control by "democratic" means *has* been exaggerated (by, paradoxically, that same anthropocentrism White also displayed). However, these limitations do not come from an abstraction, "culture," but from concrete institutions, and of course from human behavior itself; and this same behavior provides the means to modify the outcomes. The basic question is to what extent the outcomes can be controlled and the society still retain a degree of political liberty.

[9]The case for traditional subsistence systems as superior modes of adaptation to (particularly) specialized environments has been set forth repeatedly by anthropologists, but without the forcefulness the issue deserves, considering its significance for the uncritical worship of "development" among the Western nations and the new "emerging countries" alike. Indeed, the first important study of tribal subsistence systems, predating cultural ecology by a decade, was Audrey Richards' study of "land, labor, and diet" among the Bemba of Africa (1939), which made the point that the *citimene* system of managing tree litter to serve as compost for crops in a subhumid scrub woodland region was the best possible system and, at least with respect to millet, productive of yields superior to any of the introduced European techniques. (For references to other recent studies with comparable themes, see Netting, 1968, pp. 8–9; Bennett, 1973). For a detailed presentation of the problem with reference to attempts to increase animal productivity by sedentarizing nomads, introducing cattle into tribal regions of East Africa, and related problems, see the symposium edited by Darling (Farvar and Milton, 1972). Other references will appear in context in subsequent chapters.

CHAPTER 3

Human Ecology and Cultural Ecology

Ramón Margalef, a theorist in biological ecology, defines ecology as "the study of systems at a level in which individuals or whole organisms may be considered elements of interaction, either among themselves or with a loosely organized environmental matrix. Systems at this level are named ecosystems, and ecology, of course, is the biology of ecosystems" (1968, p. 4).

Is there an ecology of humans that fits this definition? Of course. Human individuals interact among themselves, and the interaction patterns can be described as systems; people also interact with "environmental matrices," and these interactions within the group of organisms and between it and the milieu, also can be considered to be a system—ecosystem, if you will. These human systems have biological properties that are susceptible to measurement (although often very difficult to make), and they possess regularities that might form the basis of theoretical constructions.

In other words, man is an animal who moves on Earth, through its spaces and properties, consuming what he needs to survive, dealing with other species, and, like other animals, largely unaware of the complicated relationships among the phenomena that he disturbs or changes—and that may disturb or change him. All this can be included in Margalef's definition. There is, however, another aspect of "human ecology," one that is *not* included in the definition: a pattern of purposive behavior involving a matching of resources with objectives, a transforming of natural phenomena in order to meet these objectives, and a capacity to think about this process objectively without actually going through the

35

physical steps. This form of behavior also contains the capability of becoming aware of the disturbances created by humans in the milieu, and how these might be avoided if there is evidence of danger. The question that cannot be answered by purely biological conceptions of ecology is how effective the regulation and how complete the awareness can become. It is possible that because of the nature of human emotional makeup, it may be easier to consume than to stop consuming—voluntary deprivation (austerity, abnegation, renunciation), our special kind, is perhaps the most difficult of all kinds of self-regulation,[1] and this may be why it has played such an important role in the universal religions. High fertility is another important factor: we breed rapidly and well, especially under sedentary conditions, and control of this fertility does not, on the recent historical record, seem to be easy. Hence there appear to be strong forces, apparently not available in the ecology of other species, working toward tipping Nature's balances in human ecology and responsible for intellectual, social, and ecological problems.

Those who would advocate the position that human ecology is theoretically assimilable into a general biological ecology might point to the fact that the Margalef definition is generalized: it does not specify the *means* of "interaction" nor the nature of the "environmental matrix," and therefore it includes the human case. More importantly, the argument is made that even though humans act and interact on a cognitive basis, with purpose and will, the *results* of this activity are "ecological"—that is, the processes and their outcomes are at higher levels of generality than the actions, or "men know not what they do."

Of course all this is true at a high level of generalization. But it begs the question underlying this essay: if we act with will and purpose, then how is this to be controlled when will and purpose become willful and purposeless and Nature suffers? When this question is asked, the focus of theoretical biohuman ecology changes: the problem is not how biological man fits into Nature, but how his social actions affecting Nature are to be modified. And, at this point, the question arises as to whether or not human ecology is, for all important theoretical and practical purposes, a special case.[2]

Equally problematic is the methodology and scope of human ecology. The potential coverage of such a "science"—if it includes the social factors leading to the use of Nature and their control—is breathtaking: no facet really can be ignored—the biological and the cognitive; the chemical, emotive, temporal, economic, political, social. The study of these many subsystems, if that is what they are from a comprehensive ecological viewpoint, have been divided among a number of intellectual-social systems that in the past century have crystallized as "academic disciplines" with their vested interests in particular procedures and prestiges. This makes it extremely difficult to devise a scheme for the study of human ecology that realistically can be matched by an organization of scholarly and practical effort (Sears, 1954). To deal with a major problem of human ecology scientifically, or for purposes of reform, it is necessary to throw bridges across these professional bodies as well as attempt to link their separate terminologies and bodies of knowledge, all of which is often no easier than bringing together the rich and the poor, one nation and another.

Therefore, the great complexity of the processes represented in human ecology, and the immaturity of a general science of the field, means that for the time being different schema or paradigms must be developed for different purposes. We have two main objectives: first, to provide a conception of human ecology that will permit us to define *cultural* ecology—that is, where, in the overall corpus of human ecology, does this specialized field find a place? The second objective is to find a paradigm for human ecology that includes the socially problematic aspects of man's relations with Nature, in order to build a sense of policy-relevance into the science.

THE PARADIGM

Figure 1 represents a conception of human ecology that is biased toward social phenomena, though it does not exclude the biological. In this conception, ecological problems are defined as the consequences of human interventions in the physical environment: it is a process of human behavior that implicates biology and Nature, and is not a matter of mechanical or biological events taking place in some statistical or material realm out of awareness of the organisms involved. I hasten to add that such out-of-awareness consequences of human actions *do* take place (although nobody knows how often, or how many) and that there is room for a conception of human ecology based on this. However, it is not *my* conception, and the justification for this position is found in the social policy sphere: that the course of mental evolution has been toward ever-increasing awareness of the cultural absorption of Nature and recognition of the need to bring this under some form of control; that is, the scientific conceptions of human ecology cannot remain static because human ecology itself undergoes an evolution.

The second point to be discussed before we review the paradigm concerns the relationship of human ecology to cultural ecology. The

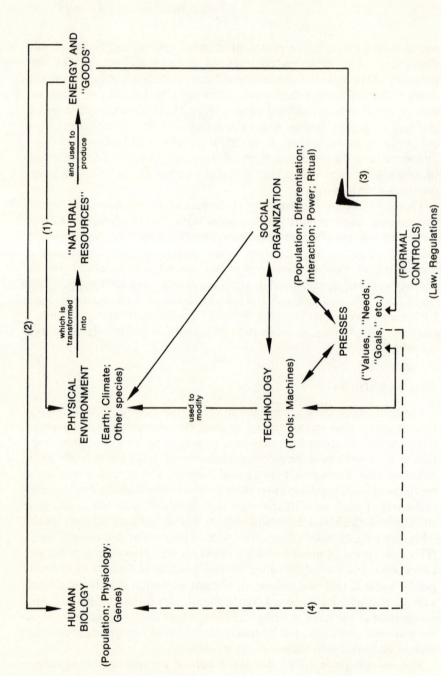

Fig. 1 A paradigm of human (or cultural) ecology, emphasizing the output function.

ENERGY AND "GOODS"

and used to produce

"NATURAL RESOURCES"

(1)

which is transformed into

(2)

PHYSICAL ENVIRONMENT

(Earth; Climate; Other species)

used to modify

TECHNOLOGY

(Tools; Machines)

SOCIAL ORGANIZATION

(Population; Differentiation; Interaction; Power; Ritual)

(3)

PRESSES

("Values," "Needs," "Goals," etc.)

(FORMAL CONTROLS)

(Law, Regulations)

HUMAN BIOLOGY

(Population; Physiology; Genes)

(4)

answer is simple; in my approach there is no important difference. That is, the bias in the definition of human ecology simply makes it, for scientific purposes, virtually identical with cultural ecology. However, if one wishes to narrow down cultural ecology for ease of management of specific issues, then the feedback loop No. 3 on the diagram, which concerns the relationships between energy output and social and psychological components, may be considered as cultural ecology *sine qua non*. However, as it may become clear in Chapter 5, other varieties of cultural-ecological research can have broader perspectives and include the wider range of phenomena indicated in Fig. 1.

The diagram is composed of capitalized components, which are linked by lines and loops. The components can be considered to be similar to "function boxes" in systems or energy-flow models, but there are important differences: each function component can be considered a subsystem, or a bundle of subsystems in its own right, operating by the same rules characteristic of the system as a whole, or by its own rules, often contradictory to those of the larger system. The complexity of each box is suggested by the various terms in parentheses underneath the label. In addition, each of the boxes can issue its own messages and its own input and output signals, often quite independent of the other boxes.

The lines, loops, and arrowheads represent interrelationships among the components, and also lines of flow of information and influence. The shorter arrows indicate direct causal influence or function—e.g., technology acts on physical environment, etc. Other and longer lines are numbered (1) through (4), and represent major feedback loops, or circuits of reciprocal and interacting influence or causation—various things, really, in this highly generalized paradigm. Some of these loops have arrowhead symbols at both ends, some at one end only. These suggest particular kinds of relationships I want to emphasize, and not necessarily invariable functions.

The diagram, as noted in its caption, emphasizes the "output function." This is important because it also represents one of the biases of this book: that it is human energy-transformation actions that have created the major problems of man on Earth: the growing pressure on Nature, and on ourselves.* If biological systems can be represented on the whole by

---

*This chapter was written before the "energy crisis" of 1973. The energy and other shortages have indicated that the problem of reducing consumption, which is treated quite pessimistically in this book, may be taken out of the hands of the people and made a matter of conformity to national policy. That is, the difficult problem of compelling people to choose a lower standard of living may not arise acutely if shortages force a rationing system.

stability and balance between organisms and Nature, human "ecology" may best, over the long historical span, be described by the reverse properties.

ENERGY TRANSFORMATION

The most obvious implication of the very term *human* ecology is, as already suggested, that man is a special or unique case and that human ecology must be studied with methods and concepts differing from those used for plants and animals. This is certainly the case when, for example, we are concerned with the capacity of the human organism to transform energy at exponential rates, or to produce "economic goods" that are provided with value based on their symbolic meaning and not derived from their function as biological necessities. In these phenomena we are confronted with human traits and capacities lacking in other species.

Of course, humans can be included in purely natural or bioecological studies. Human social arrangements, taken as givens, can be seen to affect breeding habits and consequently the frequency of certain genes in the population; the spread of disease through a human population can be found to obey rules found for nonhuman species. Man can be viewed as one organism among many with regard to a particular food chain or competition for resources in a particular locale. In these cases it is quite possible to see man as another natural species functioning within the general milieu, and there is no reason to cease such inquiries. At the same time, however, it must be remembered that cultural considerations—symbolic values, tradition, socially stimulated wants—underlie every human relationship with Nature, directly or indirectly; in the long run, all human ecological study must deal with this. Indeed, the principal mission of cultural anthropology should be to point this out and keep it in view at all times.

If culture—the superior human capacities for symbolic meaning, the storage of precedents, and the accumulation of adaptive solutions—is the mediating factor in all human transactions with Nature, then it is also necessary to observe that in the last analysis, human ecology is a science concerned with the problem of how our relations with Nature are controlled by forces within collective humanity—Society—and not solely in biological aspects of the transactions. That is, in other species, the biological transactions with the surroundings—predation, fighting, food intake, physical movement—tend to control the size of the population and its pressure on its surroundings. Or, in ecosystemic terms, balances can be reached between species with other species, between organisms with their surroundings. Among humans, on the other hand, the size of the population, and the amount of exploitation of natural substances, is governed by concerns that arise inside of the social organ and are based on mental constructs that may be independent of any organisms-milieu interaction. James Faris puts this in neo-Marxist terminology (1974). He argues that "social production" is the distinctive human method of "population management," or that the evolution of Homo sapiens involves the constant tendency to accommodate Nature to population and its needs and wants, and not the reverse. This is equivalent to our emphasis on energy transformation as a major instrumentality, and the high want-generating capacity of the human species. However, in specific historical instances, the forces described can also work toward temporary balances between output, population, and resources; the existence of these stabilized systems must be a part of our theory of human ecology. Still, the overall direction of human history appears to be toward imbalance.

The special characteristics of human ecology include just about everything distinctive in human thought and behavior and its projections into social institutions and organizations. But it is possible to narrow these down if our objective is simply to evolve a useful paradigm in order to get on with business. I believe this narrowing procedure can lead us to focus on two properties of human ecology: (1) The first is the tendency for feedback between human actions, and between actions and the surroundings to be "open": to freely exchange energy and information; for system components to be capable of emitting their own signals; or, in general, a large proportion of unanticipated or unexpected factors. (2) The second property is the tendency for humans to transform energy at exponential rates, and for this tendency to become more marked as human history proceeds. (We should remember, also, that both of these properties are expressed *within* the social organ as well as between it and the "natural" surroundings; that is, social events and changes are highly dynamic, and social energy—organization, power—like physical energy can accumulate exponentially. Or, more generally, we act on Society just as we act on Nature, and our actions toward Nature may be defined for us by actions on Society. Hence Nature becomes Society.)

Now we can begin our detailed discussion of Fig. 1. The basic component of the diagram is the transformation process:

PHYSICAL ENVIRONMENT →(which is transformed into)→ "NATURAL RESOURCES" →(and used to produce)→ ENERGY AND "GOODS"

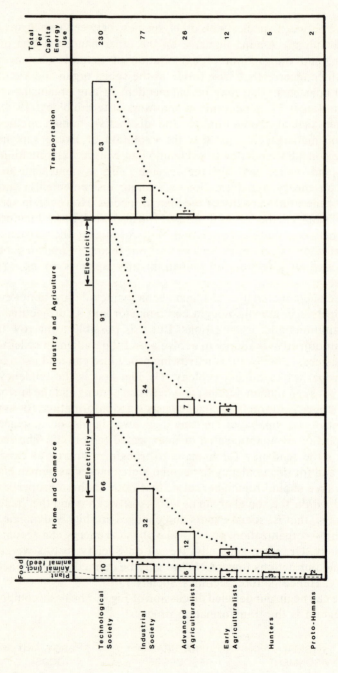

Humans act upon the physical environment and extract substances from it that are transformed symbolically into "natural resources" and are then used to produce or transform energy. The "natural resources" do not exist for other species, because these species do not have the cognitive ability to conceptualize substances as a new kind of phenomenon, nor can they place arbitrary values on substances—values that can arise out of economic and cultural arrangements internal to the social organ and do not emerge directly out of nutritional or energetics concerns. While other species act upon the physical surroundings to transform or produce energy, only man inserts this cognitive-symbolic step; it is this step that makes the difference.

Likewise, the output or production end of the process includes something in addition to energy: "economic goods." Here, again, there is a distinctive human capacity not found in other species: the capacity to value goods symbolically—that is, in terms that arise out of the social process itself and are not necessarily determined by an existing culture-environment relationship system. This being the case, the output end of the basic human ecological process has an open door, an invitation to "blue sky" energy transformation, provided that the technology is up to it. In terms of cybernetics, there is no automatic governor for the

Fig. 2A *Per capita energy consumption by humans at different levels of technical development.* This diagram shows the amount of energy per capita consumed by humans at six technological stages or points in history. The general shape of the curves created by the increasing energy consumption is exponential—as would be a curve showing the total per capita energy use. The total figures in the right-hand column represent the numerical data for such a total curve. The first, or "proto-human" position is taken from the archaeological materials associated with Australopithecine remains in East Africa, who are considered to be the descendants of ancestors of true humans. The energy consumed by them is very small, consisting solely of the food taken from the physical environment (plants and small animals) and eaten. Hunters (the people of the Paleolithic of Europe, Asia, and Africa about 100,000 years ago) added the use of fire for cooking and heating. Note that the addition of fire alone nearly doubles the energy consumption. Early Agriculturalists (as, say, in the Near East about 6,000 B.C.) added plant crops and domestic animals to the sources, the Advanced Agriculturalists (northern Europe, 1300–1500 A.D.) used peat and coal for heating, water power, wind power for sails and windmills, and animals as beasts of burden. The Industrial Society of the late 18th and 19th centuries had the steam engine and a series of mechanical devices designed to extend the power of the human arm and the efficiency of simple fuels. Finally, Technological Society (a term used to describe the present electrical and nuclear-power age) has extended the production and use of energy further in less than a century than in all previous periods. (Redrawn, with modifications, from a diagram in Earl Cook, "The Flow of Energy in an Industrial Society," in *Scientific American*, special issue on energy, September, 1971. Copyright © 1971 by *Scientific American*, Inc. All rights reserved.)

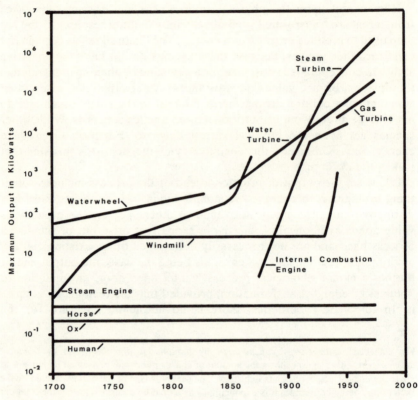

Fig. 2B *Amount of power energy produced by basic devices.* This diagram shows the exponential increase in the energy output in the form of "power" (that is, power to do work), produced by humans since the 18th century. We start with the 18th century since in all of the previous centuries and millenia the amount of energy produced by power devices was so small, being limited to the human arm and beasts of burden, that it would be insignificant on this diagram. Also, as indicated by the bottom lines, the power outputs of humans, the ox, and the horse have not increased appreciably due to physical limitations. However, the power energy supplied by most mechanical devices has increased drastically. This reflects not the increasing use of each device, but rather an increasing amount of power output due to technological improvements. Some devices, like the windmill, appear to terminate abruptly, but this does not mean that they are dead; serious discussions about reviving and improving windmills for rural energy production were under way as this book was being written. The diagram, of course, omits some of the very latest sources of power, such as rocket engines used for space travel. The jet engine is subsumed as one of the improvements under "internal combustion engines." (Redrawn, with modifications, from a diagram in Chauncey Starr, "Energy and Power," *Scientific American*, special issue on energy, September, 1971. Copyright © 1971 by *Scientific American*, Inc. All rights reserved.)

amount of energy transformed, or at least no guarantee of a governor operating on any permanent basis. Hence the exponential curves in human ecological history. (Note that this paradigm is historically generalized—it does not negate the fact that for segments of the process, certain places, times, circumstances, such governance does exist or can be arranged.)

I shall discuss the question of the energy output first. I assume that the amount of energy produced by humans in their transactions with Nature is greater, or always potentially greater, than that produced by any other species. I also assume, of course, that the actual quantity of energy produced will be relative to the biological needs and culturally defined wants of particular populations at particular times. The amount of energy produced by a hunting-gathering society is vastly less than the amount produced by a thermonuclear plant, but in both cases the amounts produced and the potential rate of increase are much greater than that which can be produced by any other species.[3] From an ecological standpoint then, the major characteristic of Homo sapiens is the transition toward increase of energy output, which has exponential properties—or, at any rate, very rapid increases. Some of these patterns are diagrammed in Figs. 2A and 2B.

When I use the term "exponential," I do so in some cases literally (meaning a case of accumulation where the increment multiplies by a factor of itself, producing very rapid increases) and sometimes rhetorically (referring to any steeply rising curve). Many of these increase curves in human phenomena are L-shaped: a long, almost level onset, with a sudden, steep rise. Others level off after a start of this type. The arithmetic curves for human population, interpolated by prehistorians and demographers from earliest hominid times have an L-shape, as in Figure 3A.

However, some of these curves, when treated logarithmically, turn out to have steps or jumps in them, reflecting increases in the rate of increase associated with particular episodes in cultural history.

The curve in Figure 3B differs from the previous arithmetic curve in that it exaggerates the sudden jumps in population apparently associated with the development of food production or agriculture (around 10,000 years ago) and with the development of modern technology and the industrial revolution (beginning around 1500 A.D.).

The "exponential" curves suggest that the human way of using Nature is more or less unique, not duplicated exactly or consistently for any other animal species. The symbolic capacity of human thought makes possible a form of resource use that is adjusted to wants that arise in society—the idea pool—and that may have no relationship to the capacity of local resources to support their satisfaction. But, at the same time, the shape of the curve suggests that human adaptations are not all alike, that the "species" level of similar behavior is always qualified by other curves that differ one from another. Humans at the point of food production are not the "same" as humans at the point of nuclear energy production. There has been an accumulation, a change in mental content. In human ecology, we can define quite different adaptations developed by different population groups in the same species—something that is absent, extremely rare, or only marginally present for other species.

If the exponential curve or something like it characterizes the long span

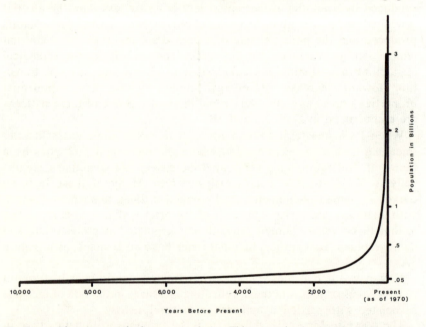

Fig. 3A *Arithmetic curve for human population.* This curve simply plots the total numbers of people on the Earth from 10,000 years ago to the present. Of course, population is estimated before the 19th century, since the census is a recent development. However, demographers and anthropologists have devised a number of quite accurate methods for estimation of population size and density. The curve is exponential; the steep upward swing is associated with the development of superior sources of energy (see Fig. 2A), especially those produced in the Industrial Revolution. (Redrawn from a diagram in Edward S. Deevey, "The Human Population," in *Scientific American*, special issue on the human species, September 1960. Copyright © 1960 by *Scientific American*, Inc. All rights reserved.)

of Homo sapiens' history, then curves of energy transformation of varying shapes characterize the particular adaptive styles of historically bounded population groups or societies. Or, not all human societies show the exponential increase curve of population, energy, and tools. Some show plateaus—that is, stability in one developed system of resource use; others display curves of decline and collapse of resource systems, with a return to simpler, less exploitative systems. To use the terms introduced by Marshall Sahlins and Elman Service (1960, p. 12), there is a difference between general evolution (the exponential curve) and specific cultural evolution (the many historical change patterns of specific societies).

It is also important to remember that there is a long-term limit on the human ability to transform energy since the resources of the Earth are finite. Sooner or later, unchecked exploitation of Nature will feed back into the human system, and population will "crash," as such catastrophic demographic declines are called by animal ecologists. In other words, the exponential rate of increase in so many human relations with natural phenomena obviously cannot continue forever. However, this is not the issue. The problem is to find ways of bringing the present rates under

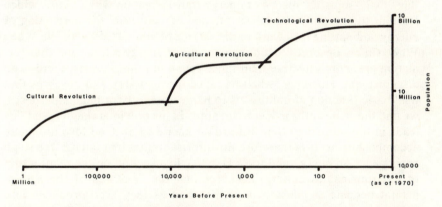

Fig. 3B *Logarithmic curve for human population.* This curve is plotted on a much longer time scale than the arithmetic curve; but the intervals between dates on the scale are systematically smaller as one goes back into the past. This gives a different type of curve: one which shows a series of major jumps in population size as associated with particular events—the production of food by plant crops and domesticated animals, around 10,000–5,000 B.C., and the Industrial Revolution of recent times. There is also the beginning of a rapid upswing after 100,000 years ago, associated with superior methods of hunting and incipient agriculture. Redrawn from a diagram in Edward S. Deevey, "The Human Population", in *Scientific American*, special issue on the human species, September, 1960. Copyright © 1960 by *Scientific American*, Inc. All rights reserved.

control so that we can avoid crashes and other disasters, which will control them willy-nilly.

But let us return to the human capacity for transforming energy. This is basic and elementary anthropology, but it seems that anthropologists have often misread its implications. Leslie White (1954; 1959A) is the anthropologist whose name is most closely associated with the theory of the importance of energy in the development of culture and in the theory of culture generally. However, he defined culture in "superorganic" terms (as some kind of emergent property or phenomenon in its own right). While in my opinion White was responsible for a great deal of intellectual confusion by taking a heuristic mental construct (culture) and defining it as a substantive reality with its own laws of operation, he deserves full credit for his emphasis on the significance of the energy factor. And this, curiously enough, is the most neglected aspect of his work.[4]

White's general position on energy release in the human species is summarized by his doctrine that man has an "extra-somatic mechanism which he employs in the process of living," and that this means "an organization of energy transformations" (1959A, p. 38). White identified this "extra-somatic" means of energy transformation with *culture*, which led him to say that "the basic function of culture is the harnessing of energy and putting it to work in the service of man" (1959A, p. 39). When White simply observes that human means of energy release and transformation are more effective than those found in other species, there is no disagreement. However, when he takes the next step and observes that the "basic function of culture" is to harness energy for human purposes, we find the same anthropocentrism noted in the previous chapter, and this leads in the same direction: toward an uncritical attitude toward human accomplishment. It is therefore no surprise to find that later in the same basic paper on energy and tools (1959A), in a section on the relationship of environment to culture, he notes that the "features of the natural habitat become significant only when and as they are introduced into cultural systems and become incorporated in them as cultural elements" (p. 51).

This last statement has two implications. It can imply that men take no notice of Nature unless it becomes useful for them—in which case the position is a classic 19th-century utilitarian (or ethnographic-possibilist) conception of human behavior. Or, the statement can mean that men take no *responsibility* for any portion of Nature that is not involved in culture; it is this latter implication that is easy to read into White's context in the light of the current world ecological situation. I do not believe that White meant the latter, only the former. But even so, the utilitarian position is precisely that philosophical position that rationalized industrial "progress" and directed our attention away from the constraining ethic of responsibility and a realistic and humane consideration of the costs of our actions. The important point is that these ideas are ingrained in the anthropological conception of man-environment relations, as they are in Western culture generally.

Related to this is of course White's emphasis on man as a unique creature, capable of doing things no other animal can do. This view is not false, and we share it; the fact itself is not the issue, only what you can make of it. Here anthropology's mood has significantly changed in recent years toward a willingness to see the continuities in human and animal behavior.[5] Human accomplishments, therefore, can have evil as well as good consequences, and this is gradually being incorporated in social science frames of reference. The fact of human superiority in the relationship with environment is cause not for theoretical blandness and implied celebration, but for serious concern and objective examination of the consequences.

To return to Fig. 1.

If the transition in energy output is one of the two major characteristics of human ecology, then presumably the measurement of energy should be one of the major objectives of a science of human ecology. No general description of the properties of ecological systems can be made without reducing the terms of the exchanges and feedbacks to a common language; general systems theory or, more specifically, energy flow measurement, provides such a language.[6] The terms of this language include the sources of energy, the pathways in the system through which it flows, valves to control this flow, storage sinks for conserving energy for future use, "function boxes"—or actions dependent on the flow of energy, and a large number of models of particular kinds of energetic systems—biological, mechanical, and socionatural systems such as agriculture.

The application of energetics analysis to human systems is an important but extremely complicated task. Quantification of much of the data going into such analysis is required, but even without precise numbers, the modeling operation itself—equivalent to systems analysis, and capable of analog computerization—represents a gain in the clarification of human systems. The difficulties are equally apparent; the extreme flexibility of human systems, the proliferation of subsystems and parts, and the constant switching of pathways of flow of information or energy make it difficult to generalize them and to create models with which to understand the operations of real systems. Equally serious difficulties exist in attempts to handle biological and behavioral variables in the same analysis, since no common measures of such phenomena have been developed. Many energetics analyses of social phenomena end up as intriguing analogies and little else: to model an economic transaction as if it were *equivalent* to an hydraulic or electrical flow system is to oversimplify the economic transaction to the point where the distinctive and important characteristics are lost. But, despite these risks, the analysis of human data on energetics or, more broadly, general-systems models is a potentially useful enterprise. We shall have more to say on all this in later chapters.

The second major characteristic of human ecology listed earlier—that it consists of open systems, receiving energy and information from the surrounding milieu, and can generate its own signals from component parts without necessary control from external inputs—means that the rate and amount of energy transformation often will be subject to demands that have no necessary relationship to biological survival. That is, the activities can be performed for purposes indigenous to the social system and are not necessarily generated by the relationship of the population to its physical milieu. This means that energy transformation is not usually a goal in itself, but is a means to accomplish some other goal. This also introduces the problem of purposeful behavior. I am not necessarily implying that all energy transformation is purposive, either as means or ends, and I acknowledge that often energy is transformed as an incidental by-product of human activities. However, we are concerned here with the long historical process, not the short-run empirical cases, and in this historical sense the great increases in the amount of energy transformed by man in the course of his Homo sapiens history has been purposive and largely a means to other ends. This also implies that if there are dangers associated with this transition, the communication channel from the output end of the process back into the governing system has been relatively poor in recent centuries, since we seem to have difficulty controlling our energy uses or delaying action on the production of more energy until we have developed pollution-free sources.

Back to Fig. 1. Beneath the transformation sequence are two terms: "Technology" and "Social Organization." For the purposes of this paradigm, both of these are considered to be instrumentalities, or means to further the objective or process of production and energy transformation (again, whether it is consciously purposive in all cases is immaterial at this point). But it is also apparent that both technology and social organization can be ends in themselves, generating their own needs, wants, precedents, styles of action, and the like. That is, they become subsystems or milieux that must be maintained, and energy is required to do this.

Technology, of course, implies tools and machines—and, increasingly in human ecological history, the replacement of hand tools by powered machines. *Social organization* as an instrumentality means that in order to produce goods the society must be mobilized in a certain manner. An adequate population base must be present, labor must be supplied, and talents must be recognized and employed. It is assumed that the basic cause of differentiation in human society arises from the need to find individuals with diverse skills and set them to work on the various tasks of environmental transformation. This process of differentiation will become more marked (and, usually, more unequal or exploitative according to some value frames) as the magnitudes of population, energy, and product increase. One of the distinctive aspects of human society is the fact that cognitive understandings pertaining to social phenomena need not be precisely isomorphic to the instrumental requirements: for example, a society can uphold egalitarian values at the same time that its energy conversions require greater differentiation, thus creating conflict.[7] Or, a society can insist on increasing satisfaction of wants, even though a net loss in resource capacity may result. Hence, many institutional conflicts, so painfully evident in modern industrial societies, arise out of a fundamental ecological process involving typically imperfect feedbacks in the social system and between the social system and Nature.

Since both technology and social organization can function as instrumentalities, the effort required in supplying the energy needed for energy transformation can be furnished by various proportions of human labor and machines. The transition in human history reflected in the exponential curve of energy transformation is in general terms the result of reducing the amount of human labor and hand tools and increasing the output of powered machines involved in the process. Since machines require relatively large quantities of energy (fuel) to accomplish their ends in the short time required to make them efficient, they have a more massive impact on the environment (at least some kinds of impacts) than human labor sufficient to accomplish the same end. The environmental impact of a pyramid built by human labor is probably limited to the hole in the quarry where the stone was removed, but if the same pyramid were built by machines, large quantities of fossil fuels would also be removed from the earth.

The cause of this transition may or may not be one of the mysteries of human history. My view is that there is no mystery at all: the shift to large resource-consuming instrumentalities was motivated, by and large, by mankind's increasing desire for comfort, security, wealth, and the sheer exercise of ingenuity to do what it wished. These elementary motives, elaborated by ideology and configurated in political and economic systems, accumulating their own vested interests and stakes in the process, led to an ignoring of the resource costs—costs that we have become fully aware of only recently.

Therefore, the term "Presses" is placed below the two instrumentalities in Fig. 1 to signify one generalized motive force for the process. This term includes *tension-reduction*, or the need to complete the action under way; Paretian "residues" and "derivations," or *values*, preference positions, which define the reasons for action; the *desires*, *needs*, and *wants* of the people involved; the *purposes* defined, and any other directing forces conveniently locatable in the mental functioning of the population. Obviously such "presses" to motivate technology and social organization to act on the environment come from various sources, and also from each other. For example, social organization and technology can be considered as sources of values, and our second major characteristic of human ecology implies that when the internal components of the process generate the impetus for more output, without reference to possible consequences, there is likely to be danger.

The presses, of course, include subconscious as well as conscious drives. There is also no doubt that press factors generated by forces inside the culture and social system *can* function to limit, as well as to enhance, the operations of the energy process. Such values can be consciously conservationist or only incidentally so. That is, when a value concerning some feature of human behavior seemingly not related to the man-Nature nexus, or only distantly related, operates in some way to control the energy transformation process (or the impact on Nature of human actions), we may be confronted with an automatic process operating outside the sphere of conscious purpose and probably even awareness. Some anthropologists have written extensively on this issue, and discussions will be presented in later chapters. For the time being, we should observe that if such subliminal regulation exists in the human ecological system, it has not been historically sufficient to preserve the system from abuse and overuse of resources. That is, there is no evidence of automatic controls operating in the system consistently in all societies.

Hence I have inserted the term "Formal Controls" below presses, more or less outside the diagram proper. This indicates that the system, while it does possess channels for information exchange and feedback, is imperfectly constructed in this regard as compared with other natural systems. In order to maintain a condition of sustained yield, to reduce impacts, it is usually necessary to introduce a formal, conscious set of controls, which of course must work through social organization. All large industrial societies are presently engaged in this process. However, it is not hard to visualize tribal hunting societies also confronted by needs to regulate the kill of certain favorite species from time to time, with conferences held on the matter for devising ritual proscriptions against indiscriminate killing. At least, such proscriptions were found by ethnologists to be embedded in the cultures of many such tribal groups at the time of observation. We need not assume that all such rituals must have emerged unconsciously. It is equally likely that they were the result of conscious planning, but in most cases we will never know.

Off to the left side of Fig. 1 is the term "Human Biology." This has been inserted in order to indicate that the output of energy will have an impact on the human physique and gene pool, as well as on values and social and technical apparatus. One element of the "human biology" factor is population, but since population can also be handled as a part of "social organization," we include it as well in that component. One of the principal issues in Vayda and Rappaport's (1968) analysis of anthropological ecology is their desire to bring human demography out of its cultural matrix and treat it as an independent variable, subject to the same measurements developed by bioecologists for animal population. Although it is recognized that there are problems that require treatment of a human social factor in its exclusively biological context, our bias suggests that cultural factors are always in the picture, and therefore population always has social implications that must not be ignored.

THE CONCEPT OF FEEDBACK

Now, having anticipated the topic at length, we arrive at the problem of feedback. Some general observations on this important concept should open the discussion.

The concept of feedback is associated with general-systems theory, but, more specifically, with an antecedent and component of that theory: the field of cybernetics, which may be defined as the study of processes of control or regulation resulting from output being fed back into the system producing it, thereby governing the output function. Ramón Margalef (1968) considers that cybernetics is the underlying approach to natural ecosystems: ecosystems are, essentially, self-regulating entities, governed by feedback:

> Cybernetics refers to systems. Every system is a set of different elements or compartments or units, any one of which may exist in many different states, such that the selection of a state is influenced by the states of the other components of the system. Elements linked by reciprocal influences constitute a *feedback loop*. The loop may be *negative*, or *stabilizing*, like the one formed by a heating unit and a thermostat or the mechanisms regulating sugar level in the blood. Or the loop may be *positive* or *disruptive*, like the spread of an annihilating epidemic. A characteristic of negative feedback is that not only the entire system but also some selected states of the system show considerable persistence through time.

The first issue to arise is whether or not these definitions really apply to the scheme of human ecology represented by Fig. 1 or whether the concepts might better be reserved for smaller (and more easily analyzed) separate subsystems within this larger system. A second question is whether a definition that is constructed mainly for the analysis of living organisms behaving according to relatively automatic controls is applicable to the human species, with its large quotient of adaptive behavioral variation due to cognition and symbolizing.

With respect to the first question, the full discussion is reserved for Chapter 4, but for the time being the following may ba said: as Henry Selby has pointed out (1972, pp. 301–305), there is first a difference between the application of *systems analysis* (or "energetics") to known and bounded events and processes in human society, and the application of *general-systems theory* to events or institutions as a rhetorical, philosophical, or analogical exercise. That is, when concepts relating to ecosystems—or any type of system—are applied to carefully defined, bounded empirical cases, and the properties of the systems are measured and empirically related, the results can be fruitful and revealing. The other type of operation yields ambiguous, generalized results and tends to blur detail and thus mask some of the crucial properties of human systems. But, in any case, for the analysis of human events, systems concepts must be used exactly the way any other theoretical concepts are used: as tools that may or may not reveal something. They must never be imposed on the data. The proper attitude of the investigator with respect to the question of whether human ecology is systemic, or ecosystemic, is agnosticism.

Second, there is a difference between *mechanical* systems and *eco*systems—a distinction that is not clear in Margalef's presentation and in many other published discussions of the systems business. The terms in Margalef's definition of feedback pertain to the general model of systems as developed originally in the 1930s and '40s.[8] In these early discussions by Norbert Wiener and others, the illustrative examples of systems were mechanical, not biological or social, and the basic ideas of feedback and self-governance or servomechanisms were derived from mechanical functions. It is of course true that biological and social analogies to this type of systems conception appeared almost immediately (e.g., Bateson, 1949; von Bertalanffy, 1950), but this simply means that the concept of ecosystem was heavily influenced by these mechanical images of reciprocal function.

The two most commonly used examples of systems in the earlier literature were the 18th-century steam engine (with its flyball governor) and the thermostat, which regulates furnaces. In both cases, the feedback involved is of a specific type: when output reaches a certain level, the mechanism sends a message back through the system, which automatically controls the output-generating functions, which in turn modify the operation of the mechanism. This type of feedback—quite a distinctive thing, really—is usually distinguished from "open-sequence control systems," arranged in a linear fashion, in which a signal from one end simply travels down the line and controls something but does not travel back up the line to inform the components of what it has done—a switch, in other words, rather than a thermostat. Such linear systems (something analogous to "linear causation" models in other reality contexts) *are* systems, but they are not systems on the special cybernetic model. The cybernetic model was so intellectually attractive that it came to be the starting point of most attempts to build systems models, or do systems analysis, and this was done often without carefully qualifying the definition of a system.

So: the original notion of *eco*system received a heavy dose of cybernetic theory and, as in Margalef's definition of ecosystem, it is often portrayed as having the same properties as mechanical systems. When these properties are imputed to biological and social systems, in terms of a model for analysis, the mechanical imagery may be extended to phenomena somewhat less amenable to analysis in such terms.

Moreover, true cybernetic or interdependent, self-governed systems have their distinctive problems. Variations in inputs from the outside, the lags inherent in message flow, and various imperfections in working parts introduce oscillations in the system or waves of performance. If these waves are regular—the same shape over and over again—the oscillation is stable, or homeostatic. But oscillations can be quite irregular, or can have complex patterns of regularity and irregularity. The functions presumably governed by feedback can then "overcorrect" and the system begins to "shake itself to pieces"—like a thermostatically controlled furnace that begins to shut on and off with increasing frequency.

Therefore, biological systems involving plants and animals must be expected to be *less* regular and self-controlled than mechanical systems, but *more* so than human behavioral and social systems. Or, putting it methodologically, biological systems can be analyzed with the use of idealized cybernetic models and considerable knowledge can be gained in the process, even though it is known that the actual systems are less regular than the ideal ones. It follows that the application of perfect cybernetic models (or even the modified biological ones) to human social-behavioral or social-ecological systems are likely to produce much less useful knowledge, and might even seriously distort their reality.

Or, with special reference to feedback: whereas in mechanical and to considerable extent in biological systems, feedback can be measured in terms of *directional* energy and information flow (measurable accumulations of output that have predictable governing effects on input and other functions of the system), in the case of human social systems, feedback usually defines a process of *reciprocal interaction* between the components or subsystems of the suprasystem, and this interaction may or may not modify its functions. Moreover, the messages themselves may be emitted by any of the actors in the system without regard to properties of the system as a whole—that is, through random, spontaneous, or emotional responses about which it is extremely difficult or impossible to know in advance.

The next issue in the feedback problem concerns the distinction between "positive" and "negative" feedback. In the quotation used earlier, Margalef defined negative feedback as a stabilizing condition, and positive feedback as disruptive—these definitions obviously referring to notions of entropy, or the process by which energy is used, transformed, or conserved and retired. When such terms are applied to the human case, confusion is likely to arise for at least two reasons. First, "negative" connotes something undesirable, and "positive" connotes its opposite. Since all actions and changes in human affairs will be defined by values and preferences, there is a tendency to assume that negative and positive feedback are equivalent to undesirable or rejected states on the one hand, or desirable and sought-after conditions on the other. But there is no such regular relationship: desirable or undesirable states in human affairs can be the result of either positive or negative feedback, depending on the circumstances. (A similar confusion is likely to emerge over the concept of *adaptation*—what is adaptive for X may not be adaptive for Y, but since the term "adaptation" has generalized connotations of desirability, its use is likely to lead to an assumption that any adaptation is generally good and applicable.)

The second reason confusion has arisen over these terms defining feedback is that the flexibility and open quality of human systems means also that they are *open-ended*: they usually change not by returning to former states, as do biological systems that retire energy (negative feedback), but by "adapting"—that is, by innovating, borrowing from outside sources, and then selecting, from these innovations, the most adjustive variety (a process that has been called "deviation-amplifying positive feedback"—quite a mouthful). This means that true negative feedback is rare in human systems, or at least is not the usual or most important way humans cope with environment. This means also that "equilibrium," a concept closely associated with negative feedback and stable energy states, is also not the most appropriate concept for a general theory of social behavior. The fact that this concept did become such in the functional theory of society can be attributed to certain versions of negative-feedback theory creeping into social science—or at least into Talcott Parsons—from early versions of systems theory. (We discuss this in greater detail in the next chapter.)

What seems to have escaped some of the workers in this field is that there is a hidden value judgment in the biological concept of system: a bias toward, or ideal-typologization of, stability and regularity which misrepresents the biological realm as well as the human, though perhaps not to the same extent. There is an increasing disposition among biological ecologists to set aside the whole issue of stability and regularity and view natural ecosystems as energy systems, with measurable, and changing ratios of input to output (the so-called "International Biological Programme approach," since it was developed in IBP conferences). If this view of bioecosystems should predominate, much closer research articulation between biological systems and social systems can be expected. The preoccupation with the stability issue has tended to drive the two fields of inquiry further and further apart.

But, whatever the biologist's confusions, there is no doubt that to apply positive feedback in the bioecological sense to human society as an invariably disturbing or disruptive force is to ignore the fact that humans also solve their problems adaptively—that is by "disturbing" systems that work poorly and reforming them. For better or worse, we use positive feedback to adapt, and this means that we can formulate goals and apply selected means in order to change things. Feedback, then, is at least partly a cognitive and time-binding operation in human mentality and in social life. It is in our power to analyze the workings of feedback, something no other species can do.

There are, then, two things to consider, not one: there is the feedback process as defined by Margalef for living organisms, including humans in some contexts (though the functions are extremely complex); and then the other process—preferred behavior, or controlled purposive behavior, involving the "rational" manipulation of feedbacks for particular purposes, operating in the sphere of society, or generally, culture. While it is possible that the two blend at some high level of generality, since the behavior may simply become part of a macro feedback process, they must be clearly distinguished at the subsystemic level when one is concerned with issues of social control or planned change. For the time being, we shall continue to use the feedback rhetoric, but in Chapter 9 we shall shift gears and consider the cultural-ecological process in terms of the concepts of *adaptation* (desired) and *maladaptation* (rejected). There is then, a possible four-fold matrix:

FEEDBACK

		Negative Feedback	Positive Feedback
BEHAVIORAL PREFERENCE AND CONTROL	Adaptive Behavior		
	Maladaptive Behavior		

Fig. 4   Preference and feedback in human ecology.

To avoid confusion between these analytical concepts, we shall not use the terms "positive" and "negative" in this book, but simply discuss the functions of feedback empirically. (It is always necessary, in human ecology, to explain from whose point of view the analysis of feedback, and adaptation, is defined, since what is adaptive for one person or group may be maladaptive for another.)

Still another issue pertains to Margalef's emphasis on self-regulation of ecosystems. The actions of humans in social systems can, at some level other than full awareness, result in control of these same actions. However, once again there is another analytically separable function: the *conscious seeking* of controls through the medium of "deviation-amplifying" (Maruyama, 1963) planning or reform, and its opposite—the *deliberate disruption* of control systems. The implication of this, which we shall develop in subsequent discussions, is that a policy-relevant approach to human ecology must always distinguish the two kinds of regulation. Control is not always, if ever, automatic; frequently, the system must be cognitively objectified and arbitrarily modified, or at least an attempt to do so must be made. However, once again, at a high theoretical level these two can be combined in a generalized process analysis.

Still another distinction concerns the way feedback is apprehended in human systems. Here one can distinguish between indirect effects (gene frequencies, physiological rhythm changes, and so on) and those that are cognitively perceived (i.e., through the flow of linguistic information). In some dimensions these blend, of course, but others are analytically distinguishable by the existence of language and literacy. One of the critical problems of feedback in human ecology is the different rates of movement along channels: some effects (e.g., gene frequencies and microevolutionary changes) take a long time to work, and even longer for awareness on the part of the affected individuals to develop. But others (e.g., sensory or nutritional deprivation) can be perceived immediately. Linguistic information can be fed into the feedback loops and can travel rapidly—unless blockage occurs, and in that case the rate of flow can be very slow. One really cannot generalize about rate of flow between the two channels—both can be either fast or slow, depending on circumstances.

Finally, because of the volitional and emotional character of the message senders and carriers in human systems, feedback frequently operates in exactly the reverse way as defined for mechanical and biological systems: the efficient sending of information from the output end back through the system actually contributes to the *mal*functioning of the system, rather than its opposite: governance of the process to insure a steady output and general maintenance of the system. There is widespread concern at the present moment in history concerning the efficiency of newsgathering and transmission: that messages are so numerous, and sent so quickly, that events have no time to die in secret, work themselves out, etc. The system suffers from a surfeit of messages that demand, in accordance with current values, some appropriate immediate action from too many people—the action often serving to worsen the crisis.

THE FEEDBACK LOOPS

Now back to Fig. 1 and its feedback loops. We noted earlier that the social and behavioral components of the human ecological system can alter the direction of flow and can change the content of the messages in an almost random or at least exceedingly variable manner. It is also evident that the operation of feedback generally in the human system is subject to culture—that is, to particular definitions of the situation, or particular needs existing at particular times for reasons that have nothing to do with survival, breeding, population size, or the state of the resources used.

This means that the number of potential feedback loops in the system modeled in Fig. 1 is very large. Any effect can influence any component of the system: A "want" can stimulate the social organization to mobilize technology to use resources to produce the desired good, and this output then can stimulate the technology to produce at a higher or lower rate, depending upon changed economic values resulting from the production process. (The example just presented concerns feedback loop No. 3: the relationship between the energy transformation process and the instrumentalities and presses that fuel it. This is, of course, the key loop for cultural ecology.)

At the same time, it is evident that no particular feedback is inevitable or required on the basis of theory. Feedback may or may not occur; preferences and particular social arrangements may block the channels or divert and change messages. It is now apparent that the ecological transition has had consequences for the social system that are beginning to be perceived as undesirable ("maladaptive"): increased density of population in industrial areas, overstimulation of wants, high anxiety, and eventually the social differentiation accompanying high technology that results in social unrest and desperate attempts to reorganize society to fulfill promises. Karl Marx was on the track of some of these in his famous "contradictions" of capitalism, although one could hardly consider Marx an ecologist.

Feedback in the general domain of loop No. 3 also relates to the effort to seek causes for contemporary ecological problems. Commentators on the situation will tend to fix on one or more components of the system and make these the prime factors: Paul Ehrlich emphasizes population (part of our "social organization" for the moment); Barry Commoner—technology; Garrett Hardin and Rene Dubos—various elements of the "press" constellation (values, ethics). These attempts at explanation are, of course, partial since it is apparent that the system functions as a historical system, with all components involved, but the great complexity of the process requires focused discussions or piecemeal analysis.

Functioning of feedback in this loop is not confined to conscious wants. Energy conversions can increase sustenance, which permits population growth (facilitated by social organizational changes promoting longevity), which in turn increases the supply of labor, requiring more production and increased environmental disruption. This loop may then encourage the emergence of anti-human values and pro-environment perspectives.[9] Still more subtle effects would include those proposed by Joseph Birdsell for Australian tribal populations (1963), where rainfall and food-getting activities may influence the structure of marriage ties and other social phenomena (similar problems, but handled in a cross-cultural evolutionary manner, are presented by Harner, 1970).

In contemporary society rapid-acting feedbacks concerning social and production phenomena may operate without implicating the value component. For example, a certain division of labor may have been created to provide for a given level of output, but this same social arrangement may then set up needs that require a change in the output. Often such effects are felt, and acted upon, without alterations in the values. Consequently, we can have, as in the case of contemporary Japan, cultures with traditional conservationist values and respect for Nature, who nevertheless energetically exhaust their scarce resources and pollute the environment. The decisions to do the latter are made pragmatically (Firth's concept of "organization" in his 1954 essay) without resorting to the "structural" or value area. In cases such as this, the terms of the diagram need revision: the "social organization" component can generate its own presses, which short-circuit what may be from our preference position an adaptive (i.e., not destructive of sustained yield) function of the existing value presses.[10] Thus, to achieve a given level of output, humans will adjust technology and social organization appropriately; but, once output increases, its new magnitude can alter relationships in the social-behavioral systems, requiring further adjustments. The process is especially common in systems of power, and has become increasingly dangerous with the escalation of technology and the quest for power.

As previously suggested, the content of the information flowing within the loop can vary due to the operation of various kinds of censoring screens set up in human value systems. These may prevent the operation of feedback loop No. 3 in such a way as to eliminate controls over damaging effects. Eugene Odum made this a major theme of his paper on ecosystems (1969), where he is concerned with the tendency for human actions to intervene in the normal process of establishment of orderly energy-exchange systems in Nature. We shall discuss this in greater detail in the next chapter.

Loop No. 3 also contains the mechanisms for control of man's use of the environment. This involves the difficult question of conscious or unconscious operation of feedback. In a paper by D. H. Stott, to be discussed in Chapter 6, it is proposed that a steadily increasing human population will automatically develop conditions for the selection of biologically and mentally substandard individuals, whose unenergetic and passive behavior might well feed a steady state in society and technology, introducing controls over further population growth and the pressures on Nature. This type of feedback would presumably operate through a combination of loops Nos. 2 and 4, from energy transformation back to human biology, *via* some features of social organization and values.

Roy Rappaport proposes the existence of control mechanisms operating through ritual observances (social organizational and values components) in relatively isolated tribal groups, but whether these observances function as controls serendipitously or whether the group developed them in order to obtain control is not known. Nor is it clear whether the members of the society are aware of the ecological control functions of the ritual. In any case, the position taken in this essay is that automatic controls have not been sufficiently effective to introduce long-lasting historical control over population and the use of resources.

More specifically, loop No. 4 is represented in the diagram as a dashed line, indicating its highly tentative nature, and the immature state of research bearing upon it. It hints at possible effects, induced by energy transformation, on the cognitive and physiological functioning of human individuals. One such case is the possible constraint on "intelligence" or learning ability exerted by particular nutritional regimes (Harrell et al., 1955; Cravioto, 1968; Eichenwald and Fry, 1969). Other candidates would include the Stott effect, mentioned previously, and possible genetic selection of human traits resulting from migrations due to economic development measures and the resulting changes in breeding population size and practices.

We turn now to loops Nos. 1 and 2. These are represented on the diagram as leading from the output end of the transformation process back to physical environment and human biology, but the arrows are single-headed—that is, information is not shown to flow back to the output end. This is a deliberate omission, designed to dramatize the way the system tends to function at macrolevels. In other words, in the historical episode of industrialization, and to some extent in the entire urbanization process in Homo sapiens history (from ca. 3500 B.C.), humans have been reluctant to act upon biological and environmental consequences of their own actions where the needs being satisfied are important in the hedonistic and power spheres. Or, if they have acted, it has been ameliorative rather than designed to change the workings of the system—seeking new sources of fuel, or new regions to pollute, or inventing medical science to repair the human damage, but not removing the institutional cause of that damage.

With respect to loop No. 1, the effects on the physical environment are both direct and indirect: direct in the obvious sense that any alteration of Nature is its own consequence; indirect in the sense that alterations in one sector will have spin-offs in others. Contemporary environmental pollution provides abundant examples of the indirect chain effects: the application of fertziler to soil changes the edaphic environment and releases energy, but the runoff of nitrates and phosphates from fertilizers or detergents into water supplies causes eutrophication, a change in the nutritive status of the fluid resulting in overproduction of algae, which then decay, encouraging the growth of oxygen-using microorganisms.[11]

The three processes in this feedback loop of major importance for contemporary problems are: pollution, erosion, and aesthetic-inconvenience effects. These are often equated or confused and strong sentiment can be generated without reference to the actual amount of ecological damage. Thus, of the three types, *pollution* is the most serious, since it contains dangers for human health and survival, as well as possible irreversible effects on Nature. Air pollution exemplifies the first of these; eutrophication of lakes illustrates the second. The *erosive* effects are mixed: some, like natural resource exhaustion, are damaging since they cannot be modified or reversed. Others involve less biological damage, though they often permanently change the landscape. The encroachment of highways and tourists on wilderness areas is an example. The purely *aesthetic* or *inconvenience* effects are the least dangerous and are feedbacks to social environments, on the whole, although they often attract the most vociferous action—the ubiquitous beer can and urban dilapidation are examples. Social action focused on these aesthetic spoilages can divert attention from the ecologically and socially more dangerous phenomena.[12]

In the background of these definitions lie controversies over the nature of polluting effects. The term "pollution" is a difficult one, since it inevitably contains value judgments as well as objective measurements of effects. The principal issue concerns whether a state of pollution is to be defined in terms of a provable destructive effect, or whether any intrusion into an existing environment of substances known or suspected to be dangerous in any degree is to be considered as pollution. The sense of urgency is the critical factor here: if one feels that such intrusions are dangerous *per se*, then pollution will be defined in the second sense. A more cautious approach, which demands clear proof of specific effects, will reserve the term "pollution" for the demonstrated cases.

Another basic issue with regard to pollution concerns the widespread assumption that a perfectly clean environment actually exists, or can exist, provided humans mend their ways. Recent studies of the quantity of "polluting" substances in the atmosphere have tended to show varying background amounts, which presumably have existed for a long time, even though some of these (like sulfur dioxide) have risen as a result of industrial activities. A recent study at the University of British Columbia may demonstate that the growth of certain plants, cultivated and wild, is actually stimulated, or reaches normal levels, in the presence of certain pollutants in the air (J. P. Bennett et al., 1974). The authors conclude that "..., clean air is a misnomer.... It seems unreasonable to assume a zero level for many air pollutants when there is no supporting evidence.... The evidence already cited suggests that for most pollutants for which plant growth data are available, the levels which cause stimulation are close to those which can frequently be found in nature." (p. 39)

A related issue concerns the mix of scientific and public-informational objectives in the ecology action movement, and the contradictions between methods and objectives resulting from this. Again, if the sense of urgency is great, there is likely to be a disposition to imply meaning to incomplete or inconclusive bodies of scientific evidence or to feature these data in public announcements. Even when the actual claims are modest, the fact of announcement, given the habits of news media, inevitably confers authority on the results, however vague they may be. Another problem concerns the tendency of the scientist to scorn the cleanliness and aesthetic side of the movement, since, as noted in the text, this issue is not always environmentally significant. However, it should be noted that the milieu of public attitudes often functions on an all-or-none basis; that is, attention to the damaging phenomena often can be created by generating excitement over less important but culturally valued things. All these issues have produced considerable strain within the scientific profession and between scientist and nonscientist members of the environmental movement.

Feedback loop No. 2 runs from the output end of the equation back to human biology. The most obvious process here is sustenance, or nutrition, and its affects on human survival and population dynamics. However, the indirect effects are equally important. Examples: carcinogenic substances in food additives or combustion; the alteration of genetic structures by radiation; direct poisoning by pesticides or nitrates; and the various diseases and functional disorders associated with tropical water impoundments. A recently discovered case is milk intolerance: a genetically determined deficiency of the lactase enzyme, especially frequent in Negro and possibly Asian populations, which prevents the individual from properly digesting lactose, causing gastrointestinal illness (Bayless and Rozenzweig, 1967; Davis and Bolin, 1967). Precisely how this trait emerged is not known, but it is suspected that a process of environmental-cultural-genetic interaction or selection comparable to the sickle-cell disease (Livingstone, 1958) may be responsible (McCracken, 1971). In any event, the condition has attracted considerable attention in the civil rights movement, since for generations well-meaning whites have encouraged the ingestion of milk among ghetto populations, many of whose children cannot digest it properly.

Only recently have we become fully aware of such biological effects. Since a course of human action can perseverate indefinitely due to the cushioning effect of surpluses, or because of the inconspicuousness of impacts on ignored minorities, biologically deleterious behavior can likewise continue until extreme consequences or social action force a sudden change (a "step function" as we shall call it in Chapter 9). Food supplies may be sufficient to permit human populations, or at least a significant fraction, to survive at optimal levels for a considerable period ("buffer mechanism"), and hence the information concerning the harmful consequences may not be fed back efficiently into the system, especially if vested interest in the damaging action is present or if the damage is considered to be a culturally tolerable "cost."[13] In other species, deleterious habits may more quickly or efficiently become "known" in the sense of influencing migration or adaptive genetic patterns and thereby introducing inevitable corrective change. Man's actions are so extensive, so quickly operating, and so heavily influenced by relative judgments that possible regulative feedback effects sometimes cannot be detected until considerable damage has been done—damage that in the early stages, at least, often has more serious social than biological consequences, in the sense of requiring special care for the damaged specimen or in the sense of spreading anxiety and alarm and encouraging sociopolitical conflict.

If the effects of energy output on the physical environment are not fed into loop No. 3, so as to create changes in the values governing the instrumentalities, the consequences are likely to perseverate and accumulate at various rates. Therefore, as noted above, the slowly accumulating effects may generate adaptation in the sense of *tolerance* of dangerous conditions, which can last almost indefinitely, and usually require deliberate mobilization of public sentiment (the Nader effect) before the change in perspective and anxiety level emerges. The system thus breeds a positive social function for anxiety or fear, a common process in contemporary society. In any case, the occurrence of lag phenomena at various points and phases of the feedback process means that *time* becomes a critical variable in the human ecological system and information flow and control are always matters of temporal concern. If we read the ethnological literature correctly, many tribal groups at the time of observation had achieved balances in their local systems, and in only a few cases have ethnologists been able to stay around long enough, or to reconstruct history, so as to obtain evidence showing how these balances evolved. There is also evidence in the record to suggest that existing balances were frequently upset in tribal societies through innovation, warfare, and migration. Tribal man differed mainly from industrial or urban man in the level of his technology, which required more humility in the face of Nature—in other words, more restraints on human behavior.

SOME FURTHER IMPLICATIONS OF FIG. 1

First, it may be pointed out that social organization and values can be substituted for the physical environment component without change in the fundamental processes represented in the diagram. Man can act upon sociocultural phenomena—"social resources"—with technology to produce "social goods" and to release "social energy," just as he can upon the physical environment. This process is formally embodied in the concept of social and economic "planning," but it is evidenced in the routine manipulation of social phenomena by human individuals to obtain their objectives. This social process combines with ecological relationships so as to require the necessary incorporation, in human ecological research, of sociocultural data of various kinds: for example, in studies of air or water pollution, the power structures of municipal politics and industrial enterprises must be researched if amelioration is the objective.[14] At the other end of the developmental scale, certain religious rituals of New Guinea tribalists apparently must be included in a study of the use by these people of the physical environment and the effect of the whole system on human and animal populations (Rappaport, 1967A; 1967B).

A second implication concerns the evident significance of economic considerations in human ecology.[15] Following Lee (1969), we hold that economics is a strictly human phenomenon since it is based on a division of tasks and, accordingly, a symbolic differentiation of the value of the "goods" or product—something nonexistent or at best borderline in other species.[16] The sheer magnitude and complexity of the production process means that different tasks will have greater or lesser significance, leading to differential rewards. These effects are least visible in hunter-gatherer groups, but emerge clearly on all developmental levels above this. The presence or absence of market exchanges or monetary values is not especially important at this level of analysis, although it is at others.[17] Or, more concretely, all human groups, even the hunter-gatherers, display "economics" in the human sense of valuing goods, although as Lee points out (Vayda 1969B version, p. 49), the hunter-gatherers display the most "elementary form" of such economic behavior and, for some purposes, can be taken as "closer" to nonhuman animal ecological processes.

The third observation takes us back to feedback loop No. 3: the relationships between technology, social organization, the press component, and energy. As noted previously, while some informational feedback is always taking place, this varies in kind, quantity, and above all, in the degree of awareness of it on the part of the people involved in the process. However, it is at least probable that in different phases of the ecological transition greater or lesser effects of feedback on the system, and/or awareness, will be found. For example, if the energy transformations typical of tribal societies feed back into the social system in such a way as to control population, then it is also evident that controlling functions of this particular feedback mechanism have been inoperative, ineffectual, or ignored in many contemporary societies. The historical record makes it appear that, as technology and social organization have become more effective and energy conversions more efficient, a progressive loss of control (for better or worse) over the whole output system has been experienced due to the growing autonomy of individual economic behavior and of subsystems (institutions, organizations, vested interests) and their tendency to escalate power;[18] this loss being marked at various historical time horizons by rapidly increasing populations (e.g., those associated with the onset of effective food production, advanced trade and urban nucleation, and powered industrial production).

Other causes of loss of control can be found in certain value-presses concerning man's domination of Nature (especially important in the Western world) and in the removal of the majority of human populations from direct contact with the physical environment and such tasks of energy conversion as food-producing activities. Such sustained contact with Nature *via* subsistence labor, with the social reinforcements of shared reciprocity, must have had its cultural consequences in the form of attitudes of humility toward and subjection to Nature, respect for other species, and conceptions of partnership between man and these species. At least, all of these attitudes are indicated in ethnological studies of tribal peoples and nonmachine civilizations.[19]

A moral view of the problem blames the loss of control on the general secularization of our attitudes toward environment, or, more particularly, that which is defined as pure and impure, clean or unclean. Rigorous definitions of these are to be found in social systems of considerable homogeneity, like tribal societies, but are difficult to achieve in pluralistic societies of any size, where all views are considered equal competitors, and where government and other macroinstitutions therefore eventually introduce their own "rational" conceptions of the situation—which then get into conflict with the local and subsystemic versions. The lack of an overall social consensus on how to define environment and to control human uses of it undoubtedly contributes to the breakdown of controlling feedbacks in loop No. 3, but simply pleading for a consensus in a pluralistic system of subcultures will not help much. Public debates, the making of political choices, and planning are necessary, and scientific standards of "purity" (ambiguous and defective as they often are) will remain the only ones we have for some time.[20]

DIVISION OF PROFESSIONAL LABOR

The scope of human ecology will continue to require cooperative effort by a number of disciplines, and anthropologists increasingly will find it profitable to work in teams with biologists, nutritionists, economists, and others with the requisite skills. Anthropology's habit of attempting to create, out of its rather specialized knowledge, its own comprehensive theories of man and his relationship to environment, will probably change toward a more specialized role as research and theory become more of a cooperative undertaking. It is possible that this role will not be directly concerned with ecological problems, but rather with some standard aspect of anthropological research that is defined as one facet of the total ecological complex. Economic exchange involving cultural definitions of consumption wants, and how these generate pressure against resources, is an example of a topic that could easily become an anthropological specialization for a multidisciplinary cultural ecology (Sahlins, 1972).

We can use Fig. 1 to describe the division of labor among the various professional fields concerned with human ecology. Figure 1 as a whole does not conform to any recognized academic discipline; there are no "departments" of human ecology, although in recent years cross-departmental programs of study have emerged at several universities with rather modest success. The term "environmental sciences" is sometimes used to imply a general field of human ecology, and has been used as a label for some of these interdepartmental study programs. However, the term is misleading, since it does not provide a theoretical rationale for human ecology. Environmental science is a congeries of physical and natural-science approaches to practical problems of pollution, weather changes, earth movements, and natural resources, with a growing component of legal and administrative skills.[21]

Few really practical suggestions for bridging the massive disciplinary boundaries have been offered, despite the considerable amount of rhetoric. Obviously affirmative actions beyond the usual research-team level is needed. Probably a major reorganization of fund-granting agencies along the lines adopted by both the Ford Foundation and the National Science Foundation in recent years will be needed—that is, major and sustained allocation of research funds to research in environmental problems defined as interdisciplinary from the outset, with the awards going only to large efforts involving researchers from several fields. But even this type of thing will not help as long as we continue to operate with limited theoretical frames of reference.

Feedback loop No. 2, from the output end of the transformation process back to human biology, includes the human-adaptability and demographic studies by those concerned with bioanthropology (Baker and Weiner, 1966); by medical researchers concerned with environmental medicine, epidemiology, and ecological causation of disease (Dubos, 1959, 1965; Alland, Nurge & Ng, 1974); by geneticists concerned with similar topics and with population (Reynolds, 1960); and by physiologists concerned with the effects on man (and other species) of pollution, food additives, and the like (Woodwell, 1970). This general field may be called *human bioecology*, and it alone, among the several efforts in human ecology, is a reasonably well-established interdisciplinary or at least interdepartmental operation. Its unity is conferred by the common framework in biological science.[22]

Feedback loop No. 2, from energy and production of goods back into the environment itself, is obviously represented by scientists concerned with pollution and also by the ecology-action and conservation movements, from concern for water and air pollution to preservation of wildlands and species.[23] These groups are often divided and in conflict on various issues—e.g., the quarrel between preservationists and conservationists, between radical environmental-quality people and more temporizing positions advocating moderate pollution in one sector as the price for cleanup in some more important sector, between those who see technology as the villain (Commoner, 1971) and those who blame population (Ehrlich and Holdren, 1971), between those who visualize ecology as a separate issue and those who see it as a phase of a necessary revolution in social and economic institutions. The field blends into the "psychology of space," an approach dominated by urban planners and assorted ecosophers who define environment largely in terms of human needs for and conceptions of space and surroundings.[24]

Within this heterogeneous group of ecological actionists, conservationists, planners, architects, and others, there are serious value conflicts, many of them beginning to surface at the time of writing (1972). Physical-environmental protectionists are willing to abrogate many humanistic values in favor of the natural landscape and wild species, while the social-environmentalists advocate clean, orderly, spacious cities or other arrangements, requiring transformation of the natural environment. The basic issue around which all the conflicts revolve is whether we have the right to conceive of environment in wholly human-centered terms or whether we must ake our cue from existing natural phenomena. This issue will be one theme in ideological, religious, and social-reformist debate for the next generation.

Behind the conservationists and planners is research carried on by biologists and physical scientists concerned with specific consequences of human interventions. Studies of the nitrogen cycle (Commoner, 1968; 1971; Schuphan, 1972); geological effects of nuclear experiments; eutrophication (Hutchinson, 1973); consequences for the soil of artificial chemical fertilization; the alleged "greenhouse effect" due to heavy output of carbon dioxide; chemical interactions between the natural and man-made components of airsheds; radio and light pollution (Riegel, 1973; Swenson and Cochran, 1973); and lead and mercuric poisoning—all are examples.[25] Social scientists have begun to join this effort, in order to suggest how political and socioeconomic mechanisms lead to these environmental consequences (Ridgeway, 1971; Klausner, 1971).

Cultural ecology[26] can be given a narrow definition as the topics covered in the feedback system represented in loop No. 3: the reciprocal relationships between the production of energy and goods, cultural values, social organization, technology and population. However, in line with the interpretations of human relations with the environment made in this book, cultural ecology is really equivalent to human ecology—or is rapidly becoming so. Several disciplines operate in this field: anthropology, geography, sociology, economics, and a number of offshoots and special-izations of these. Anthropological cultural ecology has been particularly concerned with the way these reciprocal relationships function in rela-tively isolated, low-energy societies, often living in specialized environ-ments. Existing works in the field seem to alternate between approaches that take the environment as the starting point (e.g., arid lands or the tropics) and then see how these specialized settings have influenced social organization and cultural ideas and those that take the subsistence system (e.g., pastoralism, or swidden agriculture, and its social concomitants) and see if similar patterns have emerged in similar environments.

The research produced by anthropological cultural ecologists will be discussed in Chapters 6 and 7. In Chapter 6 I also provide a topical classification and history of the field. However, it should be said that the field is not tightly organized around specific theoretical principles and hypotheses but, like most of anthropology, is a loosely assembled body of studies of particular societies on the basis of certain distinctive features. There is the usual ethnological emphasis on providing variant examples of particular phenomena, although particular problems (e.g., the work on "predatory expansion" of tribal societies and its political, military, and ecological significance) can capture the interest of field workers for a time and become the topic of a series of studies.

Other cultural-ecological approaches may be treated briefly. *Sociologi-cal ecology*—at least the dominant branch focusing on the geographical distribution of social components in space—has indirect connections with my frame of reference for human ecology, since it is only marginally concerned with energy conversion and its effects on Nature and Society.[27] However, at least two rural sociologists have shown considerable interest in natural resources and kindred problems[28] and have tried to produce some general theory as well as empirical studies.

The key issue in sociological ecology is the presence or absence of a voluntaristic element in theory and analysis. Hawley (1950), in a classic sociological ecology text, acknowledged the importance of a concept of adaptation because it introduced a "rationalistic" (i.e., choice, decision) factor into the theory, but relatively little research featuring such concepts has been produced by sociologists who have preferred, on the whole, to stick to descriptive presentations of sociocultural, psychological, and spacial correlations. Organic analogies, including homeostasis, have figured in sociological ecology for a long time, but with one or two very recent exceptions (Emery and Trist, 1973) there seem to be few linkages between this older tradition and the newer systems theorists in sociology (Buckley, 1967; Berrien, 1968; Breed, 1971; Ackoff and Emery, 1972). In general, systems theory in sociology has not been considered to be ecology.[29]

Ecological interests in *psychology* are represented by two subfields, both relatively new.[30] "Ecological psychology" is a highly technical investigation: a kind of quantitative cultural anthropology or ethnology of the way surroundings bring forth specific stylized behavior; e.g., football playing and watching occur at football games. As Barker (1968) has expounded it, the field involves quantitative specifications of various attributes of the social environment and some features of the physical, although only insofar as they are encompassed in social milieus. Prediction of behavior appears to be the general goal. The use of the term "ecological" here is misleading, although it is in harmony with one theme of our approach: the need to specify the dimensions of the social environment.

"Environmental psychology," the second subfield, is a conscious attempt by psychologists to relate to the environmental movement. A survey of its characteristics is available in Downs and Stea (1973) a collaboration between a psychologist and geographer. The field aims at showing the relationship between behavior and thought patterns to the physical environment and the use of resources. A specific research example, involving an explanation of the differences between responses to tornado danger exhibited by residents of the northern and southern United States, is described in note 1, Chapter 8. The field obviously blends with the "environmental perception" movement in geography, described below.

Cultural or *human geography* has a mainly descriptive tradition, with an emphasis on distribution of cultural phenomena in space, much like classic sociological ecology. Geographers have always been aware of the relationships of their field to ecology (e.g., Barrows, 1923), and recently organic analogies, including the ecosystem, have attracted their attention as a possible unifying frame of reference for the whole discipline

(Stoddart, 1965; 1967). Stoddart's own research on island ecology constitutes one major contribution of this approach; several other geographers, some teamed with natural ecologists, have also pursued the island topic, since the role of man can be more easily analyzed in these bounded habitats than in larger continental contexts (see Fosberg, 1963, for a symposium of these island ecosystem studies including the human factor). Another current approach, inaugurated by Gilbert White, is concerned with human perceptions of the environment, and the way cultural values shape human response to the environment.[31] This approach has much to contribute to the description of the feedbacks in the loop No. 3 area.

Economic geography is of course concerned with energy conversion, although its approach has generally been more descriptive than processual.[32] However, one important technique produced by economic geographers is the analysis of settlement location as a function of time and distance variables in human instrumental activities. Although an essentially empirical science, it is based on a geometric model, built on the "least effort" assumption (Zipf, 1949): other things being equal, people will seek to minimize the cost of movement for obtaining the things they want and need. If these movements are theoretically perfect, and no factor other than the most rational expenditure of energy, time, and money is influential, settlements will arrange themselves on a two-dimensional surface in regular geometric patterns, with "central places" (e.g., major service towns) always fewer in number than the secondary centers, and so on down through a hierarchy of nucleated centers with varying amounts of services. The central places thus would come to be surrounded by regular grids of secondary and tertiary, etc. centers. The model works best in geographical conditions where transportation arteries are evenly distributed across a relatively featureless surface and the economic occupation system is also evenly distributed: e.g., an agricultural plain. It turns out that one part of the globe where the model is closely approximated is the Great Plains of North America.[33]

There is of course a question as to whether this approach, with its great potential use for anthropology, really belongs in our definition of human ecology. The phenomena it concerns appear to be contained somewhere inside of the processes represented in loop No. 3, but it is not directly involved with energy production and the effects of this on society and environment. It describes certain conditions under which transformations may take place, but it does not analyze the process in detail.

Historical accounts of man's use of environment have interested a variety of disciplines, although generally these studies seem to fit into geography. Walter Webb's study of the Great Plains (1931) is the American classic in the field; Carl Sauer has contributed much of this (e.g., 1966); in Britain, a group of economic historians and natural ecologists have turned to historical studies: Tubbs' account of the New Forest of England (1969) illustrates the empirical approach; Russell's general account of "Man, Nature and History" (1967)—the synthesizing mode. Ladurie (1971) presents a semi-popular history of climate and its effects on man. To some extent, these historical studies replace the old Huntington style of interpretation, which assumed more environmental influence than was actually there—although the attempt to recount man's historical dealings with Nature was a valid and useful one.

I shall not discuss the range of research associated with feedback loop No. 4, since it extends beyond the topic of the book. Obviously, these studies are carried on by bioecologists, psychologists, and occasionally, anthropologists, and the references for the earlier discussion of Fig. 1 provided some samples.

To summarize: the major purpose of this chapter was to provide a definition of human ecology and the division of labor among scientific specialists concerned with it. Our special subject, cultural ecology, was seen to center on one component of the larger one, and we represented this focus by a feedback loop connecting energy output with a series of components emanating from human behavior: value and need presses, social organization, and technology and other cultural factors. By its nature, this network of feedback channels occupies the center stage in contemporary issues of human relationships to the natural environment and resources, but anthropologists to date have shown relatively little concern with these issues.

The next chapter continues the discussion of human ecology with further analysis of the problem of the extent to which man can be studied as part of Nature or requires a special frame of reference.

NOTES

[1] Let me hasten to add that if this sounds like a reversion to instinct theory, nothing is farther from my thoughts. In the first place, it is clear that human behavior contains the mechanisms for its own control—as well as a great deal of creative and destructive capacity. It is also clear that the capacities for exceeding reasonable limits in acquisitive and want-satisfying behavior occur under certain kinds of cultural conditions and are not a constant. I am fully aware of the oversimplifications of issues of this type which Ardrey and Lorenz or Tiger and Fox (but especially Ardrey) have offered, and I insist on qualifications. However, I suggest also that there might be a long-term bend in the direction of acquisitive or want-satisfying or creative—or in any case "output-oriented"—behavior in Homo

sapiens, which may show itself most clearly over long periods of time, or especially when favorable cultural conditions are operating over long periods. In other words, the human species is not "perfect" or neutral; it may have a bias built into its evolutionary status that has accounted for its ecological dominance. *Something* has to account for this dominance. (In any case, a typical example of social action related to the acquisitiveness issue is represented by the current debate over suitable methods for the control of pollution. Both "carrot" and "stick" methods have been advocated, but a third approach sees the problem as one of "pricing" the waste-disposal capacity of the environment, and charging for its use—a combination of both "carrot" and "stick" approaches [Solow, 1971]. That is, to make use of existing institutions—in this case the market economy—to encourage a change in practice.)

[2]Cf. J. Bronowski: "Man is above the other animals not because he is alive as they are, but because he has a life unlike theirs" (1971, p. 6). I do not like the word "above," but Bronowski may not mean it quite that way—he is referring to the stubborn fact that humans do live differently, think differently, and hence have a different relationship to Nature—and, in addition, also share in Nature as do the other species. Dualism is both a necessary view, for some analytical purposes, and also a dangerous one when it creates an exaggerated or false dichotomy between man and Nature. But the point is that humans can *think* in such terms, and *that* becomes an ecological fact.

[3]Reviews of the energy situation, with discussions of exponential curves of increase in energy consumption, are found in the September 1971 issue of *Scientific American*. Somewhat more technical appraisals are found in several issues of the *Technology Review* for 1971, and an article by Boffey (1970). The world picture of energy resources and the economics of energy production is summarized by Manners (1964). An appraisal of the energy-generating potential of modern technology, in relation to projections of population growth, is found in an article by Weinberg and Hammon (1970). However, they do not consider the degradational effects on the environment of the enormous magnitudes of energy we are capable of producing (they point out that a standard of living comparable to that enjoyed by the "developed countries" could be maintained up to a level of 20 billions of people—although they acknowledge the existence of social stress if the attempt is made). The pioneer philosophical exegesis of the energy-release potential of man, taking the form of an analysis of man as *the* major geological transformation agent, was contributed by Vernadsky (1945). This 1945 paper includes the same uncritical appraisal of human potential that was noted for Leslie White.

[4]Likewise, Leonard Cottrell's book, *Energy and Society* (1955), has been generally ignored by sociologists. While utilitarian ideas have saturated social science, there has also been a perennial critique of them. In the case of the energy theory of cultural development and human behavior, the objectionable implication has been identified as "Marxist" or "materialist"—that is, an equation of attempts to compare cultures and social systems on the basis of their energy outputs, with an anti-humanist position. Well and good, but the humanist position is equally involved in the failure to incorporate an ethic of responsibility for Nature and Earth.

[5]This is, in broad terms, the view of Vayda and Rappaport (1968), although both qualify the argument in ways to be discussed later. Other examples of the willingness to see human ecology as part of natural ecology are to be found in the writings of contemporary group of ethologists and ethological commentators summarized by Ashley-Montagu in his essay, "The New Litany of 'Innate Depravity,' or Original Sin Revisited" (1971). More analytical critiques are presented by Callan (1970), especially in the final chapter, and by Alland (1972). I am in complete accord with the attempt to see human behavior as problematic in its

effects because of its "natural" or "animal" basis (see Hallowell, 1960, for the pioneer attempt), but the critics are right when they point out that this, too, is a one-sided view, a swing to the complete opposite of the anthropocentric position. Alland's critique of Ardrey, Lorenz, Morris, and others makes the useful point that territoriality and aggression are not "instinctive" in humans but are subject to social directives and incentives. However, there are some serious ambiguities in Alland's argument. For example, in his discussion of Ardrey's territoriality instinct, Alland (1972) notes that

> ... Julian Steward has demonstrated that patterns related to the organization of work can be seen as specific adaptations to ecological conditions. If, on the other hand, territoriality were instinctive, and if its most perfect expression were in capitalism, we might ask: why did it take so long (two or three million years!) for this basic instinct to find its proper expression in human behavior? For Ardrey, the incentive which drives humans is not only property but affluence.... Marshall Sahlins has shown through a careful analysis of ... hunting and gathering bands that such people shun abundant possessions. (p. 70)

In the first place, a persistent tendency or tilt of some kind in human behavior need not be comprehensively represented in all instances and times, and if capitalism is territoriality's and acquisitiveness' pinnacle, it could have been reached over a long period of human history; time is strictly relative here, it is no proof or disproof of the "instinct." Secondly, the fact that hunter-gatherer groups shun possessions (though they do have territories!) does not necessarily mean that they lack the "tendency"—they might simply suppress it for good reasons. Although I concur with Alland and others that "instinct" theory is wrong, his type of argumentation does not refute the fact that human behavior displays long-term trends toward increasing organization of resources and possessory allocations.

[6]The discussion here of energy measurement is indebted to a paper by Emilio Moran (1973). Energy measurement is largely equivalent to general systems theory and modeling, and the two terms are often used interchangeably. (For introductory treatments of general systems theory and systems analysis, see Berrien, 1968; Rapoport, 1968.) The term "energetics" is sometimes used as another equivalent, although some anthropologists use this term to describe studies of work in human groups in which food intake and energy output in the form of labor is measured. Howard Odum's book, *Environment, Power, and Society*, discussed in the next chapter, represents an attempt to model human systems on the basis of energy flow mechanics and other elements or systems analysis.

[7]The distinction between "cognitive understandings" and needs for "differentiation" represents a distinction related to Firth's "social structure" (the cognitive-normative map of society) and "social organization" (the actual, ongoing activities with their own rules and pragmatic accommodations, which may or may not conform to the map). This distinction has not been adequately utilized in cultural-ecological studies, but, as I shall argue, it is fundamental for a socially relevant approach (see Firth, 1954; 1955).

[8]See Wiener, 1949; 1950. As noted earlier, all the basic illustrative examples in the classic statements of the cybernetic process were drawn from machines, and this persists today: perhaps the most common illustration of feedback processes in contemporary discussions is the thermostat. For a more recent discussion of feedback in the context of society and economy, with comparisons to biological cybernetics, see Hardin, 1963. A good elementary introduction is presented by Nagel and Tustin (1955). A recent book edited by Van Dyne (1969) uses feedback or "ecosystem" as a new approach to natural resource management. In this sense, the concept refers to the consideration of *all* costs and effects of resource use, in

an effort to attain greater control or regulation. (More on this issue in the next chapter.)

[9]Reflections of this point of view, from varying professional and preferential perspectives, can be found in the following: Bertram, 1959; Medawar, 1960; Boulding, 1962; Cole, 1964; McKinley, 1964; Glacken, 1966; Brown, 1969. The view emerges frequently in the pronouncements of spokesmen for the radical wing of the ecology action movement, where it can be seen as part of the general alienation from and disenchantment with man characteristic of the times ("We have met the enemy and he is us"; or "Man: One of Evolution's Mistakes"—Koestler, 1969). Commoner (1966; 1971) takes a more positive view—namely, that man's fate is in his own hands and he must rely on his abilities to introduce a measure of control and regulation over his attack on Nature. (Even so, there is no room for false optimism, and we will be hard pressed to control our wants.) As a general rule, most proponents of "anti-human" action see increasing population as the major cause of the difficulties. While human populations certainly are part of the problem, a static or reduced population in itself will not necessarily solve the problems of environmental deterioration, since wants are relative to population, not strictly correlatable with it. A reduced population could continue to use resources at the same or even an enhanced rate. In addition, many of the current ecological problems are caused by maldistribution of population, not by specific overall magnitudes. (For contrasting discussions of the role of population, see Coale, 1970; Commoner, 1971; Ehrlich and Holdren, 1971; and later discussions and notes.)

[10]An example of the complexities of feedback in loop No. 3 can be provided. This concerns the socionatural system of the automobile and its noxious emissions, which create smog problems in all large cities. Originally, the internal combustion engine was developed as a source of a moderate amount of power at the cheapest possible price. Gasoline was expensive; incomes were modest. As the economy "developed," and as gasoline became abundant, the demand for more power started a cycle of engineering attempts to increase the power of the engine. At no time in this history was any consideration given to the question of wastes produced by the engine: its nonpolluting capacity in its early days was not the result of deliberate design but was a secondary effect of the small numbers in use and the modest power generated. Hence, when the power was increased, this was done without concern for emissions. Since the power enhancement requires a higher proportion of fuel to air in the mixture fed to the carburetor, there has been a greater chance that hydrocarbons will escape unburned—actually the increased power is created at the cost of rather inefficient combustion and, of course, greater emission of by-products of combustion. When these gases escape into the air, the effects of sunlight, temperature inversions, and other things result in photochemical smog. The problem now is that we had permitted a rising dependence on the automobile as a transportation device, until the public transport facilities of many cities were allowed to deteriorate or not to expand to accommodate needs. In addition to this, the commercial exigencies resulted in a cultural change involving heavy symbolism in the automobile as a source of ego gratification, prestige, and the like. The combination of vested financial interests, essential transportation, and emotional need-fulfillment creates a massive sociocultural investment in the automobile. The case suggests that the entire monster was created or rather incepted by a single cognitive omission: the failure to be concerned, at least to any significant extent, with the problem of wastes by an optimistic society on a development kick. If wastes had been a significant factor at the beginning, the engineering development would have been different: toward an engine (not necessarily an internal combustion type) with higher power and lower emissions. In systemic terms, the feedback down the line kept reinforcing the value press toward higher power, symbolic status

functions, and the like, without reference to the pollution dangers. Information relevant to wastes and their effects was ignored or disbelieved—or, the functioning of feedback loop No. 3 was defective. By now the knowledge is public, but little has been done because the automobile complex represents such a massive economic, social, and psychological investment. There are three grand alternatives: the development of new or revised forms of transportation, serious attempts at control of manufacturing of the automobile, or drastic rationing of automotive fuel. Moves by government are being made at the time of writing along all these fronts, but they are running into heavy opposition. Specialists in the field seem to feel that the development of alternative transportation facilities is a way around the political risks, in a permissive egalitarian democracy, associated with curbing investment and individual want-gratification.

[11]Although I emphasize the environmental impact of modern technology, tribal technologies also had their effects. Low population and simple technology meant that impact was usually specialized, in the case of the effects on trees in the Great Plains by bison-hunters (Wedel, 1960 argues against significant impact, but Wells, 1969, presents paleobotanical evidence suggesting that grass firing associated with the hunts may well have reduced the extent of forest "islands"). The specialization of impact or the moderate use of resources meant that balances were struck with nature in which the band or village could exist indefinitely without seriously damaging the environment or preventing its regeneration. However, in some cases, as in the salinization of irrigation works or denudation of plant cover in the ancient Middle East, the impacts could become substantial over long periods. In other cases, the impact of tribal settlements could substantially alter the native flora and fauna, but not in the sense of destruction or diminishing resources (as in the probable impact of early agriculture on forests in northern Europe—e.g. Clark, 1945; and in northeastern North America, Maxwell, 1910 and Day, 1953). Recently some paleontologists have suggested that early hunters in North America may well have been responsible for the extinction of the large native fauna typical of the Ice Age (Krantz, 1970). Still another effect occurred when tribal peoples encountered Europeans: population increase or intensified production using traditional methods has often meant increased environmental impact (for North America, see Crosby, 1972). "Peasant" agricultures are typical examples (e.g., for the tropics, Janzen, 1973). For environmental consequences of pre-industrial agriculture in Europe, see Darling, 1964 and Jones, forthcoming). An early account of tribal and premodern civilized impacts on Nature is in Thomas, 1956B, Part I. We shall return to the problem of tribal impacts on Nature in Chapter 5.

[12]See the article by Carpenter (1970) for a classification of "current environmental concerns" from the standpoint of practical policy and action considerations. It should be noted also that the militant wing of the Black civil rights movement, and the New Left political movements, have opposed ecology action as diversionary (Neuhaus, 1971). An example of the kind of listing of environmental problems that attracts this accusation is the following, issued in 1970 as an information sheet by the World Wildlife Fund: (all terms are quotes) too many people; too much trash; polluted air; poisons; atomic radiation; too much garbage; food adulterants; too much sewage; water wasted; wasted rainfall (overpaving); noise; lack of privacy; destruction of night. Each of these is described briefly and remedies are proposed, but the extremely complex problems of comparing benefits with costs in each case are not discussed. (A different mood is presented by Leiss, 1972: a Marxist analysis of the environmental crisis that is concerned particularly with the close relationship between the exploitation of humans and Nature.)

[13]A pioneer study with implications for these problems is Allan Holmberg's report on the Siriono of eastern Bolivia (1950). Holmberg deliberately chose this group because he wanted to study a people who were "perennially hungry" in order to find out what effects

food-anxiety would have on the culture. Among other things, Holmberg concluded that the Siriono compensate for severe and chronic hunger by allowing great license in the sphere of sexual behavior. Prestige, magic, hunting behavior, child socialization, and many other things also were seen to be related to the strong hunger drive. Newman (1962) outlines the ecological and social dimensions of nutritional problems, noting that malnutrition affects different segments of a society differently, thus having implications for evolutionary changes. Gross and Underwood (1971) provide an empirical case for Brazil: how a substandard diet among sisal laborers results in the man receiving the lion's share of food energy, with women and children getting a substandard diet. (For a general review of the ecology of food on a species level, see Brown and Finsterbusch, 1972.)

[14]The linkage between politics and urban and natural resource ecology is hardly new, since it has lain in the background of natural resource theory for years (see G.-H. Smith, 1965, for an example of a text on resources with a standard, more-or-less "establishment"-oriented approach to the problem). However, an explicit approach to the political or power dimension of current resource and pollution problems is very recent. Among some recent formulations: F. E. Smith, 1966; Anderson, 1970; Eisenbud, 1970; National Research Council, 1970; Ridgeway, 1970; Sax, 1971.

[15]McHale's (1962) suggestion that human or cultural ecology is really "econology" is certainly acceptable to the writer although I have had some difficulty adopting the term. Lee's (1969) paper on Bushman subsistence is a good example of the contribution an economic analysis can make to ecological studies at the tribal level. Lee's analysis also demonstrates how feedback from the energy-transformation system comes back through the social and technological system to limit use of resources (discussed in more detail in Chapter 6). Only a thoroughgoing economic analysis can document this vital control, apparently greatly diminished in contemporary industrial societies. Piddocke's (1965) reanalysis of the Potlatch data is another example of econological analysis insofar as he shows that the potlatch "counter(ed) the effects of varying resource productivity by promoting exchanges of food from those groups enjoying a temporary surplus to those groups suffering a temporary deficit." He calls this a "function," thus following the ethnological tradition of unwillingness to attribute rational purpose to tribal men. The writer suspects that at least some Kwakiutl knew full well what they were doing, no matter how elaborately they dressed the activity in ritual trappings (cf. Firth's "structure"-"organization" dichotomy). Turning to contemporary econological analysis, Crutchfield and Pontecorvo (1969) propose that traditional biological conservation measures to preserve the Pacific salmon population are bound to fail, since they completely ignore the fact that the salmon is an economic good. They would substitute control of the numbers of fishermen and the nature of their gear, in order to promote greater efficiency of operation and, hence, conservation of the fish. We cannot be sure that they are right, but their argument documents one basic point of the book: that man's relation to Nature is a projection out of his institutional activities, and has to be governed through the rules of those activities.

[16]Once again it should be noted that I seem to argue here for relative human uniqueness, and that this appears to conflict with ideas in current evolutionary interpretations, which view animal and human characteristics as continuous rather than discontinuous. I have no intention of reviving the simplistic notion of "culture" as a unique human emergent property, not rooted in phylogenetic development, which man shares with other species. However, the problem explored in this essay is not evolution but behavioral exploitation of the environment on a nonrecoverable scale, and for this we have few or no important analogs in nonhuman animal behavior.

[17]I am referring here to the formal vs. substantive definitions of economic theory in the

field of economic anthropology. The formalists, represented by Dalton (1961), hold that the absence of true markets in tribal and other simpler societies prevent the use of modern economic theory in analyzing them; the substantivists (e.g., Scott Cook, 1966) argue that economic theory is not exclusively applicable to developed economies with markets and extensive use of monetary standards, and that barter and other forms of nonmarket, nonmonetary exchange are as common in developed economies as in tribal. The only problem is quantification: the economic systems that lack true markets may require rather specialized modes of analysis since many of the exchange values are qualitative. This may, in fact, be the only issue at stake between the two positions, which represent, in the writer's opinion, a spurious controversy in which data and theory are confused. (For discussions of the controversy, see Cohen, 1967; Kaplan, 1968; Edel, 1969; Schneider, 1974.) However, the controversy may be serving a useful end in that it calls attention to the fact that a broader synthesis is needed in cultural anthropology—a synthesis of economic, ecological, and social anthropology, in which social exchange theory may play the crucial role.

[18]This point has been developed in various economic, political, philosophical, and sociological writings. For the escalation issue, see Meadows et al., 1972. Crowe (1969), in a commentary on Hardin's "The Tragedy of the Commons" paper (1968), points out that a major "myth" of our time is that of "common values," and that the increasing proliferation of divergent value systems in a pluralistic society leads to difficulties in establishing a consensus on direction and regulation. Strong (1970) explores the destructive consequences of pluralism for land use, pleading for a new uniform "land ethic." Caldwell (1970) provides a most useful synthesis of modern social and ideological needs and issues arising out of the "environmental quality" problem. Actually all societies are really mosaics of separate value systems, which can move into conflict whenever competition or deprivation becomes felt (the "folk community" is a passing state of being, a *phase*, not permanent *thing*). In anthropology, the rise of "conflict theory" in political studies is another instance of the growing awareness of this fact. Blau (1970) provides a sociological analysis of the effects of increasing size of the social organ: he holds that marginal productivity results from indefinite increases in size due to increasing problems of articulation of segments.

[19]One of the earliest and most impressive attempts at portraying this constellation of humility-concepts was Frank Speck's *Naskapi* (1935), which demonstrates how a hunting-gathering people in a forbidding natural environment conceptualized their humble status in the face of Nature with the Windigo notion of an all-powerful, sweeping, but tenuous force largely contemptuous of mere Man—a concept reminiscent, of course, of early Judaic notions of Jahveh, developed among desert nomads. (On the other hand, Judaism also found a role for the prophets, who were anything but humble.) Turnbull (1972) phrases the "humility" theme differently, noting that in a low-technology society there has to be considerable "adaptiveness" (conformity) and interplay between the physical and social dimensions of life.

[20]Rene Dubos (1969), however, feels we need more: his pamphlet is entitled *A Theology of the Earth*, and in it he advocates a new religion of man-environment relations on the basis of the fact that we have confused religion and science, looking to science for the kind of moral guidance that only religion can provide. (See also, Revelle and Landsberg, 1970B: "Ecology as an Ethical Science.") Mary Douglas takes a somewhat related view, though with greater emphasis on ritual, in several pieces (1966; 1968; 1970). In the 1970 essay, on the role of anthropology in the contemporary ecological crisis, she begins by citing familiar materials from tribal studies, showing that their views of environment are rooted in their social systems and cultural values. For example, beliefs and taboos concerning ritual purity, which

simultaneously define what is clean and unclean in the environment, also provide mechanisms of social control—hence such notions of purity and cleanliness parallel our own concepts of polluters and pollution; or, how tribal societies gain a conception of climate from their "timetable" of subsistence activities, a conception that is always relative to the actual parameters of temperature, humidity, etc. She concludes with a culturalistic argument concerning the basis of an environmental ethic: that a less destructive view of man-environment relations must be rooted in a moral consensus—"Community endows its environment with credibility." She adds that this concensus is a developing and changing thing, and that we "*must* [italics hers] talk threateningly about time, money, God and Nature if we hope to get anything done." That is, controversy over the environment and the dangers to it must exist as part of the move toward consensus, and this controversy should never cease. Her argument, while intriguing, is somewhat hard to follow, due to the highly literary approach of the essay. It is not entirely clear to the writer whether she supports rational scientific planning for environmental change as our only hope, or whether she more or less opposes it as unhuman, uncultural, mechanical; or perhaps she recognizes that if we plan without a clear consensus, we run the risk of authoritarianism. "The day when everyone can see exactly what is on the end of everyone's fork, on that day there is no pollution and no purity and nothing edible or inedible, credible or incredible, because the classifications of social life are gone. There is no more meaning." Is she saying that we need a little pollution in order to permit us to define pollution—that is, to preserve a sense of good and bad as well as clean and unclean? Whatever she means, she is right about one thing: the lack of consensus, the scientization or secularization of our concepts of clean and unclean that creates difficulties in defining a substance as dangerous, when "scientific" tests are ambiguous. This is particularly evident for things such as drugs, foods, food additives, pesticides, and fertilizers. But Douglas is basically hazy about the difference between a homogeneous and a pluralistic cultural system, and does not seem to recognize the difficulties of reaching consensus in the latter and the need for a more regulative, planned, incentive-finding approach.

[21]For a survey of the environmental sciences, see Pitts and Metcalf, 1969. For a discussion of the general problem of synthesis in human ecology and its components, with a strong emphasis on the cultural basis on human ecology, see Sears, 1954. A discussion of the inadequacies of contemporary university academic structure for handling human ecology is found in Hare, 1970.

[22]The medical ecology segment of this field has also produced some remarkable examples of scientific journalism relating disease to social phenomena. A favorite of the writer's is an analysis of a socionatural system by Powell (1949): the interplay of the level of medical knowledge, social stratification and elitist ideologies, and disease in the yellow fever epidemic in Philadelphia in 1793. Economists are beginning to include biological "costs" in their calculations of the price equity problem in new technological advances (e.g., Sagan, 1972, for the human costs of nuclear power). Boyden (1970) presents a symposium on various biological consequences of civilization.

[23]The environmental movement has produced a large number of original books and anthologies in the past three years. Shephard and McKinley, 1969; Helfrich, 1970; Boughey, 1971; Wagner, 1971; Ehrlich and Ehrlich, 1972; and Smith, 1972 are examples. Boughey and Smith are the first to include substantial reviews of anthropological ecology—especially prehistoric and paleontological aspects. See Sills, 1975, for a review of the environmental movement.

[24]The field is represented by extremes of "loose" and "strict," or at least specific

approaches. The "loose" range from sheer urbanistic fantasy (Soleri, 1971) to deliberate attempts to use aesthetics as the model for planning (Ewald, 1967–68) to an elaborate attempt by McHarg (1970) to combine ecological and space-utilization themes in a grand design. The "strict" is represented by Litton (1970) in a general essay, Halprin (1970) in a theory of the planning process, and Lansing et al. (1970) in concrete attempts at residential planning on ecological principles. In a class by themselves are Gottman's "megalopolis" scheme (1961) and the "ekistics" approach of Doxiadis (1967; 1970); these two approaches dealing with formal theories of man's use of spatial relationships and processes of communication and interaction. Chapple (1970) presents an anthropological conception of spatial patterns in culture, called "proxemics" by some practitioners; Watson (1972) gives a current review of the field; Douglas (1972) applies spatial organization ideas to domestic arrangements. In these anthropological efforts, as in the architectural and planning field, space is transformed into a wholly cultural or cognitive entity and the relationship to ecology is specialized.

[25] A convenient source of semitechnical reports on such phenomena is the magazine *Environment*, published by the Committee for Environmental Information, St. Louis. For more technical data, the AAAS publication *Science* is probably the best single source. The compilation edited by Farvar and Milton (1972) provides reviews of research on environmental and biological consequences of economic development programs in emerging nations.

[26] As may be apparent from earlier discussions, until recently, cultural ecology and its antecedents tended to usurp the ecological interests in anthropology, but this is no longer the case, as anthropologists from other subdisciplines have entered the field. There now exist distinct branches of anthropological ecology in prehistory (Watson and Watson, 1969), bioanthropology (Baker and Weiner, 1966; Baker and Dutt, 1972), demography (Polgar, 1971; 1972); nutritional studies (Newman, 1962), and others—references are supplied to all of these at various points in the book.

[27] For a survey of sociological ecology, see Theodorson, 1961. Hawley's (1950) remains the best general textbook. Abu-Lughod (1968) and Willhelm (1962) present critiques along the lines suggested here. Klausner's book (1971) is an attempt by a sociologist to handle the contemporary environmental issues. The classical study of technology's influence on society by sociologists has an indirect bearing on the ecological problem (Ogburn, 1956).

[28] Although none of these has shown much interest in the problem of man's impact on the environment, and on man. Some typical research: Gibbs, 1958; 1964; and a theoretical statement by Firey, 1959. Both Gibbs and Firey appear to be concerned mainly with economic growth and rationality. Gibbs' 1964 paper is a case in point: he shows that the artesian well-drilling farmers in west Texas behave "rationally" in the sense that they make accurate accounting of costs in getting and using water and profiting by it, but he fails to recognize the damage these wells are doing to a probably irreplaceable subsurface reservoir. If this long term cost factor is considered, the short-term, individually adaptive behavior cannot be considered rational or adaptive. (For a detailed history of the west Texas wells, and an analysis of the socioeconomic forces responsible, see Green, 1973.)

[29] A recent book by Samuel Klausner (1971) represents one attempt at developing a sociological approach to environmental questions outside of the traditional sociological ecology frame. In some respects the book complements mine, especially in discussions of what he calls "resource decisions" and other socioeconomic aspects of the contemporary situation, the nature of interdisciplinary cooperation, and aspects of social planning. However, since Klausner's attempt to develop a general social theory of ecological issues is

little more than a restatement of familiar ideas and categories from the functionalist social theory of Talcott Parsons, he fails to penetrate the distinctive issues of society in a capitalist or economic-growth framework. The important role of social stratification in providing differential rewards is largely ignored. The basic difficulty with Klausner's approach is that he bases his theory on neutral, descriptive propositions about behavior, whereas a sense of problem is required, i.e., that man is capable of performing destructive actions or that an ideology of equality in an unequal allocative system results in massive pressures on the environment.

[30]For a collection of papers on various aspects of ecological and environmental psychology, presented to the 1971 meetings of the American Psychological Association, see Wohlwill and Carson, 1972. These papers include reviews of the "crowding" syndrome in the behavior of animals and man, effects of room size on hospital patients, architectural aspects of prisons and effects on inmates, and others. A detailed research report on a major investigation in "ecological psychology" proper is available in the work of Barker and Schoggen (1973). This is a study of two small rural towns, one in Kansas, the other in Yorkshire, England. The research attempts to account for differences in the behavior of residents of the two towns by precise analyses of the differences in community physical setting, layout, and social ecology. No reference is made to comparable, though less quantitatively specific, approaches in sociology and cultural anthropology; indeed, the term "culture" does not appear in the book, so far as I could determine. Nevertheless, the methodology has many intriguing features and community-study social scientists could benefit greatly from a careful study of the approach.

[31]For some examples of research in perceptual geography, see Kates, 1962; Kates, et al. 1973; Burton and Kates, 1964; Saarinen, 1966; 1969 (his 1969 paper is a general review of perceptual geography); Gilbert White (1966) applies his frame to the problem of public attitudes toward environmental issues. (More generally, Mikesell, 1967 identifies many ecological interests in anthropology as geographical in disciplinary locus; and for examples of such papers, with mixed geographical and anthropological themes, see Kristof, 1959; Curry, 1952; Price, 1955; Duncan, 1962; Johnson, 1957; Murphey, 1951.)

[32]An excellent introduction to the techniques and models used by economic geographers is provided by Chorley and Haggett (1967). An especially illuminating example of economic-geographic analysis (though produced by an agricultural economist) is a paper by Anderson (1950). This paper and others by students of the Great Plains and other sparsely populated regions of North America (e.g., Kraenzel, 1967) show how the rising cost of services produced by diminishing population density create deprivation, which in turn may generate Populist political and economic movements. The latter have been extensively researched by sociologists and political scientists, although the specific role of environment and adaptational strategies have been taken for granted rather than systematically analyzed.

[33]For a review of settlement location theory, see Garner, 1967. The available anthropological data probably most susceptible to locational analysis are from archeological surveys, where a large number of settlements with systematic estimates of their population and range of productive activities have been made. Published applications of the technique had begun to appear at the time of writing: Gregory A. Johnson, 1972. Robert Canfield has attempted to apply generalized central-place theory to data on settlement and politics in Afghanistan (1973A and 1973B). Other possibilities of application exist for studies of tribal boundaries and areas, which up to now have been handled largely in terms of cultural factors such as identity and similarity-difference ratios, although Leach and others have explored questions of power and movement (Leach, 1954, 1964; Barth, 1969).

CHAPTER 4

System, Ecosystem, and Social System

Much has been written about systems, and much overwritten. There is always that yearning for certainty in social science, a reaction to the vagueness of categories that depend, in the last analysis, on mental constructs of reality and not measurable reality itself—that search for hard categories filled with hard data, or for imposing rhetoric and terminology that seems so much better than "soft" language based on interpretation rather than consequence. Systems theory when applied to human affairs unfortunately often feeds these very human but also borderline authoritarian impulses, and we can do no better than to cite the judgment of C. A. McClelland (1965):

> Although we are still at the beginning, general-systems analysis being *general*, being specific to any wanted degree in application, and being indifferent to the dividers usually set up to keep subject-matters apart, appears to have good prospects for the study of social systems.... Yet for all that promise, it should be kept in mind that the general-systems approach is neither a formula nor a doctrine, but a cluster of strategies of inquiry; not a theory but an organized space within which many theories may be developed and related. (p. 271)

General systems theory emerged in the 1950s as the umbrella for a series of related theories, philosophies, and empirical inquiries related to the interdependence of parts in any natural process, including human society. In the previous chapter, I mentioned some of the antecedents and accompaniments of general-systems theory, especially energetics and cybernetics. The latter provided the crucial idea of feedback. The discussions centering around cybernetic phenomena merged in the early 1950s with related inquiries in biology, psychology, anthropology, and other fields, to reemerge as "general-systems theory", signaled by the appearance of Vol. I of the *General Systems Yearbook* in 1956.

In much of this early work, as now, distinctions were not always made between several things: first, between general-systems *theory* and systems *analysis*. The first is an attempt to use system as a generalized model for reality; the second, an empirical attempt to discover interdependencies, or energy flows. The former commits the analyst to system as a definition of reality; the latter, uses systems concepts heuristically, in order to discover possible regularities in real phenomena. The blurred distinction was the result of the early focus on general theory and the lag in the development of methods for studying actual systems. The basic theoretical concepts have not changed fundamentally since the 1940s; the interval has been spent mainly in devising ways of studying actual sets of interdependent parts. In biology, for example, as ecosystem analysis has proceeded, there is a tendency to discover that the expected stability and self-regulation are often as hard to come by in the natural world as in human systems—and especially since humans have intervened so extensively in the natural world.

The second blurred distinction is between *general-systems* theory and analysis on the one hand, and *eco*system theory and analysis on the other—a distinction especially violated in many of the attempts to apply systems theory to human affairs. While the two types of effort do blend, because both have the same source in cybernetic theory, at the empirical level there is a considerable difference. From the point of view of human systems, ecosystem theory is an especially extreme case, whereas the application of some of the descriptive elements or principles of general-systems theory and systems analysis techniques to human society is a less risky or committal undertaking.

The language associated with general-systems theory contains the following terms:

Open systems: those that receive and accept inputs from the outside.
Closed systems: those that receive only messages internally generated.
Components: the basic units of a system, however defined, but this generally means things that the received inputs use to produce some kind of output.
Boundaries: how one separates one system from another, or where— often an arbitrary or extremely difficult task, and may be resolvable only as an operational decision—that is, one cannot really "find" the line.

Inputs: the messages, information, energy impulses, etc. received by a system from external sources ("external": by definition). Various kinds of inputs: some simply maintain or restore the system to previous states; others require the system to function, to produce something.

Outputs: whatever the system produces.

Feedback: (already discussed in Chapter 2).

Storage: way of dealing with needs to delay response to inputs; also way of handling excess output so it does not unbalance the system.

Black box: a concept assigned to any function within a system that is not fully understood, but whose effect can be measured or observed.

Coupling; interface: and other terms referring to relationships between systems, or subsystems or a larger system.

As noted above, this is essentially a language, or a linguistic model; it should not be confused with reality. That is, systems "exist" in the sense that the language is useful when talking about a particular group of interdependent components—to say that these "constitute a system" is a potentially misleading reification. They are "systemic"; or they are interdependent to such and such an extent—both of these phrasings are superior, in my way of thinking, to *identifying* them as systems, although it is hard to avoid this rhetoric, and I have not been entirely successful in doing so. I believe this to be as true for biological as for social systems, but certainly the dangers are greater for social systems because of their many subsystems, inherent dynamism, and vagueness of boundaries.

SYSTEMS AND SELF-REGULATION

In the discussion of systems in Chapter 2, I noted that the original cybernetic models were mechanical, and that these have influenced subsequent attempts to think of biological and social phenomena in terms of interdependencies. However, the original idea of system, in its dictionary definition, is far simpler. The word "system" is derived from the Greek *systema*, and it means "an assemblage or combination of things or parts forming a complex or unitary whole" (*Random House Dictionary of the English Language*). This meaning has not changed through the ages, although in various applications there may be shifts of emphasis—in some cases on the parts, in others—on the whole. The concept of system is also an excellent example of the capacity of human thought to perceive both parts and the way they function or interact. This effort to understand the interrelationships of parts probably has been the prime effort of science since the late 19th century, and every scientific and scholarly field has its own history of efforts to deal with this problem. The history of these fields in the late 19th and 20th centuries is also marked by complex cross-fertilization of systems concepts, and a few highlights may help.

In biology, "system" or "systemics" originally referred to taxonomy: the emphasis here was on the parts. The descriptions of all life forms in terms of similarities and differences would permit grouping the forms into categories at different levels of specificity. The transition from this descriptive or assemblage notion of system to a concept referring to the *functioning* of organisms emerged first in physiology. For a long time, this field was not considered to be in the central evolutionary and taxonomic corpus of biology, but represented a medical speciality. Claude Bernard, in the mid-19th century, initiated the modern study of the physiological functioning of organisms, which led him to theorize about the relationship between "vital phenomena"—physiological processes—and the governing physical and chemical milieu. He noted that vital phenomena are distinguished from inorganic by their dynamism: growth and regeneration, developmental cycles, and interactions. The regularity of these processes led him to call vital phenomena "deterministic," a concept very close to the concept of a self-regulative system. Bernard even philosophized about the resemblance of social phenomena to these physiological organism-milieu processes.[1]

Walter Cannon's work on emotions and physiology—*The Wisdom of the Body*—in the early 20th century, and L. J. Henderson's *The Fitness of the Environment*[2] established the systemic properties of the organism, and also continued the speculation with social analogies: Cannon discussing, for example, the way emotions become forces in society, setting irreversible processes, like war, in motion (Cannon also seems to be responsible for the term "homeostasis"). Henderson went further: he taught a course in human society based on the idea of systemic functioning, the lecture notes for which were compiled in 1970 by sociologist Bernard Barber. Henderson had explored systems in his physiological and biochemical research, but had been especially impressed with J. Willard Gibbs' writings on physical and chemical systems. Henderson was also attracted by Vilfredo Pareto's ideas of social equilibrium and his concepts of "residues" and "derivations," the latter pertaining to the sentiment-value-preference domain in human behavior. However, the central theme of Henderson's brief writings on the social system was *equilibrium* as the consequence of mutual interdependencies, or what later was called feedback. His influence found its way into emerging functional theory in the social sciences, especially Talcott Parsons' version (1951), which used equilibrium as a primary rationale. But at the same time, Henderson was deeply concerned over the unpredictable and unforeseen, sometimes capricious, processes in systems, especially social systems. He ascribed most of these to the sentiment-residue factor—a viewpoint that we share, and emphasize as the crucial aspect of human "systems".

As suggested above in the reference to Willard Gibbs, another important early source of systems concepts was the growing understanding of basic resource processes in the physical world, the air and soil, by chemists, physicists, agricultural scientists, and climatologists. The carbon, nitrogen, phosphorus, and sulfur cycles, and their ties to biological systems through photosynthesis in plants and food chains among animals, were appropriate examples of functioning systems with loops. These physical-systems models differed from the biological and behavioral largely in the way they dealt with feedback: feedback was present, but on the whole the system operated through energy exchanges and recycling of substances rather than message switching. The physical models of natural systems therefore have not been influential in social analogies (although at one time Gregory Bateson was talking about the statistical theory of gases as a possible analogy for the movement of individuals in a human society: the random movements of molecules generate patterns of interaction or fluctuating rhythms that move through the social organ, and so on).

Coming down into the 1930s, the new science of ecology began evolving its own version of systems concepts as biologists began to make microscopic studies of small populations of plants and animals in carefully defined environmental contexts. A. G. Tansley seems to have used the term "ecosystem" for the first time in 1935, in a general article in the then-new periodical, *Ecology*, where he discussed a number of concepts referring to plant growth and change and advocated "ecosystem" as a term to refer to the "physical systems" of Nature. The investigations of Frederick Clements[3] and others into the development of plant populations in specific environments established the idea of *succession* of species toward a "climax," and began to extend the concept of system, or ecosystem, to larger assemblages of interacting species in particular milieu, over spans of time—a body of concepts that had a major influence on sociology and anthropology. The significance of the ecosystem concept, in fact, lies in its extension outward of the system idea from single functioning organisms to the interrelations of organisms in the environment. This was a historic step.

While these developments in bioecology were taking place, mathematicians and communications engineers were exploring the processes of information transfer and the distinctive ways computers and other machines operated. The new information machines multiplied by many times their dependence on the medium of self-regulation or feedback for continuous and accurate operation. The process is by no means new—every machine with some kind of power source, from water to electronics, is to some degree dependent for efficient or productive output on this principle. The new machines, however, had *information* as their primary product; in this sense, the concept of self-regulation was double-barreled—it really implied the construction of machines that could "think." Thus, W. Ross Ashby, a neurologist and physiologist, joining the movement,[4] began constructing electronic turtles that could move around on command in an effort to learn about the behavior of organisms. Norbert Wiener, mathematician and one of the founders of cybernetics, was deeply concerned in his 1950 book *The Human Use of Human Beings* that the computer and its extensions might reduce men to the status of ants: "I am afraid I am convinced that a community of human beings is a far more useful thing than a community of ants; and that if the human being is restricted to performing the functions of the ant and nothing more, he will not even be a good ant . . ." (p. 61). Here Wiener was specifically concerned about the reconstruction of society on information-machine models, in which feedback would control the functions of humans so that they would have no latitude, no choice—each individual, or group, would become one of the "function boxes," or one of the information channels, and the open quality (the adaptive potential in human behavior) would be lost or suppressed. The current political struggle over the desire of bureaucrats and businesses to computerize and centralize information on every citizen, along with other developments since 1950, make his warnings quite timely.[5]

Associated with Wiener in the 1940s were two anthropologists—Gregory Bateson and Margaret Mead—both of whom participated in the Macy Conference on cybernetics, along with ecologist Evelyn Hutchinson and others. These seminars were of historic significance in the evolution of scientific ideas in the 20th century: they marked the coming-of-age of the concept of system and self-regulation, and a fusion of the parallel understandings that had grown up in physiology, ecology, information theory, and the social sciences. A large chunk of contemporary science is based on the intellectual stimuli produced at these conferences.

Bateson seems to have constructed much of his subsequent intellectual career on the fruits of the Macy Conferences. His recently collected essays (1972) are known as *Steps Toward an Ecology of Mind*; his first cybernetics-influenced book was *Communication: The Social Matrix of Psychiatry* (Ruesch and Bateson, 1951); and his first published application of cybernetic concepts to culture—"Bali: The Value System of a Steady State (1949)."[6] All these titles have an obvious significance, but the "Bali" paper is especially intriguing since Bateson combined the old American-ethnological idea of "whole culture" with the cybernetic notion of regular feedback and self-regulation of a system. Bali was portrayed as a self-contained entity; its relationships to the outer world were not specified, nor were they a factor, according to Bateson's presentation, in the self-regulating system. In essence, this system was one of a "steady state"—that is, *not* "schismogenic." This latter term is Bateson's, and by it he meant a pattern of human interaction characterized by build-ups in hostility and competition, or "maximization" of certain stimuli that would tend to lead toward conflict and intense climax. In steady states, on the other hand (and here Ashby's modeling research was cited—Bateson [1972 re-publication version, p. 124]) if any attitude or behavior began to increase in strength or tend toward maximization, some other part of the system would send out messages to stop it and retire the energy, thus returning the system to an original calm or regularly functioning state. Likewise, according to Bateson, the Balinese child learned to avoid response to provocation and lapse into "awayness," thus reducing the potential for conflict and irregular operation of the behavioral-cultural system. Such a culture would remain largely without change. On the other hand, with the Iatmul (a Melanesian tribe studied earlier by Bateson and Margaret Mead), the pattern of interaction was schismogenic rather than steady-state.

This was pure social psychology, without reference to features of social structure or to external stimuli that might serve to modify the system. Since Bateson's article was never followed by a detailed monograph clarifying its theoretical ambiguities or describing alternative behavior patterns and exceptions to the portrayed regularities, it has been difficult to evaluate it or to appraise its theoretical significance. The essay stands as a challenging but isolated attempt to model whole-culture on a more-or-less closed-system cybernetic basis.

As such an attempt at whole-culture portrayal, the imagery was basically similar to many other descriptions of "cultures" or "tribes" that appeared during the 1930s and that occasionally still appear: external inputs and forces, or internal innovative or conflict processes, are either downplayed or considered to be special cases and not part of the idealized time-slice, monographic "culture." Bateson's addition of a sophisticated scientific model and a philosophy of reality was not picked up by cultural anthropologists, who were skeptical of just that faddishness, that supersophistication, and who saw the self-containment of cultures more as a style of writing monographs and less as a theory of the nature of culture itself. And then, too, anthropologists were beginning to move toward social-structuralism, with its avoidance of behavioral analysis.

There was something rather curious about this emphasis on self-containment and bounded systems on Bateson's part, because the application of systems theory to complex systems, in both biology and society, took the process out of the context of a single, bounded machine or organism and applied it to much more complicated phenomena consisting of many organisms of different types functioning in a relatively open milieu, the boundaries of which were hard to determine. In fact, the concept of milieu now became relative: the environment was anything that was not the immediate organism, which meant that it could be the organisms themselves, interacting with each other. Yet this interaction of organisms was also capable of being reified as *the* system, the superorganism that was in a state of feedback control. In other words, by taking the idea out of its single-machine-organism context, many of its primary terms of definition became relative to the ongoing process that was to be defined by them.

Just as the steam engine or the thermostat became favorite illustrations of feedback systems in mechanics and electronics, so the aquarium and the terrarium became familiar examples for biology. These were microcosms, clearly bounded, with known or measurable inputs and with recycled resources contributing to the continuous functioning and survival of the enclosed organisms. The writer's own introduction to such systems occurred at the age of 13, when he began work on balanced aquariums of tropical fish—back in the days before pumps, aerators, heaters, or chemicals, when it was necessary to do it all with plants, fish, snails, and the right spot near a radiator, (but not too close) in the winter. Perhaps his caution with regard to systems theory is due to the fact that he discovered that no matter now hard you tried, something always went wrong; that the system might work for a couple of weeks and then something began to oscillate; that unless the operator, the *deus ex machina*, intervened, all the fish would die or the tank would fill up with snails or algae. In other words, the aquarium model is a man-made thing, its boundaries do not exist in Nature, and unless one gives it continuous supervision, or has costly machinery to maintain it, it won't work.

However artificial the models, the application to biological multiorganism-milieu phenomena was a useful one since under ideal or undisturbed conditions, these complex phenomena do often appear to work out along cybernetic lines. For example, there is the situation in which a group of species in a given milieu exploit different "niches"—use different substances as food—thereby staying out of each other's orbits and controlling competition. Such a system functions so as to maintain optimum populations. Fluctuations or oscillations in food supply, temperature, humidity, and so on trigger appropriate adaptive responses among the organisms, which cause populations to fluctuate regularly. This kind of situation, with its regular wave-forms in the data, encountered in natural ecology, does resemble the idealized descriptions of cybernetic systems based on machines.

In biology, the bridge between system as a single unitary phenomenon and system as supersystem—as composed of many separate but interdependent or interrelated units—was created by the concept of diversity. For some time it was assumed that the more diverse the units (i.e., the populations of living things) the more stable the system—that is, the greater its homeostatic tendency to return to its original state after some disturbance. New evidence, however (e.g., Holling, 1973), has modified this approach, finding that stability is a relative thing: some very simple or unitary systems (like human agriculture) can be extremely stable for long periods as long as major changes in the milieu do not occur. If they do, the system lacks "resilience" and may collapse quickly. Diverse systems or supersystems have greater resilience. But there is a sliding scale here, and it is clear that the stability or changeability of any system is related to many factors, not merely its diversity or simplicity. The finding, of course, has a plausible applicability to human-Nature relationships, since it can appear to confirm the growing fear that human technological solutions tend to create greater risks of breakdown in the midst of their illusion of greater control.

A closer reading of some of the concepts so frequently cited in ecological research using ecosystem concepts is desirable. There are three closely related ones that need distinguishing:*

*The language is based, to some extent, on Walter Buckley's presentation (1967).

Steady state: the system functions with no apparent change or fluctuation; all subsystems continually reinforce each other. Systems in a steady state are characterized by minimal complexity, and in social systems, reciprocity relations tend to be fixed or ritualized.

Equilibrium or stability: terms used to describe a particular state of a system when the self-reinforcing characteristics of steady state are visible. However, a system in equilibrium at point *x* may not be so at point *y*. That is, equilibrium need not imply that the system remains static.

Homeostasis: a process characterized by cycles of equilibrium and disequilibrium; the system moves or fluctuates in response to inducements to change or adapt to new inputs or conditions. Organization and reciprocity in social homeostasis are reasonably complex and capable of change, as long as the same average conditions are maintained over time.

In addition to the bias toward stability or at least fluctuating continuity, the concepts (true to their single-organism origin) stress self-containment of systems—the system exists and receives information from external sources, responding to disturbance from the outside in homeostasis, or existing in steady states when disturbance is minimal.

Viewing social systems from the standpoint of these concepts, it is clear that the fit is not very good. As Amos Hawley (1973) has observed, human systems are very broad, and their boundaries are hard to determine; the flow of energy and the emergence of signals are hard to trace, and constantly changing. There are also unique phenomena in social systems that are difficult or impossible to duplicate in biological systems—social differentiation, for example. Relationships between human systems are not determined by physical factors entirely, but also by cognitive and affective factors. One can add that the precise state of a social system is often a matter of values and not objective measurement: equilibrium, oscillation, steady states—these are all ambiguous sociologically, and are interchangeable or easily confused. Human systems do not always return to original conditions, but move toward new patterns—that is, they adapt, and the nature of this change is often more usefully described in valuational terms. Above all, while in animal systems the behavior of the organisms is easily absorbed into the systemic processes, human behavior often moves in opposition to such processes and must be taken as an independent variable. While all of these factors do not make the application of biological-systems concepts to human affairs impossible, they make them very difficult or ambiguous. As Scott Boorman remarks, "Work in biological ecology and in population biology as a whole can at most stimulate human social science; it can neither subsume nor be subsumed by it" (1972, p. 393). Clearly human social systems are their own kind of system; or rather, to call human affairs "systems" is a heuristic or experimental exercise, and not an identification of substance.

THE ADAPTIVE SYSTEM

Therefore, there are at least two approaches to the application of systems concepts to social phenomena: (1) In the first approach one rules at the outset that social phenomena are interdependent or systemic—as are phenomena in all realms, more or less—and the analysis then proceeds to the next step, which is to accept certain obvious empirical criteria that demarcate systems for analysis, e.g., "subsistence system." The third step is to determine whether or not the system is operating in terms of particular processes of feedback that confer stability or change. (2) The second approach takes the applicability of systems theory to social phenomena as an empirical question or hypothesis. The systems criteria are used as "models" and they are fitted experimentally to the data to see if they help to explain why certain things occur. This approach assumes that not all behavior or social phenomena are systemic, but that systemic properties emerge in human affairs when people want them to, plan for them, or when behavior is predictable enough to permit them to emerge. It assumes as well that people can react against or respond to systems in accordance with the objectification capability of human thought.

As suggested in Chapter 2, the metaphor for social system most congenial to the position taken in this book is the one called by Walter Buckley, the *adaptive system*. The properties of this type will be explored in subsequent chapters, but a preliminary definition may be presented here. Adaptive systems are open systems—they freely exchange energy with the environment, and contain internal innovation. Adaptive systems are dynamic systems, because the innovative solutions to problems tend to create new problems, which must be coped with at some future date. Adaptation is a behavioral process that seeks satisfactions for present needs, with greater or lesser concern for the future: where there is great concern, the system will change slowly, and undesirable consequences may be avoided; where the concern is weak, the systems will change relatively rapidly and easily, and the problems will accumulate. Human social systems are all adaptive: some are more dynamic than others. Human or cultural ecology is a study of how adaptive systems influence the physical environment and the human environment as well.

While general systems concepts and analysis can be applied to human affairs, our key question is whether the ecosystem is a good model with which to analyze adaptive systems in their many varieties and shadings. The position taken in this book is that ecosystem has some advantages as a model when the more traditional varieties of social or cultural-ecological systems are the focus of concern. However, when the interest shifts toward the more dynamic cases, or to episodes in the history of any social system when tradition gives way to change, ecosystem is an inappropriate and awkward model. It tends to impose an image of order and predictability upon something that is often (or usually) engaged in adaptive coping, or searching for congenial outcomes without knowing precisely how it will all turn out.

It might be argued also that "ecosystem" should be used in cultural ecology only when biological factors are explicitly included as independent variables.[7] There is something to be said for this, but even here the problem is a sticky one. Certainly one can argue that in any biological system that includes humans (studies of diseases, epidemics, or humans as part of a food chain including other species), ecosystemic analysis may be used with profit. But in any analysis of human use of natural resources it is impossible to exclude social-behavioral and valuational factors, because it is these that shape the resource practices. And it is these behavioral and institutional factors that are difficult to handle with ecosystemic ideas. "Human ecology," as I define it, then, is a *mixed* system—it is not wholly biological, although it includes some elements from biology. It is not wholly behavioral, although it recognizes the importance of social phenomena. It is not wholly ecosystemic, although it may profit from some of the concepts derived from natural ecology. *Cultural* ecology is simply human ecology with a little more emphasis on the social factors involved in the process.

We turn now to some varied attempts to apply systems concepts to human ecology, with special significance for the problems of the book.

PLANT ECOSYSTEMS AND HUMAN ECOLOGY

Eugene Odum, in a widely read article on problems in plant ecosystem theory (1969), attempted to characterize the differences—rather than the analogical similarities—in human systems as viewed from the perspective of natural ecology. As befitting a biologist experimenting with plants, he emphasizes homeostasis and a directional movement toward a balanced state, in which the physiological functions of the plants begin to approach a regular fluctuation. He does this by using a series of symbols of great clarity and economy:

B = the total biomass,
P = "primary production," or photosynthesis in plants,
R = output, or respiration in the case of plants.

In early stages of a succession, or when youthful plant systems are trying to establish themselves in a given habitat, the amount of P will exceed R, so that the P/R ratio is greater than one. In mature systems, as the ratio approaches one, or unity, succession of the new species becomes established—or, in other words, the amount of energy fixed in photosynthesis tends to be balanced by the energy cost of maintaining the system. So long as P is greater than R, biomass (B) will accumulate in the system (the plant population increases), which means that the ratio P/B will tend to decrease. This suggests that the amount of biomass supported by the available energy increases to a maximum quantity and then ceases, the amount being maintained with minor fluctuation thereafter. The theoretical laboratory results have, according to Odum, been observed in Nature, although there is no way of counting the incidents nor of determining how long such mature succession systems lasted.

The basic idea here is the distinction between "young" and "mature" systems, the former characterized by dynamic buildup, the latter by a stable balance with no further increases in biomass. Applying these concepts to the human case, Odum observes that there is "a basic conflict between the strategies of man and nature" (p. 266). But this conflict turns out to be based on the fact that human systems are of the "young" rather than the mature type. That is, man, as a rule, seeks the youthful "bloom" type of situation in which the P/R ratio is greater than one. Or, in other terms, man seeks a *high* P/B efficiency as a permanent condition, whereas Nature "seeks" (moves toward) the reverse: a high B/P ratio. All this means is that humans try to get as much out of the environment as possible, at the lowest cost. This pertains especially, of course, to agriculture, where we have developed efficient crop systems by manipulating all the factors: varieties of plants, fertility of the soil, and availability of water. We have done so, however, at certain costs that are now beginning to become evident: water pollution by fertilizers; destruction of soil texture by removal of humus; and injury to various regenerative chemical processes in the soil, water, and air. The "boom and bust" strategy of production may provide immediate rewards, but at delayed costs that eventually must be paid.

So man seems to reverse the law of natural ecosystems: plants may define efficiency as the state of affairs where there is no further need for additional population or product, and the goal of existence is the maintenance, without conflict, of the existing amount. But humans try to get the highest yield—to reorganize energy, to resist entropy or the retirement of energy to simpler states, thus conferring a teleological property on human systems.

Odum's model is really a very specialized one—not general or theoretical. His argument excludes humans from the giant natural system: his natural systems are those of plants; humans break into these systems with agriculture, forestry, and mining, and prevent, (Odum seems to be saying) Nature from attaining these ideal states of mature succession. Or, in my terms, Ecology is incorporated into Culture. It is important to know the limitations of Odum's model: in it, Homo sapiens is artificial or outside of nature, and not part of natural ecosystems.

This view is not false, but only part of the truth. In larger conceptions of systemic functioning, humans would have to be included, and this is especially the case if we become concerned about the problem of control. A system of "sustained yield" of resource use can produce at a high level but not degrade the environment or generate unpaid costs. That is, not all human systems are just the "young" type—there are examples of combinations of both "young" and "mature" systems that provide high yields, but without the hidden, concealed, or unpaid costs. Trade-offs are often required between costs in one subsystem and returns in another. A simple example is found in crop rotation, where yields and returns remain reasonably high, but the soil is protected against abuse by rotating between nitrogen-fixing and nitrogen-using species. Moreover, Odum's doctrine oversimplifies cultural history: sustained yield systems, with all the attributes of Odum's "mature" systems, characterized many food collectors and early agriculturalists—although the ecological transition demonstrates that these balanced systems really had the seeds of imbalance.

The lesson here is that an understanding of the human ecosystem cannot be limited to a single analogy of contrast with the biological, any more than such understanding can be reached by oversimplified analogies of identity or similarity. It is not only what humans do that is different from or similar to Nature's ways, but also how our actions interact with

Nature and, finally, how we can construct our own rational ecosystem state—sustained resource yield—and still maintain a reasonable level of living. We shall return to this problem at the end of the chapter.

Clifford Geertz made the initial attempt to apply ecosystem theory to agricultural ecology in his 1963 book, *Agricultural Involution: The Processes of Ecological Change in Indonesia.* In his introductory chapter he defends the approach as follows:

> This mode of analysis is of a sort which trains attention on the pervasive properties of systems *qua* systems (system structure, system equilibrium, system change) rather than on the point-to-point relationships between paired variables of the "culture" and "nature" variety. The guiding question shifts from, "Do habit conditions (partly or completely) cause culture or do they merely limit it?" to such more incisive queries as: "Given an ecosystem defined through the parallel discrimination of cultural core and relevant environment, how is it organized?" "What degree and type of stability does it have?".... (p. 10).

In the next chapter, Geertz defines "two types of ecosystems"— swiddening or shifting cultivation, and wet-rice production. Swiddening, in contrast to rice paddy, is "integrated into, and, when genuinely adaptive, maintains the general structure of the pre-existing natural ecosystem into which it is projected...." (p. 16); whereas rice culture more drastically reorganizes the nature structure. Well and good, but the phrase "when genuinely adaptive" is of course the sleeper: later in the chapter he notes how swiddening, under various social pressures, can turn destructive when the interval between cultivation is shortened. He also suggests that the rice system tends to result in human population concentrations, due to its capacity for increasing yield and needs for labor, whereas the swidden system results in a dispersal of population due to its inherently limited yield. These and other conclusions have been subjected to criticism:[8] for example, extensive agriculture apparently *can* support large, concentrated populations given the requisite social and political organization (e.g., Dumond's claim, 1961), as supported by a number of observational studies of modern Maya swiddening—that swiddening in Yucatan was adequate to supply the Maya cities. The issue illustrates the point that, when dealing with human systems such as agriculture, an analysis of the "natural" properties of the cultivation as ecosystemic does not tell us what the long-range potentialities may be. Although swiddening may be closer to Nature, wet-rice production has perhaps less degradational potential, since even with the pressures of increasing population and corresponding intensification of production, the system, according to Geertz, is "virtually indestructible." But *both* systems *can* turn destructive if they are not maintained properly, or if certain social features require them to produce more than the resources can sustain. The key variable is the *social* system—that is, human needs, skills, anxieties, population—all of which can be in interaction with subsistence techniques—but are not "determined" by these techniques. Their long-run function is to push subsistence systems to produce at varying rates.

Thus, while the stability of homeostatic properties of human agricultural systems may be subject to some ecological rules, such as the one cited earlier concerning the relative lack of resilience of simple or unitary supersystems, these have to be qualified by the social arrangements available for sustaining the system. Rice agriculture is certainly a simplified system, and possibly subject to swift degradation by major climatic changes. However, the important factor here is time—or really human history. Wet-rice agriculture has survived and thrived for a long time: that it may some day give way to a different system goes without saying. This change can be induced by climate or it can be created by humans who require or desire a different method of food production.

When Geertz brought social phenomena into the analysis, he moved away from a consideration of tropical agricultural systems *per se* and became involved with familiar economic, political, and historical events: the exploitation of Javanese peasants by native and foreign groups involved in Dutch colonialism, so that fewer alternatives for innovative change in the agricultural economy were available. The description of these historical processes has a generalized systemic quality, but the story makes equally good sense if told in ordinary historical or institutional language. The climatic and hydraulic components of the system occupy precisely the same place in ecosystemic theory that they do in the possibilistic frame of reference Geertz criticized and wished to replace by ecosystemicism: a set of limiting or shaping conditions for the institutional arrangements. In other words, ecosystemic analysis was appropriate and meaningful in the presentation of the nature of agriculture as physical systems, but does not appear to carry over into the portrait of "agricultural involution" in any decisive manner. This does not make the picture of involution any less ecological; only that the heart of an ecological inquiry involving complex human events and actions is basically a sociological analysis.

BEHAVIORAL ADAPTATION AS SYSTEMIC

Another approach to systems analysis can deal with a particular adaptive change in human behavior as its problem, attempt to explain this, and note its consequences for a series of institutional and environmental phenomena. Thayer Scudder and Elizabeth Colson have done this for Tonga tribalists, after their relocation following the construction of the Kariba Dam in Kenya (Scudder, 1968; 1972A). The total system observed consisted of the following important components (or "subsystems"): the river as a fluctuating resource, the government and its connections with overseas development agencies, the Tonga as a tribal population, Tongan techniques of subsistence as related to climate and soils, Tongan culture and religion, and relationships of Tongans with tribal neighbors. Previous to the building of the dam and resettlement, Tongan subsistence and the cultural pattern that validated it were in a state of slow evolution toward a particular form well-adapted to the climate and land features. The dam flooded out their home territory and they were forcibly resettled by the government. It was at this point that Scudder encountered them, and his research then came to focus on just one subsystem: the adaptive strategies developed by the Tongans to cope with the changed conditions. They were required to discover new resources and methods of agricultural production and to cope with the shocks and hazards of a new habitat and a new set of tribal neighbors, all of which required a series of psychological, social, and ritual adjustments. The consumption of new, wild, vegetable foods required new medicine and curing routines, since some of these were poisonous and may actually have contributed to the increased death rate after resettlement—the dismay and fear accompanying increased mortality itself requiring adjustments. The analysis is an example of how ideas related to ecosystem theory can dramatize a process called "culture change" in traditional anthropology.

However, Scudder has not yet investigated the effects these new adaptations will have on natural resources over a period of time.[9] Recovery of psychosocial balance—satisfying cognitive and affectual adjustments between men—is often secured at the cost of environmental damage (human adaptation at the price of environmental maladaptation).[10] Thus, to some extent, the "permanent war economy" of the United States and other nations in the contemporary period represents such an imbalance between one system and another: Man-Man is kept in reasonable quietude at the cost of Man-Nature, which appears to be degradational. In many ancient civilization systems, balance was maintained for certain periods by high infant mortality or by resource-utilization systems like large water impoundments that functioned effectively for varying periods of time before collapsing (see discussion in Chapter 5).

INSTITUTIONAL PROCESS MODELS

A familiar type of application of ecosystem theory to human affairs is found in the attempts by biologists and ecologists to develop models of institutional processes on the basis of ecosystemic analogies. Until recently, these were often quasi-literary essays, works of imagination more than analysis. Garret Hardin's influential paper, "The Cybernetics of Competition" (Hardin, 1973) was one of the first of these. Hardin noted that "negative feedback" seemed to describe the idealized Ricardian theory of price—prices fluctuate as the number of manufacturers and quantity of goods fluctuate—but also observed that the model assumed a lawful naturalness about the process which did violation to the social reality of competitive advantage, or of the proclivity of economic agents to make deals preventing the system from operating according to prediction. In his discussion of the "competitive exclusion principle," Hardin was concerned with the well-known ecological concept that there can be no such thing as "perfect" competitition since two parties using the same resources eventually conflict and one wins over the other. The idea relates to the theory of *laissez faire* economics, in which the producers, by competing with each other in a "free market," and eliminating inefficient and unfair operators, create a stable economic system with the regular fluctuation noted previously, prices and other factors returning to some optimal state, with the public presumably the beneficiary. However, Hardin notes that the total freedom of the market is a high price to pay for "stability"—we seek controls in order to eliminate the constant and destructive competition—and also to guard against what he calls the "positive feedback of power," which tends to corrupt the workings of the system—*i.e.*, the need for a countervailing force to ensure co-existence of various groups who must *share* resources. Hardin's appreciation of the evident limits of applicability of ecosystem theory to human affairs shows a sophistication not always encountered in other attempts to apply biological analogies to society.

A more recent attempt to apply the principles of the ecology of animal predation to—of all things—real estate speculation in the Puget Sound region, by Crawford Holling (1969), reduces the biological analogies to specific rules which can be researched in a particular and specific institutional process, presumably yielding empirical generalizations useful for social analysis. The basic analogies developed by Holling are presented below (Holling's Table 1, p. 32):

Table 1. Analogies Between Predation and Land Acquisition.

Predation	Land Acquisition
Populations (quality and quantity)	
Prey population in generation n	Lots available for sale in market period n
Predator population, generation n	Bidders for lots, market period n
Prey quality (size, etc.)	Land quality
Predator qualities (size, etc.)	Bidders by bidding price
Unsuccessful predators (predator morality)	Unsuccessful bidders
Alternative prey species	Alternative land qualities and alternative geographical sources of land
Processes	
Attack process (generates number of prey killed in n)	Market process (generates number of lots sold in n)
Prey reproduction (generates number of progeny in $n + 1$)	Resale process (generates number of developed lots for sale in $n + 1$)
Predator reproduction (generates number of predator progeny in $n + 1$)	Population and economic growth (generates demand in $n + 1$)
Dispersal (generates net number of prey immigrants)	Speculation (generates number of new lots in $n + 1$)
Motivation (e.g., hunger)	Final selling prices
Competition	Competition (between speculators and bidders)

The objective of the ecological studies of predation has been to determine how predatory actions serve to control animal population fluctuation. The processes involved have been found to be extremely complex, due to the large number of variables involved: rates of searching for prey, hunger patterns, learning attack strategies, diet, topography, cover, age distributions in the animal populations, and so on. The interactions of these variables produce a variety of models of predator-prey populations, each with its own characteristics of stability and fluctuation. Predatory tactics will vary when past circumstances and changing conditions feed back information into the animal population, so as to stabilize the system and "dampen" the population oscillations. Thus, reasonable overall stability of population can be achieved—though how often it actually is, or was, is not usually specified.

In the land speculation model,

a population and economic growth submodel generates regional population by income and family size each year. This population is converted by a recreational demand submodel into a population of bidders [for lots] according to bidding prices by using a function that relates the proportion of the population desiring land to income, family size, and distance from home. This output of bidders then represents demand. Supply of lots for sale includes unsold lots developed by speculators in the previous market periods as well as developed lots that come up for resale. The amount of this supply is classified in seven categories that define the lots' qualities for cottage development. Both demand (bidder = predators) and supply (number of lots for sale by quality = prey) come together in a complex submodel that mimics the peculiar properties of the' real estate market process, and this submodel generates the number of lots sold, the final selling price, the unsold inventory, and the number of unsatisfied bidders. These outputs in turn serve as inputs to a speculation submodel which moves underdeveloped land into the next year's market in relation to the size of the market and the rate of price appreciation over the previous three years. Finally, an ecological feedback model stimulates the effects of intensity and duration of use, shifting the amounts of land between quality categories in response to regional and local density effects. (Holling, 1969, pp. 133–134)

These operations generated a model of land speculation that showed properties similar in form to those produced in the studies and simulations of predation and animal populations. Omitting much detail, the properties concerned the way prices responded to changes in population and the supply of lots, and *vice versa*. Oscillations in these were controlled (damped) in a manner similar to the animal cases: past events tended to control present behavior—that is, the systems achieved stability over time since the "memory" of past events modified present action.

The exercise provides a view of the ecosystem analogy in human affairs that features the application of particular mathematical techniques derived from biological phenomena to the behavior of humans in institutional life. No implication is given that human behavior is somehow like animal behavior; the relationship is purely mechanical, processual. There is no doubt that such applications have intrinsic interest and serve to illumine the institutional process, but it should be remembered that the results— the portrayal of stability or regular fluctuation—is usually the result of the particular model, or the particular topic, used for the experiment.

The biological model itself is biased toward finding control or stability, as noted; there is a serious question as to just how often animal predation itself functioned to regulate population, but one can suppose that it did so with fair frequency. However, the question of the frequency of predictable outcomes in land speculation is quite another matter. Due to the inherent dynamism of the human case, the fact that an external factor (market conditions) is constantly changing and introducing new rules suggests that a comprehensive study would show that self-regulation is a more variable condition than the pilot project would imply. However, it is conceivable that if government decided to intervene decisively in the land economy—socialize all land ownership and subject it to regulation—its regular movements could be maintained. In this case we would not be dealing with a "natural" system, open to discovery, but with a planned institutional device for controlling and regulating change. "Ecosystem" in this instance would be transformed into social policy.

Environment, Power, Society

The most ambitious attempt to apply generalized systems concepts and systems analysis (not ecosystem, necessarily) to human institutions is Howard Odum's *Environment, Power, and Society* (1971). This book will repay reading with many fascinating insights and certainly the fullest collection of diagrams of feedback in Nature and society in the literature, although they are not all equally clear or relevant to the text. However, Odum's basic scheme is underlain by the following ideas and objectives:

1. Energy, or what he calls "power," is the common denominator of both natural and social processes. Power is the "rate of flow of useful energy" and is a measurable quantity, hence it provides a quantitative basis for studying mechanical, biological, and social processes in a single frame of reference. This is true as far as it goes, but the difficult problem is how to quantify *social* power, a question which Odum sometimes answers by substituting measurable equivalents (like the monetary value of fossil fuels) or by avoiding the issue completely and concentrating only on those technological processes (like agriculture and raw materials conversion) where measurable material energy budgets exist.

2. To focus on energy budgets and the power aspect of human systems, is to take what Odum calls a "macroscopic view" of human systems. That is, such a view provides what he calls a "detail eliminator," which avoids concern with motives and logic as found in particular social systems and processes at particular times, and focuses on that lowest common denominator of all systems, regardless of content: power or energy. Stated differently, Odum is saying that the evolution of culture had taken the direction of a growing convergence of process and our cognitive understanding of process—that is, the systems concept. Or, historically, cultural evolution is working toward interdependence of all human systems on a global basis; as this occurs, it becomes increasingly possible—even necessary—to apply the systems model in order to find

out what is happening and how to control it. However, once again we come up against Wiener's queries: who is going to control whom and what? Odum, like most of the systems analogizers or modelers, does not deal with this question.

3. The "language of power" is the language of the feedback network—that is, the familiar mechanical-biological model we have discussed. This is where the diagrams come in—nearly one a page. Odum considers a diagram to be not simply a visual aid, but an inherent step in the analysis of systems: a true model of reality. His version of the feedback network is, as already indicated, a matter largely of tracing energy flows:

> Everything and anything that takes place on earth involves a flow of potential energy from sources into dispersed heat through pathways driven by directed forces which originate from energy storages. The essence of cause, Newtonian physics, and the laws of energetics are irrefutable on these principles, but only recently have these laws that were developed for simple physical systems been applied to nature's complex ecological system or to the even more complex system of man's civilized activities in the biosphere. The flows of energy through complex food chains and complex economics systems follow the basic laws, and we may use these quantitative relationships if we realize that the flows in the macroscopic world are primarily flows of populations of large and small parts, including populations of molecules, cells, organisms, people, occupational groups, and other associations of active components. (1971, pp. 40–41)

This is explicit enough: from food chains to economic systems; plants and people—all are equated in the rules that govern the power network. The models are consciously reductionistic: they permit the kind of generalizations that the 19th-century scientist sought so assiduously: the grand laws of Nature. One of Odum's examples concerns energy storage—a process met with in networks because the amount of force or energy required to set in motion a particular process may be greater than is needed farther along in the process; hence a storage "sink" is developed. The force stored in the sink "is in proportion to the storage whenever the storage function is one of stacking up units of similar calorie content. Most ecological and civilization systems have such storage systems" (1971, p. 41).

Money saved in a bank might be an example of a storage of force against needs developing later in the system, and of course the monetary units in this case make it easy to measure. However, it is an open question as to whether the replacement of a concept such as "cash savings" by "excess energy storage" clarifies anything; or whether the diagrammatic rhetoric of energy flows makes any contribution to the already-well-worked-out science of economic transactions and cash movement. The problems become much more complex when we consider that the storage function in human cultural systems must also include knowledge, information, delayed reactions, bided times, and other phenomena that can be thought of as energy or force reserves, but that are mental and behavioral and therefore difficult if not impossible to subject to the quantitative measurements required in order to reduce them to Odum's modeling procedure.

Odum's own analogy on the savings issue is as follows:

> Savings represent the money flows into storages for work services done and thus provide flexibility and time delays in the reward loop of energy expenditure. An equivalent in the ecosystem is the holding of fruits made in summer for planting in winter. The energy has already been expended in preparing a complex product, but an important material of low-energy value is fed back upstream and has the capability of developing new circuits. With the saving of both money and seeds, what is being used as a loop reinforcement is critical information. In seeds it is in the genes; with money the critical information is already stored as the acceptance of the symbolic nature of currency as a measure of value by the network of people. (1971, pp. 191–192)

This seems plausible, but the analogies are fuzzy, or forced. Putting savings in the same category as seeds is not an accurate analogy between culture and Nature, since the saving of seeds means that seeds become capital—part of the economic institution. Odum ignores the fact that natural substances are incorporated into human affairs, and the "natural" aspect—the growing of fruit trees—becomes a cultural phenomenon. Both fruit seeds and cash savings become part of social systems, whatever natural ecosystem they may be part of. To me, the important problem is not whether human systems are ecosystems, or can be modeled on ecosystem diagrams but, rather, the relationships between natural and human systems and their interpenetration, especially in systems of production when natural substances are consciously exploited.

Odum's major attempt to deal with the behavioral components of institutions is in his Chapter 7, on "Power and Politics." He notes that:

> The organizations of man provide for decisions and actions that serve to open and close important circuits and control the rate of power flow in them. The acceptance by individuals of interindividual organization structure constitutes the essence of the circuits. Mental concepts form a part of the structure. Through feedback pathways actions of individual voters on committees, of duly appointed authorities, in general elections, and through other institutions, control valves ensure continued flows of their own energy and those of the organizations they represent.... Successful institutions ... have positive reinforcement loops which keep the control upstream working in a sensitive way to effect the best output downstream. A successful political

organization is an energetic control that provides for energetic loop reinforcement. Successful systems of power budgeting require the positive programs of power delivery to necessary new activity as well as defensive budgeting to prevent power leakages to crime, useless activity, and unnecessary wars. Failure to control the system toward group-rewarding aims results ultimately in redirection of component power flows and reorganization of circuits to deliver greater loop reinforcement. (1971, pp. 207–208)

Now, just what kind of a political system—that is, from the standpoint of the thing that concerns men, ideology—might this represent? It is, I suspect, neither a dictatorship nor a democracy, but something in between: a benevolent, authoritarian oligarchy, with systems managers monitoring the energy flows and power budgets, controlling the information, and seeing to it that everyone is happy and amused, as well as hard-working: a familiar image, that of the science fictioneers and their portrayal of the future technocracy—or, perhaps, Plato's philosopher-kings. Even though Odum is not trying to design political systems, but only to supply a model for analyzing existing ones, his model is *not* politically neutral. The model imposes particular conditions on reality, as do all models; in the political sphere, this becomes equivalent to a particular type of social order.

Later in the chapter Odum attempts to deal with the freedom issue in terms that are consistent with the implications in the quotation just presented.

Thus basic energetics require some loss of freedom of control over one's power budget in order to gain freedom over the pestilences of the environment and to receive injections from the rich flows of fossil fuels which cannot be utilized by simple individual systems. (1971, p. 217)

This is quite true: the simplistic notion that individual freedom can be absolute, so prevalent in recent years, flies in the face of everything we know about scarcity. But, again, the translation into power-flow analogies dodges the issue: what kinds of trade-offs between freedom and protection, liberty and security, are offered to the individual by the political leadership, and how much choice may he have among them? It is possible that this problem of choice and decision can be modeled in ecosystemic terms, but there is nothing in Odum's attempt that shows us how, or even if it would be a useful enterprise. The issue dramatizes the central point of this essay: that human ecology needs to be analyzed in human terms—that is, in the terms of human behavior, or what we call the adaptive process.

In the end, Odum becomes almost mystical, verging on outright reification of impersonal processes:

> ... the many compartments and circuits that constitute systems of man and nature are themselves special-purpose computers. When manipulated they provide calculations of the consequences of their own activity. (1971, p. 270)

> Let us first fantasy the nightmare of an electronics technician. After a week of exhausting tedium, soldering circuits and completing a large network of wires connecting thousands of tubes, transformers, and transistors, he goes to bed with the feeling of a design completed. Then with the veil of the dream the parts begin to breathe. Next he sees them grow and divide, making new parts. Then the wires become invisible. The new and old parts disconnect themselves and move into new patterns, reconnecting their inputs and outputs, replacing worn members, and together generating functions and forms not known before. Soon the new system with its vast capabilities is growing, self-producing, and self-sustaining, drawing all the available electric power. Our hero awakens when he pulls the switch removing the energy source. To some visionary engineers the nightmare may seem a preview of a machine world. Our ecosystem, however, is already the nightmare. (1971, p. 275)

In the first quotation he is serious, descriptive; in the second, it is a dream, a nightmare. But the point is that if the components design themselves, as in the first quotation, and if the components are humans, then the nightmare is the result—that is, Odum's own system model generates the nightmare. And it *is* a nightmare, as Wiener foresaw.

Environment, Power, and Society is a preliminary statement of postulates and frames; its author is supplementing it as this essay is being written by a more practical and focussed approach to the energy question. Dr. Odum has reduced the systems element to a technical operation involving the computation of difference between *gross* and *net* energy costs of particular technological solutions. Net energy is simply the amount liberated from any process designed to produce it, minus the amount of energy required to fuel the process itself. The computations should permit assessment of the full costs of resource practices, perhaps even combining both social and environmental costs in the same measurement. If this comes to pass, the basic truth in the Odum concept of system will pay off handsomely: the use of the systems metaphor for the analysis of concrete human decisions and their consequences.

The important ingredient of human institutional systems is the behavioral element of voluntarism: purpose, accomplishment, social control, decision-making, and of course cognitive evaluations of these. Human systems are not simple matters of food chains or predator-prey relations (although they can be shown to be mechanically similar to those), but include conscious objectives and techniques, the buying of time, the "trade-off," and the willingness to borrow from Peter to pay Paul. Since these complex adjustments and exchanges configurate into world-wide systems, it is doubtful if much will be gained in the immediate present by the application of systems concepts based on the proposition of self-regulation, unless such analyses are used for the purpose of constructing control systems. But the seeking of control over the use of resources and a new framework of choices and priorities that give a greater value to sustained yield should retain a framework of democratic decision and choice, and the role of systems analysis in this process is ambiguous.

This has become evident in the issue of pollution in both the developed and emerging nations, where the introduction of new substances and techniques into existing systems of resource use, however stable or unstable those may have been previous to the change, has resulted in a variety of major and minor disasters, most of them avoidable if proper investigation had preceded the innovation (for examples, see Farvar and Milton, 1972). While the omission of adequate study of the whole systems can be attributed to scientific atomization and to the Cold War, which induced the big nations to compete with each other in the economic aid field, fault is equally present in the eagerness with which the new nations seized on development as a path to power and rivalry among themselves. Once again, ideological and power issues underlie ecological problems.

The minimum requirement for practical dealings with systems in human interventions is to ascertain, with the greatest possible accuracy, the *whole range* of systems that may be involved in a given form of resource use. To show, as have some cultural ecologists, that a particular tribal or peasant society has reached a state of balance with Nature, and to attribute this to internal cultural patterns (without at least an attempt to discover whether it is not some external factor such as a government regulation or market process that permits or encourages this sustained-yield situation), is to commit a crucial error: to confuse historical actuality and the means-end nexus in human behavior with some automatic process at work in Nature. Moreover, in cases such as these, it is more than possible that the sustained-yield situation in one locality is being maintained at the expense of some other resource complex.

THE SOCIONATURAL SYSTEM

Examples of complex socionatural systems are beginning to accumulate as ecologists and economists collaborate on particular problem-cases of environmental or social damage resulting from human use of resources. An example is provided by recent studies of the sardine fisheries off the coast of South America (the most complete or at least most readable account is by Paulik, 1971). The story begins with the American demand for fish products during World War II, the Peruvian response to which was to build a new commercial fishing industry. Following the war, the American demand collapsed and the Peruvians developed a fish meal and oil industry as a substitute. This new field resulted in an economic boom of unprecedented proportions, and the rapid development of dockage and processing facilities all along the arid Peruvian coast. As a boom enterprise, it rapidly became overcrowded and, at the same time, overfishing began to reduce the available stocks. Since the birds of the coastal strip also depended on the anchovy for food, and since men had collected the guano for fertilizer (for centuries one of the few means of making a living on the coast), the new fishing industry threatened the guano stocks. The new human population on the coast began predation against the birds, further threatening the guano industry. A sanctuary policy was introduced by the government, which has worked "fairly well." This tied the guano industry to the fishery business.

To protect the fish supply, the government has resorted to closed and limited seasons, which of course introduces a serious economic problem: what to do with the excess supply of human labor and technical facilities. To bring these things into balance, an extensive economic and biological control program has been generated, to institute ways of harvesting the right amounts of fish and guano to maximize yield, but at the same time to maintain the supply at a sustained-yield level. Accompanying this must be a system of spreading gains among the entire population serving the fish industry—requiring a government-supervised allocation system or a system of supervised cooperatives. Political factors are vital in this program, since the fishery business, due to its meteoric rise in the 1950s, became the supplier of almost 55 percent of Peruvian foreign exchange. As usual, in cases such as this, the industry is inclined to give undue consideration to measures that provide short-term advantages, ignoring some of the long-range problems.

International relations have been involved in the system insofar as the fishmeal and other products of the industry are purchased by foreign nations for advanced uses—uses not anywhere near as important in Peru. This has generated accusations of natural-resource imperialism: that Peru is harvesting a valuable natural resource and selling it for peanuts to nations who realize much larger gains from its use, while the Peruvian masses go hungry; or, even worse, that the fish meal is processed in the United States into human food, which is then sold back to Peru in economic aid schemes. Peru also has had difficulty controlling the price of the various products, since the sales are governed by the markets in the industrialized countries: thus, the population dependent on the fishing and guano industrial system experiences severe income fluctuation from this source as well as from the conservation measures.

This complex system has given rise to a fantastic amount of research on the biology and nutritional conditions of the anchovy schools, the movement and temperatures of ocean currents, international relations, economic alternatives, labor conditions, community studies, and so on through a long series of specialized disciplinary researches. The case illustrates the nature of socionatural systems under modern conditions of macrosocial forces and relations. Whether one calls these ecosystems or something else is of course beside the point; the main issue is that these systems to an increasing extent involve attempts at rational control and organization—creating far-flung networks of communication and tying the biological and human loci into the macrosystem, for better or for worse.

System and Subsystem

It is obvious that the anchovy fisheries system is composed of dozens of subsystems, each with its own rhythms and characteristics. But, in turn, each of these subsystems is composed of analytically distinguishable systemic components.

Something like this is visible in some of the writer's data on North American agrarian contexts. In a volume under preparation,[11] Dr. Kohl and I refer to the macrosystem of private family entrepreneurial farming as the "agrifamily system." In this conceptualization, we see the family unit managing natural resources in such a way as to provide a living for its members and seizing opportunities for profits over and above subsistence. If continuity of the family enterprise is a goal, the management of resources will be carried out in such a way as to conserve them, which means avoiding "maximization" pressures emanating from the national economic system and consumer culture, since such stimuli are not controlled by conservationist considerations but function, by and large, on the basis of gratification values.

However, one can perceive "subsystems" within the agrifamily system that respond differentially to these pressures. Among others, we have distinguished the following:

1. The *enterprise cycle*, which begins with establishment, proceeds through development, reaches a relatively stable plateau where its returns

satisfy the family needs and desires, may undergo redevelopment, and finally is transferred to a successor, who is likely to begin the process of development all over again in response to external economic pressures and higher standards of living. This cyclical high P/B efficiency system is marked by steady accumulation and elaboration, acknowledging occasional pauses. It is not supposed to be homeostatic, although it may develop cyclical properties if economic conditions preclude accumulation or induce recurrent collapse.

2. The *agrifamily household population cycle*, which begins, typically, with two persons, expands as children are added, contracts as children leave, although usually one will be retained (the successor, his wife, and offspring), then contracts finally as the parents die or leave, and begins over again. This cycle is homeostatic, although its regular fluctuation is due to the generally increasing scale of economic values, which exert constraints over the number of people who can be supported by a family enterprise. The interesting thing here is that the same forces that tend to propel the enterprise subsystem toward increasing use of resources tend also to control the population size of the family, keeping it small. In addition, there are forces for conservation of resources built into the system, as in the case of a father wanting to conserve his resources in order to hand over a viable unit to his son.

3. The *agrifamily instrumental network*, which is a subsystem consisting of numbers of people—relatives and nonrelatives—who assist in the operation of the family enterprise. At one point in the family cycle a predictable increase in the numbers of persons in the network occurs: marriage, when a new set of kin are added to the existing group. That is, whenever a marriage occurs, especially to a male member of the family who will succeed to the enterprise, a new body of helping hands is supplied to the enterprise. However, at all other points in the cycle of the family enterprise, the numbers of people in the instrumental network will vary, depending on actual needs for assistance (labor, loans, etc.), the personality of the operator and his skills in cooperating with others, the presence of good neighbors, and other factors. That is, while part of the network subsystem is under the control of cyclical events (and therefore displays a degree of homeostasis), the rest of it is not; it is controlled by factors operating with a degree of randomness. The larger the network, the more obligations the operator and his family develop toward others, and this also tends to result in pressures on the enterprise to produce.

LARGE-SCALE SYSTEMIC PROCESSES: THE DEMOGRAPHIC AND MOBILITY TRANSITIONS

It is fitting to close with what may be the best-established feedback processes in the ecological transition: the population dynamics and human movements associated with economic development.[12] Like all systemic processes, they operate when the conditions are right—they are not universal and not automatic—although their operations are not something within reach of awareness of every member of the society. Nor is it always easy to ascertain if these changes actually take place in particular cases; there are complex problems of data analysis and interpretation.

In its classic formulation, the demographic transition has three stages: (1) The first stage is defined as the typical state of affairs for most of human history: high birthrates balanced by high death rates, with a slowly growing or fluctuating population. This describes India, China, and most of the countries of Latin America and Africa until recently, when modernizing institutions altered the picture. (2) The second stage, considered to be the true transition, occurs when improved nutrition and medical care, associated with early stages of industrialization and modernization, results in a lowered death rate while birthrates remain high; this results in rapid population growth. This process has been operating to a greater or lesser degree in non-Western countries for the past century. (3) The third stage is associated with low birth- and death rates, and a low rate of population increase. This comes about as levels of living rise, education spreads, and people begin to "trade off" fewer children for a better way of life. This stage has also been called the "transition."

The second stage is considered to be the principal problem of demography in the developing countries; it affords an example of how population phenomena are interwoven with economy, resources, and key social institutions. The drop in mortality was due largely to the fact that disease-prevention could be introduced relatively quickly and cheaply—more so than significant economic changes and the construction of a consumer attitude, which take at least two generations. The resulting population increases tend to cancel out small gains in economic status, since the increase in wealth and goods is immediately consumed by the increasing population. In order to pay for the support of increasing numbers, these countries must then export raw materials to the developing nations, resulting in a loss of basic resource capital. Economic aid and social assistance, thus, has had a serious demographic and environmental impact on these countries.[13]

Such cases of partial transition are therefore generated by the development programs of the United States and other countries, which have had their strongest emphasis on industry and health. The effect of the latter on reducing mortality has been mentioned. The effect of industry on fertility is established through the fact that industry benefits the existing urban populations more than the rural. While the urban begins to change toward middle-class values and smaller families, the rural remains in large part in an agrarian condition and continues to possess the labor incentives for large families. Or, a characteristic lag develops between the aspirations for better living and the preference for smaller families. These effects, clearly visible in countries like Mexico and India (though with many details of difference in the various countries), can be considered to be consequences of post-World War II foreign aid policy and constitute an excellent example of how political and economic institutions, operating on a large scale, can influence ecological relations.

The demographic transition may be seen to operate by a series of feedbacks. These have been diagrammed and discussed by public health specialist Harald Frederiksen, and modified versions are presented below. The first, Fig. 5, shows what happens when economic development does *not* produce synchronous declines in both fertility and mortality—or, rather, the case in which feedback does *not* operate. The diagram consists of a series of causal linear chains—one thing leads to another; although the economy develops, the *per capita* share decreases because the population continues to increase. The assumption here is that the system of failed transition does not contain the necessary reinforcing loops that would give the desired result of "high levels of production-consumption, but low levels of fertility-mortality." The messages are not getting through to the birth-generating system—that is, to men and women.

In Fig. 6, Frederiksen diagrams the case of a hypothetical successful transition. This diagram contains lines that show feedback taking place: for example, the interaction between increasing health, increasing fitness for work, decreasing fertility, and increasing production to raise levels of living. If these loops function, then the population reaches a stage of equilibrium with decreased numbers of very young and very old—"decreasing dependency": a relatively young, economically productive population that practices "family planning." This is an idealized approximation of the population of countries such as Holland or the British

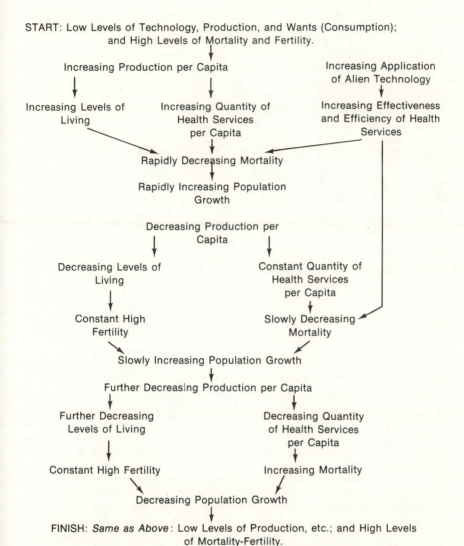

START: Low Levels of Technology, Production, and Wants (Consumption);
and High Levels of Mortality and Fertility.

Increasing Production per Capita

Increasing Application
of Alien Technology

Increasing Levels of
Living

Increasing Quantity of
Health Services
per Capita

Increasing Effectiveness
and Efficiency of Health
Services

Rapidly Decreasing Mortality

Rapidly Increasing Population
Growth

Decreasing Production per
Capita

Decreasing Levels of
Living

Constant Quantity of
Health Services
per Capita

Constant High
Fertility

Slowly Decreasing
Mortality

Slowly Increasing Population Growth

Further Decreasing Production per Capita

Further Decreasing
Levels of Living

Decreasing Quantity
of Health Services
per Capita

Constant High Fertility

Increasing Mortality

Decreasing Population Growth

FINISH: *Same as Above*: Low Levels of Production, etc.; and High Levels
of Mortality-Fertility.

Fig. 5 Failure of economic-demographic transition. (Modified version of Fig. 1, "Neo-Malthusian model of failure of economic-demographic transition," in Frederiksen, H. "Feedbacks in Economic and Demographic Transition," *Science*, vol. 166, November, 1969. Copyright 1969 by The American Association for the Advancement of Science. Used with permission.)

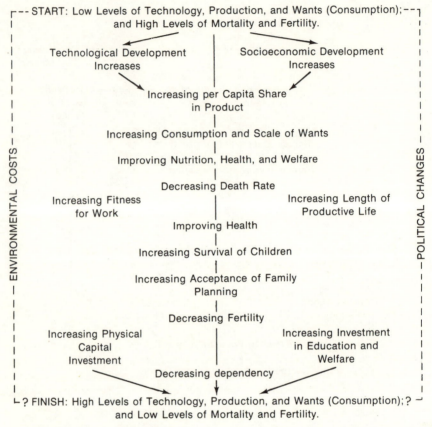

Fig. 6 Proposed successful transition with high levels of living combined with low mortality and fertility. (Modified version of Fig. 3, "Alternative model of successful economic and demographic transition," in Frederiksen, H. "Feedbacks in Economic and Demographic Transition," *Science*, vol. 166, November, 1969. Copyright 1969 by The American Association for the Advancement of Science. Used with permission.)

Isles—old and very mature industrial nations with very modest rates of population growth and a strong middle-class culture.

As noted, the key to the process outlined in Fig. 6 is the reduction in mortality—which, in the arguments of anti-population-explosion proponents, is often viewed one-dimensionally as one of the causes of population growth, not its control. Frederiksen and others sharing his views propose that reductions in mortality would lessen survival anxiety in a population and encourage the adoption of family planning customs, which in turn reduce fertility. The critical factor in this is, of course, the growth of a particular cultural pattern consistent with this hoped-for operation of the system. This would require changes in other institutions in order that the necessary attitudes will emerge.

Japan, a recent high-economic-growth case, appears to have entered the transition—largely as a result of national fertility policy and legalized abortions. Increasing educational levels and effective cultural communication permitted the widespread acceptance of both mortality and fertility control measures, resulting in a close-to-zero population growth by the late 1950s. However, since 1969, the year of publication of Frederiksen's paper, the Japanese have been engaged in a national debate on population control, and the birthrate has begun to increase as the country experiences labor shortages due to the high demand for youthful, energetic workers—the category of the population in shortest supply due to the control measures. (In other words, the entity, "increasing fitness for work" on Frederiksen's diagram, is defined differently by industrial managers and population experts!) Whether the pattern will really reverse itself and fertility rise drastically, as it did during Japan's early modern or transitional period, is not clear at the moment. However, the possibility illustrates the fact that these processes do not work automatically, but always in relation to particular social, economic, and political policies.

Another ambiguity in Frederiksen's scheme (as suggested by my modification at the left) is the lack of specification of environmental costs associated with achievement of the goals. The high levels of technology, production, and consumption are considered to be achievable as a matter of course, and their control for purposes of environmental health is not specified. Here again the case of Japan is revealing: there is a clear association between her achievement of demographic transition in the 1950s and degradation of the environment by her burgeoning industry and agriculture (Bennett & Levine 1975).

The scale of human wants and consumption is not a fixed or permanent affair in modern societies—it has, up to now, continued to rise; the economic actions required to promote and to maintain an increasing scale, as in the case of Japan, require intensive development of industry—especially the big polluters such as chemicals and metals, which supply needed foreign exchange for capital. These processes create both ecological problems and the need for control of human actions—yet, at the same time, the complexity of the system makes control difficult to achieve and "breakdown" becomes a probable result.

Still another ambiguity in Frederiksen's scheme is the lack of specification of any sociopolitical process accompanying the transition from the top to the bottom of the diagram (I have added copy to the diagram to suggest this). The nature of the power system seems to be taken for granted, or perhaps as a constant, while great changes and reversals are made in contemporary institutions governing the relationship of technology, economy, and culture. As in other papers to be discussed in later chapters, social change and social preconditions for change are simply ignored, and yet these are often the issues on which the desired improvements really turn. Changes of the magnitude proposed here will obviously require increasing controls and intensified indoctrination—"education." Just how all this is going to happen seems to be the most important issue of all, and certainly the one most urgently requiring public discussion.

There are also unsolved problems concerning fluctuations in fertility in the highly developed nations such as the United States, presumably within and beyond the stage of demographic transition. The population-increase curves of these nations do seem to move downward and level off, but they frequently (as in the United States during the 1950s) develop sharp spurts in fertility that are difficult to explain. Clearly the motivations for births are different in the developing and the developed nations. However links between fertility, consumption attitudes, needs for labor in the farm or the factory, cultural styles favoring the having of children, women's liberation movements, and many other things will influence fertility and result in short- or long-term departures from the expected transition.

Closely related to the demographic transition is the *mobility transition* or "laws of migration":[14] another set of demographic processes related to economic development and its social changes. These regularities have been noticed for years. In a recent attempt at formulating the hypothesis, geographer Wilbur Zelinsky (1973, p. 219) lists the following related propositions (paraphrased and supplemented):

1. As a community or society experiences modernization, there is an increase in both physical or geographical mobility and social or status mobility. That is, the society changes from a relatively static, locality-dominated system to a more dynamic one, with networks and movements covering the entire population.

2. The mobility transition parallels (goes along with) the demographic transition. That is, in a community undergoing changes in fertility and

mortality, there also will be increased migration and change in social and occupational status.

These two key propositions are followed by a number of detailed hypotheses concerning the stages and rates of spacial and social mobility, forming a body of complex hypotheses concerning the feedbacks between economic development, urbanization, and demographic and social phenomena. Many of these hypotheses have not been adequately tested in research, and there is in general a tendency to be overly mechanistic, as if we were confronted by natural laws. Zelinsky uses the term "axioms" to refer to both—and in other passages he talks about "hypotheses," "paradigms," and "principles." Underlying the mobility transition is the principle of "least effort," which we discuss in other chapters. (It concerns the tendency for humans, over sufficient periods of time and ignoring the many exceptions that mar the regular functioning of the principle, to do things in ways requiring the least amount of effort: go the shortest distance, work the least hard, and so on. The principle also has much to do with consumption behavior, and advertisers and merchandisers have played on this theme for years.)

To simplify the quite complex stages and patterns in the mobility transition, we can distinguish the following:

After the "traditional society" has begun to modernize:
1. there occurs a large movement of rural residents to the city to take new jobs and improve life chances;
2. many of the better educated people emigrate abroad, either for additional training or to improve their position;
3. a small number of skilled and educated people from other countries immigrate to the new country.

In later stages of development:
4. the rural migration to the city slacks off, and movement between cities, seeking better jobs, increases;
5. emigration out of the country diminishes; immigration into the country increases;
6. social mobility increases greatly, with large numbers of children receiving better education and jobs than their parents and moving their residence as they search for opportunity. In other words, internal migration and social mobility becomes a norm.

It is not hard to see how the demographic and mobility transitions are related. As mortality drops and fertility drops even more so, the rising level of living and general opportunity-seeking behavior of the population is manifested in the various migrations and employment upgrading characteristic of the mobility transition. A feedback is established: as people get more, they want more—success and aspiration create more of the same, and behavior adapts to the means for achieving the goals.

If the key to the demographic transition is the reduction in mortality, then the key to the mobility transition is the improvement in opportunities. In fact, both of these processes really boil down to the consequences of improvement in health and welfare, and improvement of opportunity. The movements of people created by these developments, in both social and physical space, might be considered the irresistible forces of modern world history, and the outcome is logically the "homogenization of the entire inhabited world" (Zelinsky, 1973, p. 248). This is assuming, of course, that the reinforcements and feedbacks continue to operate—that is, whether environmental and political costs can be met. We will have something to say about that possibility in the next chapter.

In the meantime, these processes of the ecological transition operating on a large scale are best viewed not as laws, or "axioms," but as social facts—as current historical events. Whether the processes involved, fueled by least-effort and other common behavioral phenomena, are to be seen as unique to man or as greatly enlarged versions of processes found in all animals is perhaps not the main point. What is important is their impressive magnitude, their testimony to the enormous power generated in human systems, and the way human behavioral proclivities can produce massive consequences for the environment and for man himself.

NOTES

[1]Claude Bernard's major work is *An Introduction to the Study of Experimental Medicine* (1927; original edition, 1855).

[2]W. B. Cannon's two basic works are: *Bodily Changes in Pain, Hunger, Fear and Rage* (1915) and *The Wisdom of the Body* (1939). L. J. Henderson's classic work is *The Fitness of the Environment* (1913; revised and republished in 1958). His essays and lecture notes on social systems have been published as *On the Social System* (1970).

[3]Tansley's original formulation, and its relationship to Clements' work in plant succession, is indicated in the following quotation from his paper (1935)

> I have already given my reasons for rejecting the terms "complex organism" and "biotic community." Clements' earlier term "biome" for the whole complex of organisms inhabiting a given region is unobjectionable, and for some purposes convenient. But the more fundamental conception is, as it seems to me, the whole *system* (in the sense of physics), including not only the organisms-complex, but also the whole complex of

physical factors in the widest sense. Though the organisms may claim our primary interest when we are trying to think fundamentally we cannot separate them from their special environment, with which they form one physical system. (p. 299)

The emphasis on the physical, the material, the non-sentient factors, or rather the absorption of sentiency into the physical, is clearly evident in this first statement of the ecosystem concept. (Clements' pioneer effort was *Plant Succession*, 1916. B. W. Alfred and Edith S. Clements, 1949, provides a selection of F. E. Clements' key writings.)

[4]W. Ross Ashby's two lay works are *An Introduction to Cybernetics* (1956; and *Design for a Brain* (1952; 1960). It is in the latter book that Ashby identifies adaptation in behavior as equivalent to stability, a point of special concern to the argument of this book, since it imposes a biological model on human behavior.

[5]Wiener's major works are *Cybernetics: Control and Communication in the Animal and the Machine* (1949) and *The Human Use of Human Beings: Cybernetics and Society* (1950).

[6]Bateson's "Bali" paper appeared first in 1949, in M. Fortes (ed.), *Social Structure: Studies Presented to A. R. Radcliffe-Brown*, and has been reprinted in Bateson's recent collection of essays (1972). A history of Bateson's involvements with cybernetics and systems theory appears in a *Foreword* to this collection. Cybernetic principles became a fad in the early 1950s in all the social disciplines. For such applications of systems theory to economics, see Boulding, 1956B; Mayr, 1971; to psychology, see Stagner, 1951; McClelland, 1965; to urban social organization, see Mesarovic and Reisman, 1973.

[7]Ecosystem now is advocated by everyone as the master concept for a unified science of human ecology, or a general ecology including man (Ripley and Buechner, 1970). For other discussions of the concept, see Hall and Fagen, 1956; Kalmus, 1966; or appropriate sections in any general text in biological ecology. A good summary of the concept in both economic and bioecology is found in Boulding, 1966. He reviews some of the analogies to natural ecology and evolution to be found in economic science and social science generally. Expositions of ecosystem theory in relation to resource management, economics, and other fields are found in Van Dyne, 1969.

[8]See, e.g., M. Moerman, 1968, pp. 81–84.

[9]The construction of large dams and water impoundments in tropical regions (Africa, Southeast Asia) has received considerable attention in recent years by a number of disciplines (medical research and epidemiology, natural ecologists, hydraulic engineers, geologists, anthropologists). The work constitutes a model of multidisciplinary ecology in which the role of the cultural ecologist, as partly illustrated by Scudder's work, emerges clearly as one of doing before-and-after studies of behavioral adaptations. For a review of these studies, see the recent papers by Scudder, 1972B; 1973.

[10]Small-scale examples are found in the new communes of the counter-culture movement: the communalists, despite the best of intentions toward Nature and the restoration of balanced relations between man and Nature, have in some cases been responsible for serious soil erosion, injury to forests, and stream pollution. Intentions are simply not enough; balance has to be achieved by detailed knowledge of environments and careful adjustment of human needs and wants to the capacity of the environment to support them.

[11]Bennett and Kohl, forthcoming.

[12]For accounts of the demographic transition, see Thompson, 1929 (the earliest formulation); Cowgill, 1962–63; Thomlinson, 1965; and the definitive large-scale test of the hypothesis on 53 nations presented by Satin, 1969. For accounts of the problems associated with the failure of transition and the accompanying population explosion in transitional

countries, see Geertz, 1963; 1964; Kunstadter 1972; Stolnitz, 1964; Ehrlich and Ehrlich, 1972. Hillery (1966) presents an example of a microscopic study, which involves a comparison between Navaho Indians and Kentucky Hills people. The Navaho are just entering the transition; the Hills people are leaving it. The article also illustrates the connections between the demographic and the mobility transitions, although this is implicit.

[13]The process is beginning to become the subject of study by anthropologists concerned with cultural-ecological studies of particular tribal groups undergoing a shift to a cash from a subsistence economy. The Miskito Indians of Nicaragua is one group that has been studied by a number of anthropologists and zoologists with respect to their subsistence dependency on the green sea turtle (Helms, 1969; Neitschmann, 1973; Ward and Weiss, 1973). This reliance on the turtle has shifted from subsistence to cash, as the Indians have entered the market economy. This hunting of turtles for sale has threatened the animals with extinction and threatened the tribe with a loss of both its subsistence resources and cash supply.

[14]Zelinsky's paper is the best recent formulation of the mobility transition. The antecedent theory of migration is treated in Ravenstein, 1885; Thomas, 1938; Lee, 1966. A technical analysis of the relationships between mobility and the demographic transition is presented by Chung (1970), where the demographic transition is handled as a diffusion process—that is, the mobility transition becomes the diffused demographic transition. In many respects, this combined analytic approach seems preferable to formulating the two "transitions" separately, as axioms or processes.

CHAPTER 5

The Ecological Transition: From Equilibrium to Disequilibrium

The transitions in population and mobility are only facets of the grand transition in human relations with the physical environment. This is not a single transition, but a great many, involving both natural resources and social structure, the human species and all other species, the surface of the Earth and the settlement of humans. The ecological transition is equivalent to the ecological history of humanity; it is also largely equivalent to what anthropologists have called cultural evolution.

The enormous span of time and historical complexity of the processes mean that we can describe it from many points of view and frames of reference. There are typologies and histories, evolutionary "laws" and empirical generalizations, regularities and exceptions to regularities, and contradictions galore awaiting the single-factor theorist. The process is characterized by both broad, unidirectional evolutionary trends and by evolutions or histories of specific human populations that may or may not exemplify the sequence demonstrated in the evolutionary pattern.

There is, also, the fact that the portrayal of cultural evolution by western scholars was deeply influenced by the doctrine of progress. This has meant that the emphasis was on human accomplishments, rather than failures; upward and onward, rather than stagnation, decline, and fall. For the ecological transition, this implied a tendency to ignore the consequences of human use of Nature in favor of what was seen as increasing control over it—ignoring, in the process, the destructiveness and fragility of systems based on increasing dependence on finite or scarce resources for the support of increasing populations. While it is true that over the long span of history, the human population did increase, and the disasters often recouped, this was usually accomplished at considerable cost to the Earth's supply of resources. The Malthusian process *does* operate in the very long run; its short-term effects may be less evident or applicable.

If we choose to fasten on one particular facet of the ecological transition, which appears to explain more phenomena than others, it would seem to be the question of how human societies do manage to maintain a sustained-yield balance with resources and control over population increase for reasonable periods of time; and how these same societies move away from such balance toward demographic and economic-technological growth with its more intensive use of resources. What forces impel this change, and how can the change (if it should endanger survival) be halted or the process reversed? While there exists anthropological data on the evolutionary growth process, information on control, destructivity, stagnation, or decline is much less abundant.

We shall discuss the transition from two approaches: the first concerns material progress: the archeological record of the move toward more intensive use of natural resources and support of an increasing human population. The second approach concerns the problem of how equilibrium, achieved for a time, gives way to disequilibrium between resources and population.

THE ECOLOGICAL TRANSITION AS MATERIAL AND DEMOGRAPHIC EVOLUTION

The modern approach to the material evolution of culture in southwest Asia begins with V. Gordon Childe's work in the 1930s and '40s (1936; 1942) on southwest Asia* and Europe. Although the factual outline has been greatly supplemented and the details modified in many respects,[1] the proposed sequence of basic events has undergone no substantial change. Before Childe, the course of material evolution was illustrated with tools and the materials used for making them: the Old Stone, New Stone, Copper, Bronze, and Iron Ages. Even here, while it is common knowledge now that the developments associated with the sequence include far more than tools, and the divisions were by no means as sharp as the 19th-century inventors of the scheme assumed, the outlines still stand. The movement from stone, through beaten copper, and then on to smelted

---

*"Southwest Asia" refers to the large region from the Indus Valley to the eastern shore of the Mediterranean, including Egypt. "Middle East" refers to a smaller area: roughly the western half of Iran to the Mediterranean and Egypt.

metals (bronze and iron) does represent the historical southwest Asian pattern of technological evolution, or increasing sophistication in the use of raw materials and their conversion into resources.

Childe's improvement on the materials-tool sequence was to shift the emphasis toward the use of natural resources for subsistence purposes, and the way these adaptive postures evolved one from another. He was not, of course, much concerned with the initial step from non-tool-using to tool-making, since at the time he wrote archeologists deferred to the bone men (the human paleontologists) because the evidence was locked up in fossils or in stray bits of tool-like objects encountered in geological deposits that may or may not have been associated with the man-like fossils. Childe's interest was in the later two steps: the food-producing "revolution" (his term for the old Neolithic or New Stone Age) and the urban "revolution" (his designation for the Bronze Age). Both of his revolutions, and his evolutionary theory generally, were based on archeological data from the Middle East: from the Indus Valley to the Palestinian shore of the Mediterranean and, of course, down to Egypt.

To begin the exposition, we should take a look first at the population concentration of human communities under preindustrial forms of adaptation to the physical environment. A great deal of work has been done on this in recent years, and more or less well-founded estimates have been produced for hunting bands and village communities in all parts of the world where the archeology can provide some evidence. The local figures vary, of course, and no one set of figures that averages the population for particular places over particular periods will be identical to other estimates. However, the proportions will be similar, and the historical pattern of growth seems the same the world over. In 1957, Robert Braidwood and Charles Reed proposed some figures for the early Middle East which, although very approximate, indicate the pattern of growth of the human population with which I am chiefly concerned. The following are revised and supplemented versions of their figures and categories, beginning with the earliest:[2]

1. *Food-gathering* of the Old Stone Age, including the collecting of vegetable foods, the killing of small game, occasional killing of large game.

Population concentration: 3 persons per 100 sq. miles to 1 person per 1 sq. mile.

2. *Food-collecting*, or intensified food-gathering associated with late Stone Age peoples, and the populations of "Mesolithic" semi-sedentary hunters, fishermen, and plant-gatherers.

Population concentration: 12.5 persons per 100 sq. miles to 1 person per 1 sq. mile.

2A. Food collecting, *plus vegeculture.* This technique is characteristic of the tropics, and it refers to plants that can be propagated easily by sticking roots, stems, or leaves in wet soil. Such "agriculture" need not have large, tilled fields, regular rows, etc. The technique is visible today in various parts of Africa, Southeast Asia, and the Pacific Islands.

Population concentration: Around 50 per sq. mile. More recent data indicates the range is from lower figures than the above to as high as 400 persons per sq. mile. These later figures are for modern peoples emphasizing vegeculture, under "swidden," or shifting cultivation regimes, and of course these represent more highly developed types than would have been characteristic of the beginning stages.

3. *Incipient agriculture.* Includes sowing seeds of wild, or semi-wild plants, and possibly the domestication of some animals. Food-collecting still persists: the diet is a mixture of wild and semi-cultivated foods. Production probably still not sufficient to provide a stored surplus for the fallow season.

Population concentration: The authors refused to estimate, but later evidence suggests that the range would be similar to the estimates for vegeculture, above—that is, a considerable range, from 50 to several hundred per sq. mile.

3A. *Primary village-farming community* ("Neolithic"). Major reliance on cultivated crops and animals; sedentary village life, with full range of agricultural technology.

Population concentration: 25 per sq. mile in the drier parts of the Middle East; up to 500 per sq. mile in wetter regions.

4. *Combinations of farming villages and trading towns* (late Neolithic, early Bronze Age). Here the basic population supported by food would be enlarged by others subsisting on trade and commerce. Religious bodies and government officials would also swell the total.

Population concentration: 50 per sq. mile and up.

5. *Pastoral nomadism.* Special adaptation: people living with herds of animals, subsisting on the products of the animals and also on vegetable foods bartered from farmers. A mobile life, involving moving with the herds to pastures.

Population concentration: Difficult to generalize, because of the mobility and the great variation in the quality of pastures, which permit varying numbers of both animals and humans. Braidwood and Reed give a figure for the ancient Middle East of between 3 and 15 persons per 100 sq. miles.)

If we exclude the inserted special cases, such as pastoral nomadism and tropical shifting agriculture, the grand sequence or ecological transition for the Middle East is something like this:

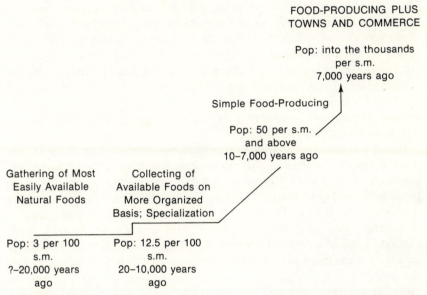

Fig. 7 Approximate population concentrations for evolution of material adaptation for Middle East.

Figure 7 indicates that as time passes the increase in population density forms a curve with several sudden jumps. While this seems reasonably well established for the Middle East, it is not necessarily the case elsewhere in the world. Sharper increases, fluctuation, or less dramatic increases are found, but the general pattern of increase as the range of natural resources utilized and the amount of energy extracted from them increases, is found everywhere when the time period is long enough.

However, as noted, the population figures are indicative, not definitive. The precise state of resources in different climatic and topographic zones will of course affect population within any given technological regime. The data represent, with qualifications noted, the situation for southwest Asia or the Middle East—a generally arid land with marginal subsistence conditions. Population concentrations at the same levels of technical development were different in more humid regions, though always within a general range, but it is these very regions that have proven refractory to archeological methods depending on maximum preservation of the crucial remains.

As the sequence of technical developments proceeds upward, the ability to predict precise demographic magnitudes probably decreases. That is, under simple food-gathering and food-collecting regimes, populations were probably very similar the world over, regardless of climate. However, as food-producing technology increased in sophistication, the ability to build specialized subsistence systems on particular resources increased, and therefore the influence of different resources in different regions would be considerable. There is reason to believe that "cultures"—the distinctive mental systems characteristic of relatively isolated communities—probably emerged along with this distinctive reliance on distinctive resources.

It was the growing awareness of population increases in the past, and those associated with intensive resource exploitation in the 18th and 19th centuries, that started European scholars speculating about the long-range relationship of man to Nature. Thomas Malthus is responsible for the most influential of the theories of the relationship of population to resources, although both John Stuart Mill and David Ricardo made significant modifications of his theories (Barnett and Morse, 1963, Chapters 3, 5). The issues raised in these early studies really revolved around the question of the nature of resources: could they be taken as fixed or finite, as Malthus assumed, or must one make a distinction between amounts and quality of resources (principally agricultural land), as did Ricardo and Mill? The models of population growth relative to resources provided in these commentaries are all considered too simple today in light of the enormous development of technological devices and techniques to modify productivity of resources—such as fertilizer, soil texture modifiers, deep tilling, land recontouring, scientific animal breeding, and many others. For example, until recently in many parts of the Northern Great Plains of North America, sandy soils were considered worthless, and human and livestock population densities on them were low. Today, while the human population density has not increased in these areas, or has increased very slightly, the soil itself is worth a lot of money, since ways have been found for making it produce excellent pasture grasses on which an increased livestock population flourishes.

Essentially, these early attempts at analyzing population-resource ratios held that as population increased, and the resources had to be worked harder to provide for the greater number, the amount of added product decreased per amount of work it took to produce it; and/or that as the resource declined in quality, the number of people it could support would also decline (that is, people would press against the resource and eventually survival would be threatened). As we noted above, these generalizations have to be heavily qualified today, and in a subsequent chapter we will examine Ester Boserup's theories on the relationship of agrarian development to population growth. At the same time, there is a large zone of imprecision around these concepts—that is, the quality of resources and the effects of technological means to modify that quality are both subject to change through time. We are also learning that many of our resource-enhancing strategies are injuring the resource itself: fertilizer pollutes water, tilling increases wind erosion, and so on. Many people in the environmental movement have, in effect, returned to the early, unqualified Malthusian doctrine of finite or fixed resources, at least for the *long run*: the "space ship Earth" idea, because it is safer—it increases respect for the Earth's substance, which we must continue to rely upon.

Whether food-producing should in fact be considered the primary characteristic of the Neolithic is a matter of argument among archeologists that does not concern us here (P. E. L. Smith, 1972A, pp. 3–4). From an ecological standpoint, Childe was right in singling out food-producing as the major development, because more than anything else it signifies man's distinctive way of using resources and the consequences of such use. The onset of food-producing is still imperfectly known because it is always extremely difficult in prehistoric research to find the exact point of beginning of anything—largely because there *is* no exact point in most cases. Food-producing is not a single thing even though the term "agriculture" implies the unity of all peoples who are shown to practice it. Food-producing involves knowledge of topography, soils, weather, climate, moisture in the air, running water, moisture in the ground, plant species and their distinctive habits, and the technology of digging sticks, hoes, plows, baskets (for storage of plant foods), sedentary life, and many other things. Food-producing is a new way of life, since it leads to a new material adaptation: *settling down* and making more or less intensive use of the same general piece of land year after year.

However, the development of this sedentary form of life was preceded, of course, by experiments in plant and animal domestication of varying degrees of intensity: in all of the world's tropical regions, various types of semi-sedentary agriculture, using different types of root and grain crops, still survive. Much attention has been paid recently to these extensive forms of agriculture, often summarized in the terms swiddening or shifting cultivation (Conklin, 1963; Harris, 1972B; Weiner, 1972). In early studies of swiddening, attention was given to its apparent ecosystemic properties: it does not drastically modify natural ecosystems like intensive agriculture, and the recurrent abandonment of fields for varying intervals permits regeneration of soils and natural humus. However, as Geertz pointed out (1963, Chapter 2), swiddening can be harmful when the interval is short, when the burning of plant cover preceding cultivation of a plot is too extensive, or where unusually friable soils are put into use. These tendencies have been observed in many places (see Bennett, 1973, for a summary and references).

Food-producing is based on the domestication of plants and animals. The human behavior involved is basically the same as that in trade and commerce: the removal of objects from natural settings to places where they will satisfy human needs more efficiently. In doing this, man alters Nature and changes his own social relationships in the process. In significant instances, the environment is permanently altered, and new problems arise for men to solve.

The ecological theory of plant domestication in southwest Asia, emerging in the work of Reed, Flannery, and others,[3] has the following points: (1) In regions of relatively abundant resources, food-collecting peoples may persist indefinitely, benefiting from the relative ease of living, and (2) population is likely to flow outward from such regions into areas of less abundant or available resources, where the need for new subsistence techniques and resources arises. (3) However, with a heritage of "broad spectrum" (a term Lewis Binford [1968] uses to refer to the old "Mesolithic" or various forms of Braidwood's "food collecting" plus "incipient agriculture") food-collecting from many different life zones, these migrant populations would bring some of these techniques and plants to the new territory, thereby changing their habitat and altering their adaptive capacities. This is "domestication."

The consequences for the physical environment of plant domestication in the Middle East are summarized by Kent Flannery (1969) as follows: (1) Many varieties of wild, edible grains and legumes were eradicated and pushed into refuge zones in order to make way for cultivated varieties; in their place, new weed crops invaded cultivated areas (a process repeated many times in the history of agriculture, including the recent North American agricultural frontiers). (2) The technique of fallowing resulted in a replacement of many varieties of grasses and legumes by pasture plants, which in turn became forage for domesticated sheep and goats, thus building up large areas of grazing land, which until recently were assumed to be "natural." (Again, the same process occurred in Western North America, where midgrasses in many regions were replaced by short grass, under grazing pressure.) (3) The development of irrigation created new environments along the canals and ponds, where leakage and subsoil saturation permitted the growth of palms, vegetable crops, and weeds. Siltation and salinization due to imprecise engineering and improper maintenance was an additional problem (Jacobson and Adams, 1958; Helbaek, 1969; Dimbleby, 1972). Other forms of deterioration also were evident: destruction of savannah and forest, soil erosion, and others—not all unregenerative, however. Although agriculture has been viewed in the material context as one of the great triumphs of mankind, its movement across the land has left great damage. As E. Hyams (1965) has suggested, agriculture has survived in those parts of the world where the soil and weather could sustain the destructive impact of the early stages of trial-and-error farming.

The impact on the human social environment involves two main questions: (1) What did food production do to the bands of hunters and food collectors who had, up to this time, been more or less nomadic? (2) What consequences did food production have for subsequent developments in human society? In the first question, the development of food production was an extension out of specialized and intensive food collecting, so the process of settling down had been slowly evolving for a long time. When the balance tipped away from the necessity for a degree of roaming in search of food to the production of all or nearly all of it in a territory small enough to permit foot travel back and forth in one day from all important resource loci, the "village" emerged. This is a small nucleated population unit, usually surrounded by fields and woodlands, and is a place of residence and a natural-resource processing and storage center. Its existence is dependent on food-producing nearly everywhere except in a few famous cases (e.g., the Northwest Coast Indians, whose food-collecting from the rich natural crops of salmon and vegetable foods permitted sedentary life short of actual production).

The second question—the subsequent developments made possible by food-producing and its accompaniment, the village, as summarized by Kent Flannery (1969) and Philip Smith (1972A) were as follows: (1) population became concentrated in larger centers, accompanied by an unequal possessory allocation of the relatively smaller amounts of land used to support the growing population, leading to social stratification based on property rights and power—a localized "Malthusian" process. That is, town and urban population nucleation and social structure were not merely products of economic surplus produced by farming, but of changed relationships between population size and the amount of land it depended on for subsistence. (2) The nucleation of population also was responsible for vast new cultural and technological developments: architecture, decorative art; city planning; military organization; intricate division of tasks and labor; advanced trade and craft manufacturing. It should be noted that in this paragraph we have made the transition to Childe's "urban revolution," because the food-producing revolution provided the basis for the growth of towns and cities.

The domestication of animal species is less well known than that of plants, but the basic processes appear to be the same, and most of the same effects were present. Nearly all the animals presently used by man for food, transportation, and tame pets were domesticated in southwest Asia, though Southeast and East Asia had some of their own species (the pig, the water buffalo, or perhaps even cattle). The details are still obscure. Each domesticated species is a separate problem, since its habits are distinctive and man's use of it differs. Nor are the precise circumstances of domestication of particular species known in detail. The relationship to plant domestication is generally assumed to be fundamental: for example, Eric Reed (1969, p. 367) appears to feel that in the Middle East village life and at least a specialized "broad spectrum" pre- or incipient agricultural base would necessarily precede full domestication (controlling-protecting-breeding the animal) of the important food species, if not the pets. (Dogs are generally considered to have "joined" man as a hunter and food-gatherer.) Flannery (1969) has suggested that the sheep-goat-cow triad of southwest Asia may have emerged as a response to the high-risk agriculture of the arid region. Surplus crops, acquired in high-moisture periods, as well as the abundant arid-adapted pasture plants, made the storage of food in animal bodies a logical and efficient solution to fluctuation. This is, in general, the key factor in animal domestication: the animal is used as an energy converter to supplement crops, and of course in that sense it replaces wild game protein in the diet.

The sequences of the ecological transition in Middle America are less well known than those for southwest Asia, but the basic pattern of food-gathering or collecting, to incipient agriculture, to full village agriculture, to nucleated population centers with advanced trade and institutions is the same. However, the wider variety of life zones in the New World—southwest Asia was pretty uniformly dry—meant that the exact sequence of development in particular localities differs considerably (Coe and Flannery, 1964). Three such areas intensively studied are the Mexican valleys of Tehuacan (MacNeish, 1972), Oaxaca (Flannery *et al.*, 1967), and coastal Peru (Patterson, 1971). In all three cases, the archeologists have revealed a series of minute, shaded, combined adaptations to differing "microhabitats" and food resources by contemporaneous and sequential groups. The emergence of cultivated forms of corn, beans, avocado, peppers, cucurbits, and others takes place under differing circumstances and combinations in each case. Irrigation has been a matter of some controversy, insofar as archeological work has not revealed its presence in the formative stages of urban life as convincingly as in the arid southwest Asian region, although recent work is beginning to suggest that it was indeed present.[4]

As with plant domestication everywhere, the development of a cultivated variety means considerable genetic change, some of it irreversible. Corn is a supreme example of this—the genetic changes have made its precise origins in wild plants a matter of continuing controversy (Mangelsdorf *et al.* 1964; 1971; Mangelsdorf 1974). However, the basic objective of domestication of corn was similar to that for the dryfield grasses such as wheat and barley in Asia: the conversion of seeding structures from easily opening rachis, to facilitate wild seed dispersal, to closed structures in which the seeds are held tightly to prevent accidental or wind-scattering (the "head" for the grains; the "ear" for the corn).

An important environmental impact of corn domestication has been the progressive extermination of some of the wild plants known to be involved in the plant's history, even though the details may be somewhat obscure. This is the grass *teosinte*, which has continued to hybridize with corn in peasant farming in Mexican valleys, to produce new viable strains. However, progressive destruction of wild flora in Mexico, with conversion to cultivation, has systematically reduced teosinte's range. Wilkes (1972, pp. 1076–1077) has pleaded for deliberate conservation of these wild strains in order to facilitate continued hybridization. Similar problems are approaching for many other cultivated plants. They all need reinvigoration from the wild ancestors from time to time.

One issue associated with intensive preagricultural adaptations is forest clearance in northern Europe (Clark, 1945). Simmons (1969) summarizes available evidence for Britain and concludes that the burning of woodland and brush by Mesolithic inhabitants for the purpose of clearing hunting areas would initiate cycles of occupance of the burned areas by game, to take advantage of the improved grassland, followed by a slow regeneration of certain stages of forest growth. In some areas soil deterioration resulting from such use of the land might permanently inhibit forest growth (Keef *et al.*, 1965). Accounts of possibly comparable impact on the forest by northeastern American Indians have been provided (Day, 1953; Niering and Goodwin, 1962). Pastoralists everywhere are known to occasionally fire grasslands to herd wild game—the habit was particularly prevalent in Western North America, and some paleobotanists have concluded that this practice might well have reduced the extent of the islands of trees in certain elevated parts of the Plains and along rivers (Wells, 1969).[5]

Even the food collectors and hunters are turning out to have their impact on Nature—although it is always specialized. The most elementary technologies, like fire and stone implements, can have permanent effects on vegetation if the applications are persevering (Iversen, 1949), and the case of extinctions of large game animal species at the close of the Pleistocene is a much-debated issue at the time of writing (Krantz, 1970; Martin, 1973). There is also evidence from the Great Plains bison kills and other slaughter sites in Europe that hunters sometimes killed animals far in excess of subsistence needs, and that grassland and savannah burning was sometimes practiced for sheer pleasure (Bartlett, 1956).

Still, viewing the material transition over long spans of time, it seems apparent that the food-producing "revolution" was the turning point. Up to that time, humans had a modest impact on the physical environment because their numbers were too small and the technology they used to transform energy was limited or sharply focused in its destructive potential. Food-producing, however, concentrated human activities, required greater energy sources, and also increased the range and scope of human communications through trade and commerce, as well as by the more sophisticated technical processes. Innovation in human societies proceeds more rapidly under such circumstances, in general (Barnett, 1953), so the seeds for the subsequent developments with much greater environmental and social impacts were sown (pun intended). The more or less exponential curve of energy conversion and human population begins its upswing at the point of food-producing, and perhaps its next leap upward was in the Industrial Revolution (see Figs. 3A and 3B).

THE PROBLEM OF STAGNATION

The process of material evolution obviously does not explain the cases of cultural stagnation—or, in more ecologically appropriate terms, restraint of demographic and economic development. Such cases are well known in the ethnological literature, although anthropologists have always been puzzled by the phenomenon and have been unwilling, or unable, to explain it. The most obvious cases are the living populations of hunter-gatherers—like the Bushmen of South Africa, the Australian aborigines, and a few others—who existed at a food-collecting level of subsistence in their respective regions for as long as 10,000 years. Attempts at explaining these cases by genetic differences in innovative capacities long ago collapsed. Nor can the ambiguously defined factor of "isolation" be used to explain cultural stability. Perhaps more light can be shed on the problem if we remember that in every case for which we have some archeological or historical evidence, the population exists in a geographically remote "refuge," with limited or refractory resources that no one else wanted; and/or it was driven into this area by hostile neighbors with, for that moment, superior military technology. Thus, there is the hint that the key factor in the process may well be social stratification, with its accompanying process of exclusion and suppression. The answer to the ecological question is to be found, if this is indeed the answer, in the human social process and not in geographical isolation *per se* or in man-as-animal.

But even this does not completely solve the problem, because there are other cases where social exclusion and forced migration did not lead to ecological stability and cultural stagnation. Perhaps the other variable in the picture is the level of technological development of the population at the time the exclusion process begins. The movement from food-collecting to food-producing is a big one; it does not happen overnight, and the evidence for the process in the Middle East and Meso-America suggests that it required considerable experimentation by many peoples and communities before a viable style was developed. Thus, the collective explanation for the case of ecological stability at low energy levels involves the social exclusion of a relatively low-energy society by a relatively high-energy one, involving physical movement to a remote geographical region with refractory resources. The combination of these factors seems to produce econological stability at a low level of energy conversion. The system becomes self-maintaining; it becomes one of the few instances of "ecosystemic" functioning in human phenomena over relatively long spans of time.

The argument may be strengthened when we look at the other most prevalent case of stagnation at a given level of resource use: the peasants. The case is not quite parallel to the hunters, because peasant agriculture has had a more obvious deteriorating effect on the environment, and peasant populations have persistently increased. But there are similarities just the same, and here the role of stratification is clear enough: the peasants are people who do not modify their basic subsistence or ecological posture, or do so slowly, because of exploitation by the people who control them. Their energy output is too low for successful resistance or revolution—at least not very often.

But these attempts at evolutionary interpretation of the causes of stability in resource arrangements really do not get us very far. Anthropologists do much better at the microlevel of the inner structure of the societies that most often exemplify the lack of, or extreme slowness of, econological growth. More enlightenment—at least from the standpoint of what anthropologists have done best—can be furnished by examining the social dynamics of these societies in order to obtain a picture of systemic processes which, for a time, have sufficient feedback so as to reinforce a given ecological posture and discourage the movement toward a higher level of energy conversion. Since this is really a matter of the findings of contemporary cultural ecological research, we shall reserve the discussion for the next chapter.

THE ECOLOGICAL TRANSITION AS A PROBLEM OF EQUILIBRIUM

We turn now from material evolution, with its overall record of progressive use of resources and increase in human population, to a different approach: the interpretation of the econological postures of human societies as ideal types. An ideal type is a controversial, often tricky, but useful device for representing historical differences and changes in culture. Robert Redfield used typology in his effort to portray the transition in social life from small communities, and their shared common understandings, to the larger, more impersonal urban social systems. The former, the "folk" societies, would be characterized by direct contact of nearly every individual member with the subsistence quest; the latter, urban type, would have the majority of its members separated from such contact.

If we look at the ecological transition from the standpoint of systemic functioning, we can reduce the complex and gradual changes of the historical process to two types: societies that find an equilibrium with Nature and those that do not. The first are adaptive systems that have stabilized their internal affairs and their technology; the second are those that allow for substantial change in these. By "equilibrium," we mean managing or using resources so as to sustain their yield without significant deterioration—for varying periods of time. Equilibrious societies would then approximate ecosystemic relations with Nature: use of resources would fluctuate, perhaps between cycles of overuse and regeneration, on a homeostatic basis. The judgment of sustained yield or homeostasis in the resource system would be made for specified groups, with defined boundaries; or it could be made on the basis of generalizing a number of societies in a large region over a period of time. Some of these might well abuse their resources, but the average of them all would indicate minimal destructive impact.

Culturally, equilibrious societies would be those in which for at least the period of time they were under observation, their meanings and goals of life were made to conform to a sustained-yield system of resource use. Although behavior *vis-à-vis* Nature would be controlled in part by values having nothing to do with natural phenomena—social constraints or supernatural ideas and rituals—even these would function so as to permit a balance with the physical environment. Such societies would be characterized by a philosophy of continuous existence without substantial change in technology or energy levels—that is, "traditional" societies. They would avoid the risk of altering their present level of survival, avoid jeopardizing their future. That is, the ecosystemic qualities of their life would be a consequence of their culture, and one would not necessarily find an explicit conservationist philosophy. Equilibrious societies would also be those that are, in a sense, two-dimensional with regard to physical settlement. They would be bound to a particular geographical range of resources, and all their necessities (as well as any luxuries) would have to be supplied from this range. Their small population would familiarize every member with the state of the resources.

These are obviously idealized requirements, because they tend to neglect trade and commerce. But craft manufacturing and trade between low-energy societies is performed by simple technology with minimal communication and does not have significant environmental or cultural impacts. In any case, it is not sufficient, in our ideal type, to alter the rule of sufficiency of local resources for survival. Such societies also use *primary* resources: land, water, air—there is minimal conversion to secondary resources and processing.

The disequilibrious society is the opposite of the equilibrious type. It has more complex internal and external relations: it is in "free space," not bounded space, since it seeks resources wherever they are to be found, and thereby does not need to depend on a local supply for survival. Such societies may have a philosophy of social continuity, but it is expressed by growth and change—development, improvement, increasing satisfaction not tradition—hence they are dynamic in the context of resource use. They require larger amounts of energy, and they consider Nature to exist primarily for satisfaction of human wants.

Figure 8 lists the characteristics of both ideal types. The left-hand column contains the criteria; the middle column, the equilibrious case; the right-hand column, the disequilibrious. If we think of the two sets of characteristics from the standpoint of social control, the equilibrious type is one where considerable discipline exists over the use of home-range resources; the latter, where little discipline exists over the use of either home-range or externally-derived resources.[6]

In terms of energetics, the equilibrious type concerns human societies that relied primarily upon sunlight as the major source of energy, structuring their social systems, cultural values, and ritual practices in order to manage the energy provided by sunlight to plants and animal species dependent on plants—that is, technologically simple hunting-gathering, pastoral, and agricultural regimes. The limited amounts of energy available from these sources provided constraints on institutional growth. Rewards and tasks in these ecnological systems were distributed to individuals in proportion to the amount of work they could perform to maintain the flow of energy from natural species, or simple domesticates and cultigens. Since intervention into natural processes was limited by the sources of energy utilized, human impact on natural ecosystems was relatively slight—again excepting some classic cases of destruction even under the simplest technological regimes (Kunstadter 1972B; Turnbull 1972).

This pattern changed toward the disequilibrious type as man discovered new sources of energy in his own economic organization, his technology, and in fossil fuels. The tendency to allocate tasks and rewards in accordance with performance output in the primary production system has changed (and did so by degrees throughout human history) as the wealth provided by the increase in energy permitted large numbers of people to achieve their wants and amass property without paying the full costs of the resources. This process resulted in the proliferation of particular cultural features labelled "civilization" or "human creativity"—attributions that are not completely wrong, but that underrate the obvious efficient causes of fuels, chemistry, and the machine.

The first thing to note in Fig. 8 is that the phenomena used to construct the types are heterogeneous: population; contact with environment; range; sustenance; gratification; and technology run the gamut of the

	SOCIETIES IN EQUILIBRIUM WITH ENVIRONMENT	SOCIETIES IN DISEQUILIBRIUM WITH ENVIRONMENT
Population Dynamics	Small, Controlled	Large, Expanding, Weakly Controlled
Contact with Environment	Direct Contact by Maximum Number of People	Direct Contact by Minimal Number of People
Range	Restricted to Local Resources	Resources Available From External Sources
Sustenance Needs	Close to Minimal; Defined Largely by Physiological Needs	Maximal; Defined in Large Part by Cultural Wants
Gratification Expectations	Low; Controlled	High; Promise of Continued Expansion
Technological Capacity	Low	High
Feedback Loop #3	Functioning to Control Resource Use	Functioning Only to Promote Resource Use

Fig. 8 Ideal types of societies based on degree of ecological equilibrium.

academic disciplines; in the same order, the criteria are represented by: demography and sociology; geography and anthropology; economic geography; biology and nutrition; psychology; engineering-anthropology-history. This also reaffirms that ecology is a frame of reference or point of view toward human and natural phenomena rather than a field or discipline of knowledge.[7]

The second conclusion to be drawn from Fig. 8 is as follows: Since the types represent a progression from low-energy societies to high-energy civilizations, the underlying technical processes used by humans are the same—the only difference is in the quantitative properties of these techniques, and the only difference between contemporary technology under industrial conditions and that of the past is the sheer amount of energy converted and the extent of use of natural substances.[8] At this level of the discussion, cultural evolution gives way to a recognition of basic similarity in all econological postures: men at all levels of cultural development can be seen to have similar behavioral tendencies, which provide them with the means to modify and pollute Nature—if circumstances encourage them to do so. As Edmund Leach points out (1972):

> History does *not* show us that there has been a repeated failure to achieve a balanced relationship between human beings and the environment. There has been no such *failure* because it is in only the most extreme kinds of environment, such as those found in Australian deserts or Greenland icefields that the simpler peoples have become in any way aware of the possibility of ecosystem balance. It is only in such extreme circumstances that human beings of the past have been in any way motivated to achieve balance between their society and the environment. (p. 39)

That is, there is no built-in mechanism restraining the human proclivity to use, and expand the use, of natural substances—this has to be consciously developed under special circumstances. In all other cases, the historical record is one of progressive expansion of resource conversion and growing impact on Nature.

Thus, important material processes in cultural ecology exist and are repeated at intervals. In the Middle East, the deterioration evident in the archeological record argues that there were cycles of overuse of resources with consequent deterioration; then depopulation and technical devolution back to simpler energy-conversion systems; then slow rehabilitation of damaged resources; and finally, a return to the systems of overuse and overdependence.[9] If these cycles (homeostatic?) do exist, then many evolutionary propositions in current use for cultural ecology are too simple, being based on unidirectional or unidimensional concepts. There is the suggestion that while economy and technology do "grow" or increase in complexity, the key issues may not always be associated with growth *per se* but rather with the relationship of growth to social phenomena, since the consequences of growth may turn out to be proportionately similar at different levels of energy output (e.g., the effects of breakdown of irrigation systems on the Middle East population in Sassanian times might have been no greater, or no less, than the effects of comparable degradation of the environment may be on the modern population).

However, despite the evident importance of material phenomena, the role of ideology also deserves attention. The emergence of high-energy technology in the West may well have had its basis in Judaeo-Christian philosophy and its emphasis on a man-centered universe.[10] Conversely, the lower energy solutions to civilization practiced by Asian countries before the onset of "modernization," may have been rooted in the greater emphasis in these civilizations on man-in-Nature ideals, as Northrop (1946) has endeavored to show.

THE CASE OF JAPAN

The case of Japan is often cited in this dialogue since the nation has moved from an Asian low-energy, preindustrial culture to a high-energy, industrial type with rapidity and efficiency. Caudill and Scarr (1962) did an interview study with questions designed to tap responses to the Kluckhohn-Strodtbeck (1961) classification of value orientations.[11] They found that the dominant Japanese orientation is "mastery over Nature," with "man and Nature in harmony" as a secondary category. Man's "subjugation to Nature" was a distant third. The problem was picked up again by Tatsuzo Suzuki (1970), who reported on responses to somewhat similar questions on a Japanese national attitude survey repeated at intervals of five or ten years. The results confirm the Caudill-Scarr findings in one sense, but present more of a man-Nature-harmony profile in another:

QUESTION: "In order to be happy, man must":

	Adapt to Nature	Make Use of Nature	Conquer Nature	Other	No Response	Total
1953 Survey	27%	41%	23%	1%	8%	100%
1963 Survey	19%	40%	30%	1%	9%	99%
1968 Survey	19%	40%	34%	1%	6%	100%

Fig. 9   Data on Japanese attitudes toward nature (from: Suzuki, 1970).

The Caudill-Scarr concept of "mastery" straddles the "make use" and "conquer" categories of Suzuki's surveys, and "harmony" is more or less equivalent to "adapt to." The national surveys did not use the "subjugation" concept, so the comparison is hard to make. However, the "make use" category is less severe than either "mastery" or "conquer," so if one adds together the responses in "adapt to" and "make use of" and sets them against "conquer," one obtains a large majority for something less than an outright "mastery" notion.

There may be a hint here that the Japanese, despite their economic-technological growth and its expected ecological effects, remain somewhat more congenial to concepts of respect for Nature than most Westerners, which might suggest that they will be more receptive to controls over destructive practice. Such receptivity is doubtful at the time of writing, however.[12] Moreover, Befu (1971, pp. 171–172), who also presents a summary of the attitude data on this question, concludes that in the past the Japanese must have believed more strongly in "subjugation by Nature" than at present, because in the 1953–63 period, the surveys used by Suzuki show an eight percent reduction in the "adapt to" category, "which in terms of the continuum on man-nature orientation stands between 'subjugation' and 'mastery'"—and also, a nearly similar amount of *increase* in the "conquer" category. Thus, Japan's rapid economic growth and development of a consumer culture is apparently having its attitudinal effects.[13] (However, the problems of translation between Japanese and English, and the problem of obtaining precisely comparable results in the presence of the many shadings of attitude and rhetoric in interviewing, make this sort of thing less than reliable, and one is inclined to look at behavior rather than attitudes as a guide to man-Nature relations.)

A more fundamental issue concerning the Japanese ecological posture is available in the literature on the Japanese equivalent of the "Protestant ethic" of Western civilization. Robert Bellah (1957) explored this at length in an effort to provide an ideological explanation for the rapidity and efficiency with which Japan accomplished her modernization. Bellah noted that the stress on achievement in Japanese feudal culture was functionally analogous to a similar emphasis in the Puritan heritage, although in the Japanese case the rewards for achievement are to be found more in the satisfaction of living up to the expectations of one's groups rather than, as in the Western case, fulfillment of individual aspiration.

The Japanese achievement ideology was based on Confucian economic morality which features a strong emphasis on the moral duty to produce, but also to restrain consumption, in order to avoid self-seeking and consequent social dynamism and disorder: "Production is in order to attain sufficiency and economy is to see that sufficiency is not upset" (Bellah, 1957, p. 110). A variety of laws and sumptuary regulations were enacted in order to enforce this policy of production—plus austerity. The strict Confucian view, which certainly influenced Chinese social theory and practice, was therefore based on the concept that the society and the state are made self-sufficient at a fixed or balanced level by a feedback process—the output, when adequate, informs people that they should not want more, and this in turn sets up constraints over production and use of resources. This Confucian view of the relations of man, economics, and Nature is similar to concepts now urged by ecological philosophers (e.g., Hardin, 1968; 1972) as a means of restraining economic growth and its abuses; or in terms of the discussion of our Fig. 1, the feedback loop from the output end of the production process toward the sociocultural components functions so as to control technology and the use of resources.

However, the Japanese version of Confucian economic doctrines contained an important implied qualification: that diligence in production and modesty in consumption are to be carried out by the *samurai* in the service of his lord; that the primary aim was not to produce social stability by avoiding self-seeking and gratification but to serve one's master loyally and efficiently. Moreover, few *samurai* in preindustrial Japan were actually engaged in business, and the merchants and some of the lords who were, were not always motivated by Confucian values. The point is that the achievement emphasis in the Japanese ideology was a loophole: it eventually led to as strong an emphasis on production, wealth, and consumption as that in the West. Japanese today achieve and consume for the greater glory of the state and nation, the family, the peer group, and the company, and there are few visible Confucian restraints in operation. This suggests that, whatever the Japanese values concerning Nature, there has always existed an emphasis on output and achievement in Japanese culture that is not substantially different from the Western experience.

The recent acceleration of economic growth in Japan offers some valuable opportunities for viewing the ecological transition in a modern context. A whole series of craft industries that existed through World War II and into the 1950s have vanished or been greatly curtailed in the past 20 years: a change comparable to a shift from the crafts of early 19th-century America to the present situation: from wood and bamboo to metal and plastic. Whole chains of resource uses have vanished: the timber and wood-products industry formerly operated so as to consume every portion of the tree: the leaves and litter for agricultural compost, heavier branches for firewood or charcoal, substandard sections for wood packaging, smaller logs for mushroom production, timber for lumber and interior house fittings, and so on. *Genya* (hardwood bush) furnished material for charcoal on a sustained-yield basis for centuries without need for special renewal processes.

The wood-products sustaining chain has been broken into by new methods of rice-paddy tillage, which lessen the need for forest-litter compost; by the substitution, on a widening scale, of gas and electric appliances for space heating, eliminating the consumption of wood for fuel; by the substitution of plastics for packaging materials, and many other fabricated materials, involving the abandonment of useful substances available at low cost (or, at least, at low financial costs but with relatively high labor inputs). Since many of the substitutes are produced chemically, with imported substances at the base of the process, there is a decided shift away from modest self-sufficiency toward increasing dependence on foreign sources. A similar process can be seen in the growing industrial pollution of bays and inshore areas along Japan's seacoast and the corresponding interference with the supply of fish—a major staple. This loss is not felt immediately because at the same time there is an effort to shift the meat protein content of the Japanese diet toward beef. However, successful large-scale beef production in Japan is dependent upon imports of feed grains; and, of course, the foreign exchange gained by industrial exports currently pays for the losses due to pollution, or the added cost of shifts toward beef. Since such dependence on foreign resources and supplies is contingent upon stable international relations, and since Japan's position in this respect is precarious or at least hard to predict, some legitimate economic (not to mention ecological) questions can be raised about this creeping abandonment of reliance on available resources.

Each of these cases for breakage of old cycling systems, or substitutions of new substances for old, involves a cultural change as well (Bennett, 1967A). The Japanese phenomenon involves the creation of a mass consumer culture in the span of a very few years (bare beginnings in the 1930s and substantial development in the '50s and '60s) and a partial shift of values from a group-controlled consensus pattern to an individualistic or hedonistic pattern. This change is of course by no means a drastic one if one considers the fact that Japanese culture had precedents that could be drawn upon to reinforce these changes without conflict: for example, the tendency for consumer styles to emerge as a mixture of individualistic gratification and socially defined standards appropriate to the reference groups for the individual—the latter, for Japan, even more sharply defined than in the American case.

The Japanese case once again raises the specter of human wants getting out of control, and the problem of how to deal with this. In Fig. 8, the equilibrious type is indicated as having its "gratification expectations" in a "low" state; that is, they have not yet responded to the forces in economic growth that encourage the "revolution of rising expectations." The inner dynamics of the control systems in the small, "equilibrious" societies studied by anthropologists will be discussed in the next chapter; some important contributions have been made by cultural ecologists in this sphere. The factors that induce a "low" level of expectations and wants to change toward a "high" are both internal and external: they involve the combined processes of technoeconomic growth and increasing population and social differentiation, which can emerge within a society by inner dynamics (as they did in part in Japan during the hermit stage in the 17th and 18th centuries). However, the process is usually accelerated when the influences come from external sources: "developed" societies. The inequality of development throughout human history—the fact that there were always some societies, somewhere, that were "ahead" of others in their energy potential—has been one of the major causes of continued economic growth and social differentiation. This process has simply become faster (another "exponential" effect) in the past few decades, but it is by no means unique to our era.

This is why one must not lose sight of the fact that homeostasis, or steady states, in man-Nature systems in any society are situational or historical *events*, and not permanent states-of-being, held in place by biological controls. They will last as long as people want them to, as the internal reinforcements or external inputs let them, as the institutions that protect them continue to exist, and as the technology requires. Moreover, the existence of a systemic stability in any man-Nature context has to be "profitable"—either monetarily or some other way—for the people involved in it, and it appears that the emphasis on certain forms of profitability in a modern capital-oriented market economy are more prone to exert pressure toward resource exploitation than are others. So culture—values—in the form of precedents and cautions against certain practices will play a role. But not an automatic one, and certainly a highly variable one.

CHANGE

The equilibrium typology can also provide a frame for the devising of particular hypotheses about change. As noted previously, Robert Redfield's work in Yucatan (1941) succeeded in isolating a number of particular communities and groups at varying levels of technology and economy, and he arranged these groups—already arranged along a geographical gradient—in a gradient of typological change. This was formalized as a theory of change from the "folk" to the "urban" type of society. While criticisms of the theory tended to take the form of showing its empirical errors (pointing out that change in other places did not follow the gradient), the important contribution of the exercise was to provide a series of hypotheses about change that could be tested. The critics of the Redfield theory showed that changes in "culture," in social organization, or in instrumental aspects of social life do not necessarily follow the same courses.[14]

As long as we remember that the criteria in the two columns in Fig. 8 are idealized, they can be combined in various ways to furnish hypotheses about change and control. For example, is it possible that low-energy-technology societies also can experience rapid population growth and pressure on resources even though the latter are listed as characteristics of the high-technology type? The answer is "yes," when we consider this happened in the monsoon Orient, where an improvement in the minimal technology of rice production, plus the effective mobilization of services through cooperative intervillage organization on labor and irrigation, provided new food energy, in turn triggering rapid population growth around 1500 A.D. This suggests that in some instances social instrumentalities can be as effective as technological ones in increasing production and the transformation of natural resources into energy and goods. One of the more controversial examples of evolutionary generalizing in cultural ecology and its related fields revolves around this proposition. Karl Wittfogel (1957) argued that "Oriental despotism" arose out of the need for large-scale bureaucratic organization needed to control water resources, which led to another sobriquet: "hydraulic society." This thesis was immediately examined by specialists on other preindustrial civilizations, and it has been reworked to show that despotism and bureaucracy can *precede* large-scale water and other resource developments, as well as follow it; or that the particular *use* of the water—e.g., irrigation vs. flood control—is the significant cause of particular social forms.[15]

There is, however, another kind of ecological transition available for study in the history of these ancient empires dependent upon large-scale water control for sustaining population and agrarian-based wealth. This is the reversion to simpler systems of resource use—a devolutionary process. An illuminating paper on the history of one of these cases is provided by Rhoads Murphey, for ancient Ceylon (1957). The Sinhalese constructed a stupendous series of waterworks in the dry zone of the island, accompanied by one of the great architectural complexes of ancient civilization: the vast ceremonial-political complex of Anuradhapura, with its enormous stupas, baths, and public buildings. The Sinhalese effort was only one of a series of these developments produced around the 9th to the 13th centuries in Cambodia, Siam, Burma, and Java. All of them collapsed in the 13th century or later.

Murphey has sorted through various theories advanced to account for the remarkably similar pattern of civilization buildup and collapse, with water development a central feature: military invasions and conquests, climatic change, soil exhaustion, salinity and siltation of the irrigation works, and epidemics of malaria. Murphey discards most of these as the primary causes, although he acknowledges that they all might have contributed to the decay and collapse. His own reasoned theory rests on the need for large numbers of docile laborers, controlled by a powerful administration under an absolutist monarch, to build and maintain the works (for a contrasting theory of Sinhalese hydraulic society, see Leach, 1959). The irregular rainfall of the dry zone can result in disastrous floods, which can sweep away major engineering works in a day; if labor is not available to make instant repairs, the system can begin to decline and rapidly slip out of control. Internal weaknesses of the bureaucracy, inevitable in all aging political (especially absolutist) systems, plus invasions, plus rainfall—in short, any factor that would help to weaken the system of labor—would bring the system to a point of collapse, and this is what Murphey believes happened to Anuradhapura-Polonnaruwa. In other words, the key to the devolutionary transition is in the sociopolitical system, like all large-scale human ecological processes. The body of accumulating knowledge on civilizational growth in the past (and the present?) testifies to the instability rather than the stability of large-scale socionatural systems and the increasing uncertainty, rather than control, resulting from technoeconomic growth.

Or, reinterpreting these events in terms of concepts of self-regulation, we could say that during their heyday, these systems were not stable or equilibrious, but rather the reverse: typical human systems with increasing quotients of "organization" and increasing tendencies to defer the payment of inevitable costs—high P/B efficiency schemes or positive feedback. Their breakdown, on the other hand, can be defined as a case of a *return* to preexisting equilibrious or homeostatic systems with lower levels of organization and with less cost to the related subsystems (negative feedback). Such returns to more primitive systems thus have a dual meaning: in terms of human affairs, or history, they imply social breakdown or instability; in terms of a comprehensive ecological perspective, they represent a reversion to some kind of equilibrium.

This also reaffirms that generalizations about stability and instability in human societies need to consider the factor of time in order to obtain an accurate perspective. The tendency in cultural evolutionary thought to consider states of being at particular moments in time as sufficient evidence for generalizations about process leads to erroneous judgments. The issue is paradoxical because of the great interest in history and change exhibited by these evolutionary approaches.

A position with greater concern for policy would propose that there exists in human behavior a constant potential toward overexploitation of resources or pollution of the natural environment, granted that in certain historical circumstances and institutional arrangements, the effects may be minimal or phased out over relatively long periods of time. Humans can assert control over environmental deterioration by conscious discipline or planning, by ritual regulations, social interaction, or cultural precedents, and/or by very occasional automatic feedback mechanisms operating outside of cognitive awareness. A generalized cultural ecology obviously must include models pertaining to *all three* possibilities, although for highly developed pluralistic societies the conscious planning process is the only realistic course.

Still another kind of change process can be seen in attempts to combine some of the criteria listed in Fig. 8. These hypotheses concern the possibilities and circumstances of preserving the technological and consumption gains of the present but reducing the pressure on the environment.[16] Therefore, the questions may be put:

Is it possible to combine the characteristics of the equilibrious and disequilibrious types so as to:

a. maintain a high technology but reduce the scale of human wants?
b. maintain a high technology but reach a stable population growth?
c. maintain high standards of living without polluting effects?
d. maintain a dynamic and innovative technology, but bring it under the control of society; i.e., permit feedback loop No. 3 to function as a control system?

(The logic of these questions resembles the arguments about Redfield's theories of typological change, especially when debates occurred over whether the "folk" and "urban" criteria were really distinct, or were overlapping. We noted earlier how typology tends to provide the basis for creating imaginative hypotheses, providing one does not confuse the types with reality. More concretely, the main danger of culture typology is its tendency to carry an assumption of cultural determinance of behavior and thought: that in the presence of cultural pattern A, A-type behavior will always occur; and that since cultural patterns A and B are frequently associated, they must have some basic affinity. The logic of this thinking can obscure two important facts: (1) that human experience is configurated in several different systems, not just one, and these systems can change and develop with varying degrees of independence; and (2) that humans have the capacity of reacting to patterns and systems, of combining opposites, and bending existing systems in unlikely directions in order to achieve ends.)

The theme of combination of opposites is discussed by economists U. Ayres and A. V. Kneese (1971) in a paper concerned with the possibilities of creating a world with a stationary economy and population and a controlled degree of pollution. They observe that the pollution rate has been increasing faster than the rate of population growth—a point also developed by Commoner (1971). The issue here is, of course, the attempt to maintain a high economic growth rate by providing more jobs and income for people to purchase the commodities—which are produced as cheaply as possible. Because of hidden subsidies or policies of ignoring the costs of resource damage and exhaustion, the cheapest modes of production have required the use of synthetic substances and metals (like aluminum), which are notorious polluters. Ayres and Kneese point out that this does not mean that population growth has no relationship to pollution, since the concentration of large masses of people in cities and of course the sheer numbers of consumers obviously aggravates pollution in various ways. But a technological basis for reducing pollution does exist: the curtailment of especially damaging processes.

However, Ayres and Kneese also note that enormous pressures to maintain high rates of economic growth arise from the expectation of wealth and leisure engendered by the rise itself, and that attempts to curtail pollution and economic growth will inevitably affect the capacity to meet these standards—and social unrest is bound to follow if they are not met. We might add that in an increasing number of cases labor has joined business in opposing pollution control measures. In other words, pollution cleanup, like control of economic growth, is becoming a political problem of great magnitude. The obvious solution is to inaugurate policies involving a switch from polluting to nonpolluting industries, but this will take a consensus, detailed planning, and new incentives.

After discussing various possibilities, some of them optimistic, the authors conclude with a distinct note of pessimism based on their doubts about the capacity of human social arrangements to handle the increasing complexities of a world out of control (not to mention the capacity of science to continue to produce the kinds of new technology, and corrective technology, that the new world of nonpolluting activities will require):

The large world population of a century or more from now might be sustainable at relatively high levels if the technologies one can optimistically foresee can be successfully applied. For some of the major ones, this assumes that "everything goes right," with social and political institutions, nationally and internationally, and for very long periods of time. This is quite an assumption, for historically everything has gone right only momentarily in terms of the time scales we are discussing. (Ayres and Kneese, 1971, pp. 20–21)

Moreover, with continued experience of failure, the managers might begin to minimize risks and make choices of safer but less rewarding processes, giving us a vision of a crowded world in which no one starves, but everyone exists at a drab level of living and in a state of compulsory conformity—that dismal image of the science fictioneers.[17]

Much of the discussion in this field centers around the problem of a value consensus. The dilemma, as portrayed by Crowe (1969), is simply that in a social system increasingly characterized by theoretically "equal" subcultures with their own "non-negotiable" demands and definitions of life, government can only play a temporizing role, permitting each social group or institution to realize its objectives with minimal conflict with others—an "incremental" approach to regulation. This process does not provide much optimism for the achievement of the far-reaching changes necessary to achieve a state of sustained yield. It would involve, among other things, a considerable change in the power of the corporation.

A more optimistic view holds that the interplay of the semi-autonomous groups contains the grounds for a pluralistic solution: the making of deals, trade-offs, and bargains among the actors so that environmental health, or a reasonable level of pollution, becomes profitable for all. That is, the very forces that seem to prevent control may in fact provide the means. In ideological terms, it is a question of the kind of balance that might be struck between a coercive totalitarianism and a pluralistic, balance-of-power democratic process.

What role might the anthropologist play in this situation? Monica Wilson (1971) visualizes it as follows:

It is the business of the anthropologist to show the Peter Pans who refuse to grow up, who reject the responsibilities of largeness of scale, what tiny societies are like; to show yet again, that the "noble savage" in Arcadia is dream, not reality. To seek a return to smallness of scale is no cure for our present disorders; rather we must examine very closely what aspects of scale necessarily hang together. Can we have the close-knit warmth and emotional security of an isolated village without stifling individuality? Can one enjoy the fruits of science and industrial production without smothering the personal? (p. 107)

These are deceptively simple objectives. They speak in the language of the traditional anthropological preoccupation with the small society, the microsystem, but they also require a serious attempt to struggle with the macroinstitutions of national and world society and show how they affect local systems. As we have noted elsewhere, anthropologists will require extensive training in the institutional social sciences before they can move in this direction.

NOTES

[1]For ecologically-oriented descriptions of the development of food-producing and urban civilization in the general southwest Asian area, see the following: Steward, 1955; Braidwood and Reed, 1957; Wittfogel, 1957; Adams, 1960; 1962A; 1962B; 1965; 1972A; Evenari, 1961; Braidwood and Willey (eds.), 1962; Flannery, 1965; 1969; Dales, 1966; Raikes, 1967; Binford, 1968; Hole, Flannery, and Nealy, 1969. For Europe, see G. Clark, 1952; J. G. D. Clark, 1954; Waterbolk, 1962.

[2]For other discussions of population units and settlements associated with various subsistence adaptations, see the following: Millon, 1962; Adams, 1972B; Flannery, 1972B; Forge, 1972; Harris, 1972B; R. B. Lee, 1972B; O'Connor, 1972; Smith, 1972B; Trigger, 1972; Woodburn, 1972.

[3]Current discussions of the work of plant and animal domestication and their ecological and social consequences, are found in Flannery *et al.*, 1967; Ucko and Dimbleby (eds.), 1969; Struever (ed.), 1971; Smith, 1972A.

[4]For ecologically oriented accounts of cultural development in the New World, see the following: Heizer, 1969; Sanders, 1962; 1968; Flannery *et al.*, 1967; Patterson, 1971; MacNeish, 1972.

[5]For additional data on the impact of preindustrial man on the physical environment, see the brief articles by G. W. Dimbleby, D. Brothwell, and D. M. Dixon, in the book of essays, *Population and Pollution*, edited by P. R. Cox and J. Peel (1972).

[6]One of the writer's earliest published papers (Bennett, 1944B) concerned an attempt to interpret the use of resources in a midwestern region by prehistoric and contemporary agricultural peoples on the basis of a typological distinction between equilibrium and disequilibrium. The paper also proposed that adaptive-maladaptive criteria be included in anthropological studies of man-Nature relationships, and that superorganicistic conceptions of culture were inappropriate for ecological research.

[7]Cf. Netting (1972, p. 1), who quotes Bates (1953) and Shephard (1969) to the same effect.

[8]At several points in this paper we note that among the various systems preoccupied with economic growth, monopoly capitalism probably exerts the greatest pressure on resources. This issue is by no means settled, and the roles of capitalist and collectivist economies in the ecological "crisis" have not been clearly distinguished. One argument for the position that monopoly capitalism is more environment-destructive than collectivist-socialist systems concerns the much greater attention paid to the intensification of human wants by the private sector. Another is that the greater measure of central planning in collectivist economies permits a more efficient corrective response. On the other hand, the Soviet Union is experiencing acute pollution problems, due to its high technology and resource conver-

sions, and the arbitrary personal direction characteristic of some phases of Soviet resource policy has resulted in extensive deterioration—witness Krushchev's "virgin lands" experiment. For surveys of Soviet attitudes toward and experiences with ecological problems see Pryde, 1970, on water pollution; Pryde, 1972, on resource conservation; Luscher, 1970, on nature conservation. Goldman (1972) presents a comprehensive review of pollution in the Soviet Union. These works at least suggest that maximization and growth attitudes are as important in Soviet resources policy and institutions as they are in capitalist systems.

[9]For a recent study of ecological deterioration associated with Neolithic village-level agriculture, over a period of several centuries, see Helbaek, 1969. The study is part of a monographic presentation of prehistoric resource development in the Deh Luran plain of Iran. The extensive time period represented by this type of study provides a dimension of analysis not usually encountered in ethnological studies of cultural ecology. Another significant contemporary development in the field of prehistory is "landscape archeology" (Armillas, 1971), which aims at portraying the way men have shaped the physical environment in their quest for resources. William Sanders' study of the ecological and cultural history of the valley of Teotihuacan, in central Mexico (1965) provides another example of the archeological approach to ecological study, where the long time periods involved permit an assessment of the possibilities and social consequences of various alternative resource uses. Struever (1968) provides a scheme for the ecological study of small sites and geographically mobile populations, emphasizing the variety of settlement types characteristic for such groups.

[10]Studies of the Judaeo-Christian tradition and its responsibilities for ecological crisis are found in the following: Yi-Fu Tuan, 1970 (the West compared to China with respect to attitudes toward environment and resources); Orleans and Suttmeier, 1970 (the possible superiority of the "Mao ethic" of Red China over the Western approach to the environment); Darling, 1955-56 (the evils of man-Nature dualism); Lynn White, 1967 (an indictment of Nature-exploiting tendencies in Western and Christian thought); Moncrief, 1970; Marx, 1970 (arguments similar to White's); Black, 1970 (a more sophisticated argument, with recognition of the existence of a medieval concept of stewardship over Nature that was abrogated in the post-Renaissance decline of faith and the onset of growth-oriented cultures). Nisbet (1969) provides a history of the concept of social and economic growth in Western philosophy and social science, which shows how the idea has influenced the pattern of development in the Western world and our methods of interpreting this development. In my opinion, the crucial issue has centered around the concept of "rationality" and its misuse—particularly the assumption, inherent in any growth-oriented, technology-centered culture, that any clearly stated purpose, or any efficiently contrived relationship between means and ends, is inherently rational. This assumption has led to the ignoring of hidden costs and disbenefits in the entire process, as well as a distortion of basic philosophical issues. In general, however, I am inclined to place rather less emphasis on ideological matters as providing explanations for adaptational postures at any particular time than on economic systems and on pragmatic schedules of human wants. At least, every civilization has produced both Nature-respecting and Nature-destroying values; social and economic forces will push the system toward either pole, and the appropriate values will be used as reinforcements or rationalizations at different historical periods. It is probably true that human-centered traditions in Western culture had an early causal effect on vectors of activity, but, thereafter, the activities and institutions became their own ends.

[11]Briefly, these orientations are: (1) Human nature; (2) Man-Nature; (3) Time; (4) Activity (action, accomplishment); (5) Relational (to other men).

[12]The difficulty with arguments such as this, which take the form "because the X culture has thus and so, the X people will do thus and so," is that values (read: "culture") cannot really be used to predict behavior except in the most carefully controlled circumstances—that is, *only* when one can be sure that it *is* these values and these alone that are the critical causal factors. The point is that most cultures will contain viewpoints and rationalizations for almost any action, and even if some happen not to exist, they can be invented—a point made in the previous chapter with respect to the possible short-circuiting by Japanese of conservationist (man-in-nature, etc.) values in order to accomplish some immediate, subsystemic end. The writer was concerned with a problem of this type in his study of the attitudes and practices of forest owners and timber merchants in Japan during the Occupation (1963, Chapter 7). Reverence for forests as the home of important spirits and aesthetic values and a respect for conservationist practices on the part of all the people concerned was certainly present. However, needs for cash in the postwar period, a growing interest in profits, and pressures from the dependent timber workers who had to be supported by the merchants and owners for paternalistic reasons led to excessive cutting in the forests. In other words, traditional values alone do not tell you very much about what people are likely to do to their natural resources. (For a recent discussion of Japanese attitudes toward Nature which fails to appreciate this point, see Watanabe, 1974.)

[13]A conclusion reached by the writer with very different data, in a survey of the growth of Japanese consumer culture in the early 1960s (Bennett, 1967A).

[14]For Redfield's writings with ecological significance, see 1941; 1953; 1955. For some evaluations of his folk-urban theory, see Gross, 1948; Miner, 1955. (More in chap. 7.)

[15]The term, "irrigation civilization" had been used by Julian Steward (1955A) before Wittfogel published his major work. Wittfogel appears to return to the earlier Marx-Engels concept of "Asiatic type of society," avoiding Stalinist distortions of this concept, and it is this "Asiatic type" he calls "Oriental despotism." At minute levels of research, the approach has produced some interesting studies of the relationship between water resource development and social organization as this results in parallel institutional development in historically unconnected cultures (Beardsley, 1964). For some key discussions of the Wittfogel et al. thesis, see the following: Leach, 1959; Adams, 1960; 1965; Millon, 1962; Sanders, 1965. The Leach paper is particularly interesting, since he shows that Wittfogel tends to ignore another major type of Asian "hydraulic society": the Indian-Sinhalese. This type has a great many village-level irrigation works sustained by cooperative labor, and grandiose water impoundments engineered and financed by the king—the latter largely for ornamental purposes and for the watering of the royal gardens and fields. These vast works were not built overnight, and emerged over several centuries on the basis of grants of land to local magnates. Hence, in Leach's view, these enormous water systems were not accompanied by the appearance of an authoritarian bureaucracy, and village autonomy was maintained. (Murphey [1957], however, may dispute this.) Sanders, for the culture and ecological history of the valley of Teotihuacan, seems to support the generalized Wittfogel hypothesis, stressing water shortages resulting in crises as population increased, and subsequent social conflict—the two factors stimulating the emergence of large-scale bureaucratic control over water systems and the state. Others concerned with the Valley of Mexico have emphasized different cultural-ecological relationships—in particular, the question of large vs. small population centers. Blanton (1972) proposes that the Classic period was dominated by Teotihuacan, with an absolute monopoly on resources and trade, leading to the decline of smaller centers, while the Aztecs encouraged small settlements, due to reliance on a dispersed network of economic and trade systems. These differing patterns

would have quite different implications for resource use, population growth, and social structure: the network system, with its encouragement of smaller centers on the margins of important resource supplies, would tend to develop strong leadership and innovative aggression in the smaller, marginal communities—as in the case of the Aztecs and their many rebellious clients.

[16]A recent quasi-official policy statement by the U.S. government, which adopts this combined position, is presented by Garment (1970). This report also introduces the concept of "quality of life" as a focus of regulatory action, to replace the naive growth-for-growth's sake orientation of most contemporary economic policy. This same orientation has characterized some anthropological studies of cultural ecology, particularly those produced in the applied tradition. See Boulding (1966) for a much-quoted paper in which he distinguishes between the present "cowboy economy" and the controlled, recycled "spaceman economy."

[17]These speculative projections or world-systems models of population and resource systems have become a distinct subdivision of the ecology movement. Perhaps the most persistent world-systems modeler is Jay Forrester (Forrester, 1971; Schwartz and Foin, 1972). Just after this chapter was written, the most controversial one of all appeared: the Club of Rome's report, *The Limits to Growth* (Meadows et al., 1972), which gives the results of a modeling project carried out by an MIT group. The findings are pessimistic: if present trends in population growth and resource use are projected into the future, the "limits to growth on this planet" will be reached within a century, and "the most probable result will be a rather sudden and uncontrollable decline in both population and industrial capacity" (p. 23). The report is based on the assumption that present exponential growth trends in population and industrial production will continue without change as long as the present social system with its incentives to growth does not change. Exponential growth is defined as the result of positive feedback operating without significant restraint; a condition that eventually (within 100 years) will change itself into a negative feedback system with catastrophic social consequences—a "crash" in ecological terms. Proposals are advanced for achieving "equilibrium" by planning for reduced growth rates, although the report admits that the basis of this would be new social and value systems, their nature unspecified. The basic pessimism of the report lies in the fact that whether planning for limitations to economic growth takes place or not, growth eventually will cease, accompanied by agonizing social adjustments.

The Limits to Growth has now been countered by *Models of Doom* (H. S. D. Cole et al., 1973), a critique by a Sussex University team more positively oriented toward economic development as a means of modifying inequality, accepting as inevitable a certain amount of environmental consequence. But more important is their more optimistic view of the human response to problematic situations, or the issue of control as we discuss it in the present book, Marie Jahoda, in a wind-up chapter, points out that the fundamental concept in the *Limits to Growth* modeling experiment was the exponential growth (of population and resource use), in a presumably finite world—"space ship Earth." If it is assumed that there are no built-in controls over such growth patterns, then disaster is on its way. Jahoda—and the whole Sussex team—assumes that "negative feedback loops" (mainly social and political) *are* built into the human system so that the exponential growth tendencies will be checked before—before what? they get out of control? But in many cases (and here I would agree with the MIT team) they are already out of control. Jahoda points to such things as the demographic transition in the developed countries as evidence for these "negative feedback loops" in operation, forgetting that it is the *failure* of the transition in the emerging countries that is causing the population problem. On the other hand, and in a technical sense, Jahoda is right: the MIT group did exclude social and cultural responses in certain of the subsystems of the model, and Jahoda's message concerning human adaptive techniques echoes our own:

> Man is not pushed by a unified system mechanistically into intolerable conditions but assesses the circumstances around him and responds actively by adapting his goals and values . . . . Such adaptations occur as a persistent process when the strains of life are experienced. Man's fate is shaped not only by what happens to him but also by what he does, and he acts not just when faced with catastrophe but daily and continuously. (p. 211)

This is a generally acceptable argument but it perhaps is overly optimistic as to its inevitable working. Things can go too far, in other words, so that human constructive action can be too late to avert catastrophe. What Jahoda ignores, I believe, is another social process: the increasing rigidity of institutional systems. In any case, the two books are worth reading and comparing, as examples of how world-systems modeling obtains different results depending on the inputs. (It should be remembered that world-systems modelers rarely discuss the political and ideological implications of their experiments, and behind the predictions of disaster, however modified, there lie technocratic and often authoritarian implications of control, as suggested in the Schwartz and Foin review [1972] of the Forrester models.)

CHAPTER 6

Culture and Ecology: The Use of Biological Concepts

In this and the next chapter we shall review some contributions of modern cultural anthropology classifiable as cultural ecology, and we shall describe some of its successes and failures. The two chapters divide at the point where biological factors cease to play an important role in the analysis, but both chapters are introduced in the first section of this one.

INTRODUCTION TO CHAPTERS 6 AND 7

Up to this point we have offered three interrelated definitions of cultural ecology. The first was concerned with social policy: cultural ecology is that field which examines the consequences of human actions toward the physical environment for the environment and for humans, with a view toward modifying or controlling these consequences. The other two definitions concern the scientific means of accomplishing this. The first of these is very general: cultural ecology is any inquiry into human relationships with the physical environment, including biological factors, that seeks to understand the phenomena in terms of human purposes and activities. The third and most specific definition views cultural ecology as the study of the interactions involved in the feedback loop No. 3 of Fig. 1: the way the energy-conversion process is related to social and psychological components of the total system. Although I emphasize *physical* or "natural" environment in the above definitions, social factors often blend with physical, or are coped with by people much as they cope with physical phenomena; hence cultural ecology merges into general social and economic analysis—or Ecology becomes Society (or Culture).

However, "cultural ecology" is also an academic category—a relatively new effort in cultural anthropology, and one that will undergo great changes in the years to come. Robert Netting, in a concise review of the field (1972), defines it as follows:

> If cultural ecology were a little older, rather less diverse, and not so lively, it might be possible to develop a connected theoretical and methodological summary . . . . I believe that such an overview is premature—we are too busy dealing with the details of specific subsistence systems, instances of microevolution, and limited regional comparisons to begin the process of definition and synthesis which characterizes a more mature discipline. There is only one way to explain what cultural ecology is: to show what it is doing. (p. 4)

This is putting the best possible face on the situation; of course Netting is right, but what he sees for modern cultural ecology has also been true, by and large, for traditional cultural anthropology: a tendency to focus on data-gathering in an effort to collect as much material from exotic contexts as possible—to be concerned more with description than with explanation. Basically these characteristics stem from the methodological bent of cultural anthropology or ethnology: the attempt by single workers to do fieldwork in particular communities in order to obtain comprehensive portraits of these entities. While this orientation has been greatly modified in recent years, the concept of the unique society, with its unique relations with Nature, tends to persist. It will continue to persist as long as anthropologists work in geographical and social areas with a high proportion of unknowns. Under these conditions, it will remain difficult to make comparative studies of particular segments of ecological relations and processes across several cultures on the basis of a consistent theoretical viewpoint. And when such studies are done (as they have been from time to time), "comparative research" is likely to be something done on the published literature, by a scholar mining his data from the many separate studies of distinct groups.

Netting's[1] table of contents provides a conspectus of topics studied in the field:

Hunter-Gatherers
   Privation or Abundance
   Band Flexibility
   Territoriality
Northwest Coast Fishermen
   The Nature of the Environment
   The Potlach
   Competition and Control of Resources

> *East African Pastoralists*
>> The Cattle Complex
>> The Herding Habitat
>> Economizing with Cows
>> The Advantages of Large Herds
>> Pastoralist Personality
> *Cultivators*
>> System and Knowledge in Non-Western Agriculture
>> Shifting and Extensive Techniques of Cultivation
>> Functional Links between Farming and Social Organization

Of the major topics the first and last deal with societies classified by an evolutionary step or stage of subsistence. "Hunter-gatherers" and "cultivators" are considered by definition as having distinct cultural ecologies, and the materials summarized by Netting do not include some that feature hypotheses about processes common to both: for example, studies of input-output bioenergetics, which pertain to social or physiological regularities overriding specific dietary sources (e.g., regardless of whether food intake is from wild or cultivated sources). A shift toward ecological research of this kind will have to treat the evolutionary-stage categories as empirical phenomena, not as fixed differentiae in human experience.

The other two major topics listed by Netting pertain to specific geographical areas—and again, evolutionary-stage classifications are in the picture: the Northwest Coast people became a major focus of interest in the past because while they did not practice real agriculture or animal husbandry, they were sedentary, village-dwelling people with sophisticated arts. The pastoralists have been of interest for comparable reasons: the main issue being whether a herding existence limited cultural development. To sum up: many of the substantive topics of contemporary cultural ecology have arisen not from scientific propositions but from earlier ethnological work based on an evolutionary or cultural typology.

The subtopics in Netting's list cover the waterfront, suggesting a wide-ranging curiosity rather than an orderly unfolding of scientific hypotheses. A few will serve to indicate the pattern. First, the "privation or abundance" theme, which heads the list for hunters-gatherers, is actually the result of an illusion created by the failure, as Netting makes clear in his text, of ethnologists to live with H-G groups long enough to make systematic studies of their round of life and their bioenergetics. A few studies of this type (e.g., Richard Lee's work on the Bushmen, discussed later in the chapter) were finally made in the 1950s and 1960s, with the finding that many H-G peoples had an adequate food base on the whole, did not have to work very hard to obtain it, and lived to a "ripe old age with few signs of anxiety or insecurity" (Netting, 1971, p. 5). These studies in the ethnological context have been reinforced with prehistoric and paleontological data, to constitute one of the better cases of time-depth analysis in anthropological ecology (Lee and DeVore, 1968).

The "territoriality" issue is a product of work on northern and northeastern Canadian H-G bands by a handful of ethnologists over a couple of generations: the problem arose as one topic in the study of social organization: did these migratory groups stay within designated geographical areas before or after white contact and the fur trade, or both? Julian Steward had made proposals (1938) concerning social organizational adaptations to subsistence technology, and the territoriality issue was one of these. However, the literature of the period suggests that the topic of major interest was the ethnohistorical issue: whether these bands were sufficiently sophisticated before white contact to have had a concept of territorial ownership; that is, cultural evolutionary or social-developmental concerns, not ecology, were the major interest. As noted in Chapter 7, the current best account (Knight, 1965) suggests that the data are not really good enough to lay the acculturation issue to rest—we may never know whether the territories did or did not precede the Hudson Bay Co. However, the data *do* show that the size of the hunting band is positively related to the availability of large animals and negatively related to population density.

Progress *does* happen: Netting shows, in his wind-up, that the collective findings on land tenure indicate that typological or stage theory regarding the relationship of particular forms of social organization to land occupancy has given way, in cultural ecology, to the finding that particular kinds of resource use require certain adaptive responses, regardless of stage development. In other words, one would not expect to find rigorous stages, but frequent adaptive convergences *between* stages when uses were comparable—something that one would have thought could have been taken for granted on the basis of the Boasian refutation of the *a priori* stage typology of the 19th century "comparative" or evolutionary ethnologists.

The Indians of the Northwest Coast are represented by the potlatch; this topic, like the interest in the half-hunting/gathering-half horticultural subsistence system of these Amerinds, is also inherited from past generations of ethnological research. The potlatch has been studied by successive generations of ethnologists, like the famous Sun Dance of the

Plains Indians (Bennett, 1944A), and each intellectual generation has interpreted the ceremonial differently, the ecological approach simply being the latest in line. Throughout this history, the thrust of the effort has been to explain a particular *cultural* feature, the potlatch ceremonial, and this applies to the contemporary ecological mode as well. Succinctly, the latest approach finds that the potlatch, with its dramatic exchanges of property and conspicuous consumption, stimulated production and the use of natural resources, and thereby would confer a "selective advantage to the groups practicing it" (Netting, 1971, p. 11). Similarities in this behavior to the environmental-exploitative techniques used by modern man with his high technology are rarely considered seriously, and the key factor—an open system of social stratification—has not received the attention it deserves. While the Northwest Coast people might not have abused their resources, since their population was small (although we probably will never know if they did or not), their human-centeredness, the pressure on resources from a status-achievement orientation, and the notion that natural substances were there to serve man, did not differ from the contemporary situation, providing another example of how a true cultural ecology will contain generalizations across stages of cultural development.

Pastoralism is one of the oldest topics in ethnology, and the insistent question asked through the years (starting with Ibn Khaldun, in the 1300s) has been: what generates a pastoral way of life—especially when it is a specialized, constrained existence as seen from the viewpoint of settled peoples? Many answers have been given to this question, and the ecological is only the most recent of these. (The question, of course, is a largely false one since pastoralism, like any other way of life, emerges at some point or other in a particular socionatural system as the best alternative, and people put up with it as long as nothing better shows up.) Spooner (1972; 1973) proposes that the investment in herds rather than in land is the critical factor in pastoralism: as long as the herdsmen have no permanent attachment to the land, they are free to move. This seems to say little more than that nomadism is its own excuse, and attempts like this to find ultimate or determining causes in ecological factors are not especially revealing. That is, the ecological explanation for pastoralism is nothing more than the environmental aspect of the description of pastoralism.

Pastoralism and also swidden agriculture, one of Netting's key topics in the "cultivators" section, have recently acquired policy relevance. In the case of pastoralism, the tribal, low-yield farm appears to some anthropologists as preferable to the high-yield, domesticated-breed regime introduced into East Africa (the Dyson-Hudsons, 1969; Box, 1971). In other words, the costs to the health of humans and animals, and to pasture, in a specialized tropical environment argue for a simpler level of technology and a particular variety of animal, better adapted to a specialized and disease-prone tropical milieu. In a similar vein, the swidden studies speak for maintenance of these lower-yield but often less abusive practices in a friable biosphere: tropical jungle and scrub, where soils are leached and easily erodable or laterized. In both cases, the implication is clear: the human and environmental issues are better served with smaller and controlled human populations, existing at simpler, sustained-yield systems of resource use.

Not only has cultural ecology tended to seek its problems in issues emanating from social and cultural topics, but elaborate "schools" of interpretation of Culture-Nature relations have developed for particular small portions of the Earth's surface. An example is the New Guinea Highlands, where at least ten cultural ecologists and cultural geographers have explored tribal agriculture during the past 20 years, spawning a whole series of controversies over the origins of agriculture, lineage vs. local-group interpretations of kinship, the relations of agricultural intensity and development to population size, and other matters (see the summary in Waddell, 1972, Chapters 1 and 8). On the basis of the most "micro" studies of particular hamlet units, imposing generalizations or alternatives to the generalizations of others have been reached: Waddell, for example, hopes in his study of a tiny sample locality to shed light on Boserup's (1965) thesis that intensification of agricultural techniques and production is caused by increasing population density and, also, that increasing intensification is responsible for a decline in labor productivity. The results, as one might expect from the examination of such a small system, both confirm and deny the Boserup thesis, which is based on a much higher level of generality and on a "peasant" rather than tribal mode (see later discussion). Obviously, as Waddell notes (p. 218), labor returns may be higher in some intensified agricultures than Boserup's thesis would anticipate; and the fact that he *did* find intensification associated with increased densities, does not mean that the opposite is not true somewhere else. A theory with the scope of Boserup's is a matter of trend and tendency. If enough cultural ecologists study enough small agricultural localities, it is possible that a sample of sufficient representativeness to provide some relevant comment on the Boserup thesis will be compiled. But surely there must be a better way—planned surveys of particular portions of agroecologies in different geographical areas, with problems and methods attuned to the precise issue.

Culture and Environment in Anthropology

In Chapter 1, I discussed the superorganicist conception of culture and its implicit emphasis on the idea of human independence from Nature. Of course anthropology cannot be held chiefly responsible for this idea, for it begins to appear in European thought in the late Middle Ages and, in its ultimate formulation, is equivalent to the pattern of Judaeo-Christian thought and its humanistic emphasis. However this may be, the concrete issue of environmental influence arose first when late Medieval and Enlightenment scholars realized that all humans—in appearance and in habits—were not identical to Europeans. The explanations of human diversity (or unity) were searched for either in intrahuman or external conditions: if the former, the position took the form of biological or psychobiological determinism; if the latter, the milieu was conceived as the cause of diversity and unity, and chief among the explanations based on milieu were the climatic and geographical. However, naive environmental determinism actually was rare; most writers—including Bodin (17th century), Ratzel (19th century), and Huntington (20th century)[2]—qualified the doctrine in one way or another. Nevertheless, the thrust of this older "anthropogeographic" work was deterministic, and sooner or later it would have to be challenged.

It was not until the early 20th century that the issue of culture as both cause and effect in human-environment relations was clearly formulated. This work was done for anthropology by Franz Boas and his students; the doctrine is known as "possibilism." Summarizing previous discussions, in this position environment was defined as sets of opportunities and limitations, and man as a creature making choices among these in order to attain his goals. The attainment of such goals and the standardization of subsistence techniques create patterned traditions, which are "culture." However, in this scheme culture was really prior; one started the inquiry with a cultural "given": the perceptions and wants of humans as conditioned by their social milieu. Thus, while environmental determinism, clear or qualified, had been corrected, the new ethnological position introduced a strong human or "culture"-centered orientation, and the results tended to emerge as little more than a litany for cultural relativism in the environment context.[3] The "culture area" became the key concept: a particular set of choices made in the past, manifested and stabilized in a distinct geographical milieu at the moment of study.

Since, as pointed out in Chapter 1, the crucial issue of *choice* was fudged by the possibilists, this culture- or human-centered polemic against environmental determinism by the anthropologists of this school of "historical particularism" (Stocking, 1968, especially Chapters 7 and 9) avoided problems of process and threw Nature out along with the determinism; therefore a counterreaction was inevitable. This reaction occasionally appeared as reassertions of the importance of environment over culture (Meggers, 1954, who is answered by Ferdon, 1959), but in a more sophisticated and useful form as Julian Steward's "culture ecology" (1955C). The choice of this term implied a desire to bring some element of Nature back into the equation but, at the same time, to express the notion of an interaction between man and Nature. "Ecology" was the appropriate concept since it expresses, in a single word, the idea of all components of a milieu in reciprocal interaction with each other.

What, then, is *cultural* ecology? Literally, the term means "the ecology of culture" or the "ecological aspects of culture," but this tells us very little since culture is so general a term. The phrase also seems to suggest an opposition: there is "culture" and then there is "ecology"—but clearly these two are not in the same dimension. Can there be an ecology of culture, or is there only an ecology of population, of resources, of nutrition, of genetic adaptation? A case can be made for the nonexistence of cultural ecology, but some questions remain: since Nature increasingly becomes part of human affairs, one might argue for cultural ecology (as I have already) as equivalent to human ecology: that field which acknowledges that man is the major change agent in the physical environment, and studies the consequences of this for Nature and Culture. However, one can argue also that in all dealings of humans with environment there is an element of precedent, or reinforcement emanating from behavioral perseveration, i.e., "culture," and that the study of this process is the specific domain of cultural ecology.

One motive in the development of cultural ecology was a desire to find causes for social behavior in something other than culture, as a result of dissatisfaction with the culture concept as an explanatory device. As long as anthropologists were exclusively preoccupied with small, isolated societies, culture as both description and cause was an operable concept, since the systems of these groups were self-contained and self-reinforcing: culture was as good an explanation of why people did what they did as anything. It was only when anthropologists began working with more complex situations, with many subcultures, relationships between the local system and the outside, and with evidence of individual voluntarism and innovation that the "culture causes culture" doctrine had to be supplanted by something else. Ecology as a modified form of environmental determinism, or as human relationships with Nature, was explored as one means of providing this more sophisticated notion of cause. It is here, also, that a concept of a "social environment" to which humans adapt much as they do to the physical, adds an important dimension to the concept of holistic culture.

Culture and Environment: Major Approaches in Anthropology

The first step is a brief historical review of the major theoretical positions in the line of development leading to cultural ecological studies in anthropology. There seem to be five: (1) anthropogeography, (2) environmental or ethnographic possibilism, (3) Stewardian cultural ecology, (4) cultural ecosystemicism, and (5) adaptive dynamics. Each of these builds on the other, seeking to include a growing number of variables, but with significantly different causal models. The five approaches really divide into two sets, with anthropogeography and possibilism sharing one general class and the three remaining approaches sharing another. This differentiation is based on the major objective of *description* of environmental-cultural relations in the first set and an effort to get at *explanation* of particular kinds of relations in the second set.

The causational models represented in the five positions seem to be three: (A) is *linear causation*, in which *A* causes *B*, etc.; (B) is the *feedback or systemic model* in which causation is seen as a process of interdependent, mutually influencing factors—but acknowledging varying strengths among these. (C) The third model is the *adaptive*, which sees outcomes as the consequence of human decision and choice—a model that does not reject the systemic, or even the linear, but considers these to be empirical outcomes of behavior and not inevitable workings of the phenomena concerned.

Figure 10 summarizes the five approaches.

Looking at the five approaches in terms of the models of explanation, we arrive at the following: possibilism was not fundamentally different from anthropogeography in the joint use of a *linear causal* model. In possibilism, the "cause" of the human use of environment was culture; or, culture selects from environment to cause, or create, a cultural style based on that environment. The anthropogeographic approach used similar logic, but substituted the physical environment for culture as the prime causal force.

1. DETERMINISTIC ANTHROPOGEOGRAPHY

Environmental Factors ——————— Shape ————→ Culture
(That is, environment preexists culture.)

2. POSSIBILISM

Culture Selects From _____ to ————→ Create a Subsistence Style
Environment   and Other Cultural Factors
(That is, "Culture" preexists the inquiry, "it" is the
basis of behavior. Objectives largely descriptive.
Environment entirely subject to culture. Choice or
selection is the critical step here, though it is
generalized as "culture.")

3. STEWARDIAN CULTURAL ECOLOGY

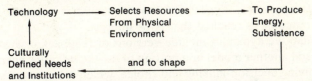

(That is, "Culture" is broken up into variables with differing
causal significance. "Environment" becomes whatever
is defined by the technoeconomic "core" or
subsistence system, but it retains some strength as a
causal agent.)

4. CULTURAL ECOSYSTEMICISM

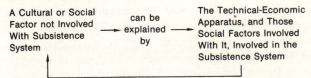

(The components are interrelated to produce a biotic or socionatural
system. No need to assign causes on theoretical grounds.)

5. ADAPTIVE DYNAMICS

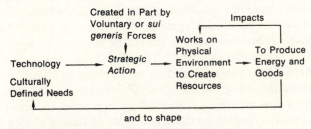

(Similar to the preceding, but the focus of research is on
the strategic behavior of the actors in making choices
and modifying patterns. More feedbacks or "impacts"
are acknowledged than in ecosystemicism.)

Fig. 10 Approaches in cultural ecology.

Beginning with Steward, the notion of *feedback* or *systemic processes* entered the models. Steward's "cultural ecology" has an implicit feedback conception in its objective of showing how the adaptation to the physical environment had an influence on other features of culture. However, Steward was not concerned with other dimensions of feedback, such as the impact of technological activities on the natural environment or on human biology. The objectives of cultural ecology as Steward formulated them (1955C) were historical and typological—to "determine whether similar adjustments occur in similar environments" and to trace these historically "through a succession of very unlike periods." Therefore, "culture types...must be conceived as constellations of core features which arise out of environmental adaptations and which represent similar levels of integration" (all refs., 1955C, p. 42).

The feedback model proceeds with Geertz' ecosystemic approach, which is limited in its explicit output to his own book, but which has influenced many other workers in cultural ecology and prehistory. Here interdependence of culture and physical factors is the primary postulate. Human activities are seen to either upset natural phenomena, to maintain them, or to create new balanced environments. Institutions then can become part of that system, to constitute a mixed biotic or socionatural entity or process. Types are not an objective; it is the process or the way the outcome is reached that is of interest.

Adaptive dynamics include versions of feedback or systemic concepts but add another model or a portion of it—the *adaptive behavioral process*, involving decision-making and choice, which *may or may not be under the control of the systemic processes.* The adaptive model modifies the systems outlook in that it considers that control or stability is reached by human decisions and bargains and not by the automatic operations of processes beyond awareness, although it acknowledges that such processes do occur in human systems from time to time. But, for practical purposes, these mechanisms cannot be assumed to work always for the good or to minimize impact. Therefore, the abstractions of "culture," "system," "ecosystem," and so on have to be translated into concrete referents reflecting human activity and action. Adaptive dynamics emphasizes one element of possibilism neglected by ecosystemicism and Stewardian approaches: the crucial role of human choice (and therefore, error).

Cultural ecology started as environmental or cultural determinism and has evolved into a modified systems approach in which all factors can be equally strong candidates as causes. This has meant a revived interest in the role of biological factors in behavior and even some tendency, as we shall note, to consider biological factors as causes of cultural phenomena. In making the selection of works to discuss, I have been guided by the following questions: how does the cultural ecologist conceive of the feedback loops in the system? Does he start from biological phenomena and work toward culture, or *vice versa*? Are man's needs and interests in the driver's seat, or is some automatically functioning process in the biosocial sphere conceived to be the motive force?

We shall begin with a general discussion of the problem of the use of concepts from plant-animal ecology to handle sociocultural phenomena. From there we shall pass to some samples of research that aim at showing relationships between biological and sociocultural aspects, and thence (Chapter 7) to a discussion of studies that have used culture as the dominant explanatory factor.

BIOLOGICAL CONCEPTS AND SOCIAL DATA

Now to begin Chapter 6 as such. When biological concepts are applied to data from social situations, there are obviously two possibilities. They can be applied (1) *analogically*, where the biological concepts and mathematical techniques are used to describe or simulate social phenomena, and (2) *literally*, in which case the actual biological or physical dimensions of the social phenomena would be identified and the same measurements performed on them. An example of the first is Frederic Barth's use of the term "niche" (1956)—which usually means in plant-animal ecology the use made of an environmental range by a particular species—to refer to the phenomenon of subsistence occupations in human society. The niche issue will be discussed in greater detail shortly, but for the moment we can ask whether these two things are really sufficiently similar to warrant the use of the same term and the generalized meanings and implications associated with it. For example, niche-occupancy among animals or plants is the result of, among other things, adaptive genetic selection, but one would be hard-pressed to find that genetic selection was responsible for the choice of agriculture or herding as an occupation among human groups.

With regard to the second case—plant-animal ecological concepts literally applied to the analysis of comparable dimensions of human behavior—there are good examples to be found in human bioecology and adaptability research, where various physiological, genetic, and energy data are collected and interpreted in ways similar to that for nonhuman species.[4] However, on the basis of our previous discussions, it seems clear that the crux of the issue is the exact meaning of the results acquired by using the ecological concepts either analogically *or* literally to analyze human behavioral choices and decisions: does this make the behavior "natural" or self-regulating? The "niche" example is relevant here again: the introduction of agriculture into a system of hunting-gathering populations will have biological consequences for the humans and the environment, and other nonhuman species will have to adjust their niche-occupancy accordingly. Something similar would happen if a nonhuman species with comparable impact were to appear—for example, a grazing ungulate with a heavy impact on the floral environment. However, the appearance of agriculture may have been due to cultural transmission or to questions of power, as when a ruler stabilizes a frontier by resettling farmers on it. Are these cultural aspects of the situation part of "niche-occupancy" or do they suggest that human ecological relations include a special form of behavior that requires a separate analytical procedure?

The use of biological or organic analogies for social phenomena are hardly new: Plato used them, Hobbes' *Leviathan* was based on them, Ratzel and Ritter established them in geography, and the Spencerian in sociology and the social Darwinian tradition in general exploited them (see Stoddart, 1967, for a review). In the 20th century, the borrowing of organic analogies and ecological concepts took a more specific form: the foundation of sociological ecology was the use of such terms as "succession" and "dominance" of socioeconomic groups across the spaces of North American cities, in a conscious borrowing from plant ecology (e.g., McKenzie, 1928).

It was proposed that populations in an urban setting distribute themselves within the community in zones due to differences in income, education, and other variables. The process of distribution creates neighborhoods that develop material characteristics (something like natural habitats for plants) appropriate to the group living in them, therefore, as the original group moves upward and out, the neighborhood is refilled by people of similar character, or by persons for whom the new neighborhood represents a step up or out of something else. These concepts had strong ecosystemic overtones (although the specific term and concept of ecosystem had not yet emerged): the city, in this approach, came to be a large system with many subsystems in a state of homeostatic fluctuation and balance. The causes of the process were considered to be beyond the consciousness of the actors—impersonal economic forces and the like.

The comparable case for anthropology was the development of the "age-area" idea and its translation into the *culture area*, a concept and a classificatory scheme that dominated a whole generation of ethnology and spread into other social sciences.[5] This concept also was a borrowing from early plant ecologists, who had found that other things being equal the older floral species were at the periphery of a geographical area, the newer—in the central portions. When the age-area idea was carried into ethnology, the qualifying factors were ignored and the impression was given that a lawful regularity in human behavior, below the level of consciousness of the actors involved, had been discovered. Dixon (1928) and others eventually showed that there were more exceptions to the rule than observances, pointing to the fact that historical (situational) circumstances affect the distribution of cultural items in time and space, and only completely ideal conditions will permit such regularities to operate at all. Linton used the telephone in *The Study of Man* to illustrate the principle of "marginal survival" of older forms (such as the hand-cranked type), but he failed to note that the telephone, with its instant long-distance communication, transforms all spacial relations of objects and ideas based implicitly on slower forms of communication (1936, pp. 329–330).

Another and much later example, this time from evolutionary thought, can be found in Campbell's (1965) and Alland's (1967) theoretical analogies between natural selection in biological and cultural phenomena. Equating cultural and biological traits, they propose that: (1) Variations *must* occur. That is, selection does not operate unless there are alternatives available—meaning that cultural variation is analogous to mutation in biology, and both can emerge at "random"; that is, without reference to specific functions (a challenge to classical functional theory for culture). However, (2) for a variation to survive, mechanisms of continuity and preservation must be available. Thus, certain mechanisms in culture— e.g., symbolic communication or increasing functionality—are analogous to reproduction in biology. A third criterion: (3) environmental selection must take place on the basis of consistent criteria in order to display regularity or direction. Since reproductive success is the single end in biology, the situation in culture is much more complex: a given trait must have a place in many different systems for strong selection pressures to favor it.

These analogies make *logical* sense, but the empirical situations represented are widely divergent—the difference between the communication flow in cultural selection and the reproductive flow in biology is sufficient to indicate this divergence. The objectives of biological or organic analogies are sometimes difficult to discern: they titillate the mind, may define very general processes, but they are ambiguous with respect to the empirical properties of the phenomena represented.

ECOLOGICAL NICHES

Our first case concerns the initial statement in modern cultural ecology involving an attempt at a disciplined application of a bioecological concept to cultural phenomena—Frederik Barth's account of "Ecological Relationships of Ethnic Groups in Swat, Northern Pakistan" (1956), which is an exercise in the use of the concept of *niche*.

We should begin with a definition of "niche" as it appears in bioecological writings and research. Eugene Odum's (1971) definition states that:

> ... the ecological niche of an organism depends not only on where it lives but also on what it does (how it transforms energy, behaves, responds to and modifies its physical and biotic environment), and how it is constrained by other species. By analogy, it may be said that the habitat is the organism's "address," and the niche is its "profession," biologically speaking. (p. 234)

That is, the important aspect of "niche" is what a plant or animal *does* in the general habitat: the food it requires and consumes, the amount or type of energy it uses and transforms. A defined position in a trophic level (a particular food source) is a niche; such niches can be occupied by single species, or competitive occupancy by more than one can occur, in which case the movement may be toward homeostatic resolution, with one species becoming dominant (see McNaughton and Wolf, 1970, on the relationship of dominance to niche occupancy). Niches also can be overlapping or partially competitive in the case of species with more than one major food source. Occupancy of particular niches by particular species may be essential to the occupancy of other niches by other species, when the energy converted by the first are vital for the survival of the others, as in trophic systems involving successive decomposition or with various species consuming each others' wastes.

While the central idea of the niche concept involves the energy-using and producing capacity of the organism, as it uses particular natural substances, it is apparent that often the concept implies a particular *place* or subhabitat: a geographical range or locus. The word "niche" is a location-term: the mental picture is one of an aperture in an existing milieu in which something fits neatly. Even in biology the term is sometimes used in this manner: not as an abstract rendition of a particular kind of energy or resource pattern, but as a place in which a natural species exists.

Barth was concerned with finding a way to describe the relationships of different human ethnic groups with a conceptual tool more applicable to the southwestern Asian scene than the classic "culture area" concept. He noted that while this latter concept was useful for handling aboriginal New World tribal distributions, it did not work in Asia and particularly not in Southwest Asia and the Middle East with its "mosaic society": A form of social organization in which groups of differing cultures display "symbiotic relations of variable intimacy" (1956, p. 1079). That is, like so many studies in cultural ecology, the kickoff problem was not ecological but cultural: in this case, classificatory problems of ethnic boundaries.

Barth noted that in the Middle East

> ... 'the environment' of any one ethnic group is not only defined by natural conditions, but also by the presence and activities of the other ethnic groups on which it depends ... this interdependence is analogous to that of the different animal species in a habitat. (1956, p. 1079)

And also:

> [as] Kroeber ... emphasizes, culture area classifications are essentially ecologic .... The present paper attempts to apply a more specific ecological approach to a case study of distribution by utilizing ... the concept of *niche*—the place of a group in the total environment, its relation to resources and competitors. (1956, p. 1079)

He deals with three groups: Pathans, Kohistanis, and Gujars. He finds that the *Pathan* territory extends to a critical ecological threshold: "the limits within which two crops can be raised each year," although they also extend into one-crop marginal areas, and that "Pathan economy and political organization requires that agricultural labor produce considerable surplus"—hence the insistence on double cropping. The Pathans are the most dominant political group, by virtue of their cohesive social system, military organization, and numbers. As for the *Kohistanis*, while they practice a similar type of agriculture, they are not restricted by this barrier because they also practice transhumant herding "as important as agriculture." Their herds depend on summer pasture in the mountains, where the Kohistanis move during this season. Consequently, the Kohistanis are not tied down to the richest agricultural zone, and their settlement and political organization is described by Barth as less cohesive than the Pathan, being composed of independent villages. The *Gujars* are "a floating population of herders," who also practice a little farming in marginal areas. They may move from transhumant herding to agriculture to true nomadism, depending on their relations with the other groups. If, for example, a Gujar transhumant group is in the marginal Pathan district, it will become tied to a Pathan leader, and will perform services in exchange for a reduced grazing tax.

Barth then shows how these various patterns are related to the natural resources available in Swat, and how the groups share and overlap in these resource zones: e.g., "Restrictions on agricultural production limit the animal and human population, and prevent full exploitation of the mountain pastures. This niche is thus left partly vacant and available to the nomadic Gujars . . . ." (1956, p. 1087). He then raises a "crucial final point"—namely, "why do Kohistanis have first choice, so to speak, and Gujars only enter niches left vacant by them?" (1956, p. 1087). He answers this question by citing "organizational factors": the Kohistanis have "compact, politically organized villages of considerable size," due to their half-agricultural base, while the Gujars' nomadism prevents such organization and forces them to become subject to better organized groups—Pathans and Kohistanis.

Barth concludes that "The distribution of ethnic groups is controlled not by objective and fixed 'natural areas' but by the distribution of the specific ecologic niches which the group, with its particular economic and political organization, is able to exploit" (1956, p. 1088). Our concern here is not with the general findings of Barth's eight-month field survey of these three groups, of which the above summary gives only the bare outline. The findings were important contributions to the ethnology of Pakistan and Southwest Asia in general. Our interest is in the use of the niche concept as a tool of analysis.

The first thing to be said is that Barth has used the concept to refer to three often-related but nevertheless analytically distinguishable features of human settlement: (1) subsistence systems or techniques, (2) the amount of production or output provided by these techniques, and (3) the particular geographical range and loci covered by the groups in pursuit of their subsistence. While it is true that somewhat comparable multiple meanings are assigned to the term "niche" by bioecologists as well, in cultural ecology one must make careful distinctions between these things because they do not necessarily coincide. As a matter of fact, Barth shows how these groups actually overlap into each others' subsistence niches: even the Pathans with their intensive agriculture share livestock and other resources with the other two. By using the concept of niche to refer to all three phenomena, Barth seems to bypass the obligation to give precise data. This omission is most serious in the case of productive output—the impression is given that the Pathans excel, but no detailed evidence is given. A careful study of food energy produced could conceivably turn up data difficult to assimilate into the interpretive scheme: the dominant Pathans might actually be producing less than the Kohistanis, in which case the Pathan dominance would be due to social and military organization and not ecologic or at least economic-technical factors. Or it may be due to the dominant sedentariness of the Pathans, which is, of course, a secondary contribution of their intensive agricultural regime.

Moreover, the geographical ranges of these groups are by no means distinct. Barth states that the Pathans, while pinned down by their double-cropping, actually extend into marginal areas where they mingle with Gujars and Kohistanis, and so on. The proximity is close enough for all three groups to help each other symbiotically, and, in this sense, the "niches" interpenetrate and pervade, perhaps compete—there is distinctiveness only at the ends of the distribution of the systems, or only for certain periods of the year. The process seems closer to ecological symbiosis, rather than niche-occupancy, if one must find analogies.

Another criticism one can make of an attempt to consider subsistence systems as ecological niches is that it adds nothing to our knowledge of the process by which the assortation of groups into different resource constellations takes place. This process, in every instance in which the history is known, is competition for resources. That is, the process is social, not "natural"—or, rather, in order to understand the ecological outcomes of particular modes of exploitation of resources, it is necessary to know the social process behind it. Southwest Asia appears to be one of those geographical areas where tribal and village groups managed to achieve a reasonably equitable division of these resources by dividing them into different subsistence systems. Even so, these allocations were never fixed or permanent; conquest and population increase would lead to further competition and new forms of division, and, as a general result, increased pressure on the marginal resources. It is probably true that when resources are scarce or marginal, human populations are increasing, and technological levels are relatively low, the outcome will resemble the Southwest Asia case—i.e., a superficial resemblance to niche-occupancy among animals and plants. There is, of course, the further possibility that the process of resource competition is no different among animals and plants than among humans, in which case niche-occupancy can be just as descriptive and nondynamic a concept for natural ecology as for human ecology.

This leaves the concept of niche somewhat up in the air. Granting a certain feeling of intellectual novelty produced by using the concept as a replacement for "culture area," the results are simply an abbreviated description of the relationships of subsistance occupations, social organization, geographical range, and political dominance in a number of Southwest Asian tribal communities. The differences among these groups seem to be based more on social organization than ecological phenomena, either in the loose or strict sense.[6] The same data and findings could have been rendered without resorting to the concept of niche; nothing, in the opinion of the writer, is lent to the analysis by the use of the term. One feature that might have made the use of "niche" a meaningful one in this case is missing: the computation of actual energy needed and transferred between the groups, and how such symbiotic processes figured in the pattern of political dominance. The issue is unresolved: political dominance in human societies is not *necessarily* an "ecologic" process, nor can it be made one by using bioecological concepts to describe it. The scientific question is how political phenomena can be translated into biological consequences or feedbacks, and *vice versa*; and this problem is not attacked in this pioneer and otherwise excellent paper.

In pioneer attempts to mingle disciplinary levels of analysis, a certain amount of analogic reasoning is inevitable—Barth himself acknowledged the analogic basis of his exercise in a quotation used previously. But biological language can be seductive. Consider, for example, the following quotation from a current paper (McNaughton and Wolf, 1970) on dominance and niche in biology:

> In the systems we have examined, we find that: (i) dominance is a characteristic of the most abundant species; (ii) dominant species have broader niches than subordinate species; (iii) species are added to the system by compression of niches or expansion of carrying capacity, or both, and (iv) community dominance is minimum on the most equitable sites. (p. 136)

Reading this with humanity in mind can be a little voyage of discovery: what species conforms more beautifully to these generalizations— humans are dominant on Earth by virtue of numbers and their broader niche; they "add" species through domestication, or at least accommodate species to their own niche by compressing it or enhancing carrying capacity (i.e., production); and, finally, within the human population, the most "equitable sites" usually contain the more dominant communities. These could be considered plausible analogies, but they oversimplify the case. Human dominance, as already noted, may not be due always to

numbers but to superior technological power; the enhancement of carrying capacity can be a destructive act, working against ecosystemic
balance; the dominant communities in the best locations are not separate
species, but groups within the same species, Homo sapiens; the accommodation of species to niches can be either a voluntary and willed act or a
processual drift due to competitive mechanisms operating outside of
human awareness.

I have said that the use of the concept of niche to analyze the
relationships of specific human groups in a given environmental complex
is scientifically appropriate only if measurements are made of the
bioenergetics of their "niche occupancy" and the data transferred to the
sociocultural materials to establish interdimensional relationships. There
is, however, another context in which niche may perform a conceptual
service for anthropological ecology, as represented by Donald Hardesty's
paper (1972) on "The Human Ecological Niche." He considers niche as a
concept applying to Homo sapiens as a single whole species, divided into
populations with differing patterns of adaptive specialization.

> The human ecological niche is viewed as a multi-dimensional space defined by the
> properties of human survival, thus offering the additional advantage of precise
> definition and quantification . . . complex, broad niches are intrinsically more stable and
> more likely to prove successful than simple, specialized niches. The fact that highly
> specialized intensive agriculturalists have become dominant should not be taken as
> contradictory. The evolutionary history of other species supports the proposition that
> dominance is not necessarily synonymous with the best chance of evolutionary success.
> (p. 465)

Well, possibly, but humanity is not just any other species, and here we
have the analogy issue again: treating humans as equivalent to other
organisms for purposes of ecological theory, when in fact they have a
unique pattern of adaptation. Although Hardesty is operating at a general
theoretical level, his data are drawn from tribal societies, and therefore he
avoids having to deal with the sticky issue of whether the economic
occupations of people responding to macroeconomic institutions can be
interpreted as niche occupancy for any useful purpose.

Hardesty also argues that Barth was not really dealing with niches, but
with "microenvironments"—although he does not recognize the point
made earlier to the effect that Barth's data concern economic occupations
more than environments. Hardesty also redefines Yehudi Cohen's criteria
for "adaptive success" (Cohen, 1968) to be in reality "several dimensions
of the human realized niche" (e.g., the ability of a human group to make
substitutions in its diet). All of this seems to be little more than rhetorical

substitutions of biological terminology for existing descriptive categories of human behavior and institutions.

Liebig's Principle

An example of what appears at first sight an appropriate application of a natural-ecological concept to human groups is provided by Joseph Birdsell's use of Liebig's "law of the minimum" to describe certain characteristics of hunting-gathering groups. The Liebig principle is formulated by Eugene Odum (1953, p. 88) as follows: "To occur and thrive in a given situation, an organism must have essential materials which are necessary for growth and reproduction . . . . The essential material available in amounts most closely approaching the critical minimum will tend to be the limiting one."

Birdsell has proposed that the population of hunting-gathering bands is determined by territoriality and the carrying capacity of the environment, or at least that particular resource which is critical for nutrition. In one of his papers on Australian tribes (1958), he found that the population density of given tribal areas correlated with rainfall (0.8 R), and that the greater the variability of the rainfall, the higher the tendency for population density to correlate with it—an illustration of Liebig's effect in operation. (In an earlier paper (Bartholomew and Birdsell, 1953), similar arguments were adduced to explain certain rhythms in the evolution of early hominid forms, such as the Australopithecines in South Africa: control of population size and density by carrying capacity would tend to result in breeding populations of maximal efficiency for evolutionary change.)

These arguments are certainly plausible and have the effect of carrying Steward's theories about the relationship of social organization to environment in hunting-gathering groups a step further into basic ecology. Another argument in favor of application of Liebig's principle in these cases is that one dealing with tribal cultures with limited technological control over the environment, and hence relying wholly on natural substances—therefore presumably subject to the same rules that animals are.

But there are arguments against the use of Liebig's principle. For one thing, it is a single-factor explanation of various phenomena—population size, density, certain patterns of mobility, and breeding habits—which are obviously subject to many influences in any human society. It also assumes that these factors are in equilibrium and that food habits

controlling the selection of nutritive resources are also relatively fixed.*
Birdsell, in his 1958 paper, cited other work on the Great Basin Shoshoni
bands that found less favorable correlations between population and
rainfall. Moreover, one suspects that the particular time when observations are taken will tend to determine the degree of correlation: these
groups had wide ranges and, moreover, were remarkably adaptive in their
use of available foodstuffs. Their populations are known to have fluctuated, and spin-offs of bands occurred constantly.

However, it might be possible, taking Liebig's "law" as a point of
departure, to arrive at a principle of comparable meaning, but with
definite social reference. "Opportunity costs" (which we shall discuss in
Chapter 7) come to mind: A group might "settle for less" rather than risk
the uncertainty of shifting to a new resource base or subsistence
occupation. In this case, a Liebig principle is at work *via* the human
cognitive route: through rational decision making. If natural-ecological
concepts are to be applied at all to the human case, they will have to take
account of the cognitive-affectual aspects of human behavior.

There is another sense in which Liebig's principle might be considered
to apply to human transactions with environment—in agriculture, where
specialized production regimes are based on highly specific and marginal
resource parameters. These situations are familiar enough in the tribal
domain, with its limited technological transcendence, but they are almost
equally familiar in developed societies. Grain crops in the Northern Great
Plains and in Central Asia are a case in point: the marginal moisture
supplies of these regions make the successful raising of grains a risky
business, and possible in many places only with finely tuned strategies
like summer fallow, snowcatch, and the choice of the right hybrid seed for
the particular locality. The difference between the tribal and the developed cases is simply the extent to which technology has been created
to cope with the marginality. This is often abetted in the developed cases
by external subsidies to cover the risks of the producers. In all these
cases, Liebig's principle is really equivalent to the strategies and technologies available for coping with the resource factors. If these devices
are limited, then the marginal resources may be seen as a physical-
environmental minimum beyond which the agricultural regime cannot go.

*After this was written, another paper by Birdsell, reviewing all the previous contribu-
tions, appeared in *Current Anthropology* (1973) along with a number of critical comments,
including one by the present author. (For an approach to the problem of the effect of the
social organization of genetic differentiation on two tribal societies, see Chagnon 1972.)

But, due to technological and managerial innovations, these limits are not rigid.

PIGS, RITUAL, AND ECOLOGICAL CONTROL

In order to pursue this question further, we consider next one of the more challenging pieces of research in contemporary anthropological ecology: the study by Roy Rappaport of warfare, swine management, and social ritual among the Tsembaga—a particular local settlement (or clancluster) of members of the Maring people, a "tribe" of some 7,000 persons occupying a region of about 190 square miles in central New Guinea. While Rappaport has featured "pigs" in his publications (e.g., 1967A and 1967B), the underlying issue seems to be warfare and territorial expansion, a topic of dominant interest in New Guinea ethnology, and of concern to ecologists because of the tendency for swiddeners—shifting cultivators—to seek territorial expansion. The curious stylized combat (sometimes purely ritual confrontation, sometimes genuine mayhem, invasion, and forced resettlement of populations) has been a topic of perennial interest because of its exotic appeal and because it offers, (like the potlatch of the Northwest Coast Indians) a kind of caricature of various facets of "civilized" warfare and international relations. The trigger problem in the case of Rappaport's research, therefore, was intracultural, not ecological. His own work, however, came to be an exercise in how an ecological approach might help explain the causes of New Guinea warfare and its territorial implications.

One basic theory of New Guinea warfare, developed in a series of papers by Andrew Vayda (e.g., 1960, 1961, 1967, 1971), concerns population increase and decrease and the consequent changes in "man/resource ratios" that might give rise to needs for more territory for gardens and pig raising, the response being hostile attacks on neighbors. This is an ecological problem since a linkage is hypothesized between population, natural resources, and a particular type of agriculture. The theoretical implications of the problem were developed in a spin-off paper by Vayda and Rappaport (1968), which criticizes the prolonged reliance by anthropologists on concepts derived from culture in their ecological studies and advocates a shift to concepts developed by natural ecologists. Specifically, the authors cite research into territorial rights, intertribal warfare and raiding, ceremonial feasting, sacred animals, and human sacrifice in various tribal cultures, from the standpoint of how these might maintain "within an adaptive range certain variables (such as size or dispersion) pertaining either to human populations or the faunal and floral populations on which these depend" (1968, p. 495). Consideration of such phenomena would be based on units of *population* and ecosystem, rather than the traditional unit of "cultures."[7]

The basic facts of the case are complex, but a study of the papers by Rappaport and Vayda on the Maring yield the following: Warfare and the absence of it among these people seems to fluctuate rhythmically, with intervals of from 10 to 15 years suggested as the pattern in various papers. Periods of peace between groups in potential competition for land appear to have an element of ritual proscription, insofar as the preparations for thanking the ancestor spirits for guidance and protection in the preceding warfare period consume a considerable period of time. Warfare must not be engaged in while these rituals are underway. Since the rituals involve pig slaughter and feasting, enough time must elapse in order to produce a sufficient supply of animals. These periods of ritual last about as long as the warfare periods—again, from 10 to 15 years. The question is whether the human population, assuming it may be one of the underlying causes of warfare due to the man-resource ratio, also fluctuates accordingly—building up every ten years or so to trigger the chain of insults, rapes, thefts, and other things associated with intersettlement competition that might result in war. During the warfare episode, with its accompanying adjustments in territorial acquisition or reduction in overall regional population due to driving out a competing settlement, the pressures begin to lift and eventually warfare ceases.

The attempts to unravel this complex skein by Rappaport and Vayda differ considerably. Rappaport seems concerned with the overall systemic features of all aspects of the system, while Vayda focuses on the ecologically based warfare pattern itself (raiding, real wars vs. what he calls "nothing" wars or stylized confrontation; territorial acquisition; territorial invasion vs. plain fighting, etc.). Vayda is more interested than Rappaport in the question of why some fights develop into true wars, and others remain at the level of what Rappaport—borrowing a term from natural ecology—calls "epideictic display" (the trading of threats in order to, presumably, make an assessment of true aggressive ability). Rappaport's sweeping objectives are indicated in his summary of his summary paper (1967A):

> To repeat an earlier assertion, the operation of ritual among the Tsembaga and other Maring helps to maintain an undergraded environment, limits fighting to frequencies which do not endanger the existence of the regional population, adjusts man-land ratios, facilitates trade, distributes local surpluses of pigs throughout the regional population in

the form of pork, and assures people of high-quality protein when they are most in need of it. (pp. 28–29)

That is, he proposes that the recurrent war-and-ritual cycles are somehow adjusted to fluctuations in the populations of pigs and people: when, for example, population pressure produces frequent need for land among these "extensive" cultivators of tropical soils, the people go to war; then they return and consume pigs. When pig populations increase, destroying the gardens, motivation for consuming pigs arises, but since pigs are to be consumed as the culmination of a warfare episode, there has to be previous warfare to provide the excuse. The consumption of pigs may relieve "physiological stress" caused by general excitement or, perhaps, by disease, and of course incidentally this puts everyone back in top condition for the next round of fighting. Thus, the ritual cycle[8] is the key not only to warfare but also to all the other functions mentioned in the previous quotation. Throughout this presentation, Rappaport applies concepts derived from natural ecology: the relationship of pigs to people changes from mutualism to parasitism-competition; the ritual behavior is likened to epigamic and epideictic display, and so on.[9] The applicability of these concepts, and the general proposal that the entire configuration operates as an ecosystemic or homeostatic process is defended on the grounds that the Tsembaga (and the larger unit, the Maring people as a whole) were relatively isolated, and constituted a population in a dynamic self-contained balance with its surroundings.

If Rappaport's diagnosis is correct, the situation closely resembles the findings for characteristic animal population fluctuation and predator-prey relationships, where changes in one component of the system require adjustments in the others *via* feedback flow. In animal ecological research, these dimensions and changes are specified with rigorously collected quantitative information. It is necessary to know precisely what any organism in the system needs in the way of sustenance, how much it acquires as a result of its foraging or other energy-transforming activities, how much physiological energy is actually generated by these methods, and how much muscular energy is used in the activities performed. The environment that sustains these efforts also must be described in detail, in terms of its energy-producing facility—its "carrying capacity." When organisms in such a milieu are in competition with one another, the point at which competition becomes decisive (involving reduction in the number of one of the organisms through predation or starvation) has to be determined with precision, on the basis of the energy-obtaining and releasing analyses,[10] since explanations for the behavior of the organism ride on them.

That is, the procedure aims at determining the causes of behavior as they emerge in biological and resource circumstances: the assumption is that the behavior of the organism is not random or willed, but is a necessary emergent from the changing forces in the total milieu. If natural-ecological concepts are transferred to humans, and studies are made of their behavior on the basis of these process assumptions, then along with this goes the assumption that human behavior is likewise largely or wholly emergent from a bioenvironmental matrix of some kind. This, with some qualification, appears to be the fundamental assumption of Rappaport's study. If the human behavior is willed, or purposive, Rappaport's model requires this to be assimilable into the natural process: perhaps he would hold that humans will in response to a perceived environmental factor, but their physiology prompts.

Rappaport's study was the best documented piece of research in cultural ecology at the time of its publication: its ten appendices provide an unmatched assemblage of data on climate, agricultural output, flora, and energy expenditures for the community and its environs.[11] However, these data are not systematically tied into the interpretive analysis of how ritual and other behaviors serve as automatic regulatory mechanisms. That is, the study is not a rigorous, quantitatively based demonstration of the ecophysiological causes of human behavioral responses to needs. It is, despite its rich data background, fundamentally an analogic operation, in which ecosystemic complexities and a generalized impression of ecological causation are plausibly suggested but never worked out in detail. That is, Rappaport followed the protocol but not the analytical operations of the natural-ecological approach sketched previously.

However, not only must the novelty and pioneer character of Rappaport's study be cited as extenuating circumstances, but the sheer practical difficulties of doing rigorous studies of this kind in remote regions, far from laboratory facilities, should be considered. There is, moreover, the question of whether the changing complexity of human systems makes it possible to adhere to the controls necessary in plant-animal ecology research to provide these precise results. I do not know whether this last consideration is completely valid; more funds and the commitment to long periods of intensive research, not to mention proper training in biology and physiology, would provide the conditions necessary for high-standard research. Whatever the answer, one thing goes without saying: if anthropologists are serious in their intention to demonstrate the existence of complex feedback systems in human phenomena, they are going to have to specify the quantitative dimensions of the processes more fully.[12]

However, the extent to which Rappaport's effort to describe the operation of an automatic feedback system involving environment, animals, flora, and people is a successful one, it is important as a concrete demonstration of the fact that the behavior of men toward each other, as well as toward Nature, is part of ecosystems. Rappaport's study is one of the best available portraits of the isolated, small, low-energy system operating more or less in balance with Nature (at least during the 11 months of his observation), and we have suggested previously that ecosystemic analysis is best applied to societies of this type.

Now, if Rappaport's generalizations are limited to a particular type of society, then the relevance of his findings for the contemporary ecological scene are limited—and certainly Rappaport does not propose otherwise. But the issue needs to be raised all the same, because ecosystemicism is a seductive idea, and others have interpreted studies of tribal ecology as if they had universal significance. The New Guinea people, according to Rappaport, seem to have only a limited awareness of what they are doing, and yet balance with Nature emerges. Emergence of such feedback in contemporary society, with its philosophy of continuous growth and constant need for resources, is a possibility only in very specialized and sheltered circumstances. Balance on a significant scale can be achieved only by political change and conscious planning. Cases like Rappaport's, unless their context is thoroughly understood, can lead to illusions about the capacity of complex societies to work out sustained-yield regimes.

There is, moreover, a factor of time that needs careful consideration. Let us grant that ecological factors and the actions of the Tsembaga did in fact dovetail so as to produce a functioning, largely automatic system of control. However, Rappaport's observations were of relatively short duration—a field period of 11 months—and there is no detailed information available on the time required for this system to emerge, nor how long it might last after the period of observation. On the basis of data from societies of comparable energy levels and sociopolitical tendencies in Africa, there is reason to believe that such systems were quite unstable and likely to give way to depredations on Nature and other men on a scale exceeding the previous limits (e.g., Sahlins, 1961; Kottak, 1972).

The time factor is crucial because various human activities that may be in some kind of balance at a given time period are not usually under simultaneous control by the same forces or institutions; hence they can change at different rates and magnitudes. This is perhaps less true of tribal and most true of contemporary societies with their many autonomous spheres of action. The writer found a systemic balance in the population of Hutterian Brethren in the Northern Great Plains during the early 1960s, in which the rate of population increase, the rate of financial savings, the carrying capacity (productivity) of the land, the amounts of land available for purchase in the region, and various religious beliefs and social practices all fitted together to result in a process of regular colony division at a population level of about 150 persons (Bennett, 1967C, Chapter 7). Setting aside the question of whether this situation is to be defined as *eco*systemic, it *is* a particular systemic, interdependent process in the relationships among various endogenous and exogenous variables, and is subject to change and to recurrent adaptive modifications of any or all of the factors (by 1971, the population level was down to 130 persons, due to rises in operating costs and colony consumption levels). (The discussion in the previous chapter of the several subsystems in the North American agrarian family enterprise macrosystem, which respond quite differently to resource utilization and conservation, should also be recalled at this point.)

The Hutterian case suggests that the question of built-in controls over environmental use is not confined to tribal societies, where it may well be an only half-conscious procedure—the consequence, as Rappaport has implied, of the mutual reinforcing power of many cultural and economic patterns. Such control can also be entirely rational, in the sense of being planned and maintained as a system of boundary-maintaining regulations, as it is among the Hutterites and also the Amish—both Anabaptist agriculturalists, but differing in their adaptive systems.

In the case of the Amish, who are private entrepreneurial farmers, self-imposed constraints are placed on consumption and on the use of powered machinery and electricity. These taboos are not religious in some supernaturalistic sense, but are designed to shield the Amish population from what they perceive to be corrupting influences from the majority culture. Among these restrictions are a number against the use of environmentally damaging techniques, including chemical fertilizers, powered cultivating implements, and excessive use of pesticides. The Amish receive substantially lower crop yields than their intensively cultivating neighbors, but they are able to live at a higher level than one would expect due to substantial savings based on their modest use of technology, simpler consumption standards, and the like (Stoltzfus, 1973).

The collective-communal Hutterites, farming the low-productivity Northern Plains, have similar controls over consumption, but use a full range of sophisticated technology and farming methods, and support relatively large numbers of people on them—larger than would be possible by individual operators on similar resources. Their savings are due to their lower consumption, communal life, and the large and efficient scale of their operations, which are far beyond that of the Amish, who remain small-scale individual farmers. Hutterite farming also takes place in the Northern Plains, where the environmental problems differ from those in the Midwest. But the conservationist pattern of Hutterite farming, which for their region is as significant as the Amish for theirs, is based on their large economic scale, which allows them to farm without "pushing" their resources in contrast to their smaller Great Plains individual-entrepreneur neighbors.

The sectarian cases indicate that it is possible for societies to develop controls over their use of environment with self-conscious methods based on a particular ideology. In both cases the ideology is of long standing, and suitable methods, equally rational, have been developed to train the children in the rules and shield them from outside influences for the critical period of socialization. Even more, the successful pursuit of these constrained strategies is based on a carefully worked out balance of relationships *with* the outside world—not only against it—so that maximum assistance can be obtained from the external system without seriously threatening the distinctive way of life. Of course the Amish and Hutterites are minority groups with unusual inner strength: they cannot be a simple model for the larger systems, but they do tell us that conscious control can be achieved over the use of resources if the conditions are right.

We have understood Rappaport as saying that the feedback states were maintained (or participated in) without conscious awareness of the underlying consequences and causes on the part of the actors. Rappaport's presentation therefore resembles a classic functionalist demonstration: the social activities of warfare, pig rituals, etc. have the function of maintaining populations and gardens in homeostasis. This is reminiscent of Marvin Harris' claim that "functionalism" in social science is comparable to biology's "adaptation" (Harris, 1960); as all critics of functionalism have noted, an approach of this type tends to neglect change, dynamism, and the purposive factor in behavior. Rappaport might reply that he has not neglected purpose and intention, and knows full well that his people are aware of the specific effects of their actions, if not the long-range balance, but that the processes represented by these actions, whether perceived or unperceived by the actors, nevertheless have these systemic properties. This is the difference between the action level and the process level in cultural ecological analysis. Lacking more details, it is of course impossible to really resolve this question.[13]

In a paper published in 1971, Andrew Vayda focuses on the problem of war and territorial expansion as a response to population pressure against the land among the Maring. Vayda reviews evidence that suggests that recent Maring warfare may have causes other than those related to "territorial conquests as an adaptive means of reducing disparities between groups in their man/resource ratios" (p. 22). He speaks of lags and perseverations in the system in a manner reminiscent of the animal ecologists (as in the piece by Holling discussed in the previous chapter): e.g., people fighting simply as the result of desires or internal social pressures without reference to the need for food-producing territory or garden space. He points out that the verification of the ecosystem hypothesis about warfare as a response to "man/resource ratios" requires ecological investigations more lengthy and comprehensive than those which have been made throughout the Maring region, or throughout any region where there has been primitive warfare in recent times .... In short, we cannot argue categorically that absence of population pressure explains the non-escalation to territorial conquests .... (1971, p. 21). He also notes that Rappaport's calculations regarding Tsembaga population and territorial carrying capacity are tentative and that there is "no adequate basis" for ascertaining the relationship of carrying capacity and food supply to warfare with present research methods. After these comments, he concludes that Maring warfare "remained the kind that could, through an already institutionalized systemic process, lead again to the adjustment of man/resource ratios whenever ecological and demographic conditions changed sufficiently to make it appropriate for this to happen" (1971, pp. 22–23). That is, even though recent Maring warfare does not lead to territorial expansion, and thus bear out the basic hypothesis, it just might some time or other.

There are, of course, less theoretically conceived explanations for the New Guinea behavior *vis-à-vis* swine that do not depend on animal analogies in human behavior nor on demonstrations of states of subtle ecosystemic balance in ritual behavior and natural phenomena. These New Guinea people appear to have a familiar livestock management problem: raising swine in unconfined spaces on natural forage. Everywhere in the world people who do this are likely to be confronted with problems of depredation by the animals on flora and also of cyclical overbreeding, and all must resort to recurrent slaughtering, which may or may not feed into market or consumption channels. Families in the Louisiana swampland used to have annual pig hunts with recreational ("ritual") purposes, involving the consumption of alcoholic beverages and other festivities (years ago the writer participated in one to his chagrin).

The difficulty and inefficiency of swine management in unconfined spaces is due to the individualistic, ranging, voracious behavior of these intelligent animals, who quickly revert to a wild state, and it is no accident that enormous effort in developed agricultures has gone into suitable technology for handling swine in confined, artificial environments.

People who raise pigs in the open thus have a recurrent problem: for different reasons, at different times, the cost of raising pigs exceeds the gain, however gain may be measured. One can visualize what Vayda, Leeds, and Smith (1961) have already described: consultations among Melanesian men on the need for control of pig populations. But other solutions could easily occur: perhaps the opportunity cost of solving the pig problem by acquiring additional land from one's neighbors might be lower than slaughtering pigs. There almost certainly was more than one alternative, and the precise role of ritual in this situation must have been a variable, not a constant. Of course, in the expanding world of modern New Guinea, there are obviously an increasing number of alternatives, and just what will happen from now on to New Guinea traditional culture is anyone's guess. That ecosystemic processes may be at work is probably to be taken for granted. But the basic question is: to what extent do they help us understand the sociocultural reality underlying the human use of Nature?[14]

ECOLOGICAL CONTROL AND HOMEOSTASIS IN SIMPLER SOCIETIES

We may now continue the discussion in the previous chapter on the problem of controls over resource consumption in tribal communities.

We begin with the hunting-gathering group, largely nomadic in its habits, which means in most cases a pattern of alternate encampment and movement—the intervals varying by season and by tribe, both depending on the physical environment and on the social organization and preferences of the group. However, these variations need not concern us, since all of these hunting-gathering societies are alike in their stable, nonexpanding economies. There is an overall similarity in behavior and relationship to environment that argues that the variations in precise patterns of residential stability and movement are probably not significant in explaining ecological stability.

The first part of the problem concerns the small overall populations, plus low densities of the functioning social group among H-G people. Of course, these populations did slowly increase over a period of time: the

Bushmen spread through the Kalahari Desert, and the Australian tribes did likewise in their island-continent. Hunting-gathering groups seem to have undergone a slow, steady population increase in regions where they were the only inhabitants—the refuge areas mentioned in the previous chapter. In other regions, where the boundaries were more restricted by sedentary or pastoral peoples on the margins, the H-G populations may have been more stable, or the excess numbers simply migrated, merging into the bordering groups. In exceptional cases, where resources were unusually abundant, H-G populations developed densities and nucleated settlements comparable to agricultural villages. However, these cases are not the ones we are discussing.

Much has been written about the reasons for the slowness of population growth among these hunting peoples, but only recently has some data begun to appear that gives the reader more than inventive arguments. While the new data is not conclusive proof of anything, its ecological sophistication gives it more cogency. Typical of this newer approach is Richard Lee's analysis of Kung Bushman population dynamics (1972A; 1972B; 1972C) and how this is changing to a more rapid growth rate as these people become sedentary. Lee argues that the low growth rates of nomadic food collectors are due basically to the disadvantages of frequent pregnancies for the women. On several fronts—the physical movement, the need to carry infants and toddlers, the need for women to share the work—the situation functions, according to Lee, to yield birth intervals of around one child every four or five years. More frequent births, under nomadic conditions, would have, in his words, high social and physical "costs" to the women and to the group as a whole. Lee backs this argument up with some data on work effort, weights of burdens, distance the children must be carried when the mother has different numbers of children, and the like. He summarizes his ecological argument as follows: "More babies and/or greater distances to travel mean more work for Bushman mothers. Similarly, work effort would decline with fewer babies and/or less walking" (1972C, p. 328). It follows that if the group begins to settle down and adopts agriculture, it will have to walk less to obtain food, and will consequently begin to shorten the birth interval—and that is exactly what Lee found in his field studies of sedentarizing groups, as compared with his nomads (Lee, 1972C).

Of course, this explanation leaves many questions unanswered. Just how the Bushmen (and other H-G groups) maintain the long birth intervals is not fully known, although taboos against sexual intercourse, as well as social rules concerning the undesirability of too many children, play a role. Infanticide, known for many human groups, is not mentioned by Lee, but one suspects that it would have to be in the picture somewhere. The mechanisms Lee describes are plausible, but they could hardly have worked smoothly or perfectly, since they require wives to keep their husbands at bay, or practicing withdrawal, for years on end. It could be argued also that the definitions of burden or inconvenience and extra work involved in having more children are subject to cultural definitions that will vary from group to group.

Another ambiguity in Lee's argument is the apparent assumption that the burden mechanism he describes as restraining births would operate consistently over long periods of time to produce a *steady*, low growth rate. It is impossible to say what the actual growth pattern of H-G populations under aboriginal conditions was, but there is an accumulation of factors suggesting that it probably fluctuated. As Woodburn and others have pointed out, resources do vary in productivity, due to microfluctuations in climate and so on, and Lee himself shows that associations of Bushmen with sedentary or pastoral peoples on their margins can induce them to adopt a more stable existence and increase births. One suspects that rather than a steady, flat curve, the Bushmen might have had a fluctuating rate of increase, like so many people without external supports for their food economy. This means that Bushman population might have had buildups and "crashes," like some animal populations. But this we may never know; even if this should turn out to be the case, it does not modify the basic facts, which are that Bushmen, like all H-G peoples, seem to have lived in such a way so as to maintain a low average population level.

Population, however, is more than mere numbers and growth rates. It is also a social datum insofar as all people have preferences concerning the size of the group with which they choose to spend their lives. Since H-G people characteristically live in small bands of from 30 to 50 persons, depending on resources and social preferences, one can suspect that the small size of this effective social organ can generate its own justification. Lee (1972B) and James Woodburn (1972) offer similar arguments concerning this process for the Bushmen and an East African H-G group, the Hadza. Lee points out that many, if not most, H-G peoples alternate between large and small encampments—the former being the assemblies of related bands in the winter dry season in which a more "intense social life" (p. 182) was lived, and initiations, courtships, and other activities could take place. At the same time, the proximity factor in large numbers meant that social conflict would also intensify and could reach a point where the encampment could break up before the season was over. (Lee also argues that the larger numbers mean that people have to work harder to produce enough food, but this argument has been challenged by Woodburn and others.) In any case, the large camps regularly dissolve into the small family bands:

> This mobility has a profound ecological significance. Fear and avoidance of conflict has the effect of keeping people apart. This perception of the threat of conflict functions to maintain group size and population density at a much lower level than could be supported by the food resources, if the population could be organized to use those resources more efficiently. (Lee, 1972B, pp. 182–183)

Woodburn presents similar arguments, although in the case of the Hadza somewhat greater tolerance of larger camps and bands seems to have been the rule. But, like the Bushmen, conflicts break up the larger camps and people move away, seeking the peace of the small units. Woodburn also adds that the breakups mean that people have to make hard choices among the relatives they wish to stay with—if a man's mother-in-law goes in one band, and his own mother in another, he will have to make a choice, and the choice becomes a commitment. Hence nomadic movement of small bands means strong commitments to particular relatives—commitments that become lifetime decisions. The small, nomadic group thus tends to build up strong justifications for its persistence. As Woodburn concludes, "The very widespread enthusiasm for nomadic movement among both hunters and gatherers and pastoral nomads suggest that its benefits for the people concerned are far greater than the obvious ecological ones" (1972, p. 205).

We may now have an important part of the story. The existence of hunting and gathering as a subsistence routine makes the small nomadic band a desirable adaptation; and the small nomadic band generates needs for low population increase rates and also social reinforcements for nomadism and small size. This is a nice example of a system, possibly an ecosystem. It operates on the basis of limited choice: it provides its actors with what must be the fewest options in human society. To maintain such a social environment, the reinforcements must be substantial and rigorous.

But another part of the solution to the stability problem among the simpler peoples is also suggested by Lee, in a paper on Bushman energy inputs and outputs (1969). Lee notes, first, that the Bushmen, like other (but not all) H-G groups, practice "immediate consumption," which means that they collect and consume a single unit of the food supply in a period of about 48 hours. That is, they have no surplus of food and no method for preserving or storing it (but it should be noted that some groups do have borderline methods). The economy is thus geared to survival rather than to "capital accumulation"—if one can consider food to be such in societies that do store it. Following the suggestion by Marshall Sahlins (1965) to the effect that simple survival goals, in contrast to wealth-producing objectives, drastically simplify social structure, Lee notes that H-G groups all practice what Sahlins and Service (1960) have called "generalized reciprocity," which refers to the sharing of food procured in the gathering activities by all members of the band (see, also, Damas, 1972, on this point). Sharing of food is the opposite of hoarding by individuals, which appears to be universally condemned among H-G groups. Since hoarding is also the basic strategy for wealth and property accumulation, its rarity in H-G groups means that a morally sanctioned force is generated against economic differentiation. Similarly, to use food as capital—that is, to pay off or finance other activities—is likely to be considered a form of a stinginess by H-G peoples. The operation of these strategies "keeps food inventories at a minimum . . . also tends to maintain 'wealth' differences between individuals at an exceedingly low level" (Lee, 1969, p. 91). As long as the moral sanctions persist, the H-G economy will persist. This explanation would attribute persistence of a balanced or sustained-yield system of resource use to the transactional social behavior characteristic of primary (family-like) groups.

Marshall Sahlins' treatment (1972) of similar themes emphasizes the economic aspects of the process, but the argument is similar. In what he calls "small tribal societies" the household is the major unit of production, and the objectives of production mainly for domestic use leads to the tendency to accept minimal definitions of economic activity, property, and labor. Sahlins' "Domestic Mode of Production" thus sets up feedbacks similar to Foster's "limited good," or zero-sum game behavior, which through fear of exhaustion of resources, controls the impact on physical resources. The argument is admitted by Sahlins to have ideal-typical characteristics, which means that it applies best to the very simplest hunting-gathering societies, and least to those tribalists who are engaged in production for trade, etc. Aside from these controversial features of his argument based on its ideal-typical properties, he has nevertheless provided a cogent exposition of the distinctive limitations, of the econology of the small, isolated society.

Lee also remarks that the H-G system could change rapidly if an individual in the band, or population, decided to "save" his resources ". . . if enough of his fellows were to follow his example, then the social fabric would be preserved and a new economic equilibrium would be established at a higher level of surplus accumulation" (1969, p. 92). Natural resources, at least the important ones, hitherto collectively "owned" or utilized, begin to drift into private or sub-group control; disparities in wealth emerge and the conversion of subsistence resources into economic goods (and hence, prestige values) begins. The "tragedy of the commons," Hardin's symbol for the process, can occur at the tribal as well as the complex-society level. (General summaries of population dynamics in various tribal groups are found in Turnbull, 1972; Kunstadter, 1972B; Weiner, 1972; Laughlin, 1972.)

Stuart Piddocke's analysis of the Northwest Coast potlatch system (1965) suggests a step in this latter direction, but one that still preserves some semblance of sustained yield and control of escalating wants and wealth differentiation. According to Piddocke's interpretation, the potlatch operated when disparity in food supply between tribal segments reached a point where one segment (usually a village) was seriously disadvantaged. At the same time, the loss of prestige of this group's chief meant that his incentive to recoup his losses became critical. The result was a potlatch ceremony, in which the fortunes of the fading segment would be revived (the wealth redistributed) and the opposing chief permitted to realize some status for having cooperated in the ceremony. In this case we have the evidence for a differentiating society that nevertheless can make compromises with the differentiation so as to achieve redistribution of goods in the whole community, and thus permit relatively equal access to basic resources and preserve the general control over the use of Nature. However, it is easy to see how this balanced system, on the verge of exploitation by the rich and powerful, could make the transition to a wealth-poverty system where resources are differentially "owned." Piddocke does, as a matter of fact, mention cases where villages would be so detached from an equal share in the economy that potlatching was impossible, in which case they would simply fade away.

Anthony Leeds' account of the Yaruro Indians of Venezuela (in Vayda, (1969B)) suggests still another pattern within the general type of the tribal society in balance with Nature. The existence of a "chief" role among these forest dwellers, with their mixture of swidden agriculture and hunting-gathering subsistence, is an equivocal affair due to the distinctive ecological adaptation. A chief is required due to the need for direction of the frequent migratory movements of the group. But, at the same time, the low productivity of the subsistence system required few needs for direction and control beyond this point, or, for that matter, opportunities for private control of wealth in the form of massing stores of food and other goods. Hence, chiefs had vague, intermittent authority. The case echoes the Bushmen, on the whole: the way of life makes it difficult for economic growth and its accompanying social differentiation, including private control over resources, to emerge.

All the studies discussed have one thing in common: they locate the explanation for the achievement of what appears to be (granting the validity of the observations) a sustained-yield strategy for natural resources—and the accompanying control over human population—in a system of *social* transactions; of dealings between men that have the common consequence of establishing a static economy and social horizon. Rappaport, on the other hand, seems to rely on ritual for sending signals to the actors to behave in ways leading in the same direction—ritual that is some sort of response to a tension between institutions, population, and environment. However, such tensions, and the emergence of ritual to handle them, must be managed by transactional social behavior and the operation of adaptive strategies to satisfy needs and the trade-offs between one set of needs and another.[15]

But whatever emphasis we give this (Rappaport's ritual mysteries or Lee's down-to-earth social materialism), it is clear enough that the methods of ecological control in these tribal societies will not work in our own. The essence of the argument is to imply that the tribal cases have *no* "control" because they do not appear to make formal, conscious decisions to use few resources—at least there is no data in the studies that suggest this, which of course does not mean that none exists. But in its absence we have to conclude for the time being that the control is more likely to become a conscious issue and a formal procedure when the system has grown *out* of control—that is, when the process of wealth and stratification has resulted in undue pressure on resources.

Be that as it may, we can still learn *something* from these cases, and it is, on the whole, the fact that human relations with the environment work through the social system—that the social system extends into Nature, and Nature becomes the social system, in effect. Our own society differs only in the magnitude and complexity of the process.

By "economizing" or "socializing" the explanations for the degrees of stability in human-environment relations, the need for biological analogies and ecosystem interpretations is minimized. These socializing approaches make sense out of the motives and strategies of the actors behaving in mixed socionatural environments, and it is this context that must be understood if we are to understand the problem of control in our own system. At the same time, the studies clearly make a case for systems analysis—that is, a close study of reinforcements and interdependencies—in cultural ecological contexts, so the orientation developed by Rappaport is not "wrong," only stretched and extended too far in the direction of biological analogies.

But of course it can be argued that Rappaport and Vayda have been saying that socioeconomic behavior has ecological consequences—that social activities have biological consequences, and hence become "biological" or "ecological." Ecology, then, for Vayda and Rappaport, appears to lie on some higher level of generality or consequence, while for this writer, it is most relevantly studied in the actions of humans.[16] Middle-level generalizations that deal with the practical consequences and the social basis of decision-making—"adaptive dynamics"—would be preferable to interpretations that find the causes of action in out-of-awareness factors, or in obscure and even harder-to-demonstrate feed-back loops.[17] But this does not mean, of course, that Vayda and Rappaport, and their colleagues, are completely wrong. The argument is, in fact, laden with reifications and logical complexities—all due to the special position of humans in the natural world and the difficulty of managing cognitive behavior in natural contexts of analysis.

If one must make a general judgment on various attempts to use concepts borrowed from biological ecology for analyzing human cultural ecology, one would start from the fact that the analogies tend not to be drawn systematically from particular domains in biology, but from any domain or level that happens to fit the case semantically. While this is the nature of analogy, the habit has created a certain amount of confusion over the nature of similarity and difference between biological and social systems in anthropological (and ethological) literature. Many of the analogies are drawn from the behavior of single organisms; others are taken from populational or species phenomena; still others from ecosystems. But no matter from what level the analogies are taken, there is a general tendency to ignore the fact that biological systems are generally more stable or more self-regulating than human social systems, and they lack the impressive capacity of social systems to adapt to circumstances by using linguistic and symbolic information. The point is that social systems are organized differently than biological systems, and no amount of analogy-building will alter this fact or make social systems more like biological.

BIOLOGY AND CULTURE IN RELATIONSHIP

We turn now to a consideration of work in cultural ecology that aims at the explication of biocultural relationships in particular cases and problems. This is different from the use of natural ecological concepts for interpreting cultural and behavioral phenomena on analogic grounds, since the objective is—or should be—to show the precise contribution of biological and cultural factors to a particular phenomenon.

We begin with a paper by D. H. Stott (1962) on the general theme of how cultural and biological factors might exert controls over the "population explosion," presumably without conscious purpose and planning being involved. He takes his cue from two Malthusian-type observations: (1) when population presses against food resources in a human population to the point where survival might be endangered, "any process which tended to *lower* the mental capacity, physical dexterity, or perceptual acuity of a certain number of individuals might mean the saving of the race" (p. 355). This is the case because Homo sapiens seems to lack capacity for fixing adaptive behavioral strategies genetically, in order to avoid behavior that threatens group survival. (2) The second assumption is that starvation is not an effective means of population control in any animal species, and fluctuation in the size of animal populations often occurs in cycles without reference to fluctuations in food supply. Such fluctuations provide built-in controls over population that serve to regulate the balance of species in a given environment and to maintain the distribution of food resources.[18]

Stott's objective is to review the evidence in order to suggest whether or not such mechanisms exist in human populations. He summarizes a handful of studies that seem to show that mental stress and lowered intellectual capacity due to adverse social and psychological conditions, substandard nutrition during pregnancy, lethal malformations leading to diminution of fertility, and various combinations of these are processes limiting human births and the survival of fertile or innovative individuals. These mechanisms serve the same functions as fertility limitation in animals caused by stress from excessive crowding, nutritional deficiencies, and exteroceptive stimuli. Stott concludes that "the predicted catastrophe of world population increasing by geometric progression to the point of starvation is unlikely to occur. It will be forestalled, if not by conscious human design, by the physiological mechanisms which have been evolved to obviate such a calamity" (1962, p. 373).

Stott is probably quite correct in assuming that things will never reach the ultimate Malthusian consequence of absolute starvation of the whole human race, and I doubt if any of the doomsayers in population ecology ever really thought this would occur. Starvation is hardly the issue: humans can exist socially at a near-starvation level indefinitely, as has happened repeatedly in India and China. The threat is not starvation, but privation: a whole world functioning at a marginal nutritional level under political regimes of increasing ruthlessness.

Besides, populations *have* "exploded," whether the mechanisms cited by Stott have been in operation or not: a population problem is already considered to exist in countries with food production problems or with subsistence technologies requiring large labor forces—precisely those countries where one might expect to find the mechanisms operating. Humans can breed very fast, and nutritional supports can usually be mustered effectively enough for a considerable time to permit net increases in population in spite of high mortality rates (what is adaptive for the individual may be maladaptive for the group). Moreover, while Stott's mechanisms may indeed operate, they may not do so equally in all sectors of a population—only in those where the subculture established the necessary conditions.

Even if Stott is right, and the future will be one of decreasing fertility and increasing mortality, not to mention incompetence, these conditions would constitute catastrophes of a magnitude fully equal to starvation or permanent malnutrition. There is little choice—both would be cultural-biological events of the most unsettling nature. Stott does acknowledge in passing that the effects of self-regulation would be "unpleasant," but he has not realized the full implications of the alternatives.

Stott's paper is a classic exampe of biologizing what is a cultural as well as a biological problem—and therefore an example of how not to relate biological and cultural factors in ecological analysis. Population is not merely a matter of numbers, but also one of the quality of life and human dignity (see Davis, 1967, for a discussion of this point). By biologizing the argument and showing that population is self-limiting, the central human issues and essential cultural dimension are ignored. Since the response of humans to a threat to the quality of life can be drastic, such responses have their own consequences in despair and destructiveness. On the other side of the coin, humans can tolerate worsening conditions if there is no hope, and this "adaptability" can block change and modification. Quality of life, aspiration for better conditions, and tolerance of the worst—these are the key cultural issues in the population question, and any ecological inquiry will have to include them.[19]

The Irish Potato Famine

A detailed case study concerning such matters is available in the literature on the Irish potato famine of the 1840s—one of the massive socionatural events (an ecological and human disaster) in European history, and a record of privation and loss of life on a scale equal to the great Oriental famines (and one conveniently forgotten by most Western commentators on such events). The definitive history of the event is *The Great Hunger* (1962) by the British scholar, Cecil Woodham-Smith. This book, by a *historian*, is one of the two or three major existing works in cultural ecology, though not usually identified as such. The book is important for our purposes because it shows in detail how human institutions can affect man-environment relations at the cost of unimagined human misery and injury to the natural and human environment.

The basic facts were these: in 1845 the blight (a fungus flourishing under certain conditions of temperature, moisture, and cultivation) affected most parts of Ireland; in 1846 the entire potato crop failed; in 1847, a small, though good crop (characteristically inducing optimism) was harvested; but in 1848, another total failure. In the next several years, one million Irish citizens emigrated, several thousand dying from diseases contracted on the substandard ship accommodations supplied on a speculative profit-making basis. By the time the sequence of famine in Ireland and deaths from other causes there and abroad had run its course, $1\frac{1}{2}$ to 2 million persons had died or emigrated—a demographic catastrophe by any standards, and, from one point of view, a true Malthusian event.

The genesis of the catastrophe is to be found in the conditions in rural Ireland developing under British control from the 18th century. As a result of laws that prohibited ownership of land by Catholics, and required equal division of land among the heirs, the Irish peasant became a tenant or smallholder, existing on tiny plots of land and required to pay cash rents—really the only "cash crop"—to the British absentee landlords (and a few Irish Protestant landowners). Division of lands and reduction of size was encouraged, since it increased rent income. The system, therefore, required some cheap, easily produced, high-yield foodstuff in order to permit survival of the human material, and this is where the potato came in. Ireland's climate is remarkably damp, especially during summer and early fall (the growth and harvest seasons), and the potato is one of the few high-yield food crops able to produce well under cool, damp conditions. Another feature of the Irish environment that encouraged the persistence of this socioeconomic setup was the availability of a cheap, abundant supply of fuel in the form of peat.

Population increased rapidly, despite marginal nutritional conditions and recurrent local famines and food shortages, because early marriage and many children were the peasant's only available adaptive response to the insecurity of old age.

Several generations of life under this system had reduced agricultural technology to the spade, nutrition (exclusively potatoes, and a little milk from an occasional cow) to a semistarvation level, and hopes for a better life to zero. The near-exclusive reliance on the potato, and the lack of any alternative agricultural response was a ticket to disaster.[20] A few voices in England were raised against the system in the early 19th century, but the power of economic and class interests, and ideological resistance to social planning, prevented any constructive modification. The sheer mass of the Irish population—almost 9 million by 1845, 66 percent of which was totally dependent upon potato agriculture—bred an attitude of fatalism and discouraged the rise of protest movements, since any disturbance in the precarious system (not to mention the repressive measures used by the Crown) threatened the lives of large numbers. Moreover, as this system went its involutional way, the attitudes of the British masters hardened in expectable molds: the Irish were viewed as subhuman creatures, ignorant Catholics, not intelligent enough to want the benefits of Progress or to seize them.

The straw that broke the back of the system was an increase in the moisture level of the climate for several years in succession. While the potato was resistant to excessive moisture, the same conditions (cool, damp) also encouraged the growth of fungi, and in 1845 such conditions during the summer produced the first total crop destruction. The initial response of the British government had a modicum of humanity. From 1845 through the summer of 1847 there were intermittent attempts at relief measures: public works (especially road-building), distribution of foodstuffs (including much corn from North America, which the Irish refused to eat), and some cash relief payments were all tried, but in small amounts or in inadequate ways. For example, the road-building projects were set up with stern regulations requiring the half-starved men to work long hours at hard manual labor and to travel great distances on foot. The pattern that came to govern the British response in coming years became visible here: a notion that if men did not work, do things to help themselves, or seek to learn new ways, they deserved their fate, and the successful had no obligation to assist them. At the same time, the Irish peasants rejected the occasional efforts to teach them to grow vegetables or to accept new foods.

Therefore, from the mid-1847 period onward, the British response was to let Ireland solve her own problems without assistance. This policy was set by a clique of government officials dedicated to the propositions described above: the apotheosis of utilitarianism, with graftings of the doctrine of progress, and what later came to be known as the "survival of the fittest" in social Darwinism. In fact, even the sporadic relief measures introduced from time to time were financed by taxing the local landowners in Ireland, who by this time had nothing left. The absentee landlords followed a policy of driving their starving tenants or smallholders from the land in order to introduce new methods of cultivation and crops, creating a vast class of landless wanderers—which, in turn, triggered the mass migrations to America. In this dismal story, there were episodes of heroism and humanitarian sense—British intellectuals and public figures who called for a change in the government dogma without success. Once the process of socioeconomic decay had set in, the magnitude of the problem would have surpassed any resources Britain might have brought to bear—the basic mistakes were the colonial system, the failure to teach or permit the Irish to diversify agriculture, and the initial inadequate measures.

This summary omits many parts of an intricate analysis of how environmental, biological, cultural, political, and ideological factors intersected to produce a great catastrophe. Woodham-Smith lays much of the blame on the British rule, which permitted the Irish peasant to rely upon a single crop—in fact, it is the classic instance of the risks attendant upon monoculture, especially when there is no alternative adaptive response, and the human material has become deeply habituated to the system. But Woodham-Smith puts equal blame on a particular ideological bent of the mid-19th century: the rationalization of stratification and exploitation in the early industrial revolution—a conception of men as free agents who seek, in utilitarian fashion, their own welfare; and if they do not, their fate is of their own making. It is, therefore, also a story of human ignorance of the nature of society and the sources of power and responsibility.[21]

There is an echo here of Stott's propositions about human adaptation to high population density. Under the British system for Ireland, the population expanded and the agriculture involuted until, as we have noted, Ireland had nearly 9 million poverty-stricken people, most of whom subsisted on nothing but potatoes and milk. In other words, as the population grew, the population became habituated to harder and harder conditions, and when the famine hit, efforts to persuade some of them to shift to more profitable or nutritious crops, or to accept new foods, failed completely. The peasants simply could not conceive of shifting from traditional methods, or risking a new round of defeats. And the results were, of course, extensive depopulation.

The pattern of events is reminiscent of Stott's doctrine that increasing population and privation will tend to favor the survival of human types who will be increasingly inured to the discomforts of a crowded world, but whose biological incapabilities eventually will result in a population drop. However, in the Irish case the mechanisms of eventual population control came as a sudden catastrophe, not as a gradual fertility drop, and their causes were not increasing biological incapability, but starvation and migration due to an inadequate agricultural system imposed by a foreign power—and, once the system existed, the fear of risking the unknown on the part of a beaten-down population. Perhaps some selection of the more adaptable (tolerant of privation) individuals occurred preceding the famine, but since there was no major out-migration previous to the famines, and since the agricultural involution process in Ireland took only about a century (not long enough for genetic selection to operate), the case is a better example of how man's cultural mistakes and inhumanity have an impact on his biological chances than it is of automatic fertility control.

Therefore, this case is important for our argument because it demonstrates that human and cultural ecology are more than the study of settlement patterns, subsistence techniques, or the effect of agriculture on kinship, but involve attitudes, ideology, and politics. Even more important, it locates biological and environmental factors in the framework of a concrete sociohistorical process. The potato blight was a natural species, a particular fungus whose growth was accentuated by the climate of Ireland and certain habits of cultivation, and by the failure of the rulers to instruct or permit a downtrodden peasantry to change its ways. Another biological factor enters when the increasingly debilitated condition of the peasants and their fear of risk in a zero-sum game prevented them from accepting the few innovations that the welfare agents occasionally tried to introduce. The failure to appreciate the possibility of disaster, to reform the system and evolve an adequate adaptive response—ideological and sociocultural as well as biological—is the heart of the episode, and it is the study of this kind of process that is the key to a relevant cultural ecology.

The emphasis in the preceding discussion has been placed on adaptive social processes as a key to human ecology—although the role of biological and environmental factors is acknowledged. On the question of conscious vs. unconscious factors, the distinction may be largely one of short-term vs. long-term processes: "agricultural involution" may be a general process taking place without clear human awareness, consisting of incremental accommodations to what seems at any given moment a secure and reliable way of life, but what is actually increasingly fragile because of the limited alternatives available to an increasing population; at the same time, the involutionary process is also an assortment of human reactions and institutional structures, all of which are knowable and familiar. That is, on a short-term basis, we would not speak of "involutionary process," but of policy mistakes, adaptive responses, external controls, ignorance, and the like.

The Sickle Cell Disease

This distinction is sometimes not appreciated in anthropology because of the peculiar schizophrenic historical perspective of the field. That is, there is a tendency to use the typical slice-of-time, short-term ethnographic situations to produce evolutionary generalizations, and therefore miss the opportunity to deal with policy issues. A partial example of this tendency is available in the case of research on the sickle cell disease (Livingstone, 1958; Weisenfeld, 1967). This is an inheritable debilitating illness of the hemoglobin cells (which become sickle-shaped), common to West African populations and their New World offshoots, but which also has the property of conferring degrees of immunity to malaria on the affected populations. A decade or more of research on this condition was expended by anthropologists, medical researchers, and geneticists, before it was fully realized that the presence of the disease in New World populations had quite different implications than for Africans: the absence of malaria in the New World made its immunological advantages meaningless, and it was simply another physical factor contributing to substandard performance of Negro populations. Research is now beginning on this aspect.

However this may be, the work on the sickle cell disease has constituted what may be the single most important piece of professional research and theory construction in human ecology, at least with reference to the problem of the relationships of biological and cultural factors. This assertion is based on the fact that it has been found that the groundwork for an increase in the sickling gene was provided by the importation and spread of Malaysian techniques of root crop cultivation, adapted to a rainy tropical environment, into sub-Saharan Africa. This introduction drove the Negro populations into the forest and, due to the high yields associated with this type of agriculture (cf. the Irish potato), populations increased rapidly. The increased density and sedentary life of these new agricultural communities led to an increase in the incidence of malaria, due to ease of transmission and stagnant water conditions associated with forest clearing. Malaria, as a debilitating disease, endangers human existence by withdrawing workers from agriculture. Unless some protection from malaria emerges, depopulation will result.

The sickle cell condition is such a protective device, and it arises in human populations as a mutation. In ideal conditions, such as those sketched above, the gene responsible for the disease is likely to increase in frequency, since it confers survival value on individuals who have a mild, heterozygotic form of the disease (the homozygotes—those who have the genes from both parental sides—usually do not survive to the fertility stage). For the gene to increase in frequency in a given population, certain conditions must be present, and considerable work has gone into the study of these conditions in the field, sampling actual populations, and in the laboratory, making computer simulations of the possibilities. To summarize a complex series of researches, it has been found that an increase in the frequency of the sickle cell gene in a population will cause a decrease in the actual reproduction rate of the malaria organism, since the number of people in the population who are susceptible to heavy cases of the disease, and the consequent high production rate of the parasite, are reduced. That is, the adaptability of the trait is found not only in its grant of immunity to malaria but in the fact that a high frequency of the trait also materially reduces the number of malarial parasites in mosquitoes. (Weisenfeld [1967] and Livingstone [1971] provide a review of this later work on the effects of the human condition on the parasite.)

The process in Africa thus extended over many human generations, and was marked by a slow accommodation of the germ plasm to a particular environmental complex, building up the genetic potential for a physical condition that would be markedly adaptive in that environment, but maladaptive outside of it—a case, from at least the humanistic viewpoint, of biological involution. It differs from the Irish case in that, as far as we know, the Irish peasant population had no visible genetic deficiency—the causes of agricultural-demographic involution were located in political and economic policy, particularly land tenure. The significance of this difference is simply that while the end-states of such ecological processes in different human populations can be similar, the etiology can differ, and the decisive factors can be either biological or cultural-socioeconomic. And, as noted previously, due to the high mobility of human populations, the adaptive value of the trait can change from high to low, or negative, creating needs for rational corrective action.

There is an additional significance of the sickle cell research for cultural ecology, and this concerns the division of labor among the several fields of specialization in anthropology. As Livingstone's 1958 paper summarizes the situation, the identification of the populations with high frequencies of the gene had to overcome a confusing picture due to migrations of West African tribal groups subsequent to, or previous to, contact with a malarial environment. This migration meant that high-gene-frequency populations were not confined to malarial regions, but could also be found in low-malarial dry regions, and that some low-frequency populations were living in malarial areas. The problem was to demonstrate that the contemporary distribution was due to migration; if the populations could be traced back into their original habitats, a perfect correlation of the gene frequencies and the incidence of malaria could be obtained.

In order to make this reconstruction, linguists and archeologists had to be called into the program. Distributions of languages, and particular archeological complexes, seemed to confirm the hypothesis that migration had removed some high-frequency sickling populations from their original habitats, and had resulted in the movement of low-frequency groups into malarial regions, where their period of residence was not sufficiently long to permit the sickling adaptation to emerge. This work also provided some mean values for the time required to build up a given gene frequency.

The pattern of research that emerges from this case provides an excellent model for ecological study in anthropology and affiliated sciences, and even suggests the possibility of an ecological approach as a master plan for the discipline, and the discipline's relationships to other fields.

Three important conclusions emerge from these reviews: (1) The role of biological factors differs greatly from case to case in human cultural situations, and can never be assumed to play a similar role on theoretical grounds. (2) The level of generality in cultural-ecological studies has much to do with the degree of policy relevance the field might attain: in order to provide such relevance, the immediate social factors involved in a particular case must be ferreted out, and the generalizations based on biological process, beyond awareness of the actors involved, must be handled with caution. (3) Whatever else cultural ecology has contributed, it has provided some portraits of the low-energy, relatively isolated society, operating largely in equilibrium with Nature. These portraits, at best, show how the social reciprocities and mutual expectations of a primary group function so as to restrain human wants and objectives and avoid abuse of resources (or perhaps the objectives implement the reciprocities). The system is circular and mutually reinforcing; hence it tends to perseverate. But, at the same time, the openings toward change and development are present in every society, however small or isolated.

NOTES

[1]See Netting, 1972, for a bibliography of assessments of cultural ecological writings. Most of those items are also cited in this book.

[2]For presentations of the old environmentalist position, see the following, among others: Hodgen, 1964, Chapter 7, for Jean Bodin, the founder of the European anthropogeographic tradition; the work by Thomas [1925] remains one of the best studies of the environmentalist position in social and geographic theory; C. C. Huntington and Carlson [1933] present the E. Huntington position, often misrepresented by critics; and the Ratzel tradition is represented by Semple [1911]. See Freilich, 1967, for a brief criticism of environmentalism and the ethnological response to it; also Steward, 1955F; Abbott, 1970.

[3]As David Damas points out (in Damas, 1969, p. 1): although Boas was probably the first anthropologist to make a convincing case for a culture-environment correlation in his demonstration of the relationship of Eskimo settlement location to the formation of sea-ice and the movements of the seal (Boas, 1888, p. 417), Boas insisted that environment has only "a certain limited effect upon the culture of man," in his famous essay criticizing evolutionary anthropology (1896, p. 906).

[4]For some available studies of this type, see the following: Lee, 1969 (a study of food intake and energy output among Bushmen); Parrack, 1969 (estimates of energy levels provided by West Bengal agriculture); Montgomery, 1972 (ms) (relationship of nutrition and health to social organization in a southern India village). Of somewhat different style is McCullough's brief study (1973) of Maya farmers' methods of coping with heat-induced stress, as sanctioned by the Maya cultural folklore concerning "hot" and "cold" phenomena and the need to balance these.

[5]Wissler (1926) represents a central statement of culture area theory. Perhaps the *very* earliest was Mason (1895), although the idea was emerging out of several types of intellectual interests and field experience of anthropologists, and there are echoes back into the 17th century and foreshadowings in the classical Greek geographers. The plant ecology material served to crystallize the modern trend, and the definitive statement of that seems to have been made by Sapir (1914), in *Time Perspective in Aboriginal American Culture*. The final product, and certainly the last detailed attempt to use culture area theory empirically, was Kroeber's *Cultural and Natural Areas of Native North America* (1939). Kroeber's chief finding was that natural phenomena and cultural patterns coincided only when historical conditions permitted. (A more detailed analysis of this appears in Chapter 7.)

[6]In the recent volume of papers edited by Barth, *Ethnic Groups and Boundaries* (1969), it becomes clear that he is interested almost exclusively in sociocultural rather than ecological problems, since he treats the multiethnic "mosaic" business here in social, psychological, and economic terms, with ecology (for most of the papers in the volume) a kind of result rather than a cause of boundary-maintenance. In his own brief paper on "Pathan Identity

and its Maintenance" he focuses almost entirely on psychological identity, presenting sociocultural and econological factors as resultants of identity rather than as causes, although the term "niche" appears as a figurative expression for something like life goals or cultural orientation; e.g., "less ambitious niches" (p. 129). Actually in one sense, the 1969 book as an ecological treatise is an improvement over the earlier paper since it deals more comprehensively with the sociocultural dimensions of adaptation. However, there is no attempt to deal with natural resource utilization and environmental impact problems.

[7]Vayda and Rappaport (1968) might well argue that their approach is not "cultural ecology" at all, and therefore has no business being considered in this paper. From a narrow or purist point of view, they would probably be correct. However, since their objective appears to be a translation of familiar cultural phenomena into ecological terms, and since this translation adds a dimension of explanation to these cultural phenomena, we choose to include their approach. Looking at their approach from the point of view of Fig. 1, it would seem that on the whole they attempt to deal with feedback loop No. 2—from NR-E/G back into biology. However, their attempt is highly specialized since they are using bioecological concepts to do it. That is, their findings concerning the impact on biology are generalized, and from our point of view they seem to contribute more to the explanation of the perseveration of cultural behavior than to such feedback.

[8]This is a very complex system, and we cannot review it in detail. Succinctly: the culminating, post-warfare ceremonial in this cycle is the *kaiko*, which lasts for approximately one year, and is begun by planting the gardens, which in turn marks the end of combat. The gardens grow until a sufficient number of pigs have accumulated through purchase and breeding and, when this occurs, the *kaiko* proceeds through the harvest of the gardens, and pig slaughter and feasting, involving ritual presentation of pork between men involved in maintaining prestige. The activities of presentation and consuming pork mean that considerable protein is consumed "during periods of stress" (1967A, p. 154); that is, in the presumably tense period of the *kaiko*. The decision to slaughter pigs is made when the consequences of the increasing pig population result in general irritation at their depredations, and fighting, which includes forcing the hamlet settlements farther apart. Rappaport apparently was unable to obtain precise figures concerning the optimal size of pig populations leading to slaughter over a period of years, although he found that over the 50–60 year period ending in 1963, there were four *kaiko*, meaning 12–15 years between ceremonials. However, he also notes that these durations are not standard for the Tsembaga or other groups. In other words, the cycles are not regular, and the decisions to slaughter are not governed by precise measurements of populations or time.

[9]The proclivity to use concepts from ethology in analogic or quasianalogic fashion is nothing new: Roderick McKenzie was doing it in the 1920s. In a series of papers reprinted in a volume of collected papers edited by Amos Hawley (1968), McKenzie explored the concept of *dominance* in international relations, urban zoning, and other social groups and segments, leading from an analogy with the physiology of organisms and how this is translated into spacial organization of animal groups—the approach developed later by W. C. Allee and others in their studies of pecking order and dominance submission relations. An early general reference to the theme of using animal behavioral analogies for human behavior is the volume edited by Robert Redfield (1942), entitled *Levels of Integration in Biological and Social Systems*. This book includes papers by Allee, Robert Park, A. L. Kroeber, C. Carpenter (societies of monkeys and apes), and others concerned with the problem. This was really a "first round" of attempts to use ethology to interpret human society; the new ethologists are discussed by Callan (1970) and Alland (1972).

[10]At the time of writing, work of this kind is just beginning in anthrolopology.

[11]Rappaport has recently reworked some of these appendix data in an attempt to portray the energy flow in his New Guinea society (1971B).

[12]The application of natural-ecological concepts and measures to archeological contexts probably has been more successful in the sense that in the absence of distracting details, with historical depth the conclusions may get at long-term processes. An example of this is the article by E. B. W. Zubrow (1971) on "carrying capacity" in the prehistoric Southwest, in which he builds a model of "carrying capacity as a dynamic equilibrium system" and applies it to a particular archeological site in an effort to "test the hypothesis that the development of populations in marginal resource zones is a function of optimal zone exploitation," which translated means that you need to make use of all available resources in order to live in a specialized environment. This is hardly surprising, but still the exercise is important for its simplicity and clarity. (I am indebted to economic historian E. L. Jones for suggesting that the problem of data obscurity in Rappaport's study—and others like it—might be overcome by studying remote contexts of advanced societies in early modern times, where sound historical data is available—for example, the Scottish Highlands or the New Forest [Tubbs, 1969].)

[13]There is an additional question concerning this matter of an automatically functioning homeostasis, out of direct awareness of the actors. The behavior itself is, of course, under conscious control, and since most of the behavior appears to be ritual, we are dealing with a high degree of control indeed—control by the sacred—or what Rappaport himself in a later paper calls "sanctity" (1971A). In the secularized, high-energy societies the control systems are regulated by instrumental considerations, or "rationality." The question is, then, if ecosystems in the special sense of sustained-yield principles are to be created, which of these two systems works best—the symbolic-sanctification-automatic control system or the rational-instrumental-planned system? The question is, of course, a largely spurious one; the difference is not one of choice but one of level of cultural development. Any attempt to impose sanctified systems of control on our own society would be equivalent to totalitarianism; that is, the political costs might be considered to exceed the ecological gain. However, this is one of the choices we may have to make in the future.

[14]Vayda has argued (1969A), however, that the ecosystem position *can* lead to an analysis of imbalance and dynamism in human ecology, since it does allow for the role of human purposes, at least in a generalized way, and does take fluctuation and change into account. This is possible, but the problem is that the systems (like Maring warfare) may not remain in equilibrium long enough to permit a detailed analysis to ascertain their ecosystemic properties.

[15]There is another issue here, not discussed, which I do not enter into because it is really not germane to my argument. This concerns the extent to which anthropologists have romanticized or exaggerated this image of serene, primary-group homogeneous tribalists or peasants. There is little doubt that they have, and a whole sector of contemporary social anthropology can be considered to be an effort to criticize this—social transactionism itself was developed in part to do it. However this may be, or however imperfect the *gemeinschaft*, the system did work by and large to constrain the impact on natural resources, and that is the topic of chief interest in this book. The imperfections of the social system of these groups could, of course, lead to breach of the restraints, economic development, and an increasing need for resources, and I allow for that throughout my argument as a matter of course.

[16]In two recent papers (1971A; 1971C) Rappaport appears to be taking a philosophical-

anthropological tack as a justification of his conviction that rituals are, or symbolize, corrective feedbacks in human affairs. He defines all feedback or cybernetic processes fundamentally as information flow, and rituals are therefore "conventional acts of display through which one or more participants transmit information concerning their physiological, psychological, or sociological states either to themselves or to one or more of their participants" (1971C, p. 25). In a Durkheimian mood, he uses concepts such as "sacred" and "sanctity" to refer to information-transmitting acts that are viewed by the receivers as "unquestionably true," hence to be acted upon. He develops these ideas at some length, using a variety of special terms to refer to the regulatory functions of ritual. One wonders how much important information in human societies is communicated by these roundabout ethological methods. Does Rappaport mean to imply that the very practical problem of deprevative pigs has to be solved by indirect ritual communications? One feels somehow that the New Guineans must have discovered that purposeful decision-making and matching of means to ends can serve the same end. Moreover, even granting the validity of Rappaport's implications concerning a smoothly operating homeostatic system, his own data show that the response to pig depredation is not immediate nor uniform: sometimes the rituals follow immediately; sometimes a considerable amount of harm is done before the system gets into operation. At best, it does not appear to be a very efficient process. Rappaport does not seem to have seriously considered the nature of information flow in human societies, or to realize that overt communication and rational decision-making is a part—perhaps the most important part—in feedback processes in human affairs. He seems to want to find his regulatory processes at some covert level below the interplay of human discourse and action behavior, and resist acknowledgment that direct methods keep the whole thing operating most of the time. My own suspicion is that there is a crucial missing factor in the Tsembaga analysis: the role of social structure. The Tsembaga seem to be one group in the region that lacks a "Big Man" system of status leadership, and it is possible that the absence of a strong leader means management difficulties in agriculture. In such amorphous political situations, ritual may be the last resort, so to speak.

[17]Studies of agricultural techniques and ecological relations that emphasize a "middle level" of generality are exemplified by Clifford Geertz' work on Java (1963; 1965), and Moerman's study of Thai agriculture and innovation (1968). Both of these, especially Moerman's, get down to specific coping mechanisms and cognitive-cultural motivations for specific actions and assessments of consequences. Likewise, the studies of swidden agriculture (Conklin, 1954A & B; 1963; Carneiro, 1956; Waddell, 1972) move in a more practical direction, even though adaptive dynamics are not always clearly analyzed. The swidden studies have been aimed at description of the relationships between the particular natural resources, the edaphic component of which in tropical forest regions is friable and ephemeral, hence unsuited to permanent cropping; the swidden techniques, which permit intermittent recovery of the soil and natural flora; and the human population supportable by swidden production. These studies have concluded that swidden is an ecologically suitable technique and sustains the maximum human population possible in the particular habitat under sustained-yield principles, although it is destructive of the environment when population increases and the cultivation round is stepped up (Geertz, 1963, Chapter 2; Kunstadter, 1972B). Some studies suggest that under optimal swiddening, high civilizations such as the Maya could easily have been supported (Dumond, 1961). Ester Boserup's theories, discussed in detail later, are also relevant here: she proposed tendencies toward agricultural intensification as population densities increase—a plausible idea, since it not only implies experiments in more productive regimes designed to better support the

increasing numbers, but also the need to keep an increasing population busy at tasks. This latter factor may underlie her corollary labor or man-productivity goes down in intensified agriculture, but more work needs to be done on the whole idea before any firm conclusions can be drawn. One of the difficulties here is that agricultural economists, who should have known better, have shown remarkable insensitivity to environmental consequences of their work in Western countries, and have simply transferred these insensitivities to the emerging countries, where the problems are even more acute.

[18]An analysis of the complex chain of physiological and perceptual mechanisms in population control *via* crowding is found in an article by Christian (1963). Edward Hall (1966) presents a summary and an overly facile acceptance of the possible applicability to human behavior. The comprehensive survey of regulatory mechanisms in animal behavior, now adopted by many human demographers, is found in Wynne-Edwards (1962). Hoagland (1963) summarizes the evidence for regulatory cybernetics in human populations. Ballard (1971) provides an example of a science-fiction treatment, with a wry sociological twist. For one of the rare attempts to use theory and analysis derived from human contexts on animal behavior, see the paper by Covich (1972). This is an analysis of seed-eating by a rodent species on the basis of economic theory (indifference curves and budget-line analysis). The results are interesting, though not conclusive.

[19]This issue of automatic controls over human population has figured in the debate between the Commoner and Ehrlich factions in the contemporary ecology movement. Commoner appears to blame technology for the crisis, and pollution as the major evil, and seems to imply that population will take care of itself through mechanisms similar to those Stott describes—or, that crowding is not really a serious threat, since social adaptations can be found to mitigate its effects. Ehrlich, on the other hand, believes that Commoner neglects social-biological issues in the ecological crisis in his emphasis on pollution, and among these is population. Ehrlich feels that population will not take care of itself, but will have to be subjected to social controls. Aside from the rather exaggerated rhetoric used by both sides, no one in his right mind could possibly disagree with either: clearly both technology and population are involved in the crisis (see Ridker, 1972, for an analysis). Ehrlich seems unaware of the economic complexities of environmental costs and fails to recognize that it may be easier over the short run to develop modifications of industrial and technological practices than to arbitrarily control population, although in a recent book (Pirages and Ehrlich, 1974) he appears to recognize the technological factor. Commoner is subject to criticism on the grounds of ignoring the social complications and uncertainties of population dynamics—his emphasis on the "demographic transition" and in other measures is possibly misplaced, and he neglects the quality-of-life issue and the many social tensions associated with large and dense populations. (For a debate between the two contenders, see *Environment Magazine*, April 1972.)

[20]One problem that Irish scholars have considered at length concerns the reasons that the fishing industry remained undeveloped. Surrounded by highly productive seas, Ireland might have come a long way toward avoiding the miseries of the potato famine, or simply improving the diet under existing conditions by catching fish. The reasons given for the failure are numerous: the difficult coastline, the lack of suitable types of ships, the lack of adequate transportation for fish, and (perhaps the most important) the resistance of the British government to anything that might threaten the Scottish fishing industry. (In addition to Woodham-Smith, 1962, see the following books for materials on the potato famine: Edwards and Williams, 1956; Freeman, 1956.)

[21]A comparable historical study of a cultural-ecological situation is provided by J. H.

Powell, *Bring Out Your Dead* (1949). This work by a medical historian, describes the great yellow fever epidemic in 18th-century Philadelphia, and analyzes the causes of the rapid spread of the disease. Ignorance of germ-causation and the role of the mosquito were obvious factors, but more significant is the painstaking analysis of the elite structure of the community and the role played by the prestigeful physician, Benjamin Rush, considered the first important figure in American medicine. His stubbornness in refusing to face up to obvious facts revealed by low-prestige foreign doctors and hospital caretakers, and failure to take the required sanitary precautions, accelerated the spread of the disease and contributed to many deaths. The interaction between Rush, the Philadelphia city government, and the advocates of the new methods presents another incisive picture of how personality, stratification, and politics can lead to disastrous ecological consequences.

CHAPTER 7

Culture and Ecology: Culture as the Master Variable

The preceding chapter was concerned with the use of biologically derived concepts in analyzing cultural aspects of ecological situations studied by anthropologists and their colleagues. We turn now to cultural ecology in a stricter sense: research in which culture becomes the starting point and also the objective: where the direction of information flow in feedback loop No. 3 is considered to be coming from the attitudinal and socio-cultural components up into the energy-transformation and producing functions, whose functioning can then be viewed as a cause, or reinforce-ment, of the sociocultural.

This approach is associated with the name of Julian Steward, and most of the work in anthropological cultural ecology produced to date can be considered to be a continuation or elaboration of his original scheme. As noted at the beginning of Chapter 6, the Steward approach was developed as a response to Boasian "possibilism," just as the latter was a response to the environmental determinism of the 17th–19th centuries. Possibilism converted environmental influence into an aspect of culture; the environment was defined as a passive agent, furnishing both opportunities and constraints, with culture providing the conditions for selection. Possibilism lacked a theory of the dynamic relationship of human actions to environment: the conditions leading individuals to make certain choices were simply synthesized as "culture," and the possibility that individuals might make choices other than those "in the culture" was not acknowledged. More fundamentally, the approach was based on the stereotype of discrete, homogeneous cultures, with all individuals equally exposed to norms and preferences, and socialized in similar ways so that the same choices would be made over and over again.

KROEBER'S VERSION OF POSSIBILISM

Lacking a dynamic theory of social behavior, anthropologists of the era proposed instead to investigate the existence of concordances between cultural styles and environmental factors. This effort culminated in A. L. Kroeber's 1939 (mostly written in 1931) volume, *Cultural and Natural Areas of Native North America*—a monument not only to environmental possibilism but to the entire "culture area" school of Boasian-historical anthropology. The objectives, as stated by Kroeber, centered primarily on culture, and not on a full elucidation of the dynamic relations between environment and culture: "The immediate causes of cultural phenomena are other cultural phenomena . . . . But this does not prevent the recognition of relations between nature and culture, nor the importance of these relations to the full understanding of culture" (p. 1). Nevertheless, Kroeber saw his mission as a kind of revival of an interest in "environmental factors" in anthropology, noting that the problem had been thrown out with the bath water in the revulsion against determinism. In accordance with this intention, Kroeber provided the most detailed and professional treatment of environmental divisions of the North American continent in the history of American anthropology to that date. Before Kroeber's book, environmental classifications were common-sensical geographical divisions: "Great Plains," "Eastern Woodlands," and so on. Kroeber provided detailed maps produced by geographers, botanists, and climatologists showing vegetation areas and their climatic relationships, and the relations of both to topography; his attempt to locate environmental-cultural concordances was based on this detailed information. In this feature, the book prefigured the increasing willingness of contemporary anthropologists to utilize precise information from the natural sciences. Moreover, Kroeber was not content with data on Indian tribes produced by ethnologists working with reservation groups; he used archeological and ethnohistorical information so far as it was available in the late 1920s and, in some updated passages, as it had become available by 1938. That is, his conception of culture and culture-environment relations contained a strong historical element: he was critical of the static "ethnographic present" conception, and emphasized that "the historic approach, remaining concerned with events as they occur in nature, always stresses the time aspects of phenomena as part of its ultimate objective." Culture areas, he felt, are only a "momentary and static organization of knowledge" (1939, p. 1).

The bulk of the monograph is devoted to attempts to find concordance between particular environmental features and particular cultural styles or areas—and this meant that the emphasis was put upon limiting or boundary setting effects of resources rather than on their opportunities. Because Kroeber was willing to consider time depth and, in general, to consider the whole problem of culture-environment relationships more critically than most of his contemporaries, the concordances are often inconclusive, with partial relationships, overlapping between boundaries, and the like. The very inconclusiveness of the findings suggests that culture area and environmental area are indeed temporary accommodations, and that the Amerinds were constantly changing their use of resources—implying a subtler meaning to the concept of possibilism and hinting that the notion of relatively static or fixed culture-natural areas was a concept contradicting one unconscious implication of possibilism: that humans are not capable of innovative decisions and choices. Kroeber was able to find extensive concordance in only a few geographical areas: for example, the Pacific coast, due to the "decisiveness of its topography" (1939, p. 204), which functioned to create sheltered zones where particular groups could develop in isolation. In other words, the typical isolated tribe, with its distinctive adaptation to the environment, tended to be the exception rather than the rule. The emphasis in the above on the inconsistencies or need for revision of extant theories is the writer's; Kroeber apparently did not perceive the theoretical implications of his work, and the paradox is that while the book is the capstone of a generation of possibilistic research, it is also the one work that did the most to cast doubt on the central themes and theories of the doctrine.

In a concluding section, Kroeber noted that "... the interactions of culture and environment become exceedingly complex when followed out. And this complexity makes generalization unprofitable, on the whole. In each situation or area different natural factors are likely to be impinging on culture with different intensity" (1939, p. 205). That is, generalization was conceived entirely in static or classificatory terms, despite Kroeber's initial avowal to handle the problem temporally. If concordance was to be found only occasionally, then generalization was impossible: the concept of generalization here is limited to simple correlation. But even here, Kroeber was on the verge of a departure: his analysis of the criteria delimiting agriculture showed a clear relationship between temperature and precipitation and archeological and ethnological evidence of cultivation, with variations by type of plant and method of cultivation (1939, pp. 209–212, 218–221). These brief sections presumably illustrate his dictum that generalizations are not possible, but in fact the findings (though since modified on the basis of better data) are good examples of cultural-ecological generalizations as they would now be visualized.

The crucial limitation of Kroeber's conceptual apparatus was his use of an undifferentiated concept of culture: "cultures occur in nature as wholes" (1939, p. 4); hence, when culture-environment concordance cannot be demonstrated for whole cultures, the assemblage of part-correlations and varying relationships between particular habitat features and particular items of culture make the situation "too complex" for generalization.[1] This fruitless search for holistic generalization and massive correlation obscured the very real value of empirical generalization concerning significant parts of socionatural systems. Out of Kroeber's brief but significant summary of his findings on agriculture and environment has grown a whole subfield of specialization in modern anthropology: the study of the circumstances of agricultural origins and growth.

As a result of the fixation on correlation, the negative cases in Kroeber's analysis—the absences of concordance—fall out of the model, since there is no theoretical preparation for handling them. Did Kroeber really believe that the absence of correlation meant chaos?—that is, that there was really only very limited regularity in nature and culture? In the terms of the book, the answer would have to be "yes"; in terms of Kroeber's wide-ranging sophistication, the answer is probably "no"—and he came to recognize the significance of the cultural ecology approach before his death. There is a note of dissatisfaction and even irritation at the limits of the existing theoretical models in *Cultural and Natural Areas*, but somehow the next step escaped him—in its place, he launched a trial balloon: the notion of cultural intensity and climax, a cyclical theory of cultural development, which he pursued to its logical conclusion in a later book, and which, like his version of possibilism, was quickly superseded (by multilinear evolutionism).

JULIAN STEWARD'S "CULTURAL ECOLOGY"

Thus Kroeber's possibilism reached a dead end. It is a matter of irony, perhaps, that the anthropologist who did most to revise and supplant possibilism—Julian Steward—was also primarily responsible for multilinear evolutionary theory, which superseded Kroeber's intensity-climax theory. Steward's new version of possibilism involved an attempt to locate the causes of cultural phenomena in production, or techno-economic phenomena, and to avoid metaphysical conceptions like

Kroeber's belief that culture causes itself. Steward was interested in explanation, not correlation, and hence interested in process rather than classification *per se*. This vision of causation and process led Steward toward the term *ecology*, a word that had been around for a long time on the fringes of anthropology (Kroeber mentions it once or twice, but he meant plant-animal distributions and processes).

Steward's work began with an attempt to define the relationship between the hunting-gathering mode of subsistence and features of social organization common to these societies (1936; 1938) even where historical contacts were not demonstrable. He conceived of hunting-gathering as a particular "culture type," a concept that simultaneously replaced both the evolutionary stage and the culture area classification. In a paper written in 1952, but published later (see 1955F), he drew a careful distinction between culture area and culture type and, in a slightly later paper (1953; see 1955B), he distinguished multilinear evolution from the 19th-century unilinear variety. The thrust of all of Steward's early work is classificatory, but was nevertheless devoted to a correction of the ambiguities of the Boasian and Kroeberian approaches to the study of life-sustaining activities. His ideas are clearly transitional between the older static mentalistic conceptions and the later dynamic adaptive orientations.

Steward's "cultural ecology" was defined in a 1950 paper (1955C), one of those highly significant single publications that creates a new style or trend, a whole subdiscipline. Reading this paper more than 20 years after its publication is still a profitable exercise. He notes, first, that the presence of culture (or, in our terms, the cognitive-voluntaristic capacity of human behavior) in relations of humans with the physical environment has always caused "many methodological difficulties," since it is apparent that humans are not "merely another organism" along with others in environmental contexts of study. These difficulties are due, he feels, to the failure to recognize that while biological ecology can be used to find causes of other biological or environmental phenomena (e.g., predation and its effect on population), the ecology of humans has been conceived as a separate descriptive discipline and not as a tool for explaining other phenomena. Steward wished to change that—to recognize human ecology as an instrument for the solution of problems: in the biological realm, human biological adaptation to environment; in the cultural, "how culture is affected by its adaptation to environment" (1955C, p. 31); or, in our terms, how the output of human activities feeds back into the institutional systems to change them (loop No. 3). This, he feels, is a different kind of inquiry than the bioadaptability studies because the apparatus with which men confront the environment is not biologically determined; to under-stand it, one must use "cultural historical concepts and methods rather than biological concepts" (1955C, p. 32)—and other methodologies de-veloped for the analysis of human institutions, such as economics.

The central concept proposed for the task he called *cultural core*—"the constellation of features which are most closely related to subsistence activities and economic arrangements" (1955B, p. 37)—and any other institutional feature that happens, in particular cases, to be closely connected with the core. This is the heart of Steward's major contribution to anthropological theory: he proposes a central causal mechanism in human society (or at least in society's ecological relations) that influences other aspects of culture—in all cases and at all times. This mechanism includes a physical-environmental component, although he did not consider this to be an independent determining factor, since humans select those features of the environment they choose to use as resources. Although he did not say so explicitly, the reader perceives some kind of balance or interplay here between the role of environment as a facilitating factor—permitting choice—and its role as a limiting factor—constraining choice. Steward never developed the dynamics of this interplay because he was not really concerned with choice or decision-making processes. Nor did he seem to realize that the causal influence of the core is logically a return to the old second-order abstraction dilemma: the use of such abstractions as *deux ex machinae*, when in fact it is a matter of people having to abide by or cope with their past decisions. Moreover, since he felt that the core caused other features of culture, but that these same features shaped the core at some past time, he had an implicit notion of systemic feedback. This implicit feedback conception is what, in my opinion, saved Steward from an out-and-out materialist position.

Nevertheless, the "cultural core" idea can be interpreted as "cultural materialism," to use Marvin Harris' term for it (the Harris version will be discussed later). If Steward is interpreted as expounding a materialist doctrine, one would have to say that in the last analysis Steward felt that humans can do only what their essential or life-sustaining resources permit them to do. This is, of course, true but the fallacy in materialism is that it is a truism, and it does not have the capacity to explain cultural phenomena that are produced without regard for life-sustaining resources or are produced unexpectedly on the basis of a new way of using old resources. If the constraint idea is examined carefully, the problem is not that there are constraints, but rather how much flexibility exists in any cultural process before the material constraint begins to operate. Steward was cautious on the materialism issue precisely because of this large zone of unpredictability; Harris was not.

More important than the materialism issue, in my opinion, is Steward's effort to find causes for cultural phenomena in some realm outside of culture itself. In an interesting brief paper on the Nuer and Dinka, Peter Newcomer (1972) shows how the subsistence systems—"cultural cores"—of these groups are interchangeable, and how Dinka and Nuer populations have become interdependent through a process of Nuer raiding Dinka and incorporating them in Nuer population, which means that at some point one cannot really distinguish between the two groups. Since one group was farmers and the other pastoralists, originally in differing environmental sectors, this means also that their subsistence systems are really distinct, but complementary. Newcomer aims his paper directly at the causation issue:

> ...I do not make use of "the environment" in any explanatory sense. It makes little sense to posit that the locus of social change lies outside of the system one is studying. Anthropological insistence on doing so produces the "receding causation" so common in its literature; i.e., social systems are dependent variables in a larger system which included climate, technology, available resources, etc. (p. 5)

This is an aggressive sociological countermove to the ecological-causation thesis; while it makes an important point, it goes too far in the other direction. That is, to locate *all* social causation in social systems is to fall into the anthropocentric trap—the cultural determinism error. The point is that in a multipotential species like Homo sapiens, causes will be found in a variety of phenomena in any human situation, or some situations will feature one major source of influence, others—a different one. Causation cannot be established by theory, only by empirical investigation. We can defend Steward in proposing an element of technoeconomic-ecological causation because it exists; we can criticize him for being something less than sophisticated about the multiple causation always present in human affairs and the shifts from one cause to another as systems change.

The methodological program advocated by Steward for cultural ecology was in line with the standard approach of all field cultural anthropology of the period: studies of particular communities, done in depth—at least as far as their cultural ecology was concerned. Three steps were proposed: the first involved an inquiry into the relationships between the productive system and the physical environment—what resources were selected and what technology was brought to bear upon them. The second consisted of a study of how the productive system and technology affected the "behavior patterns" in the core area—e.g., how particular methods of farming or hunting required particular forms of cooperation. The third step involved the extent to which these core behavior patterns "affect other aspects of culture"—the causal inquiry and capstone of cultural ecology. Steward saw it as requiring a "genuinely holistic approach" (1955C, p. 42).

Such studies of particular groups, selected with reference to known variants in subsistence systems, would then presumably yield a series of types of cultures with respect to their ecological relations: how different ways of exploiting the environment, or different types of cultural cores, created similar or differing institutions. The objective thus led straight into his "multilinear evolution" approach, likewise a typological enterprise. In a collaborative paper with Robert Murphy (1956), he explored the similar consequences to very widely separated simple cultures—the Mundurucu of Brazil and the Montagnais Algonkin Indians of Canada— of a technically similar adaptation: the collection of wild produce (rubber tree tapping for the Brazilian group, and fur trapping for the Indians). In both cases, this marginal extractive economy subjected them to similar forms of exploitation by and dependence on the majority cultures, leading to a breakup of the traditional culture and social system, culminating in an atomistic social order in which the individual families are dependent on the traders who buy their raw materials. The "core" adaptations in this case were seen by Murphy and Steward as causal, and the objective here, as in so much of Steward's work, is to explicate cultural process rather than to do ecology *per se*. The result is another "type": the resource-extractive marginals, lacking a cash surplus. (The theme has been recently picked up by Richard Gould and D. and C. Fowler [1972], who portray "parallel failures" of two enclaved tribal groups in "economic acculturation" due to their lack of integration in the market economy. See, also, Bennett 1969, Chapter 5, on a similar Amerind group).

Steward's most ambitious program of field research took place in the 1950s in Puerto Rico, where a team of students under his direction studied a series of communities, each with a differing dominant economic occupation. The resulting work (Steward, 1955E; 1956) was something of a letdown: the separate studies, although well-done did not complement each other with notable success, and since all the communities were contemporaneous segments of larger complex society, it was difficult to demonstrate causal influences emanating from the occupational core. The complex texture of micro-macro relationships obscured clear-cut differences, but even here Steward had something of an answer: his theory of "levels of integration" (Steward, 1955D), which proposed that communities existing within a national society would display differing strata of cultural traits, depending upon the varying relationships with external cultural and economic systems.

All of these themes continued to echo through Steward's work in the late 1950s and '60s. However, his interests kept returning to multilinear evolution. He showed that cultural evolution, in contrast to the 19th-century notion of fixed stages through which all societies must pass, took place along a variety—but possibly limited number—of pathways, depending upon particular constellations of technological, social, and environmental factors. For example, the "irrigation civilization" type (described in Chapter 5) implied that wherever a large society came to depend on irrigation, certain parallel features in the sociopolitical systems would emerge.

Steward's somewhat deterministic and certainly typological approach to the ecological problem is not wrong, since human activism does create a man- or culture-centered context of relations with Nature. But to focus on this to the exclusion of other things tends to avoid the question of the human impact on Nature, and to neglect the "ecology" of men's dealings with each other: the manipulation of the *social* environment and the effect of this on natural resources. For questions of long-range historical trends, an approach of this type has the merit of eliminating distracting detail, but for contemporary issues and for questions involving policy, we believe that its value is limited.

While it may be too early to make a definitive assessment of Steward's work, it can be concluded tentatively that Steward's most cogent concern was not with cultural ecology in the analytic and processual sense, but rather with the question of regularities and evolution in culture. Most certainly he never saw cultural ecology as a problem of choice or decision making in the context of social action. Although he had a concept of the production process, he lacked a clear concept of the distinction, and similarities, between natural and social resources. He tended to think of adaptive states as cultural types,[2] but in only a few cases did he show how such types emerge or the degree of flexibility they might possess under varying environmental conditions. Steward's approach, while halfway into a more dynamic solution to the culture-environment problem, ended up as relatively static and in part deterministic. Still, the isolation of a material causal mechanism, however vaguely conceived, was a considerable advance on the Kroeber position.

SOME OTHER APPROACHES

In 1942, while Steward was working on cultural ecology, Eliot Chapple and Carleton Coon produced a textbook treatment of the environmental issue in anthropology which, while adhering to some of the elementary principles of possibilism, took a quite different tack (Chapple and Coon, 1942, Part II). Building on a detailed description of natural environments based on the writings of the geographer Preston James (like Kroeber—going to the experts for information), Chapple and Coon described the various "technological adaptations" made by men to these environments, and then proceeded to describe the energy resources provided by these adaptations. The classification is the familiar typology beginning with hunting-gathering and proceeding through husbandry, but the treatment goes beyond the previous discussions by showing how these adaptations both facilitate and limit human actions: a clear precursor of the Stewardian concept of a "cultural core," but in simple empirical rather than theoretical terms (and thus not inclined to attract much attention).

But Chapple and Coon went beyond this to another theme: the way in which human interaction can configurate around technological objects and processes and thereby incorporate these into social institutions and action patterns. For example, the book (1942, pp. 184–186) contains what may be the first description in anthropological literature of how irrigation produces cooperative social forms; or how a technological process, such as weaving or potting, determines the amount of skill required and the amount of interaction among the operators (1942, pp. 138–140, summary).

Throughout this discussion Chapple and Coon did not find it necessary to deal with the rhetorical apparatus of the culture concept: they pitched their analysis on the level of action and goals, implying (at least to this writer) a notion of adaptive behavior and the development of social systems devoted to the maintenance of the action and goals:

> Each technique can be divided into four component elements: (1) the implements used, (2) the forces employed, (3) the actions involved, and (4) the amount and variety of interaction needed for its completion. This division will serve as convenient means of measuring the relative complexity of techniques, and will also furnish a background for the study of the development of institutions. (1942, p. 141)

If the Chapple-Coon approach had been taken seriously, or had been fused with the Stewardian, a rather different brand of cultural ecology might have emerged—one less devoted to the description of culture cases and types, and more to cross-cultural problems of resource use, technology, and adaptive behavior. Chapple and Coon appear to have seen the problem as not one of particular cultural styles but rather as the process of adaptive solutions to common and differing problems of fulfilling human objectives in the same and different environments. But the mainstream of cultural anthropology remained in the Boasian groove of whole-culture fieldwork and the descriptive portraits that emerged from it.

Of similar import—that is, an alternative to the culture-environment analytic style of the American anthropological tradition—is Audrey Richards' classic work, *Land, Labor, and Diet in Northern Rhodesia* (1939), one of those much-admired and often-cited works that failed to start a trend. Its major consequence in American anthropology was a series of applied anthropological studies of "food habits" in the early 1940s, stimulated by M. L. Wilson of the U.S. Department of Agriculture and quickly picked up by Margaret Mead in the National Academy of Sciences, which appointed her chairman of a Food Habits Committee oriented toward wartime studies of diet.[3] Richards' book, and her earlier (1932) and briefer doctoral study on the same topic, were taken as the pioneer studies in this field, but their broader economic and ecological significance was not understood. In fact, it was not until Max Gluckman's review essay of the Bemba book was published in 1945 that the implications of Richards' work began to be appreciated.

The book was, in the first place, the pioneer contribution to the scientific study of swidden agriculture, discussed elsewhere in the present volume. The Bemba, Richards' tribal group, practiced a form of shifting cultivation in forests, involving partial pruning of trees. Up to the time, this type of agriculture was believed to be wasteful and substandard. Richards, and other specialists of the Rhodes-Livingstone Institute working in Central and East Africa, were impressed with the careful planning and efficient procedures of *citimene* agriculture and felt that it probably provided the best food supply at the least cost to Nature—in fact Gluckman remarks in his 1945 paper (p. 75), "We are becoming accustomed to the experts' warnings against carefree interference in the ecological balance"—and continues with his appreciation of the value of Richards' demonstration of the intricacy and socioreligious reinforcements of the Bemba system. Comparable cultural-ecological studies by American anthropologists did not appear until the 1960s.

But of equal significance is Richards' detailed portrayal of the way a tribal subsistence system and use of resources were organized by the social system. This typically British preoccupation with the sociological dimension had little appeal to American anthropologists concerned with culture patterns and unconcerned with econological matters. Richards demonstrated how the subsistence system was shaped by the social organization and basic beliefs—a demonstration that almost exactly reverses the Stewardian conception of core and yet makes as much sense out of the problem. Although Richards did not regard her study as cultural ecology (because the term was not yet invented), she nevertheless traveled over paths since made very familiar by students of tribal agriculture who use modified Stewardian approaches. Many of the later monographic studies of agroecology followed her lead insofar as they focused on particular tribal systems as comprehensive socioecological wholes.

MONOGRAPHIC CULTURAL ECOLOGY

Thus, there evolved in the 1950s, stimulated by Steward's program, a particular format of cultural-ecological research: the case study of a discrete human settlement at a particular time. The findings of studies of this type are generalizable mainly to other communities in the same class, and it is this pattern of work that gives rise to the separate bodies of cultural-ecological information on such entities as swidden agricultural-ists, pastoralists, rice-growers, and the like. The subsistence economy and technology is the "core"; consequently, it becomes the criterion for selection of the case.

Although Robert Redfield was by no stretch of the label an ecologist, or even a cultural ecologist, one of the earliest and best protocols for the single-community, monographic culture-ecology style is his chapter, "The Little Community: An Ecological System," in his 1955 book on the anthropological tribal or community study approach. Redfield made an important distinction in this chapter between an "intuited whole" and a "system," and it is not too far from the truth to trace the history of cultural anthropological studies over the past 50 years as moving from the study of "wholes" to the study of "systems." Redfield stated that the anthropologist first intuits the whole; then, as he begins to understand the parts and their interrelationships, he constructs a system. The ecology of a small community is, in Redfield's view, such a system—"The ecological system is larger than the productive system and has a different organizing principle, man-nature rather than productivity" (1955, p. 27).

Redfield started his own village research in Yucatan by observing Indians plant and harvest corn in their particular version of swiddening, or shifting cultivation. He observed the actual digging operations for planting, the ceremonials, the felling and burning of the trees in preparing new or resumed *milpa* plots, the harvesting, and other activities. He noted how these were linked to one another and how the sequences varied, or remained the same, from year to year. His observations moved far beyond the original simple description to take into account strategies for different types of fields, differing intervals between planting and fallow, and the connections to marketing and family subsistence needs and activities. Finally he observed (though never intensively studied) specific environmental features: the nature of the soil, topography, the variability of rainfall, and how the *milpa* cultivator reacted to all of these. In his mind a figure began to take form: the system of maize cultivation is like a wheel: the corn is in the center and "the mind goes out from maize to agriculture, from maize to social life, from maize to religion" (1955, p. 22).

But there were other images: a map of the bush, the *cenote* or well, and the cultivated *milpa* tracts. In this two-dimensional grid would be placed the activities of the people: village life, farming, walking to and fro, gathering water. And then, finally, he moved toward another kind of system: one that is focused by an "organizing principle"—in this case the Maya concept of beneficiary of the gods: whatever man is able to obtain from the physical environment by his own efforts is a loan from on high, and he returns some of it as an offering by way of thanks. This principle governs the activities of the *milpa* cultivator and also most social activities—it is using subsistence as a "core," but, in contrast to Steward (who defined the core as technology and economics), Redfield specifically distinguished (as we noted previously) between the production system and the ecological—for him, agriculture is a cultural or ethos-type system of activities controlled by a picture in the head.*

More specifically, he distinguished between the *subsistence system*, or the tools and actions by which people gain their livelihood; *maize agriculture*, which in Maya culture includes religion; and *livestock pro-duction* (cattle, fowl), which is carried on purely for commercial gain. Finally, there is the *ecological system*, which is the man-nature nexus, guided by ethos, and a view of the gods as nature. In this system he seems to hew close to the ethnological line: he feels that only in "primitive communities" does one have true ecological systems including man, since

*This idealized portrait of the world view of a Maya peasant man in Chapter 5 of Redfield's *Folk Culture of Yucatan* (1941) is one of the most coherent descriptions of the integrated belief and activity systems of a society in equilibrium with Nature ever written. It is also a portrait of the zero-sum game: the Maya produce only what Nature, the gods, and the social system permit.

only in these communities is man truly dependent on natural resources. He notes that contemporary agrarian communities, such as "James West's" (Carl Withers') Plainville (1945), are only partly dependent on their immediate surroundings, since they obtain much of what they need in order to exist from the outside. Both good points.

This is a protocol all right, but it is a protocol for cultural ecology from the viewpoint of a thoroughgoing culturalist. Redfield was interested in the little community, and ecology is one facet—one system—of such a community. And, in the last analysis, he turns from ecology as such, and its highly technical natural history and science, to a structuralist conception in which man's mind becomes the starting point. With this we can only agree, but we would substitute "behavior" for mind or images, and "purpose" or "rationale" for ritual and symbolism. For Redfield, ecology is a tool for understanding the community; for us, the community is one form of human ecology.

It is possible, perhaps, to describe Steward's approach as somewhere between these contrasting objectives. Steward was certainly interested in culture, or the community; it was, after all, his basic unit of analysis. But he was also concerned, and specifically so, with human-Nature relationships. His qualified materialism as expressed in the "core" concept certainly underlines this interest, and the work of his students and others in the tradition he incepted has moved even more firmly in this direction— toward a kind of "agricultural anthropology" in which, as we shall see later, there is considerable agronomic expertise and emphasis.

But the basic method—the monographic community style—has certain inescapable limitations from the standpoint of a comprehensive ecological approach to culture. One of these has already been mentioned: the difficulty of formulating problems that involve processes or regularities independent of these particular technoeconomic styles, and that link societies with very different technoeconomic "cores." Another concerns the deterministic implications of the whole concept of "core." As Clifford Geertz pointed out (1963, pp. 10–11), the core concept proposes on theoretical grounds that the human activities involved with making a living and converting natural resources determine other activities and ideas. While there is some truth in this, its general pervasiveness has to be questioned. For example, in a paper on Bedawin ecology and social organization, Louise Sweet (1965) proposed that the basic unit of the social organization, the "minimal camping unit," is defined by the use of the camel, whose pastures must be sought in an arid region, requiring a small, mobile social unit. If this is the case, then it is true that the

technoeconomic sphere (camel technology, etc.) determines social organization. But Sweet also shows that this relationship is most true under
conditions of sparse pasturage where the necessary mobility requires
small groups to move their camels around, and least true in regions, or in
climatic episodes, where more luxuriant pasturage would permit larger
numbers, or many tribal groups, to associate together (1965, pp. 142–143).
In other words, the "core" prevails in some circumstances but not in
others. Where alternatives and opportunities are more abundant, the
social system can generate its own objectives, and in such cases its
interests are prior to the technoeconomic sphere. In any society, the
changing conditions of the environment in time and space, and the
changing adaptive strategies and objectives of the human groups, result in
temporal shifts in the hierarchy of cause and effect. This does not mean
that the overall or average effects cannot be stronger in one causal sector
than in another—it is possible that this is the case. But this statistical
tendency does not help us solve particular problems in particular times
and places.

In the preceding paragraph I have used the language of second-order
abstractions. This language requires the speaker to find causes and effects
in entities, many of which are really constructions of the observer. From
the standpoint of the actors in the systems of behavior, the issue is simply
one of making decisions on particular courses of action on the basis of
differing criteria. The question of whether "social organization" is
controlled by, or controls, technoeconomics is empirically a matter of
whether people making decisions about the size of their groups and the
length of time they stay in one place can make this decision without
considering the needs of their camels for pasturage. The difference
between the typological and the adaptive approaches to cultural ecology
is the difference between an approach that relies on second-order
abstractions and statistical tendencies and one that is concerned with
decision-making in particular situations and the consequences of such
decisions.

One of the best expressions of the monographic style is Robert
Netting's study of the Kofyar, a group of intensive field-crop agriculturalists in a Nigerian plateau region (1968). Netting provides an introduction
in which he outlines Steward's theoretical scheme, modifying and sharpening it in several useful respects. In particular, he specifies that the
vague Steward category of "social institutions" needs to be more
carefully defined: he wishes to establish a "priority" among these,
focusing particularly on those that have an intimate relationship to the

environment-technology system. He calls these by the useful term, *social instrumentalities*—which is similar to the interpretation given the social component in our Fig. 1. He emphasizes that Steward focuses on those features of the environment that humans pay attention to, cope with, and he extends this idea somewhat further by finding in it a definition of cultural ecology: the "cultural" side of the field should be restricted "to those factors which bear directly on the maintenance of life" (1968, p. 15). Steward made the same point (e.g., 1955C, p. 37), but in practice his approach seemed to drift toward the holistic community study. Netting achieves a sharp definition—he notes that the Kofyar study is not a total ethnography but a specialized examination of life-maintenance activities. This has its advantages and disadvantages: it provides more sharply focused analyses of technology-environment relations, but it even more drastically restricts the generalizing power of the analysis.

Netting does not depart from the Stewardian level of second-order abstractions: "The crucial terms of the ecological equation appear to be environment, exploitative techniques, and the cultural core" (1968, p. 14). That is, the "crucial terms" are entities, not processes; categories into which to sort data, not human actions and consequences. However, it is a mark of the thoroughness of Netting's research that he is able to produce a mix of descriptive generalizations and some processual ones:

> The prevailing dispersed settlement of the Kofyar, with households occupying discrete clusters of huts in the middle of homestead fields, is an efficient device for maintaining intensive agriculture. (1968, p. 227)

> Land rights are concentrated in the individual who by an investment of labor first builds up the permanent productivity of the soil and grows economic trees. Since homestead land remains an economic asset indefinitely it cannot be assigned on a usufruct basis as is commonly done under systems of shifting cultivation. (1968, p. 229)

> In the intensive farming of homestead plots, production is directly related to land area but is not affected by higher labor input. Thus a small resident group provides sufficient labor, and the nuclear family proves adaptive. (1968, p. 227)

> The direct production of their own food by small, independent households leads the Kofyar to internalize conscientious work and careful husbandry as personal values. (1968, p. 229)

That is, at the tribal-peasant level, intensive agriculture differs from shifting cultivation (swidden) by its greater stability and its value system related to the investment in land. Hardly surprising, but the anthropologist studies the societies nobody knows. This parade of descriptive ecological studies (with their limited and sometimes obvious conclusions) perhaps represents a first phase of the effort, and, in the future, we should expect a turn toward work on a wider, cross-cultural canvas.

CULTURAL ECOLOGY AND PREHISTORY

In some respects, the Steward-inspired approach, in its use of second-order concepts like settlement pattern, or technoeconomic core, seems more suitable for prehistorians, who work only with material remains and therefore must infer choice and decision-making behaviors. Fredrik Barth, in a 1950 article, encouraged archeology to move toward ecological studies, since he felt that the time-depth available in the field made possible long-term reconstruction of adaptive systems. He perceived the task in terms of his "niche" concept: treating the archeological culture as a natural organism utilizing a particular set of resources. In the absence of dynamic behavioral data, such concepts seem appropriate, and may even have the advantage of filtering out the distracting minutiae which often obscure adaptive systems in ethnologically-based studies of cultural ecology.

In a recent monograph on the "environmental archeology" of a portion of the Labrador coast, William Fitzhugh (1972) follows a pattern of analysis that has become standard for prehistorians working especially with small sites at low levels of technical development. The conceptual approach is defined by Fitzhugh as follows:

> One of the fundamental assumptions in relating man to his environment is that man is part of an ecosystem, that he cannot live without it, and that he is limited by the environment or by the extent of his ability to alter it. A second assumption is that culture can be analyzed as a superorganic system and that it is man's chief means of survival, resulting in successful adaptations in almost every conceivable portion of the globe. Culture is, therefore, an adaptive system which articulates with the environment through a complex set of patterned relationships. Following Struever (1968, p. 136), this occurs within two environmental milieus, one of which is biophysical, the other social. Anthropological investigation of culture must therefore concern itself with both aspects of the environment.
>
> For archeologists, the bulk of evidence from prehistoric societies concerns the biophysical realm. The most accessible and direct relationship between a culture and its environment is expressed in its technological and economic adaptations, and those cultural forms most closely related with these pursuits. The primary level is clearly portrayed in a culture's *subsistence-settlement system* (Struever, 1968, p. 135). The core of this system consists of a set of techniques used to extract biological energy from the environment, combined with a settlement system adapted to maximize the harvest of this energy as it shifts seasonally or geographically within the environment.... (Fitzhugh, 1972, p. 7)

This passage neatly synthesizes the progression from possibilism through Leslie White's culturology to Stewardian cultural ecology and finally to "ecosystem." It acknowledges the limitations of archeological data, which lacks information on the social environment (although some archeologists would dispute this, believing that social interpolations can be made from material remains). It makes the "subsistence-settlement system" the key concept, and as Fitzhugh notes later in the passage, the activities carried out in this system "often result in the deposition of physical residues patterned such that similar activities produce a similar structure of material remains"—which is simply what the archeologist digs up.[4]

The basic unit of the old archeology was a *site*—which was assumed to be equivalent to a complete settlement or community or even a "culture." For Fitzhugh, a "site" is merely a place from which one collects data on various vectors and transects of human existence. These involve some distinctions not made by the older generation of culture-complex archeologists; above all, the distinction between modes of subsistence-settlement of the same people (littoral, inland, etc.) and cultural styles:

> Archeological study of material culture is not sufficient to recognize these major changes in adaptation. ... The major point is that subsistence-settlement systems are adaptive and are tuned to specific environmental and cultural conditions. It is therefore improper to generalize these regionally relevant patterns to other regions even when there is otherwise complete cultural continuity. (Fitzhugh, 1972, p. 167)

In other words, "cultures" are not the same as adaptations, and in the recognition of this point, Fitzhugh and other archeologists working in this field take a step beyond some ethnological cultural ecologists who have tended to equate culture (or at least community) with adaptive mode.

Similarly, Fitzhugh recognizes that the subsistence-settlement system is a dynamic entity, even within the short span of one year: "The annual cycle of a society results in a series of different settlement types . . . . the spacial distribution of these sites is the settlement pattern . . ." (1972, pp. 7–8). This acknowledges the dynamic nature of human coping behavior: people exploit what they can in order to survive or to progress, and no human group at simple levels of technology will starve to death because summer droughts or winter cold removes the available foodstuffs.

But because Fitzhugh is operating in an archeological context, he typologizes rather than dynamicizes (apologies for the neologism). That is, he is interested in arriving at a classification of adaptive solutions, not an analysis of how adaptive solutions are arrived at, or how they may change under the impact of various endogenous and exogenous factors. Indeed, he concludes with a modified environmental determinism: ". . . these cultures appear to have behaved in a totally predictable fashion, the influence of the environment having been so strong as to almost override cultural considerations" (1972, p. 187). ("Cultures" here refers to a couple of specific ones—not all of them; and Fitzhugh recognizes, of course, that such environmental control is an empirical variable.)

In other words, lacking behavioral data, the orientation is toward history and typology, not behavioral problem-solution. Fitzhugh did make ethnographic surveys of the contemporary inhabitants of the region, which include European-derived groups as well as Indian and Eskimo, but these data do not seem to play a major role in the monograph in question. Perhaps they may in some future publication. But the issue is clear: the prehistorian can utilize the classic Stewardian or cultural-ecology framework because it is fundamentally typological—or fundamentally static, despite recognition of dynamic features in human adaptation. It is committed to a battery of second-order concepts that inevitably push the analysis in a typological and nonbehavioral direction. This is, of course entirely appropriate for archeology, since it must work largely without behavioral data—or, more precisely, without data that documents in detail how and why particular solutions to adaptive problems were worked out. It is a scheme that is also reasonably suited to tribal societies, with their simple technology and consequent tendency to stick with one adaptive mode for relatively long periods if it has proven useful. But concepts based on such an approach are simply inappropriate for the analysis of contemporary peoples faced with the need to adjust to constantly shifting parameters of both the social and physical environments over which they may have no real control.

The approach represented by the Fitzhugh monograph may be compared with still another, concerned with needs for causal explanation in archeology, the theoretical and methodological basis for which is presented in a general work by Patty J. Watson, Steven LeBlanc, and Charles Redman (1971). Systems theory lies at the basis of this approach (see their Chapter 3), and their exposition of systems theory in the archeological context is influenced by Kent Flannery's attempt to apply—or really to advocate the application of—systems theory to the development of culture in Mesoamerica (Flannery, 1968). Flannery was preoccupied in his paper with what he calls "procurement systems," or subsistence-settlement systems with a fancier name and with an ecosystemic nuance; or, in our terms, a socionatural system composed of humans interacting with specific environmental features. Each major foodstuff would then be acquired through a particular procurement system, or some combination. (This also may be "niche" again, although it has lost its biological label and acquired a special term designating the human capacity for more organized and efficient effort.) By analyzing the components of any procurement system, Flannery hopes to reconstruct the specific pattern of events leading to its development. For example, if in the collection of wild seeds it was found that some of the grasses produced more abundant (or more easily collected) seeds than others, the human collectors would then focus on that variety, making them more dependent on this particular plant. Ultimately, the collecting habit would encourage further changes in that type of plant, leading to domestication. The theory is familiar, but Flannery's language is new: he speaks of "deviation-amplifying" acts, such as the increasing choice of particular varieties of foodstuffs, mentioned above. The procurement system is thus a typical human purposeful system with constant change and adaptation.

POPULATION, RESOURCES, AND ENVIRONMENT

In Chapter 5, on the ecological transition, we discussed the development of agriculture in the Middle East from increasingly specialized methods of food collection. The unfolding evidence has done much to put the issue on a much more sophisticated footing than earlier archeological studies, which merely sought the point of origin. The problem is now cast in Malthusian terms: the precise relationships between population, resources, agriculture, and settlement patterns, and how generalizations about these relationships can be contributed by archeological research. With a more detailed knowledge of particular phases or types of settlement and use of plant and animal species, it is possible to develop hypotheses about the resource-population ratio in particular cases.

A stimulating theoretical contribution to this problem, currently much used by cultural ecologists interested in tropical agriculture, comes from the economist Ester Boserup, who proposes that agricultural development, or what she calls "intensification" (increased productivity from the same resources), is responsible for increasing population density (1965). She also proposes that the process includes a decline of man-productivity in labor, since the increased labor force divides the available tasks among its members, leading to less work per man. This describes, on the whole, the typical labor-intensive Orient, and one question is whether it describes other parts of the world. In anthropological ranks, Dumond (1965) echoes the Boserup thesis: "population growth has been the chief spur to the improvement of subsistence techniques" (p. 312). Philip Smith and Cuyler Young (1972) have tested the Boserup model on prehistoric Mesopotamian data with mixed results, although her ideas have certainly stimulated a new interest in demographic interpolations of archeological materials.

Actually Boserup's presentation goes beyond the simple correlation between population and intensification. She is responding to the classic Malthusian argument that population presses against food supply; indeed, she stands this argument on its head, proposing that population growth is the *cause* of agricultural improvement: a sort of Toynbeean "challenge and response" theory (and thus, she would hold, the population increases of the contemporary period are due mainly to improvements in welfare and medical care, and not to increases in food production).

Boserup uses a modification of a well-known classification of tropical cultivation regimes. The following is a condensed and supplemented version of her scheme:

Increasing Population

1. *Forest-fallow cultivation* (i.e., swidden, or slash-and burn). This involves the clearing of plots which are cropped for short periods—a year or two—then allowed to go back to bush, in order to recover soil fertility, a period lasting from 6 to 20 years.
2. *Bush-fallow cultivation.* Similar to (1), but with shorter intervals between cropping episodes—6 to 7 years—and with generally longer cropping episodes. (Anthropologists usually combine (1) and (2) and call them "shifting cultivation.")
3. *Short-fallow cultivation.* Very short fallow periods—about 1 year—so that only grasses have time to grow back. Has also been called "grass-fallow" cultivation.
4. *Annual cropping.* Cropping periods of a few months, usually with annual rotations.
5. *Multicropping.* Two or more successive crops produced annually. Fallowing absent or very short or occasional.

Simple tools, e.g., digging stick

to

Sophisticated tools: plows, horse or tractor

She proposes that movement from her first type, the most sketchy kind of agriculture, through the thoroughly sedentary type-five, is controlled by population pressure. Therefore, a prehistorian or ethnohistorian, armed with data on actual sequences of agricultural development in a given region and with actual data on or plausible reconstructions of population magnitudes at key points in the development sequence, might be able to test her theories or, what is more likely, find an intriguing scheme for ordering his own data.

Another reason for anthropological interest in Boserup's theory is that certain features accord well with studies of tribal and peasant agriculture made by anthropologists in recent years. Simple swiddening has been shown to provide good yields with minimal labor input (Conklin, 1954; Drucker and Heizer, 1960; Dumond, 1961), since fire handles much of the labor and there is no need for plowing or intensive cultivation. The latter techniques, on the other hand, require considerable labor, and the output per-man is likely to fall (see Geertz' case of "agricultural involution" in Indonesia). Moreover, when transition from simpler to more intensive practices takes place, this is done with the same crops rather than shifting to higher yield varieties, as a number of studies have shown (e.g., Richards, 1939, for the Bemba). By simply adding more labor units, they maintain the same schedule of work-leisure activities, which is a case of the "least effort" principle in operation.

However, a reading of the entire set of studies using Boserup's classification and theory as a guide to interpretation does not yield a consistent picture. Some studies seem to show that the productivity losses that may be associated with intensification can be accompanied by changes in social structure that are considered to be a gain. Netting's Kofyar study shows that with the transition to intensification, intra-familial tension was lessened due to an expansion in the cultivated acreage that permitted sons to develop their own enterprises, thus eliminating conflict with the father. David Harris (1969) concurs with Boserup on the proposition that while in swidden (shifting) agriculture the amount of land per person is large, the productivity per unit of labor is high. However, Harris also concludes that the demographic potential (and the degree of mobility or sedentariness) of swiddening peoples is a variable related to the specific nature of the crops, not to the cultivation technique. Swiddeners with *seed* crops have low populations and unstable settlements; *root* crops produce stable settlement and a potential for increase. Eric Waddell (1972) in his study of a highland New Guinea group, was unable to find that "extensive systems are inherently more productive than intensive ones" (p. 218). He notes that Boserup failed to include physical environmental factors that will modify productivity independently of the agricultural techniques. Bennet Bronson (1972) criticizes Boserup's typology, emphasizing that the association of particular population magnitudes with agricultural techniques is not borne out by research, and that population density responds to many factors, not merely the agricultural or technological. There is more than a suggestion in this literature that anthropologists have used Boserup's typology and ideas too literally. It is a broad-ranging, heuristic conception, definitely biased toward technological determinism; it is no substitute for the precise studies that need to be made in order to assess impact and causal relationships.

HARRIS' "CULTURAL MATERIALISM"

I stated earlier that there are two sides to Steward's work: the intimate studies of cultural ecology of particular communities, in which the technoeconomic core becomes the criterion of selection, and the other, the evolutionary interpretations of cultural growth, with their deterministic, grand-theoretical overtones. While the "agricultural anthropologists" like Netting pursue their detailed empirical studies, theorists like Marvin Harris have pushed forward into the other realm. In particular, Harris—in a massive book (1968) that is basically a history of ethnological theory, designed to replace the old volume by Robert Lowie (1937)—proposed a revived version of economic determinism from which to review and evaluate ethnological theory. He calls it, variously, "techno-environmental determinism," "techno-economic determinism," or "cultural materialism," and he defines it as follows:

> similar technologies applied to similar environments produce similar arrangements of labor in production and distribution, and that these in turn call forth similar kinds of social groupings, which justify and coordinate their activities by means of similar systems of values and beliefs. Translated into research strategy, the principle of techno-environmental, techno-economic determinism assigns priority to the study of the material conditions of sociocultural life, much as the principle of natural selection assigns priority to the study of differential reproductive success. (1968, p. 4)

The formula appears to describe Netting's study of the Kofyar, and the conclusions quoted from Netting's study nicely illustrate Harris' "similar . . . similar . . . similar" rhetoric. The problem, of course, is to define that "similar." In the Steward approach, this is equivalent to particular occupations, or in the tribal-peasant sphere, subsistence economies. Just how similar must things be to each other? Which factors are marginal, which are critical? In the context of intensive agricultural communities, the critical factor may be a single one: settled land tenure—the whole apparatus of "techno-economic determinism" in this case boils down to the question of whether one stays in one spot and owns land, or not. I am suggesting that there may be a grandiloquency about Harris' doctrine that leads us straight into some obvious truisms—but of course not entirely, by any means.

In his defense, it should be pointed out that Harris is operating at a very high level of generality: he calls his approach "nomothetic," as contrasted to "ideographic," which means that it aims at broad generalities, not description of particular cases. At this very high level of generality, as it did for my typological exercise in Chapter 5, his brand of determinism makes considerable sense—that is, if it is applied to large sociocultural entities, viewed over relatively long periods of time, one does indeed find that the technical and economic arrangements tell you almost everything you want to know about survival or decline (always excepting, of course, important failures of nerve, consensus, religious revivals, and the like, which spoil the materialist record). Considering this ecologically, while it is true that human societies can despoil their environments for considerable periods, eventually they must come to terms with resources and work out some sort of sustained-yield system—that is, the technoenvironmental rules have to be obeyed.[5] It is this type of long-run truth that characterizes the universal-historical theorems, such as Wittfogel's "hydraulic societies," and the rhetoric of these arguments always includes terms such as "tend," "similar," and "relatively."

However, Harris' determinism is not adequate for the solution of problems concerning man-environment relationships in particular societies over short time periods. While Netting's work seems to echo Harris' recipe, in actuality Netting introduces many considerations that probably would not interest Harris: details of ritual, degrees of correlation or relationship between technology or land tenure and particular social forms—all of which add up not to a case of determinism by the technological-environmental complex, but simply to the relationships that do exist between *some* features of technology and economy and *some* features of social organization and value. The issue is not whether determinism exists, but precisely how much and in what institutions. The question is empirical—not theoretical. Netting deliberately delimits the scope of his investigation; and Steward, likewise, qualified his feedback arguments by acknowledging spheres of culture and social life that were free of "core" influence.

The response of a particular farming population to a particular environmental configuration is compounded of technoeconomic factors, resource parameters, innovations contributed by external sources, cultural styles of management, consumption preferences, rituals, food tastes, transportation facilities, and settlement patterns. All or any of these factors can cause variation in the responses made by people to "similar environments" with "similar technologies." Cultural ecology must struggle with the complexities of the issue, including many nontechnological and noneconomic factors, in order to get a simple description of the situation, or to acquire knowledge for practical recommendations concerning change and adaptation. Scudder's findings about the Tonga's adaptive adjustments to the new environment after resettlement focuses on belief systems and rituals designed to alleviate anxiety—as well as on new subsistence techniques or resource uses.

While I am primarily concerned with the ecological implications of the Harris position, there are, as in most of the issues discussed in this book, ramifications extending far beyond this context. One problem in the Marxist intellectual tradition has been the unwillingness of many of its adherents to do empirical studies, particularly in microsituations. Marxist ideas thus have seemed to apply to certain levels of generality in society and not to others, an apparent paradox and one not easily resolved. There is reason to believe that the difficulty may lie in the interpretations made of Marx, and not in Marx' own views; the chief issue at stake is, of course, the exact meaning of a materialistic conception of the social process. This can be interpreted in deterministic terms, in which case one simply looks to economics and technology—material things—as the primary causes of events. On the other hand, as my colleague Edward Robbins points out, Marx also seems to have held that there is a human proclivity to reify material phenomena and treat them as if they were active agents in control of the situation. Money, for example, can be treated as an existing object in such a way as to be capable of injuring people when they lack it, much as they can be injured by a tree falling on them. When this sort of thing happens, social institutions have formed around material phenomena and these phenomena are accorded more respect than is given to men—or to Nature. This kind of interpretation of Marx leads straight toward empirical studies of cases of institutional hypostasization of material phenomena and away from determinism.

Determinism is precisely what is *not* needed in a socially relevant orientation to ecological problems. A human social system, or any homeostatic ecosystem, is not, *de facto*, a deterministic system: it is a series of accommodations among organisms and milieu factors—accommodations that change and require readaptation as factors in the system and its milieu alter. If policy relevance is the goal, we must be certain about cause and avoid overcommitment to particular causal factors. Steward had an answer to this, too: in his paper on "levels of integration" (1955D), he noted that any human society, and especially those in the modern integrated world, derive much of their continuity and their changes from factors originating outside and beyond the local scene—as well as from indigenous causes.

But the most serious charge one can level against Harris' argument is that by accepting determinism as a matter of assumption, he runs the risk of sanctioning any current ecological situation. And this is what he seems to have done in his paper on the sacred cattle of India (1966). Harris argued that these cattle, so often the target of planners and economic developers concerned over the animals' consumption of food in a country with recurrent food crises, are in fact part of the Indian ecosystem and provide important resources for agriculture. The argument has been criticized (Bennett, 1967D) for applying a theoretical approach derived from studying highly integrated microecosystems to a complex human macrocosm with many subsystems and exceptions to the rules. Moreover, Harris seems to say that because the sacred cattle do furnish dung and other products, they are a good thing—a position that ignores and explicitly derogates planning for a system that achieves the same ends with less cost to the human population by reducing the consumption of food by the animals. Harris' data concerning the cost-gain balances between the food consumption by the cattle and the contributions the animals make to the economy in other spheres have been challenged (Heston, 1971); a favorable review is provided by Odend'hal (1972).

However, Harris' declared objective was not really ecological. He was concerned about showing that the "sacred" cattle of India are maintained by the Indian people not for their sacred qualities, but because there is an understanding that they are important for the peasant economy, due to their contributions of hides, dung, etc. Harris seems to define religion as a matter of belief in the sacred. However, when Mrs. Ghandi attempted to implement legislation requiring the systematic slaughter and retirement of the cattle, more than 200,000 *sadhus* rioted for several days before government buildings in New Delhi, forcing withdrawal of the policy. Religion is more than belief; it is also a form of sociopolitical organization, and whatever else the cattle are, they are certainly a symbol of traditional culture to millions of Hindus.

Harris' sacred cattle paper is simultaneously a demonstration of the simplifications that lie at the end of the trail for one who overapplies cultural-materialistic arguments to complex human affairs, and also of the consequences of applying ecosystemic theory to human society without careful definitions. The seductiveness of this approach has tempted a great many anthropological ecologists and the results have not been altogether healthy for the state of the discipline.

EPILOGUE TO CHAPTER 7

In the early part of Chapter 6, I followed the conventional approach to the history of ecological studies in anthropology by tracing their origins in explicit concerns for human-Nature relationships. However, the development of a specialization in any academic discipline is a complex process, and there is usually much more than appears on the surface. In the case of ecology the links to other anthropological ideas are evident in the concept of culture—the single, bounded community as a setting for research; the notion of change as something that happens at intervals, rather than as part of the definition of human behavior itself; and the use of familiar institutional categories of description. These are all carryovers from standard anthropological research and are not inherently ecological. This has, of course, mixed consequences: on the positive side, it emphasizes the theme of the book—that ecology is contained within culture or human endeavor. On the negative, as Vayda and Rappaport have pointed out, it means that certain concepts of dubious theoretical or methodological significance for ecological analysis have been brought into the field.

A discussion of topics in cultural anthropology not usually designated as ecological, but which played a role in the development of the basic ideas behind the field, may be of interest.

1. *Ethnography of economic behavior.* Included in the vast ethnological compilation of ethnographic materials concerning tribal economic and subsistence systems are descriptions of the nature of property concepts and the control over natural resources, as these appear in tribal societies at various levels of complexity (e.g., Bunzel, 1938, pp. 346–350). While these materials were not explicitly pointed toward ecological questions, there is no doubt that economic data is vital for cultural ecology—"econology". If, as suggested in this book, tribal societies achieve a reasonable balance with Nature in part through the institution of collective ownership and/or use of the resources necessary for survival, then a review of these data in the accumulated ethnographic literature should be worth the effort. The issue is not the presence or absence of private property—but rather the nature and kind of property, including natural resources, that is retained as a collective good, and thereby managed by the group with a sense of responsibility. Similar comparative information also may exist with respect to the level of wants in tribal societies and how these may increase with increasing levels of technological exploitation of the environment.

2. *Acculturation research.* This product of the anthropology of the

1930s and '40s evolved without reference to ecology, but it deserves reassessment in the light of the emerging interests in the field. Acculturation research had some serious defects, centering chiefly on its tendency to use cultural concepts as explanatory devices, but it did succeed in focusing on the issue of compatibility of particular elements of culture in reality contexts where change and adjustment of these elements was required. One of the achievements of this work was to show how rapidly changes could take place under conditions of "culture contact" where the incentives to change reinforced particular interests in one or the other of the parties to the contact.[6] In some cases important ecological findings were made: the rapid shift of Canadian tribes into the fur trade economy, and the intensified bison-hunting of Plains tribes after acceptance of the horse and then again after contact with Whites and the emergence of military patterns, show how human-Nature relations even in tribal society can be altered in a very short time.[7]

Aside from the specific contributions to the study of ecological change, the acculturation research had a covert adaptive frame of reference. The central problem can be translated into the language of this book as a study of how humans confronted altered environments—physical and social, particularly the latter—and utilized adaptive strategies to cope with the new conditions. Hallowell (1945) came very close to the formulation in his classic paper on acculturation as a problem in *learning*: he observed that the stylized image of "cultures" meeting, conflicting, merging was no more than a figure of speech, and that the real process consisted of learning new behavioral routines and concepts. The missing element in this exposition was, of course, the purposive; Hallowell was unable to go beyond the abstract and objectivist posture of the time, that visualized humans as components of processes and not as active agents making decisions.

3. *Cultural patterns and technological change in the emerging countries.* This body of research by anthropologists was a by-product of the economic and technical aid programs of the 1950s, and its chief objective was to determine how tribal and peasant cultures could accommodate themselves to development programs. The chief defect of this effort was the uncritical acceptance of technological development and "modernization" as desirable outcomes for everyone—although anthropologists were also conscious of the need to help the native populations make the shift with the least amount of stress and disruption of existing patterns.[8] It is this latter theme that argues for a reassessment of this literature in the light of the needs for all populations to provide for their wants with less

deterioration of the environment. One of the chief findings of this research was related to the earlier acculturation work in that emphasis was laid on the compatibility issue: for example, the adoption by a peasant community of a new, sanitary domestic water supply was found to be dependent on the way the existing and the new water systems were related to social organization, social ritual, and value preferences regarding tastes, etc. This literature deserves a thorough review for the purpose of determining how men use resources and are willing to change these use-patterns (e.g., Bennett, 1974).

A recent study which seems to bring together the older interests in acculturation, tribal ethnology, and culture-and-personality, but in the frame of cultural ecology and multicultural comparison, is Robert Edgerton's book (1971) on his work with four East African groups studied in a general African cultural ecology research program directed by Walter Goldschmidt during the early 1960s. This book has rather little to say to the ecologists concerned with policy relevance, but it has much to say to the general cultural anthropologist searching for a more viable theoretical framework, and a way of avoiding the sterile traps of pure "functionalism" or "structuralism."

Edgerton shows that cultural ecology can be a frame, a viewpoint for the study of individual and cultural levels of behavior, in groups where the mode of subsistence is a critical variable in organizing the social system and determining cultural values—the classic Stewardian "culture core" concept. Each of his four tribal-peasant groups contains pastoralists and farmers, but the four do not have identical overall cultures—making it possible to hold the two subsistence-economy variables more or less constant and see how the four cultures vary because of and in spite of them. Another major variable is the posture of each group *vis-à-vis* European acculturation. By using various qualitative and quantifying instruments to obtain attitudes and emotional responses, it was possible to characterize cultural "response covariation" among these four groups in rather precise terms, and to locate the causal influence of ecological variables more carefully than has been done in most cultural ecological research. Among other things, he found that the pastoralists in each tribal group were more inclined to act out their conflicts and aggressions, and were more independent in spirit and act than the farmers. Farmers, on the other hand, were found to be more repressive of emotionality and showed more hostility in their interpersonal dealings, but they were less able than pastoralists to act on such feelings. Witchcraft was more prevalent among farmers. Reasons for these social-emotional profiles were located in the general ecological and technical-economic milieu of agriculture, and were importantly modified by acculturative processes.

The Edgerton book may point the way toward an intellectually conservative but nevertheless theoretically important and synthetic cultural anthropology in which the ecological and systems approaches constitute a central organizing framework.

4. *Local-national relationships.* Another important development in the anthropology of the 1950s and '60s concerned studies of the way local communities are related to the larger social, political, and economic institutions of the nation. This work emerged out of the studies of changing peasant communities and the new nations of former tribal groups, and was concerned with aspects of the breakdown of cultural isolation. In this sense, the theme involves a critique of the persisting tendency among anthropologists to frame their research in concepts based on the isolated cultural entity working out its balance with Nature on the basis of local resources alone. The research helped to broaden the concept of resources to include the services, goods, and assistance provided by the outside—as well as to point out how these same external factors provided limiting frames for local action.[9]

Such research could easily be extended into studies of the way particular local systems of resource use are influenced by the community's relationships with the outside. In the broader context, this involves the question of the degree of autonomy a community can manifest in its ecological actions, given the controls exercised by markets, tax laws, the demands of landlords, and the like. The level of generalization of many of the existing studies has been relatively low, being limited to portraits of particular communities and their dealings with the outside. The work will fail to attain policy relevance unless some effort is made to sample a wider range of communities, and to track down the sources of influences in bureaus and national-level organizations, which means that anthropologists will have to become more familiar with the institutional structure of urban-industrial nations and begin to make studies of key sectors and organizations of this structure.

Ways of using resources are of concern not only to the particular community and its survival needs and persisting or changing habits but also have to be seen in the context of national balance sheets and trends. Most communities and regions, at all levels of technical development, display mixtures of equilibrious and disequilibrious strategies—systems of resource use that vary from sustained-yield maintenance to progressive abuse or exhaustion. Pressures from national economic forces encouraging maximization and unrestricted exploitation of resources, or polluting transformations such as heavy fertilization, do not always yield these results in all localities. Sustained yield systems can develop under local conditions and preferences, even within these pressures. Alternative strategies with varying ecological implications—from the resource balance, to effects on human biology—usually exist in the local bodies of technique and precedent and can be reinforced by social arrangements. Clear-cutting and selective-cutting of forests have varying implications for regrowth, but forests can be put on a sustained-yield basis with either system, provided that the incentives and costs are handled correctly. Intensive grazing of pastures, with the land then returned to fallow for recovery, may be as effective a means of conserving the grass cover as the other methods, consisting of continuous light grazing of several pastures in rotation.

The point is that any program of ecological reconstruction in a modern nation will require intimate knowledge of these mixed local systems in order to evolve effective programs of change. Up until now this has been handled largely as a matter of providing some universal incentive, like taxation, and expecting the producers or consumers to follow suit. Such programs have not been effective when they encounter local systems that are reinforced by status, reciprocity, and cultural precedents. Farmers in the corn belt may use large amounts of fertilizer and risk damage to soil and water supplies not only because it produces the yields they require for income but also because they find it desirable to present an image of "scientific farming" as a means of maintaining their local prestige position.[10]

Anthropologists have an important role to play in providing this kind of information on local variation in ecological relations. However, they must proceed more systematically than the traditional ethnological fashion of making a series of unrelated or loosely related studies of particular communities, informed by intellectualizing intradisciplinary concerns. There is need for a different type of work in which the anthropologist becomes part of a coordinated effort to supply data on how localities manage their human and natural resources, the implications of these management systems for sustained yield at both the local and national—cumulative—levels, and how these patterns can be utilized for programs of change and reform.

Discussion of ecosystems, self-regulation, and equilibrium concepts on a theoretical level is an imaginative and intellectually rewarding task, replete with attractive analogies between species and even phyla. However, these concepts also have an entirely practical, down-to-earth aspect: the development of adequate systems of incentives and controls designed to minimize destructive attacks on the environment. At this level, the sometimes fanciful analogies of systemic functioning have to be translated into concrete terms: the complex interplay of subsystems and interests; the desirability of fluctuation in practices of overuse and recovery; of finding alternative uses for destructive capacity; the need to trade off a little pollution for a lot; and to restructure political and economic systems to avoid exploitative patterns. The dynamic and hard-to-predict responses of the human material must be in view at all times, and the relationship of microsystems to macroprocesses requires much more research. Anthropologists have an important role to play in all of these things; perhaps, especially, in the last.

NOTES

[1]The apotheosis of this particular idea was C. Darryl Forde's *Habitat, Economy and Society* (1934; second edition 1937), another major work in possibilistic analysis (though not within the "Boas school" historically) produced in the 1930s. Forde, however, was not as dogmatic as Kroeber: he did not renounce the possibility of generalization, but simply indicated that a full tracing of culture-environment connections was a difficult task. What is missing, of course, in both cases is a temporal perspective on the various cultures whose environmental relations are described. Lacking an understanding of how the various uses of resources developed, there is no possibility of generalization about process. This is why some of the contemporary studies of cultural ecology in the prehistoric perspective have more to offer a "relevant" perspective than many or most of the ethnological studies of the cultural ecology of tribal and peasant groups.

[2]One critique of these nonprocessual, typological tendencies in Steward's thought is found in the paper by Freilich (1963; *cf.* with the later Edgerton study, 1971). Freilich was concerned with a case of two populations—East Indians and Negroes in Trinidad—with similar "ecological adaptations" but differing cultural traditions and, to some extent, ways of life. According to the generalized Steward formulation, the shared adaptations should have produced more cultural similarities than Freilich found. Since according to Freilich they did not, he felt that the relationship between the "core" and cultural patterns was not at all precise and allowed for considerable independence of the cultural process. He also recognized that Steward, in that frequent encompassing imprecision of his writings, acknowledged that there could be considerable latitude in the relationship between the technoeconomic system and other aspects of the culture, and this acknowledgement of Steward's own recognition of the problem somewhat vitiates Freilich's critique. Still, Freilich, perhaps without fully realizing it, was really pointing to a basic weakness of Steward's ideas: the latent determinism hidden in the whole culture-type approach. If you posit a causal relationship, you also must determine how frequent or common this particular causal effect may be. If you do not, but merely acknowledge a vague amount of "latitude," you have really said very little, and there is a propensity to fall back on an assertion of determinism—or

vacillate, as Steward did, between deterministic-sounding statements and statements that modified these without producing hard measurements of degree or amount.

[3]This food-habits literature constitutes one of the prehistoric stages of ecological studies in anthropology and related social sciences, but one that has had almost no continuity and lacks ties to the cultural ecology style as it evolved in the 1950s and '60s. However, the recent emergence of nutritional and energetics studies in anthropology has permitted a revival of interest in the older materials. For some examples of the old food-habits research, see the following: DuBois, 1941; Bennett, Smith, and Passin, 1942; Cussler and deGive, 1942; Dickins, 1943; Mead (ed.), 1943; 1945; Bennett, 1946.

[4]Cf. Damas (his Introduction to the volume he edits—Damas, 1969): "The concept of the *exploitative pattern* ... the habitat and the tools for exploiting it—of the *settlement pattern* ...—the spacial and temporal aspects of society—and of the *community pattern* ... the organizational aspects of society—supply the bases for most of the discussions" (p. 7). Although these "discussions" consist of accounts of living tribal groups, the conceptual approach does not differ from the archeological.

[5]Rappaport's New Guinea groups may represent end-points in some temporal process of management that has finally worked out along ecosystemic lines—the "ecological imperatives" have prevailed. However, we would continue to insist on the proclivity of men to upset such balances when intrasocial action makes this necessary, tempting, or desirable, and the crucial importance of recognizing this proclivity in our theory. The risk of upset is especially great if, as Rappaport seems to imply, the strategies are ecologically appropriate at some *unconscious* level (a point also made by Vayda, 1970, p. 570). That is, if there is no general conscious control of the actions, there exist opportunities for manipulation by persons who may perceive them in the "ignorance" of the majority. This is not to deny, with Rappaport, that ecosystemicism can exist on an unconscious *or* conscious level—it is a result of any action with control functions.

[6]Some acculturation studies with ecological import are the following: Linton, 1940, which is a collection of studies from several tribes; Bailey, 1937, a unique study by a historian of the conflict of European and Algonkian peoples—also with implications for the fur trade issue, to be discussed below; Mowat, 1959, a study of the Barren Ground Eskimo, showing ecological changes resulting from contact; and a remarkable series of studies of the California tribes and Spanish and American contacts, by a biologist, Sherburne F. Cook (1941; 1943; 1946). The latter weaves biological and social consequences of contact together to create a pioneer and still unmatched analysis of acculturation as a human-ecological process. The acculturation theme plays a major role in Murphy and Steward's paper on "tappers and trappers" (1956), which is an attempt to show parallels in the social organization of Algonkian hunters and the Brazilian Mundurucu—the former having moved from hunting-gathering to the fur trade, the latter from forest hunting to rubber tree tapping.

[7]Interest by anthropologists in the social and ecological consequences of the fur trade have centered on a rather complex argument over the existence of family hunting territories, which would have been desirable for conservation of the beaver. The problem is whether such territories, if they existed under indigenous conditions, were strengthened or weakened by the fur trade, and its far-ranging competitive trapping. Knight (1965) reviews the literature and concludes that the issue is not resolvable by the available data, although he does state that the degree of "survival security" (p. 41) under Hudson Bay Co. conditions was not sufficient to permit the development of family territoriality. That is, the "material conditions of life" after the fur trade had materialized, required active, competitive trapping without regard for any hunting territories, if they had existed. The Plains Indian and the case

of the bison is somewhat better known. For the bison, see Mair, 1890; Roe, 1951; Branch, 1963. The development of large-scale bison hunting after acceptance of the horse is described by Ewers (1955). For other aspects of the bison hunt and the horse in relationship to ecology and population, see Wissler, 1936; Oliver, 1962. An early attempt to deal with both the fur trade and the bison problem is provided by Merriman (1926). For a basic reference to Plains Indian ecology, including the agricultural as well as the hunting modes, see Wedel, 1941.*

[8]For case studies of technical change and its consequences, see Spicer, 1952; Mead, 1955; Niehoff, 1966. Erasmus (1961) provides a personal account of the failures and successes of programs in South America. Epstein (1962) presents an illuminating study of the mingled social, economic, and ecological aspects of village development programs in India. Richards (1939) describes a pioneer, pre-World War II study of the effects of culture contact and economic development on the nutritional and social situation of an African people.

[9]For a sample of anthropological studies dealing with the process of local-national relations, see the following: Barnes, 1954; Pitt-Rivers, 1963; and Frankenberg, 1966, for Europe; Wolf, 1956, for Mexico; Bell, 1942; Goldschmidt, 1947; Vidich and Bensman, 1958; and Stein, 1960, for the United States. Bennett, 1967B, is concerned with the process for the Canadian Plains.

[10]An attractive program has been presented by Eugene Odum, in the paper discussed in Chapter 4 (1969). He proposes a "compartment model" that would divide the biosphere into a series of special-use categories, depending on the nature of the resources: areas with mature ecosystems (say, wilderness tracts) would be reserved as such; other areas, where exploitation can be carried out for intensive production, would be taken over and totally managed; combinations of the two would appear in the form of "multiple-use" environments; and finally, others would be taken out of the system entirely and reserved for urban-industrial use. This system of compartments, hopefully already evolving, recognizes the need for specialized relationships between different parts of the total environment, and differing solutions for the ecological problem, with the whole organized on the basis of controlled energy transfers.

*Since these comments on the fur trade and hunting territories were written, Rolf Knight has produced another review (1974) in which the issue is handled with reference to possible ideological concerns of some of the early proponents of family hunting territories. He notes that Frank Speck, who had strong positive feelings for Indian culture and survival, was funded by the Canada Geological Survey, which was interested in ascertaining the nature of Indian land claims in regions which had been ceded by the Dominion government to the provinces of Ontario and Quebec in 1912 with the stipulation that Indian claims would be extinguished. Moreover, the Hudson Bay Company (as well as the Indians themselves) were concerned over the depletion of fur animals resulting from competition from non-Indian trappers with the native Indian trappers tied into the HBC system. Hence several policy questions intersected to make a demonstration of hunting territories on the private-freehold tenure model a desirable thing. Knight acknowledges the difficulties of untangling the skein, and running down the various motives, but his remarks serve to add a new dimension to the affair, and to underline the significance of policy orientations in cultural-ecological research.

CHAPTER 8

Adaptation and Human Behavior

The principal assumption underlying this book is that the major issues concerning the human engagement with Nature are basically cultural, in the sense of human values concerning want-satisfaction; or social, in the sense of particular institutional arrangements involving greater or lesser impact on the physical environment. From this standpoint—that is, concern for critical issues of survival and well-being—human ecology is co-terminous with cultural (or social) ecology, which means that the study of major ecological problems ultimately becomes an inquiry into human affairs: humans treat Nature the way they treat themselves. The potential for destroying the physical environment is evenly balanced by the potential for destroying society.

On the basis of this assumption, it can be argued that the first step toward a broadened modern sociocultural ecology is an inquiry into those patterns of human behavior that lead toward a basic "tilt" in the relationship of Homo sapiens toward the physical environment of Earth: while humans characteristically initiate purposeful actions toward environment, the environment (including all species except man; all substances and forces) does not initiate purposeful actions toward humanity. That is, the basic anthropology of behavior—human capacities for symbolization and time-binding—has accounted for an overall exponential increase in the use of physical substances ("natural resources") since, at least, the appearance of the species Homo sapiens in substantial numbers. These capacities were responsible for what historians of culture and anthropologists formerly viewed as the "triumph" of human endeavor, or progress. There is now a willingness to

243

redefine these capacities as potentially destructive, and to argue for their control; a position which introduces profound philosophical issues and revisions of our images of humanity. The divorcement of philosophy, (the inquiry into values), from science, (the pursuit of control over Nature), has made it increasingly difficult to achieve the needed revision.

It can be acknowledged at the outset that the historical record of human involvements with Nature contains numerous examples of controls and of systemic balances with physical phenomena and other species; indeed, the ecology of tribal man, despite some cases to the contrary, did achieve a considerable degree of balance and control of human wants. That is, for particular spans of time; for isolated social systems; or for particular developmental stages in human history, controls have been achieved, or have emerged. The exponential curve, translated into rates of change and development, means that most of the destructive potential has emerged late in human history. Nevertheless, the behavioral capacities responsible for this pattern were present in Homo sapiens from the beginning.

It should be acknowledged also that the problem of environmental abuse by humans has two sides: on the one, the lack of foresight and planning, mistakes made in adjusting means to ends, the tendencies for wants to get out of control, and the persistence of destructive resource practices supported by vested interests, are all obviously causes of environmental deterioration. On the other side, the superior skills of humans in planning ahead, fitting means to ends, and working energetically and efficiently to supply wants, are also responsible for deterioration, when these functions are not guided by adequate knowledge and understanding of Nature. Both modes of behavior raise the question of control and modification of behavior in order to alter destructive attacks on Nature. Underlying both forms of behavior are fundamental drives characteristic of the species which are under only a limited amount of built-in control.

Nature, in fashioning Homo sapiens, decided to open the door to purposeful, energetic activity, but to provide controls for this energy in the form of a mental ability to reflect on the meaning of action and energy-release, and then, *after* reflection, subject it to control. For control to function effectively, there must be an intermediate step: the development or existence of values that define whether or not the action is to be subject to control. The system *must* work "imperfectly," since if *automatically* operating (autonomic) controls had been built into the nervous system, the opportunities open to humans by virtue of aggressive purposefulness would have been lost. That is, the cognition function serves both ends: it permits purposeful, generative action, and it also must supply the means for control of this action when it becomes dangerous. But there is no reliable built-in sense of danger: this must be conceived.[1]

The indirect linkage between goal-directed action and control mechanisms means that there tends to be a lag between initiation of an action sequence and the control of this sequence when it is demonstrated, or believed, to be destructive. During the time the action is effective, cognitive and emotional investments are put into it, and these result in "economic" investments as well, all of which can be defended vigorously and create additional obstacles to modification. Human memory functions to allow precedents to accumulate in social systems ("culture") and these affect outcomes in various ways, depending on the values embedded in them—they can constrain or reinforce the particular action.

This whole process is itself subject to historical change: in the development of human society, the control feedbacks in the system worked best in low-energy societies, where limits (often below the level of consciousness) were built into population growth and human wants for historical periods of varying length. Repeatedly, however, these episodes gave way to cycles of growth and development, when the control functions were weakened as technology and human wants proliferated and an ethic of want-satisfaction or wealth-accumulation came to characterize the system.

Any theory of human or cultural ecology that is based on the proposition that man's relations with Nature can be understood on the basis of methods and concepts derived from biological ecology, tends to neglect the variability and openness of the human behavioral process, and thereby detours the control and regulation issue. A policy-oriented cultural ecology cannot ignore the problem of control, nor the fact that humans to an increasing extent incorporate Nature into their systems, requiring a changing and evolving "socionatural" theoretical frame for human ecology.

THE CONCEPT OF ADAPTATION

In order to socialize human ecology one must adopt a conceptual scheme adequate to the task. This would focus on the active mode of the human engagement with natural phenomena, and it should allow for the inclusion of society as part of the environment with which men cope. The concept of behavioral adaptation provides such a framework: it is focused on action, and it is neutral on the definition of environment. It refers to the coping mechanisms that humans display in obtaining their wants or adjusting their lives to the surrounding milieu, or the milieu to their lives and purposes. It has been a largely unappreciated topic in cultural anthropology, due to the long dominance of second-order abstractions in descriptive scholarship and the persistent tendency to use them as causal explanations of behavior. Yet it is a very old mode of analysis: what distinguished Herodotus from other and later protoanthropologists was his willingness to observe adaptive coping in the peoples he described—even members of the same breed or culture group—a tendency that was not shared by most of his successors. In fact, the need to find single-factor causes, like race, climate, or culture, or the need to think of people in terms of fixed types with predictable, stereotypic behavior, still dogs the social sciences to some extent.

Two definitions of adaptation by anthropological ecologists are as follows:

> ... the process by which organisms or groups of organisms, through responsive changes in their states, structures, or compositions, maintain homeostasis in and among themselves in the fact of both short-term environmental fluctuations and long-term changes in the composition or structure of their environments. (Rappaport, 1971A, p. 60)

> ... adaptation implies maximizing the social life chances. But maximization is almost always a compromise, a vector in the internal structure of culture and the external pressure of environment. Every culture carries the penalties of a past within the frame of which, barring total disorganization, it must work out the future. (Sahlins, 1964, p. 136)

Elsewhere, Rappaport has distinguished between adaptation and system-maintenance (1967B, p. 241), defining the former as behavior that responds to changes in the environment, and the latter as behavior inside of systems designed to make them conform to preexisting conditions—that is, to maintain a steady state or homeostatic condition.

The quoted definition is consistent with Rappaport's wish to include human ecology in a larger natural ecological science: adaptation is the search for homeostasis. This definition is not consistent, however, with his second definition, where adaptation becomes an open-ended process of adjustment to external phenomena. The first definition can be criticized from our perspective as too narrow, since much adaptive behavior does not maintain equilibrium but does just the opposite: disturbs an existing state in order to arrive at a new one. The second definition can be criticized as too specialized—as only one-half of the process. From a behavioral standpoint—that is, from the standpoint of the individual—it makes no difference whether he is responding to needs for controlling or changing things that arise internally or externally—in our terms, he is "adapting" in both cases.

The Sahlins definition, on the other hand, stresses action taken to satisfy human objectives; it notes that such behavior always takes place in a cultural milieu of compromise and decision; and it emphasizes the continual emergence of new problems out of the solutions to past problems. It is a definition more congenial to the orientation of this paper.

However, Sahlins also defines adaptation here as referring to the individual's behavior aimed at maximizing his life chances. This is, of course, a normative definition, which implies that humans must inevitably seek maximization—presumably without reference to consequences, or to varying degrees and levels of satisfaction. The concept is influenced by values concerning consumption and continuous economic growth. However, the definition has a grain of truth insofar as human needs do have a tendency to escalate, and that tension-reduction is an important force in the human use of the physical and social environments.

Richard Mazess, in a paper prepared for the 9th International Congress of Anthropological and Ethnological Sciences, 1973, proposes a scheme for the concept of adaptation that has the following points: (1) the term is "all-inclusive," which means that it can be used for physiochemical, biological, and behavioral or sociocultural realms of phenomena. (2) It should be applied only to relations between the phenomena and the surrounding environment, and its criteria are "necessity and relative merit." (3) The referents of these criteria of course differ by the realms or fields of study; what may be adaptive for one level, may not be so for another. (4) In the social-behavioral level, adaptation has to be considered with reference to the individuals, the groups, and the "total cultural pattern." (5) A detailed listing of "adaptive domains" for the individual organism is provided, consisting of the following: reproduction, health, nutrition, nervous system, growth and development, resistance and cross-tolerance, physical performance, effective function, and intellectual ability. Other domains, for populations, ecosystems and other realms, are also suggested (for ecosystems, the domain is the familiar "attainment of a steady state or climax"). (6) Mazess states that no adaptive domains exist for the "sociocultural hierarchy"—that is, social behavior—and he does not propose any.

The concept of adaptation comes originally from biology, where it has had at least two meanings: first, the genetic-evolutionary, which concerns feedbacks from interactions with the environment back into the gene pool of organisms, leading to selective survival of particular traits that result in change in the organism so that it may better cope with specific environmental features.

The second meaning of adaptation in biology concerns behavior of the organism during its life-span that will permit the organism to cope with environmental factors—another feedback process but one functioning on the level of perceptual and cognitive processes, not genetic ones.

One of the major problems of biology and evolutionary psychology concerns the relationships between these two forms of adaptation in the organic domain; that is, to what extent can coping behavior in the life-span of single organisms be related to genetic adaptation or natural selection? Answers to this question clearly involve the time dimension: while coping-behavior adaptation must be related to selection, it is so on the basis of an accumulation of many small effects of decisions and actions on the part of numbers of organisms, leading (over relatively long time spans) to modifications in breeding patterns and, finally, to the selection of particular traits and the diminution or disappearance of others. The process is usually slow enough so that it cannot be observed in the lifetime of a single scientific observer; hence, methods for its inferred existence and rate must be developed.

New methods and approaches in human paleontology and prehistory have helped considerably with this problem, and it is becoming possible to make at least disciplined hypotheses or speculations about the combination of adaptive behavior and adaptive natural selection in the evolutionary process. An example concerns the relationship between teeth, hands, feet, tool-making and tool-using in the early hominids: here the reciprocal relationships of feet for running, hands for making and carrying weapons, and far-ranging hunting of game, provide a case for the emergence of a hominid type out of a more specialized and restricted anthropoid species.

In the sciences of human behavior, the concept of adaptation clearly derives from the second biological meaning: the coping mechanisms exhibited by the organism during its span of life. However, the quality of human coping differs from that of other organisms since it involves cognitive elements that introduce endless complexities. The means-end nexus of human behavior involves both purpose and value and not the former alone, which exists in other animal species, although not symbolically expressed.

The introduction of a valuing component means that the entire context of an adaptive action is susceptible of being judged—not only its effective result. This means that the meaning of adaptation differs depending on whether the individual or the group is the topic of concern: if it is the individual, the measurement of adaptation is tension reduction (Alland, 1967, Chapter 7), the alleviation of anxiety, the sense of accomplishment, or of reaching a desired end-state ("closure"). If the group is the topic of concern, adaptation usually refers to the choices made between standardized ways of dealing with situations available in the group culture. Moreover, the assessment of the consequences of adaptive behavior requires that a distinction be made between what is adaptive or tension-reducing for the individual and what is so for the group: the two may not coincide. Individuals may obtain satisfaction from warfare, but it may be maladaptive for group survival, peace of mind, and of course the environment, as in the case of defoliation and cratering of the Viet Nam landscape.

A related distinction, attributed originally to A. R. Radcliffe-Brown, but also figuring in general systems theory, is that between "internal" and "external" adaptation, used by Alland in his 1967 volume:

> A living organism exists and continues to exist only if it is both internally and externally adapted. The internal adaptation depends on the adjustment of the various organs and their activities so that the various physiological processes constitute a continuing functioning system by which the life of the organisms is maintained. The external adaptation is that of the organism to the environment in which it lives. (p. 121)

This is a strictly biological distinction, but it should be noted that the empirical phenomena involved in the two kinds of adaptation are very different: one concerns physiological processes; the other—behavioral processes. In his 1970 volume, Alland converts the distinction into a cultural-ecological mode, defining internal adaptation as cultural homeostasis, and external as at least a part of the culture-physical environment relationship nexus. Here the phenomenological gap is perhaps even wider. A similar distinction was developed by Goldschmidt (1959), but he used the term "selection" instead of "adaptation": "... in the ordinary course of events those features of a culture which are more suited to maintaining the community will continue and those less suited will disappear when two or more alternative modes are available" (p. 119)— that is, the presence of alternatives is frequently the result of contacts with external social or natural environments.

Adaptation is also a key concept in two versions of systems theory: the biological and behavioral (e.g., Ashby, 1952 and 1956, Chapters 16, 17, 18), and the social (e.g., Berrien, 1968, Chapter 8, or Buckley, 1967, various refs.). In these contexts adaptation is usually defined as a process that permits survival, or survival on terms more gratifying to the organism— tension-reducing, as noted previously—or, in some versions, as equivalent to learning, insofar as the organism, if that is what we are dealing with, changes as a result of the adaptive response.

In discussions of adaptation in general-systems contexts, emphasis is placed upon the following:

1. The existence of *subsystems* within the context of a larger or suprasystem. The existence of these requires internal adaptations or adjustments, and when such a complex suprasystem is in a state of homeostasis, Ashby considers it to be a *multistable* system. In general, the more subsystems, the more complex the adaptive process.

2. The presence of subsystems also means that the suprasystem contains a number of *part-functions*, each of which is more or less complete in itself, but each is also necessary to the functioning of the whole suprasystem. An example would be the mechanisms of an automobile—the ignition, the drive train, the transmission, etc.—all of them having separate and distinct sequences of operation, but linked together to move the whole car. Adaptation in human social behavior can refer to this process of maintaining linkages between the institutional and activity subsystems with their various part-functions.

3. Frequently the part-functions operate on the basis of *step-functions*. These are simply the discharge of energy or a performance of some kind when an input reaches a certain threshold, and not before. The discharge of nerve cells is a common example, but the logic is also extensively used in sociological analysis—theories of race riots, for example: where it is proposed that the riot begins when certain variables reach a particular level of intensity. Step-functions are relevant for adaptation in several senses, but perhaps the most important in behavioral contexts is that their existence requires immediate or sudden adaptive responses, often without preparation.

4. In human systems, adaptation is *serial* in large part, insofar as one adaptive response leads to another. This operates in two ways: a suprasystem may be put together in such a way that it will not function unless each part-function or subsystem operates in a certain sequence—the automobile is an example again. Secondly, the organism coping with such a system is required to pass through a

series of steps in sequence before it can realize its objectives or reduce tension.

Now, this rhetoric is obviously based on the mechanical and biological analogies, and therefore it presents certain problems from the standpoint of the analysis of actual social situations. It is unclear in these abstract expositions just what is adapting: the social system to itself or the human organism to the social system; the system to its external milieu or components of the milieu to the system. The language is of course devoid of any specific human context such as cognitive thought, innovative response, the accumulation of values around precedents, or other characteristics that govern human adaptive behavior, although the generalized level of systems theory presupposes such phenomena. However, the situation underlines the fact that systems theory and analysis is simply a set of verbal and mathematical tools to analyze complex events and should not become a substitute for reality.

In more descriptive social contexts, adaptive behavior can be seen as innovative, change-seeking, novelty-producing, or conservative and tolerational. The individual, or group, may adapt by finding new solutions to new or old problems; or it may adapt by simply learning to live with the existing situation and worrying less about it, or adjusting other behaviors to the prevailing reality.

"Prevailing reality" is, of course, a tricky concept since for man the reality milieu to which he adapts can be an inextricable mixture of physical-environmental and social or cultural components—a process that moves apace in contemporary civilization, as culture encompasses more and more of the natural environment. Adaptive coping thus becomes a social as well as an ecological problem: in contemporary societies, many primary producers find coping with the market economy more complicated than coping with natural resources—a fact that necessarily underlies a comprehensive cultural ecology.

Still another term used in both the biological and social realms is *preadaptation.* This refers to properties of the species or group that permit it to effect an efficient adjustment to altered external conditions without having to pass through an "adaptive" process of some kind. The inclusion of this phenomenon in the "adaptation" lexicon is probably a mistake, since it refers to an event of an entirely different class than coping behavior, which is what our concept of adaptation is all about. "Preadaptation" refers in essence to an opportune coincidence between an existing trait or condition and a new environmental pressure.

The ambiguity of "adaptation" means that it must never be used by the scientist in an unconscious valuational sense, as it is so frequently in everyday language. Adaptation is not inherently good or bad; it is, in the sense we shall use it here, simply coping, and coping can contribute to desirable or undesirable consequences. It can lead to stability or dynamism; to satisfaction for some and dismay for others; to destruction or construction. Adaptation always has to be defined from an explicit point of view and with reference to empirical consequences as well as value frames. The full context of the adaptive process must be set forth: judgments made on partial frames are likely to lead to confusion and error.

The existence of values in adaptation is evident in the term *maladaptation*, which implies the undesirable consequences of some form of action or coping. There is no harm in using the terms provided the context is made explicit, and the definitions are clear. Perhaps clarity would be achieved if all uses of "adaptation" were confined only to the valuational frame, and some neutral term like "adjustive coping" were substituted for the more empirical referents, but the wide use of "adaptation" advises against this usage.

THE ROOTS OF ADAPTATION

In the most general sense, human adaptive behavior is based on the capacity for "self-objectification" and "normative orientation" (Hallowell, 1960):[2] the human ability to perceive, or receive information on, and act upon or against the environment for the satisfaction of needs. The ability to conceptualize or perceive the self and its surroundings leads, among other things, to the conception of property, the basis of the distinctive human approach to environment that has had such massive and accumulative effects.

Man, with his impressive symbolizing capacity, creates his own images of reality, and these images may be more or less congruent with Nature. Man can deny the factual relationship of means to ends, can project upon others his own guilt or his own motives of destruction, can rationalize his own destructive impulses, can deny the fact of death and engage in a symbolic search for eternal life.[3] Likewise, humans can view Nature as an extension of will or desire; they can persuade themselves that their actions are not harmful to Nature or to themselves. Engineers in the contemporary United States build dams with the assurance that they will protect forever against floods—and then the biggest flood of all destroys the dam and everything built on the flood plain. Or, peasants farming the slopes of a volcano can wear charms against its eruption, only to have their homes and lives destroyed when the eruption comes. Out of these illusions about Nature are built human institutions, and the continuity of the institutions comes to mean more than the ecological hazards created by the illusion.

H. G. Barnett (1953) was concerned with the process of innovation as the "basic of cultural change." On the basis of Gestalt principles, he located innovation in the human ability to synthesize existing components of perceptual and experiential fields in order to create new combinations—a temporal process of change taking place as a sequence of psychological events. His analysis focuses on a major aspect of adaptation: the ability to make changes in contemporary phenomena in order to cope with future events. Barnett's presentation implied that the innovative process is inescapable in humans; they *must* perform these syntheses and recombinations, which means, in ecological terms, a capacity to manipulate and transform resources.

Symbolic representations of environment, and processes of coping and innovation, occur in a milieu of *information*, and it is here that the feedback model becomes conceptually relevant for adaptation. That is, while the information flow in systems is a universal process, the nature of this flow differs in humans by the large quantity of cognitive bits moving in the channels, and the superior capacity to evaluate or assess these bits of information in the process of decision making. When information content of feedback messages is detailed and relevant to the issue, decisions are likely to be "rational"—that is, appropriate to the ends sought or the consequences visualized. When information content is limited, or errone-ous, the resultant decisions are likely to be "irrational" or randomly related to the desired states. In such cases, fantasy, symbolic elements, or emotional factors are likely to dominate (not, of course, that they are ever entirely absent in any case). In the ecological context, if the "irrational" mode is dominant, and at the same time the technology available for use is high, environmental disasters are made more probable; when this occurs, the process of cognitive feedback offers no guarantee of survival-oriented outcomes.

But "rationality" is no guarantee of survival-oriented outcomes either. The "right" choice based on abundant information may be the "wrong" choice from the standpoint of ecologically adaptive consequences if the ends sought were destructive or exploitative. This represents the essence of the basic logical confusion in growth-oriented socioeconomic philosophy and the whole tradition of utilitarian and Puritan thought: that rational choices (that is, choices of the most efficient strategies) automatically assure good results in all possible contexts.

This is the posture of *optimistic voluntarism*—the central theme of much Western philosophy since the 16th century and earlier; positions that were themselves largely rationalizations of the prevailing and accelerating institutions of human achievement and gratification. These schemes have assumed that will or purpose is a general good—that, always allowing for some error in the system, on the whole if men are permitted to follow their purposes the ends will be good. Or, in our terms, that all forms of adaptive behavior carried out by individuals will serve the welfare of the group. On the basis of this general position, everything from colonialism to capitalism, from slavery to social stratification, from romantic love to hedonism, and of course basically, individualism, could be justified.

In a culture that has begun to find that voluntarism is a dangerous and hardly prudent stance for organisms living on a finite Earth, it may seem paradoxical that an approach designed to solve the problems must also take a voluntaristic stance. But the paradox is apparent only, and it points up the important difference between a policy-oriented approach and a purely theoretical one. Voluntarism, like output-orientation and control, generates problematic or practical issues. By emphasizing these phenomena, I am not necessarily proposing them as the major components of a theoretical model of society or cultural ecology, but simply as issues that must be dealt with if we are to do something about man's abuse of the physical environment. I do hold that adaptation is a fundamental process in human behavior—at that general level some theoretical schematizing is evident. But I also acknowledge that the kinds and degrees of adaptation differ greatly among societies and the real issue is not theory but empirical determination of these types and degrees. Humans are not always equally "voluntaristic" or dynamic in their adaptive strategies, but the tendency is there and it tends to get out of balance.

SYSTEMS AND ADAPTIVE DYNAMICS

There are two principal sets of conceptual tools in the study of a socially responsive human ecology: (1) the "systems" approach in social science, and (2) the "adaptive dynamics" approach to social behavior and social action, featuring an emphasis on decision making and exchange transactions. I acknowledge that I have had difficulty bringing these two approaches together. There is, first, an implied contradiction insofar as the former approach carries an implication of control of behavior by the properties of the system in which the human individuals are involved, while the second approach emphasizes voluntaristic rationalism, or the actions of individuals in their own need- and want-satisfying interests. In the first case, there is an implication of determinism; in the latter, an implication of free will. Of course both implications are examples of the tendency for theoretical social science to go to logical extremes, and the contradiction is more apparent than real.

The linkage between the two sets of propositions is made, I believe, by the notion of subsystem. That is, human systems are not unitary, but are dynamic and proliferational: when needs cannot be satisfied by one system, a subsystem is likely to form through the adaptive actions of individuals; or, the individual may switch his behavior from one system or subsystem to another, seeking out more congenial alternatives. The ease with which this can be done varies within and between social groups or "cultures," and the forces that protect systems from individual manipulation have been the topic of considerable research by anthropologists: tradition, conservatism, ethnicity, status, ritual, reciprocity, and so on all play their role—although the infinite complexity of social life lies in the fact that every factor that can shield systems from change can also be managed by actors to promote change.

A second major problem concerns the question of whether, due to the existence of systems and subsystems with varying rules of action (and inaction), the processes of adaptive behavior (decision making, trade-offs, etc.) are indeed uniform throughout the human population. We border here on fundamental philosophical and psychological problems, not to mention sociological and ecological problems. The solution to this problem appears to lie in a perspective that acknowledges a certain underlying uniformity in cognitive and linguistic behaviors and diversity in applications and situational determinants of components or outcomes of these behaviors—in other words, adaptive dynamics. Or, in the ecological context of discussion, the propensity for environment-exploiting actions is uniform in all human populations, but the socioenvironmental situations within which human groups live at any particular moment call forth particular expressions of this uniform potential. Change takes place when individuals and groups discover ways of modifying these situations in order to realize some kind of gain.

In previous chapters I have discussed the problems attending the use of systems models and analogies for describing human behavioral phenomena. The same problem, though possibly in lesser degree, exists in using these models to analyze any complex situation in Nature. Since most of the thinking about systems was done initially on the basis of mechanical imagery and processes, it is a fact that as one moves from mechanical systems to organic and social-behavioral, one moves from relatively closed entities, with their own self-contained generating and stabilizing features; to open entities, which may maintain a degree of systemic integrity, but which are constantly engaged in transactions with an ambiguously demarcated environment: receiving information, modifying their operations, altering their output. Since such open systems are common in biology and Nature generally, one might take the position that human social systems are part of this expanded Nature. However, there is, at the very least, a matter of degree: in general, the *most* open systems are human social systems, because of the nature of human behavior.

The crucial problem of comparison, then, is the degree of openness of the systems being compared. Anthropologists and others who have compared or analogized human behavior with natural ecosystems and related concepts (stability, equilibrium, self-regulation, homeostasis), have tended to compare less-open biological systems with more-open social systems, and especially so when they have used such terms, moderately appropriate for certain tribal cases, to describe contemporary society. By making such comparisons, an emphasis on self-regulatory process, prediction, and control is extended into complex society which is likely to distort the dynamic reality of social life, and in addition, have undesirable political and ideological undertones.

To think about contemporary social systems—or all social systems—in terms of the criteria used to define relatively closed or stable mechanical and organic systems is to confuse systems that retire energy (increase entropy) and simplify structure with systems that generate energy (decrease in entropy) and tend to increase their structural complexity. Such systems *require* a degree of unpredictability—or, in terms of the attitudes of the human actors, lack of fulfillment—in order to function. While feedback exists in such systems, it does not necessarily control the operation of the system as it does in the strict sense in mechanical and some organic ecological systems, but simply provides information that offers alternatives for action on the part of the human actors. Particular courses of action will be more or less probable in such feedback flows—here the operations of social systems are not automatic, but are subject to circumstances, which limits the applicability of a theory emphasizing predictable outcomes—hence "history."

From time to time efforts have been made to find basic causal principles that determine behavioral outcomes in a large number of cases. One of the most useful of these is the "least effort" principle (Zipf, 1949), which simply proposes that humans acting in a system to satisfy needs will do so in the manner offering the least amount of expenditure of individual energy.[4] The principle offers a nice contrast with the output principle that man is capable of releasing or producing more energy than any other species, but the two are really on entirely different levels. "Least effort" refers to choices made by individuals to cope or satisfy needs; output refers to the collective effort over time. If large output is accomplished with least effort, this is simply a measure of the efficiency of human behavior as a converter of energy. However this may be, "least effort" does not work all the time by any means, and its existence must be an objective of study, not an assumption.

It may be proposed that "least effort" constitutes an important principle of ecologically relevant human behavior in the isolated, low-energy tribal and tribal-peasant societies that have been the primary focus of anthropological research. This appears to be the chief finding of studies such as Richard Lee's on the Bushmen (Lee, 1969; 1972B), where the hunting-gathering subsistence system operated at a level of efficiency permitting considerable leisure or at least good nutrition for all at modest expenditures of labor energy. Lee also holds that work gets harder for H-G people as the size of the band increases; least-effort keeps both small. The corollary of least-effort is "controlled wants"; that is, maintenance of least-effort subsistence activity also means that wants are under some sort of culturally standardized constraint. These conditions prevail as long as the group remains relatively isolated from external stimuli, and this indicates that the human impact on the environment is governed not by built-in psychobiological controls but by situational determinants.

The behavioral and cognitive mechanism associated with the process of economic growth and the "developed" societies concerns a transformation of the concept of "marginal product" in economics. If a person has been accustomed to obtaining a given amount of product or satisfaction from a given amount of work or effort, he will be willing to work harder for the same amount of satisfaction only up to a point—that point where the work itself no longer is considered to be worth the results—that is, smaller and smaller amounts of satisfaction are gained from more and more work.

Now, at this point of refusal to work harder, if an external source of help is provided (in the form of additional energy from another source at no particular cost to the person), the person will achieve his satisfaction at no, or at only a small additional, effort. Since the assistance is furnished without any important direct cost to him, he will be unaware of the fact that the help costs someone—is valued at—precisely the same amount as he would have had to "pay" with his own additional effort.

The individual is therefore unaware of what or how the costs of his satisfaction are being met, and is not opposed to the system that supplies these services and commodities. Only adoption of an ideology, an increase in taxes, or a knowledgeable role in the system will be likely to move him into opposition—that is, he will be willing to stop short of complete or further satisfaction, or willing to put his own effort to the task and thereby pay the added costs himself. The process operates on the all-important factor of the *indirect* source of the energy required to pay the costs of marginal products. This increasing tendency to provide people with satisfactions in such a manner as to shield them from full awareness of the costs results in the buildup of expectations to the point where attempts to stop the movement or revise the costs meet with great opposition, and hence the whole system becomes politicized.

Another side of the process is the drive toward equity, which ultimately comes to characterize all large social systems—or at least does so as literacy and awareness levels rise in the population. Maurice Edelman (1964) has devoted much attention to the psychopolitical issue of the conditions creating a search for equity and the demand for increased use of resources in order to enlarge the supply and distribute it more widely. Edelman observes that in modern societies initial stages of transformation or growth mean that large sections of the population are willing to endure privation in the interest of the whole; that is, through such familiar motives as patriotism and sacrifice. The process also includes promises of future rewards made by the elite leadership in order to sustain motivation. Sooner or later, however, willing sacrifice comes to be felt as "relative deprivation," and the demands for fulfillment of the promises emerge, requiring further extensions of growth and resource conversion.

Because of the presence of cognition as a factor in human systems, the role of environmental factors is subject to constant variation and change. The environment can be a resource, a stimulus, a constraint, an informational "bit," a source of uncertainty—and so on—depending upon the other circumstances influencing and participating in the system. This is what is meant when we speak of an "open" human ecological system: the role of the environmental component is a variable, not a constant. Because of this uncertainty, it is necessary to consider the problem of control of human ecological systems in the context of conscious social regulation, however this may be accomplished (compulsion, persuasion, manipulation, etc.), and only secondarily in the context of automatic process. However, as suggested previously, the latter may emerge occasionally in these human systems when the historical sequence of events has, for the time being, reached a stable phase, and institutional mechanisms and attitudinal consensus are in a state of correlation. This kind of situation seems to occur most frequently in the isolated tribal societies, but it can also be a state to which open, complex systems revert, when they break down.

The applicability of systemic concepts of equilibrium, then, is limited to special classes of human ecological and social systems, although "homeostasis," implying somewhat greater variability and dynamism, probably has wider applicability to human affairs. The characteristic "open" type of system, defined above, is by definition never in a state of true equilibrium: it moves constantly from one level of organization to another, with the terms of its existence constantly changing from state to state. The system tends to mirror the mental processes of the actors: the human brain accepts information from the outside and then processes it internally, comparing this "bit" with stored items, and then issuing forth with an interpretation. The same piece of external information may, however, be subject to several different interpretations depending on which previously assimilated items it is compared with, and from one information-receiving instance to the next, these interpretations are likely to change. Consequently, the identical external phenomenon is seen differently and integrated into different Gestalts and action systems, from one time to another.[5]

The high probability of a random matching of stimuli to other phenomena means also that feedback in the human ecological system will function to direct behavior on different levels in a hierarchy, depending upon who is receiving the information and when. These extend from the individual's private motives of satisfaction outward into objectives of defense of various groups and other facets of the milieu. Social systems differ in the amount and kind of sanctions and reinforcements they apply to this process, and it is clear that a system that reinforces individual gratification will do so at the expense of some other vector.

The term "adaptive system" has been used as coterminous with the "open" system, since one of the characteristics of open systems is their capacity to respond to new information flowing into them in such a way as to achieve new patterns and levels of organization. In the most neutral terms possible this is what adaptation is all about and, in this sense, human systems are the best examples in Nature-at-large of adaptive-process systems. Consequently a suitable scientific definition of socio-cultural ecology is simply: *the study of adaptive social systems with special reference to the involvements of these systems with phenomena in the environment.* Again the necessary qualification: "environment" includes both physical and social phenomena although at the level of particular problems the two will often be studied separately.

The term "adaptive system" of course begs the question of the varying effects of particular human actions on other systems and subsystems. The human system is "adaptive" in terms of the objectives of its actors—that is, insofar as the system operates so as to satisfy needs and wants. This terminology is equivalent to the concept of "directed system" (Collins, 1970, pp. 3–5) or the notion that anything in culture that exists has a "function"—it is directed toward a certain goal. This formulation has often discouraged or diverted inquiries into possible *mal*adaptive effects, and "functionless" perseverations. The teleological formulation is avoided in this argument by the insistence on determining the precise effects of a given adaptation on a variety of systems (some of which are "maladaptive") and the corresponding debate over these contradictions that emerges in society. Specific criteria for ecological "adaptation" and "maladaptation" are necessary here, and in fact constantly emerge in the social process. (I discuss some possibilities in Chapter 9.) I acknowledge a degree of semantic confusion over the use of "adaptive" as a general label for a kind of human behavioral system, and the use of adaptive and maladaptive criteria for assessment of effect.

An adaptive or open system (like the human mind, from which it is a projection) is a texture of maps, rules, or diagrams for the performance of certain acts when certain conditions are present. These constitute precedents for behavior, and this would appear to be an adequate definition of culture at the systems level of discourse. Systems will differ in the extent to which these mapped precedents are open to modification by new information inputs, but human systems are characterized more by such flexibility (or, in psychological terms, capacity for *learning* on the part of the actors) than is the case generally in nonhuman organic systems. This difference in degree of adaptability is one of the foundation stones of any human ecology.

Although anthropologists have traditionally designated *language* as the key to this responsiveness, adaptability, and capacity to learn, language is not the only facilitating mechanism. The capacity to judge or apprehend circumstances, whether or not linguistic tools are used, is a general human capability and, along with explicit symbolism, it permits adaptive behavior. Language is simply one expression of the process of selective functioning and matching and the creation of cognitive maps and rules. The recent findings of experimenters working with chimpanzee communication on the basis of sign language appears to suggest that the animal "thinks" like humans without the ability to use what is considered "language" at the human level. The chimp's sign-responses, however, have certain "linguistic" qualities or at least syntax, including simple "sentences" composed of hand signals—permitting him to obtain things he needs from the environment in a manner identical to the human. This work has many ambiguities, but it has qualified the puzzling discontinuity between animal and human communicative behavior.

Another difficult theoretical issue is the "role of the individual" in the social process. In the long view, the system functions because the individuals in it make choices and decisions for action, and these choices become generalized as processes. However, in the short run, the choices and actions of any one individual may have greater or lesser effects on the macroprocesses of the system, since usually a certain *quantity* of decisions and actions is required to effect the change (step-functions). However, individuals may deliberately or fortuitously choose actions that have greater or lesser consequences, a fact that makes it possible for a single individual, and a single action, to make major changes in systems.

RECAPITULATION

The preceding discussion has described the theoretical underpinnings from behavioral science of an adaptive-dynamic approach to cultural ecology. The level of description is generalized: the social system is seen as a complex of subsystems that are suffused by tension-reducing adjustments of individuals and that lead to exploitation of the physical and social environments for human ends. The level of tension in the adaptive suprasystem is typically high, as the actors generate alternative views and thereby reinterpret the incoming information. From the point of view of the actors, the subsystems contain alternative possibilities, and choice is exercised among these to introduce change in the relationships of the actors, and the systems, to the various milieux. "Other people"— the various subsystems themselves—are part of this milieu. The social system is not always multipotential, since circumstances introduce limits to action and constraints will be set against certain choices. Accumulating choice-patterns, or means of conforming to or evading limits, constitute maps that form precedents for action; these can be binding, or open to various forms of manipulation emerging out of the process of reinterpretation and choice. The process is circular and reciprocal; it operates with feedback. However, these are not usually the automatic type found in mechanical and organic systems, but the dynamic form involving communication and especially characteristic of human behavior.

This is an exceedingly general model. The term "institution" probably most usefully refers to particular adaptive systems or subsystems centering on special contexts of life with their own objectives and rules. In the course of the Industrial Revolution, the adaptive-system model of greatest significance for ecological matters can be called the growth-oriented—in institutional language, "economic or technological growth," or even more specifically, "capitalism" (various types, including "state capitalism," but all featuring the objective of continuous growth by the reinvestment of output). This version of the adaptive system has been the historical culmination of several millenia of continuous exploration of human potential, with a tendency toward exponential increases of output based on the mobilization of resources to accomplish ends. It is this system that has posed a major (maladaptive) threat to the environment, while at the same time seeming to satisfy human needs (adaptive) on an increasing scale.

NOTES

[1] Or in more familiar terms, it is subject to cultural—experiential and cognitive—definition. Sims and Baumann (1972)—a collaboration between a geographer and a psychiatrist—provide an empirical study of precisely this problem: they addressed themselves to a problem that has puzzled weather observers and disaster researchers for some time: deaths from tornadoes in the United States are not proportionate to the incidence and severity of tornadoes. The death rate is significantly higher in the Southern states than in the Midwest and North, although tornadoes are in general less frequent and severe in the South. Several explanations have been adduced: differences in warning systems, differences in house construction, and some others, all of which Sims and Baumann indicate have defects. They propose to supplement these explanations with an analysis of the attitudes with which people in the South and North confront impending disasters. Matched samples of informants in Illinois and in Alabama were drawn, and a sentence completion test (a standard projective psychological instrument) was administered. The samples were compiled for districts with the necessary characteristics: the Illinois area had a higher tornado rate than the Alabama area, but a lower death rate. The hypothesis governing the construction of the test related to a number of psychological findings concerning the conception of autonomy and subordination in the personality: people who perceive themselves to be in control of their own fate are likely to take more precaution and respond to disaster warnings more readily than people who conceive of themselves as directed by external forces, or as subject

to the will of God. A majority of the Alabaman respondents perceived themselves as under the control of God, with relatively less control of their fate, whereas the Illinoians were more inclined to see God as a benevolent figure who does not interfere in one's active life, and therefore the individual must manage his own fate. Other questions in the IST tapped specific material on just what the respondent would do in case of a tornado, and the answers here followed the pattern—indicating that the Alabamans were more inclined to trust in fate, rather than to take active steps to ensure survival. In general, then, the findings of the study were consistent with the hypothesis, although Sims and Baumann are properly cautious in claiming solution to the death-rate differential. However, it would seem that they may have put their finger on at least one important factor.

[2]For a discussion of the evolutionary and phylogenetic foundations of adaptation in man, see Alland, 1967, although in his approach, adaptation is assimilated into a definition of culture, as it is in most of the papers in Ashley-Montagu, 1968A, or Cohen, 1968–70. Chapple (1970) includes a review of the contemporary data on psychophysical bases of behavior—an updating of Chapple and Coon, 1942, Part I.

[3]For an application of this concept of image formation to the psychological roots of social stratification, see De Vos, 1966. The symbolist tradition in philosophical thought is also relevant: Langer, 1942; Boulding, 1956A. The psychological approach to the problem of how humans conceptualize their surroundings or environment is described by Berlyne (1968). Symbolic studies in anthropology are a new and growing field.

[4]George Kingsley Zipf's *Human Behaviour and the Principle of Least Effort* (1949) is a book that defies classification. It is a work in psychology, linguistics, geography, sociology, and international relations—at least, materials from all these fields are analyzed by his "least effort" concept. The book is subtitled *An Introduction to Human Ecology*, and this provides as good a rationale as any for this sweeping attempt to combine data from a wide range of human behavior by means of a single principle. If this is ecology, then we concur on its basic concept: that human ecology must be based on a theory of human behavior. In this case, it is largely behavior in the contexts of space and time, and also social time: "least effort" means that the human individual will tend to make decisions as to goal accomplishment and rewards that have the least "cost" attached to them—Zipf calls this the "economy" of human behavior. The argument clearly prefigures the later developments of locational theory in geography and social exchange theory in sociology and social psychology, to name only two of the descendants. At the same time, it is difficult to trace definite connections between Zipf's analyses and these later specialties; sometimes he is cited as a source, but more often his work is ignored. In most cases, he draws from the same prehistoric sources that influenced these later developments (e.g., in his exposition of "The Economy of Geography," Chapter 9, he cites Auerbach and Lotka, whose work on distribution of nucleated population centers lay behind the later development of locational or central place theory [Zipf, 1949, p. 374, footnote].) However influential it may have been, the argument suffers from the usual defects of single-factor theories. While "least effort" is certainly important in human behavior, it is not universal and is always subject to cultural qualification. The magnitude of effort expended on any task is underlain by psychophysical or physiological factors, but it is greatly modified by preferences and prestiges. To establish the operation of least effort, and to avoid the ambiguity of cultural definitions, Zipf generally found it necessary to build highly idealized models, systematically excluding these reality forces in social behavior. This of course has its merits, since if often succeeds in showing that least effort *would* operate if these forces were not present. However, its contribution to an analysis of behavior in fields or milieu is specialized and partial.

[5]The statements in this book deriving from psychological theory deserve more detailed

treatment, but this seems presumptuous considering the lack of training of the writer in psychology. However, the sources of these psychological propositions include: modern behaviorism, emphasizing selective processes of perception and the integrative function of thought (e.g., MacKay, 1961; and works by Donald T. Campbell; G. H. Mead's "social behaviorism," 1934, and its transition to "field theory," involving communicative and role-taking exchanges between individuals; and adaptive behavior theory—(Appley, 1971; Foa, 1971). Some of these viewpoints include notions of feedback and trends toward resolution or "equilibrium" in individual thought and in interpersonal relations, but extreme care must be exercised in drawing conclusions about the larger social process from these micro situations. A collection of stabilized feedback relations within small groups is likely to be the cause of conflict and change at the social system level, as the interests of these groups intersect.

CHAPTER 9

Adaptation as Social Process

When we move from adaptation as a form of human behavior to adaptation as a process in social groups and populations, we also shift our criteria of what is "adaptive" from the individual and his need-satisfactions, to the group and its welfare or survival. However, in both cases, we must remain aware of the possibility that the individual's satisfactions can be an independent variable, ecologically speaking. A particular adaptive strategy followed by individuals can be adaptive for them, but either adaptive or maladaptive for the social and/or physical environment. The possibilities are multiple, and it is this multi-dimensionality or multipotentiality of human actions that creates the central problem of a policy-oriented cultural ecology.

In the sense of a policy science,* cultural ecology then becomes an inquiry into the adaptive consequences of human activities. A cultural-ecological study can be examined from the standpoint of its compre-nensiveness—not that we need demand full coverage in all cases, but at least a theoretical awareness of the potential range of adaptive and maladaptive consequences of human actions and a clarification of just where in this range the particular study may focus.

For example, a study of the potlatch ceremonial—a kind of archetype of human events with individual, social, and environmental significance—would, in order to exploit the full range of adaptive significance, need to show that it satisfied individual needs for prestige, maintained a system of

*For a definition of the field of policy science, see Lasswell, 1971. Lasswell's conception is on the whole more interventionist than mine, which views research more as an objective study of consequences, with policy implications to be determined by the readers, on the whole. However, I fully acknowledge the thinness of the line between relevant research and participation.

social ranking, and was a major spur to the production and consumption of goods and natural resources on the Northwest Coast under tribal regimes. The fact that the system had been given additional stimulus by European influences is of historical but not theoretical importance since it is precisely these stimuli that are characteristic of social action with environmental consequences.

We may also consider this passage from a recent monograph on the cultural ecology of New Guinea tribalists:

> Broadly speaking, tropical and subsistence economies are characterized by only a moderate level of general activity. A range of tasks is pursued concurrently and there is little specialization of labor on other than a sexual basis. Periodic variations in the amount of work done reflect both the controls that climate exercises over certain tasks and changes in the availability of certain foods. Finally, there is a broad interweaving of what the economist considers productive and nonproductive enterprise, in which the routine food producing tasks may involve ritual practices and incorporate social elements (as in the feasting and good natured rivalry involved in house construction or clearing new garden sites) and in which ceremonial activities provide the mechanism for the flow of goods and services that is central to the acquisition of power and prestige and to the establishment of credit which may be drawn upon in time of economic stress. (Waddell, 1972, p. 78)

Sometimes these production routines are harmless to the resource complex; sometimes they are destructive; since anthropologists have rarely inquired as to their effect, we are often given a picture of rather leisurely tribalists producing and consuming at no particular danger to the physical environment. The passage quoted above nicely illustrates the mood of many ethnological studies: the only reference to ecology consists of a mention of the "controls that climate exercises" over various tasks, and the good life is defined as "a moderate level of general activity." These do not appear to be people engaged in competing with each other or harming their resources.

But the issue is whether this "balance with Nature" was achieved because of the small population magnitudes, the weak stratification, and the highly localized nature of the adaptations, or whether there was something distinctive about the innate behavior of tribal man, or preindustrial man generally, that prevented serious environmental impact. Our answer is the former: the balance was achieved because of low technology and the social arrangements typical of small populations, but the case probably can never be proven because the ethnological literature so often lacks critical information on social aspects of environmental exploitation, resource magnitudes, and the effects of environmental use over long periods of time.

Nevertheless, the one contribution of cultural ecology to our general problem—and a contribution reached incidentally, on the whole, and not by design—has been the demonstration of how the social relations characteristic of micronetwork primary groups *can* exert control over the use of Nature. The picture of busy, noncompetitive tribalists certainly has its sociological unrealism, but, ecologically, it is not far wrong. Of course the competition (often covert) is there, and also the wants and drives, since these people are human. But there is something else as well: a system of social reciprocities that control and channel behavior (as well as sexual reproduction)[1] based on the interactions characteristic of parents and children and effective in controlling wants and social change. This kind of society can be at peace with Nature, if not with itself. However, since this system is socially-specific—based on small size and a degree of isolation—its processes cannot be expected to transfer to the macrosociety.

The micronetwork social system has communal features, which we encounter in the "intentional societies" (sectarian or other), that have been part of the Western tradition for a long time. In the intentional communal groups, as in the tribal, there exists a strong tendency toward the definition of natural resources as collectively owned—particularly those resources that are the major source of subsistence. Water, as a fluid resource, is almost always common property since it is difficult to develop private property rights over it. Grazing land is more commonly owned collectively than agricultural fields, but even in the latter case there is a tendency to consider land as a usufruct rather than absolute property, available to the users as long as they continue to use is productively.

Collective control or use of resources is a natural consequence of a communal, micronetwork society, and it is also a system that provides certain controls over their abuse. In any small community where local needs alone determine resource use, the collectivity retains a degree of interest in and responsibility for the resources—particularly the important ones, or the friable ones. There is a built-in tendency to avoid abuse since there is mutual control and mutual supervision. There may be, in addition, a feeling of stewardship for Nature: the individual resource user is an agent of the collective, and the collective is responsible to God or to Nature. Societies of this pattern also frequently have an extended time sense: a feeling that they are on Earth indefinitely, or forever, and that what they have now is what they will always have—Foster's zero-sum game concept: the principle of "limited good."

A degree of collective ownership or use does not mean that private control over some resources will not exist in all societies, nor that the collective control is an absolute guarantee against overexploitation or wastage. As a society evolves toward sedentary life and larger population aggregates, and stratification and a contest for power begin to emerge, collective use can be manipulated for gain, as it is in the tribal groups having episodes of predatory expansion, and as it certainly becomes in the case of corporate control over resources in our own society.

Peasant societies share in the communal features, but control of their resources is often vested in corporate agents outside of their own communities, and their exploitation of resources is guided by such necessities as taxes, which often do not permit conservationist practices.

When ownership of resources becomes detached from the community, other means of control must be devised. The community must take the responsibility for enforcing conservation measures; in fact, the concept of "conservation," or lack of abuse of resources and their management on a sustained-yield basis, becomes a reality only when individual owners need to be placed under regulatory control. Conservation emerges as a concept when its achievement is difficult. In the typical situation, the presence of a conservation value in the culture may have little relationship to the actual pattern of use of resources, which can be abusive due to demands emanating from sources not under local control, or to particular technological devices (Firey, 1957).

ADAPTATION AND ANTHROPOLOGICAL THEORY

The problem, then, is to move from the ecological contemplation of the small, relatively isolated community to the expanded community and its ties to the outside world. As Redfield observed in his chapter on the ecology of the "little community" (1955), most communities may, in one sense, lack an "ecological system" since many of their needs are provided by external sources. But, as I noted in the earlier discussion of Redfield's essay, this only begs the question of human relationships with Nature; it would mean that the anthropologist cannot share in an enlarged cultural ecological science since his preoccupation with the isolated community bars him from study of the more complex systems.

This implication obviously is not acceptable to the writer, and the objective of this final chapter is to suggest concepts that may help in the transition to broader research. This transition, we believe, can be achieved by adopting a different frame of reference—one that is less concerned with second-order abstractions such as "culture" or the "technoeconomic core" and becomes more concerned with purposive behavior. This shift in orientation requires a few words of explanation before we can proceed with an exposition.

It is possible to classify the basic subject matters in cultural anthropology into three grand categories:

I. *Thought.* The mental categories and rules of thinking that develop in the process of experience and thinking about experience and are given such labels as attitudes, values, logic, precedents, elementary forms, structures. "Cultural patterns" included such thought elements, although the concept also includes action behavior.

II. *Interhuman activity.* The observed categories and rules of behavior for individuals and groups in relationship with each other. This includes behavior labeled as interaction, consensus, conflict, affiliation, individualism, reciprocity.

III. *Adaptation.* The patterns and rules of social adjustment and change in behavior by individuals and groups in the course of realizing goals or simply maintaining the *status quo,* and called by such terms as coping, adjustment, adaptation, adaptive dynamics, adaptive strategies, achievement, compromise, fulfillment. The distinction between II and III is purely analytic; III is simply the aspect of II in which human purposive behavior is an explicit consideration in the analysis. II is therefore largely descriptive; III is largely explanatory.

The basic question for social science is the extent to which the three domains are integrated in any concrete social situation or society. By definition, the small, isolated tribal communities come the closest to such integration: the tendency is to organize behavior so that the rules and patterns of thought, interaction, and adaptation are mutually consistent. The approximation of this state of affairs is what Redfield called "culture" as opposed to "civilization," where the three domains are often in conflict or are disparate and rational action must be taken to bring them into adjustment (hence literacy, law, etc.). Concretely, a state of integration would exist when people's ideas defined their interaction with others and also the ways they coped with the milieu and realized their objectives.

On the whole, the phenomena considered to be "culture" by most cultural anthropologists (not the specialized Redfield definition cited above) fall into categories I and II, but *not* III. Some definitions emphasize I (e.g., "culture consists of values"); others emphasize II ("culture consists of the rules that define interaction"). Clyde Kluckhohn's definition of culture, influential in the 1940s, reads: "Culture consists of patterns of thought and action," which certainly combines I and II, and the action component (II) also contains some nuances of III. But cultural anthropologists in that era simply did not distinguish III from II in a decisive fashion. The result of this blurred distinction was a confusion between behavior as stylized and repetitive, and behavior as innovative and manipulative. There was a general failing to account for the existence of both, and hence, a failure to account adequately for change.

As we have noted in Chapter 7, cultural ecology arose in part as a reaction to this impasse, and its first objective was to supply an explanatory device for cultural phenomena by considering ecological or techno-economic phenomena as causes of cultural phenomena. This solution did not work, or worked only in particular instances and circumstances, because it ignored the purposive and manipulative behavioral mode. That is, it represented no real advance on the prior tendency to merge descriptive and dynamic features of social behavior.

The basic proposition of this book is that the adaptive dimension is essential in order to provide explanations for social outcomes. Since we view human ecology, or at least a large portion of it, as a "social outcome" (because man incorporates natural phenomena in his systems), the adaptive domain is essential for cultural ecology. The remainder of this chapter consists of a preliminary discussion of adaptation in the social context, with particular emphasis on its implications for ecological study.

ADAPTIVE DYNAMICS

Adaptive dynamics refers to behavior designed to attain goals and satisfy needs and wants, and the consequences of this behavior for the individual, the society, and the environment. There will be two major analytic modes of this behavior: (A) actions by individuals designed to accomplish ends or effect change in the instrumental contexts of life: the actions of a farmer in trying to increase his yield or simply to obtain a standard yield, the techniques of management in an industrial plant, the consumption-satisfaction habits of the citizen, and the techniques of wealth accumulation are all examples.

(B) The other mode consists of interactive or transactional behavior of individuals with other individuals in groups (often called "social exchange"), usually governed by rules of reciprocity and by various normative value components. Transactional behavior also is designed to accomplish ends, and some of these will be instrumental (as in the case of cooperative labor and machinery exchange among agrarians). However, a great deal of transactional behavior pertains to social ends: the acquirement of prestige, of mastery over others, of favorable positions in the favor-granting system, of consumption one-ups-manship.

From the standpoint of research operations, both individual actions and social transactions in adaptational behavior can be divided further into two levels of analysis: (1) the microsocial, which concerns the study of behavior in specific contexts of purpose (innovative, manipulative, coping, etc.). This milieu will also characteristically have both a formal or manifest, and an informal or covert level of operation, depending upon sanctioning values. (2) The second level is the macrosocial, which consists of the meaning of such behavior for social systems, including processes of change resulting from the many actions and transactions. When processes become fixed as systems, acquiring their own charters and rationales, they may be called institutions. The use of other second-order concepts (of which both sociology and anthropology have large quantities), is largely a matter of convenience and the demands of the particular problem of research.

The study of the microsocial is an anthropological speciality; the study of the macrosocial phenomena is the current domain of the institutional social sciences: sociology, economics, political science. The methodological problem involves the bringing of these into some kind of common frame: in most cases, to see the behavior and the secondary derivations and configurations as parts of functioning systems. Obviously the empirical, microsocial study of adaptive behavior in its many forms cannot be carried out indefinitely, on into mass society, since the population units are too large and the transactions too numerous. Selections of relevant sectors of adaptive behavior can be made on the basis of what is already known, in general terms, about institutions and processes; e.g., the competitive gratification-satisfaction systems of modern society. But the process will work from the other end as well; exploratory studies of adaptive behavior in relatively unknown or obscure social sectors may suggest explanations of phenomena at the macrosocial level. The search for alternative life styles with less harmful consequences to the social and natural environments is an example.

The key concepts for the study of individual social adaptation are *adaptive behavior* and *strategic action*—and the synthesis of the two, *adaptive strategy*. The distinction between the first two is a matter of level of generality: "adaptive behavior" is the more general term, since it refers to any form of behavior that adjusts means to ends, accomplishes objectives, achieves satisfaction, exercises choice, or avoids or refuses action or involvement in order to "adapt" or "adjust"—in other words, both active and passive aspects of purposive behavior of humans in systems. However, "strategic action" is the more specific term, and the one with special interest for our approach: it refers to active, goal-achieving behavior—"doing something about"—specific actions designed to achieve ends and consuming resources in the process. Around strategic action cluster such concepts as "rationality," "maximization," "achievement orientation," "*Homo faber*," and many others. It is the active mode, the "output-oriented" phase of human behavior.

The third term, *adaptive strategy*, is perhaps best defined as a component of strategic action: specific acts with a predictable degree of success, which are selected by the individual in a decision-making process. (Chains of strategies may constitute a *strategic design*, which we shall discuss in the next section.[2]) Every language has a large folk terminology of adaptive strategies in the generalized sense: coping, changing, rectifying, correcting, curing, ameliorating, modifying, manipulating, bringing-up-to-standard, swindling, deceiving—all are English words referring to ways of altering circumstances. Another set of terms refers to the psychological outcomes for the individual following the use of strategies: satisfying, gratifying, disappointing, making-happy, fulfilling, and many others. Other sets have emerged at the level of intellectual discourse and these are embodied in the literature of psychology, social psychology, sociology, and anthropology.

Many of the folk terms are suitable for analytical purposes, and a debate has continued in the behavioral sciences over the "phenomenological" approaches that seek to use the folk terms and avoid the misleading generalities and biasing projections-upon-the-data inherent in scientific jargon. The anthropological version of this debate is embodied in the new linguistic attempts to handle semantic concepts in the particular "culture"—the "etic" concepts, in preference to the "emic" categories of the anthropological analyst. However, these extensions of adaptational theory into linguistics are beyond the scope of this volume.[3]

The significance of adaptive strategies for ecological concerns lies in the large quotient of "fortuitous" strategic actions that foster the dynamic quality of social life and the expanding of changing impact on the environment. Traditional anthropological research seldom dealt with this component, since behavior persistently was seen as guided by fixed precedent. Evolutionary studies on behavior have had to revise this older conception since there was no way to account for the evolving and changing social matrix and its mental analogs. Political scientist Peter Corning has pointed out how the fortuitous capacity of human adaptive behavior lies at the basis of the applicability of "group selection" as a process in general human evolution (Corning, 1974).

The concept of *culture* supplies a number of analytic tools for the study of adaptive behavior. The most common use of the concept is to refer to sets of *values, precedents, models,* or *styles* ("cognitive maps"), which the individual can choose in order to guide his decisions and actions either on the basis of conscious choice, or unconsciously as the result of conditioning received in socialization. The culture concept also can be defined to include a supply of *moral precepts,* which function as constraints on free choice of models for action. The individual is not always free to make his own choices on the basis of predilection, gratification, or situational demand, but must consider norms of goodness, rectitude, and reciprocity. Room for manipulation and movement within these constrained patterns of choice exist in every social system, and the study of adaptive behavior must dwell on these manipulative patterns as well as on the conforming responses. Most modern social systems at all levels of technological development are by now mosaics of subsystems incorporating differing and competing styles and moral norms, with many individuals (often a plurality or even majority of the population) moving between them and manipulating them for purposes of gratification and gain. These adaptive strategies invest heavily in pragmatic criteria of action, and their norms are often simply rules of successful procedure (cf. Bailey, 1970; Goffman, 1969).

In the hyperpragmatic and individualistic style of the highly developed economies, the principal objective, as well as the body of rules of procedure, has been expressed by the terms "efficiency," "maximization,"[4] or "minimax strategy," all of these referring to various facets of the effort to obtain the largest possible output at the lowest possible cost of inputs. ("Optimization" has a similar meaning, although here there is consideration for possible harmful effects, and the output is governed by this concern.) However, strategies reflecting the general maximization aim exist in every society: it is fully cross-cultural, and is not confined to industrial or Western society. The difference is purely a matter of emphasis, pervasiveness, and the particular institutions in which such behavior is common or preferred. In the West, the economization of most institutions resulting from the need to support growing populations at high levels of living—itself an outgrowth of capitalist values—has meant that maximization philosophy has spread from purely instrumental contexts to many others, to become a generalized philosophy of strategic action. More than this, maximization and efficiency have become ends in themselves, in addition to being means to accomplish other ends, with their pursuit becoming a goal tending to exclude checks and balances against possible destructive consequences. Only recently has this been questioned, and optimizing qualifications introduced.

Time is a key factor in adaptive behavior. We have previously emphasized economic-technological growth as embodying a temporal process, noting that sustained yield and other forms of resource utilization can be observed only in terms of elapsed time. Strategic action takes place in a temporal continuum, and particular strategies also will be based on cultural or situational conceptions of the time factor. In some behavioral-science terminologies, strategies with immediate payoff have been called "adjustments," and the delayed-effect strategies—"adaptations".[5] We find this terminology confusing, since our frame of reference is designated by the term "adaptation," and also because we shall distinguish later between "adaptive" and "maladaptive" responses.

Critical differences in cultural style also may be found in attitudes toward uncertainty and risk. If uncertainty-tolerance is low, there will be emphasis on strategies designed to produce quick results without concern for possible undesirable long-term consequences. For example, a drop in corn yields may be responded to by the use of nitrogenous fertilizer, and the use of fertilizer over time may damage the soil's ability to fix nitrogen by natural means, thus permanently lowering yields at some future date. Market economies feature this kind of process, since they are guided by contemporary price-cost fluctuations originating outside the control of the economic operators. In agriculture, this can have a cumulative environmental impact.

The much-debated distinction between peasants and farmers has been illumined by these concepts. In this sense, peasants are agrarians who approach the caution end of the continuum; that is, they are extremely careful of taking risks due to past experience with uncertainty.[6] And because of a relatively high degree of cultural isolation, they also are inclined to invest in sacred criteria. Farmers who may be equally conservative and respectful of precedent, on the other hand, will be inclined to sanction their adherence to tested strategies with pragmatic criteria. Hence the farmer group will be quicker to respond to changes in objective conditions that seem to reduce uncertainty and risk.

The extent to which purposes are consciously articulated by actors helps to distinguish between levels of *rationality* in adaptational systems of behavior. This term has been greatly abused in our Western rhetoric, since it has come to mean any kind of conscious relationship of means to ends, without consideration of costs. Thus strategies believed to be efficient—"rational"—have turned out to be abusive of both human and natural resources. From one ideal standpoint, the most "rational" cultural-ecological system is the type of the equilibrious society (Fig. 8), since it maintains a balance with Nature, with the actions of its members involved in a system of conservationist feedback. However, this is only one available model of a rational system; obviously, balanced systems can be developed at higher levels of resource use and energy conversion.

In contemporary vocabulary, the term *planning* is used to refer to a method of articulating goals involving the rational adjustment of means to ends and the choice of appropriate strategies. The term *designing* has been used to refer to a planning process in which ideological guidance is conscious (that is, following a particular idealized cognitive blueprint). However, designing can also proceed on the basis of culturally pragmatic or *ad hoc* principles.[7]

The equilibrious former tribal systems included many cases where cultural style contained moral guides for decisions with long-term consequences, productive of sustained yield, which meant low or stable output. Strategies were therefore locally determined—that is, not geared to externally originating and fluctuating demands that compelled use or manipulation of resources without regard for long-term effects. Generally speaking, whenever human wants can remain at locally generated levels, sustained-yield resource management systems are more likely to evolve and be maintained by sanctioned reciprocity—Lee's Bushman case is the prototype. However, there is no absolute guarantee of this, given the known capacity of local systems to generate their own increased scale of wants. In general, however, the process of exploitation is usually speeded by demands originating outside local systems.

In terms of systemic models, the internal-external nexus means that the local actors learn to behave differently in different subsystems, some of them originating outside the community—a process that breaks up the stereotype of "a culture" and demands the substitution of a model of interactive systems cutting across population units. Adaptive strategies designed to cope with these differing systems can be contradictory: in some, the behavioral vector is toward gain and accumulation; in others, it will be toward conservationism and the maintenance of equilibrium. The incentives leading toward these contrasting strategies are themselves contrasting and contradictory: conflict and change are inevitable accompaniments, but these tend to become, in modern pluralistic society, the routine condition, not the exception. That is, individuals are required to adapt to contrasting demands as the condition of survival and also as the fulfillment of opportunity.

Decisions concerning appropriate strategies of action are importantly influenced by conceptions of *opportunity costs*. These can be defined simply as the cost of any course of action or sustaining activity, as compared with some other action or activity. The writer has used the concept as a tool for the analysis of the econological status of different agrarian groups inhabiting a common environment and with differing postures *vis-à-vis* the external market economy (Bennett, 1969, Chapter 10). By comparing the payoffs of current economic activities and use of resources with other alternatives created by immersion on a complex national system, the actors have some basis on which to make choices. We found that many of our agricultural operators were aware of the fact that the costs of their present activities were high, and they would make more by choosing other opportunities. However, many preferred to continue the present activities because they *liked* them; that is, their subjective evaluation of opportunity costs made them seem "low." Opportunity costs therefore constitute useful criteria for the analysis of pluralistic systems.[8]

However, opportunity costs have a much larger significance if we consider that the concept refers to the social transformation of individual valuations of what is "better" or desirable in the states and relationships between peoples. In this sense, the watershed phenomena associated with opportunity costs may well be the most significant general adaptive process in human history: it is the root cause of most of the great population migrations from the Paleolithic onward. The old homily about the better mousetrap needs to be taken with extreme seriousness: the attractions of sedentary wealth for nomads; of bow-hunting for dart throwers; of agriculture for herders, or *vice versa*; of mineral deposits for those who want and need them; of congenial climate for those inhabiting more rugged regions; of the city for the country people. Along with the search for customers by merchants, the search for the "better" adaptation has governed most of cultural evolution.

The interplay of local and external adaptive responses is responsible for outcomes in the adaptive process that cannot be predicted on the basis of a typology that assumes that culturally defined boundaries between groups or communities automatically inhibit change. This complex texture has come to light in studies of modernization of tribal-peasant societies, where frequently traditional cultural elements and self-imposed boundaries have facilitated adaptation to the outside, rather than impeded it. This process is nicely displayed in the case of Anabaptist sectarians in North American agricultural society. In studies of Hutterian and Amish agricultural economy and culture by the writer and associates, it is apparent that the self-imposed boundaries between these groups and the outside society do not necessarily result in deprivation, but in an increase in opportunity. For example, Hutterites gain by deliberately restricting their education level to grade 8, since this reduces the "pull" of the outside, discouraging emigration of skilled men (their own informal system of technical training is more or less adequate to operate their large-scale economy). Some Amish, by restricting their consumption level, are able to make up for the losses in income resulting from their very small acreages, farmed with horses, by using the saving to invest in profitable livestock-feeding and bulk-milk operations. Their level of living is higher than that of nonsectarian farmers with smallish acreages who spend more on consumption and machinery. These are cases—there are many others—where constraints and barriers to full participation in the larger society result in increased opportunity and internal change, although whether this is adaptive or not for the internal system is another question (there is evidence that it often results in increased tension).

TRANSACTIONS AND NETWORKS

In recent decades, sociocultural anthropology has begun to develop a generalized approach to the nature of social life, which Norman and Dorothea Whitten call "reciprocity and interaction strategy" (1972). The Whittens outline the foundations of this approach in the French school of sociology (Durkheim, Mauss) and anthropologists influenced by it (Radcliffe-Brown, Malinowski). They define the core concept as *reciprocity*, which of course is the sociological version of G. H. Mead's concept of "taking the role of the other."

The Whittens summarize the available materials in sociocultural anthropology produced to 1972 that reflect this approach. Some of these have already been cited in this volume. However, our purpose here is not to explore "reciprocity and interaction strategy" theory, but to use it as a basis for a cultural ecology that will permit the handling of contemporary problems. Consequently, the Whittens' excellent review paper should be consulted for the names of anthropologists working along similar lines, though not necessarily concerned with ecological problems. While the major innovators in the approach are not really to be found in anthropology,[9] Firth's role in formulating an early anthropological version (1954; 1955) in distinguishing between "structure" and "organization" (the latter the choice-determined outcomes; the former the slow-to-change normative components) has already been noted, as well as the later role of Frederik Barth, whose "transactionism" (1967; 1969) may be the only anthropological version of interactionism and exchange theory that might rank with the important contemporary sociological varieties. Marshall Sahlin's work on reciprocity and other facets of transactionism is equally significant (1965; 1972); and Belshaw's "social performance" is a major theoretical step (1970). There is also a tie with "games theory" in mathematics, but the attempts at application in anthropology have been very few in number, and the results not clear or impressive. Games theory is a specialized technique and much more limited in its applications than most social scientists realized at first sight.[10]

Transactionism is an important tool for the approach to cultural ecology explored in this book, but some qualifications should be introduced at this point. Since transactional or exchange analysis usually utilizes "economic" models of behavior, in which bargaining and cost-gain considerations are uppermost, it is an important tool for the study of instrumental contexts of social life, and its applicability to other contexts is probably questionable or limited. Or, perhaps transactionism is better defined as an empirical domain, and not a general theory or model of behavior. However, transactionism focuses attention on the important capacity of men to calculate gain in a social milieu. A degree of this is found in all human systems; however distasteful the humanist might view this capacity, it is there, it is a projection out of human behavior, and it is especially critical in analyzing man's actions toward Nature.

It is assumed that for the time being anthropological cultural ecology will specialize in the task of studying microsocial events: particular living social systems with a degree of representativeness for larger universae. Such microsocial systems can be communities, institutions, organizations, networks, enterprises, kinship groups or any detachable or discernible sector or phase of a larger social unit. In the ecological context, these microsocial systems—"microcosms" when they are reasonably representative of the processes at work on more general systemic levels—are to be viewed with reference to the way their actors use resources to accomplish their ends or produce energy and goods, and the way such use affects Nature and the social system. It is assumed that these use-patterns rarely will be determined exclusively by factors within the particular microcosm but will almost always involve interactions with larger or external systems. This means that the anthropologist will either be required to enlarge the scope of his research unit or rely upon other specialists to furnish him with data from these external systems influencing his locality. One of his major problems will concern itself with the way the actors in local systems manipulate the external groups and agents influencing their choice and use of resources, in order to obtain what they want, or to strike bargains with the external systems, in order to modify the effects of constraints imposed from within or without.

Transactionism, or social exchange, (the reciprocal exchange of obligations, favors, and rewards in the course of role behavior and social relations) is important for cultural ecology because it focuses on the most intimate level of resource exploitation: the use of resources to influence interchange among individuals. While there is no doubt that social systems vary in their use of measured reciprocity, their insistence on material rewards and equal exchange, and other "economic" or quantitative aspects of social relations, a degree of all of these characterize all social systems. Men do not usually interact on the basis of innate attitudes, but in terms of socialized responses that carry rewards in the form of affectual feeling, status, prestige, or power. The issue of importance for cultural ecology is the presence of a medium of exchange in the transactions between individuals. This can be either nonmaterial (gestures, services, etiquette) or material goods made from natural substances.

The point is that in social exchange the actors' statuses are always implicated in ways not found among nonhuman animals. The giving of gifts *obligates* others to reciprocate: this elementary transaction ("prestation"—Mauss, 1954) provides one major stimulus for the energy-transformation process in human ecology. The process also operates in contexts not involving actual obligation: examples are found in the emulation and status-competition cycles characteristic of capitalistic high-consumption societies like the United States and Japan, where the behavior is stimulated by advertising.

Social exchange is particularly important for the analysis of manipulation of social resources. The work of Norman Whitten (1969; Whitten and Whitten, 1972) and others on economically marginal groups (people lacking adequate cash surpluses for investment and/or the attitudes permitting investment) describes the strategies developed by such people to obtain survival necessities and anything else they may want. These strategies involve the creation of "adaptive networks" of social exchange: manipulation of reciprocal obligations among kin and friendship groups or employer-employee groups (Whitten and Wolfe, 1972). In such cases people lacking any access to natural resources, or to energy-conversion technology, must utilize available social resources in ways comparable to those used for natural resources. While these interactions are wholly within the context of social relations, they also represent forces generating pressure against the natural environment insofar as the population supported by such strategies is obtaining goods and services dependent on energy conversion. Often such "poverty" groups may be exerting more pressure on resources than is ordinarily realized, since conventional economic accounting usually neglects to consider the cost of satisfying them. Substandard and abusive agricultural regimes are one common consequence. Anthropologists are playing a significant role in calling our attention to these costs, by showing that although the media of exchange are not monetary, substantial quantities of goods or labor are exchanged.

Such studies also suggest that adaptations made by people owning minimal property are different from those made by people with large amounts—or, at least, those who are landless and those who have roots to the land. Landless people usually are familiar with a variety of adaptive strategies for economic and social survival, since their very mobility exposes them to a number of different possible strategies, and their mobility confers a certain necessary flexibility of choice. Areas with many such populations (as, for example, the Middle East and the South and Central American littoral) will display both competition for existing resources and also ordered "niche occupancy," where sharing of resources is worked out in intricate fashion.

A social-exchange network approach to the cultural ecology of agrarian people is necessary in order to fully understand the means used by the communities to allocate natural resources. While most contemporary agrarian societies operate under legal rules of tenure, and government controls allocation of resources, the local people have their own complex strategies for adjusting and manipulating these provisions. This is basically a matter of various forms of competition and cooperation that operate by the rules of reciprocity and obligation. In the Canadian region studied by the writer, he found that while assignments of grazing leases—the most important resources needed for livestock production—were in the hands of the government, applications for such leases were bound up in complex routines of cooperation and competition in the community (Bennett, 1969, pp. 293–294). For example, some men who were assigned to the lease either would have influential status positions in the community as well as being efficient operators or they would be small operators, in serious need of more land, allowed to compete by tacit agreement among more affluent neighbors, who felt the small operator deserved more. Some of the more enlightening cultural ecological studies of tribal agrarians, such as Sahlins' study of Samoans (1957), are concerned with these allocative devices and exchanges. Anthropologists need to extend these studies into inquiries that ask how the physical environment itself is affected by particular resource allocative measures.

Relations with external systems are especially important in determining the allocation and use of resources in arid and semi-arid lands, and for regions where symbiotic politicoeconomic relationships exist between people with different subsistence economies as arrangements to minimize or regularize competition for scarce resources. The persistence of particular types of resource use, and the social arrangements appropriate to these at a given point in history, may be based on political relationships with neighboring groups, even though they originated with reference to environmental factors. Groups in the Middle East may remain in a nomadic state as much for the purpose of avoiding contact with state political entities as for the preservation of particular adaptive styles of subsistence. The dynamic relationship of tribal groups to resources in Africa and elsewhere as a result of "predatory expansion" has already been mentioned.

An exchange model can also function to analyze the relationships among the actors in any administrative or political system involved in choices concerning resource use. Richard Adams (1970, Chapter 1) proposes a general theory of political power based on the proposition that power can be defined as control over environments—social and natural— and that the exercise of power is simply a process of controlling access to resources in these environments and trading advantage and decisions among the actors on the basis of exchanges.[11] The techniques for this control will, in most cases, have originated within the sociopolitical systems, and thus have reference to purely intrasystemic concerns, with the states of the social and natural environments (especially in authoritarian systems) usually being of secondary concern. "Adaptation" is therefore defined relative to the advantage of the actors in the situation; not usually with reference to some higher objective such as sustained yield. Adherence to higher values must become part of the rewards and allocations of the control and manipulation system before they can become policy mandates.

Thus, power systems operate so as to restrict or limit the alternatives available at any moment. The exchange process configurates around cultural precedents: it has its scales of rewards, bargains, and authority. A peasant population, encapsulated in a national social system as a power-less group, will have little say over agrarian development schemes imposed on it, even though these schemes may be ecologically and biologically harmful. However, since these systems are inherently dynamic, even "powerless" groups, with little control over their environments, can work toward such control by manipulative methods. The withholding of labor services is an example.

SOME ADAPTIVE PROCESSES

The term "adaptive process" refers to purely heuristic concepts: the delineation of such processes takes its cue from the state of the system under investigation, and the extent to which a temporal factor is included in the analysis. "Competition between social classes" is a process defined in terms of Marxist conceptions of the social system, and this may be more or less sound empirically for given cases. Processes might become systems, and can be called "institutions" when they exhibit consistency and repetitiveness: "capitalism" is a growth-oriented socioeconomic institution.

The concept of adaptive process is therefore an "emic" concept on the whole, since it refers to intellectual constructions made by a disciplined observer of the consequences of adaptive behavior (especially strategic action and strategies) over periods of time. The question of whether the actors in an adaptive system can perceive the processes at work is a matter of the extent of their ability to formulate purposes, look ahead, control the operations of the system, and objectify their own actions. All of these things, as we have seen, are variables in human systems, and even when a high level of awareness of destructive processes is present, there is no guarantee of cessation or reform, since the behavior may be reinforced many times by obligations, interests, and power combinations.

Underlying such processes are some very familiar but poorly understood behavioral mechanisms. If we are to understand the basis of institutional changes in ecological relations, we will have to know what levels of deprivation humans are willing to accept before a search for alternative paths emerges. Deprivation must always be measured in terms of both *minimal* tolerance (as in nutrition, the boundary between starvation and survival) and *habituated* tolerance (that level which the milieu has taught the individual to prefer and want). Responses therefore vary by "culture," but the *process* of adjusting behavior to necessary and habituated tolerances is cross-cultural.

For example, the presses that motivate people to migrate or to stay put are still very hazily understood, despite a good deal of work on some aspects (e.g., the "mobility transition" in Chapter 5). This is one of those problems with human ecological significance that can be solved only by close attention to diachronic events—not by descriptive studies of synchronic situations. Needed are predictive studies that assess various tolerance and aspiration levels and predict migration when these levels, in a situation known to be changing, exert pressure on populations to choose migration or geographic mobility as a desirable strategy. The process is multidimensional: biological, psychological, cultural, and economic factors all play their role. But certain guidelines, often so familiar that they are not taken seriously, exist and need to be studied in depth. "Opportunity cost" is one of these: the assessments made by people of the emotional, social, and economic costs of shifting to a new strategy when the existing ones are threatened. There seems to be no reason other than inertia delaying a search for methods of measurement of these factors as presses toward behavioral change. Laboratory studies of human behavior in such contexts are abundant enough, but unfortunately these simply do not provide the reality contexts necessary for predicting in actual situations.

Some specific processes:

1. *Strategy designs.* This concerns linked sets or chains of strategies with consistent effects. Any well-developed pattern of strategic action or transaction will contain more than a single strategic component, and any complex objective will require a series of strategies used in sequence or rotation. Moreover, such sequences characteristically accomplish portions of the objective one by one: technological processes are the simplest example, and the ethnographic literature is replete with descriptions of technical step-by-step routines: making dugout canoes, leaching manioc, coiling pottery vessels. Strategy chains in these cases have a behavioral logic that is mirrored in ritual and social behavior, linking intracultural and ecological systems through basic cognitive and muscular actions.

Moreover, commonly the employment of one strategy will predetermine the choice of the next—a process common to all economic and resource-utilization processes. A farmer will start a sequence of actions designed to shift from grain to livestock production by converting some of his grain fields to fodder cultivation, a step that requires the purchase of livestock to compensate for the income lost from grain—and so on through a series of such determining steps. This is the basis of the innovative process in instrumental contexts; when such sequences become standardized, one may speak of a "design." In ethnological terms, this is really a part of culture, since the design can be considered a precedent or cognitive map.

The next three processes concern the amount of time required to accomplish a given end by the employment of specific strategies or designs. The amount of *risk* associated with them will be a variable.

2. *Strategies with immediate effects or returns.* If these quick-return strategies are relatively certain to produce results, they are judged to have low risk. The certainty can be produced either by a situation with known resources and results or by the existence of social norms and rules requiring reciprocal behavior with high probability. The opening of an irrigation ditch in high water will be certain to produce results; the investing in real estate during a housing and lot shortage will be relatively certain to produce profits; the doing of a favor in a social system exerting considerable pressure on people to reciprocate, will be relatively certain to be returned.

3. *Strategies with delayed effects.* Again, if the effects, though known to be delayed, are relatively certain, the risks are low. However, the "investor" must be prepared to forego "returns" for an indefinite period; hence strategies with these characteristics should not be attempted by actors without adequate carryover capital. The building of a herd of cattle that will not be available for sale for a known period, or, again, the giving of gifts or doing favors that need not or cannot be repaid immediately are examples. An example from intrasocial contexts would be that of a businessman training a man to take over management of the enterprise at a future data—and of course hoping that he won't take another job after completing his training. Usually, in entrepreneurial activity, there are greater risks associated with these strategies than with the former, since time itself is a value—that is, a kind of capital.

4. *Strategies with sustained effects.* These are strategies that produce a continual flow of returns once initiated. The risk factor remains variable. Such flow may require a constant input of resources or capital, but if it is to be "profitable" the input will have to be lower than the output, minus any ancillary costs of the strategic operation. Stated this way, the category seems comparable to the illusion of perpetual motion—that is, impossible without some deterioration in the absolute supply of energy or resources. This is certainly the case, of course, for extractive industries

that continue to make profits on low-cost removal of raw materials, as long as the "cost" of the diminishing supply to the Earth's store is not included.[12]

5. It is also possible to consider strategic processes in terms of *multiplier effects* of various kinds—a concept closely related to the notion of hidden costs or externalities, and one that often describes effects common in the natural resource depletion and pollution fields. *Technological escalation* is a term applied by critics of economic development to the situation resulting from the attempt to solve problems created by one technological strategy by introducing still another technological device. The introduction of powered machinery in farming permitted production at lower labor costs, but also required a rise in prices. This process demands further mechanization in order to further reduce costs, and increasingly large and expensive machines are added to the system, until the costs of machines begin to exceed the savings, creating financial crises and permitting increased abuse of resources (although the latter consequence is not inevitable, since under some circumstances machine cultivation can protect soil and water resources). Another example is found in the response to heavy automobile traffic by building more roads, which permit a further increase in traffic, and so on. Such processes are guided by "progress" values in the culture, but are rooted in the institutions of capital, profit, and return on investment. Technological escalation is the opposite of "planning," although it is often presented as the apotheosis of planning.

6. A related process of particular concern to critics of our economic development strategies may be called *incremental change*. This refers to a pattern of attack on issues or opportunities one-by-one, instead of on a long-term strategic planning basis—really a chain of attempted immediate-effect, "quick buck" decisions and strategy choices. The accumulation of errors resulting from following short-term strategies without due regard for external costs or damage results in environmental deterioration on a widening scale: the slow but increasingly visible ("escalating") eutrophication of water resources; the increasing ("cumulative") contamination of urban airsheds by toxic substances. These results have been obtained by action designed to serve immediate ends of profit or output, without concern for future costs and without reference to the need for long-range planning for change in the whole systems.

To illustrate the sources of these concepts in strategic action analysis, we may consider the strategy of "machinery-buying" by farmers. For a given situation, this strategic action can have: (a) immediate financial effects in the form of lowered costs, (b) but with an escalating effect of increasing costs, and (c) delayed deteriorative effects on the natural resources. A second example can be found in the adherence by an agrarian entrepreneur to cautious, consumption-deferring strategies of operation. This strategic pattern affects parts of several systems (the business, the family's consumption, etc.), but it can have (a) a constant effect of savings and lowered costs on the business, (b) a delayed effect of ultimate consumption gratification for the family, through savings and accumulation of resources, and (c) a constant sustained-yield effect on the natural resources.

7. *Buffering and step-functioning.* These related processes pertain to the systemic lag phenomena noted in earlier chapters. A buffering effect is visible when a deleterious strategy perseverates because other factors encourage it to do so, in spite of visible evidence of danger. Vested interests are one kind of buffering mechanism of particular importance in all growth-oriented systems where gain is large and risk of loss is correspondingly felt to be severe. Step functions exist where, due to buffering, a considerable output or operation must proceed until enough has accumulated to trigger a demand for, or the imposition of, control. This process is particularly evident in the contemporary scene, where a sense of urgency over environmental "crises" develops in one group in the population, whose protests have zero effect because the situation is not sufficiently dangerous overall for a change to be effected. The Santa Barbara oil spill resulted in the first round of effective controls over offshore oil exploitation, and, in this case, the spill took place along a coast inhabited by the wealthy. The "step function" in this case meant that people with power had to experience the effects of the damage before controls could be initiated. Social class phenomena are visible here as elsewhere.

8. *Resource competition.* This process is an especially apt one for demonstrating the interpenetration of ecological and social phenomena, since humans compete equally for both. The process is also just as evident for animals and, in a specialized sense, for plants. One of the most promising, but as yet unexploited domains for comparative research among organisms including humans may lie in this sphere. Competition for resources proceeds cyclically in many cases, and may approximate steady states or homeostatic rhythms when the competing groups move toward an accommodation pattern in which allocations of particular resources in a scarce or marginal set are made to particular groups. We

commented on Frederik Barth's paper on "niche" occupancy among Middle Eastern village and nomadic people in this context in Chapter 6. The competitive process in humans is always dynamic; arrival at a particular allocation always involves time, and increasing populations or external inputs, conquests, and so on can upset the system and lead to renewed competition.

9. *Specialization of potential*—or "adaptive specialization": a process of considerable importance involving the increasingly focused use of particular resources over long periods of time, and closely associated with resource competition. If a larger regional unit is involved, the specialization of resource use results in particular productive regimes carried on by subgroups in the regional population. In a process of competition, the use of particular resources is allocated to particular groups, and various cultural and social patterns gradually conform to the demands of technology, work, and resources. Symbiotic arrangements can emerge between the specialized groups, as responses to the need to control competition. The process has been studied by cultural ecologists in tribal and peasant contexts.[13]

From the prehistorians, we have some data on the way these systems of specialization emerge over time, although the archeological data does not provide information on the competitive process. The work of Flannery et al., (1967) on the progressive occupancy of differing microenvironments in the interior valleys of Mexico has shown how there was a consistent movement from the plateau level by unspecialized hunter-gatherer groups, down the slope of the valley, with increasingly specialized subsistence systems emerging as the descent continued. MacNeish (1967) has shown how corn agriculture finally emerged on the floor occupation of one of these valleys. The appearance of urban civilization was linked to the more abundant water and agricultural potential of the valley floors. The work of archeologists in the northeastern United States on settlement, population, and agricultural development in Iroquois culture (Tooker, 1967) provides another example of growing adaptive specialization at the tribal level. My own work on the Northern Plains (1969) deals with comparable processes in contemporary rural settings.

Specialization exemplifies the tendency toward increasing energy output in human ecological systems and increasingly precise relationships with natural resources—tendencies that have implications for sustained yield, but also for increasing rigidity of the adaptation and vulnerability to particular environmental shocks (e.g., from large-scale preindustrial hydraulic systems). Such consequences can of course be avoided by increasing integration of differently specialized systems into cooperative macrosystems: in the Western United States experiments have been underway for a number of years on such cooperative specialization between farmers and ranchers in irrigiated watersheds: the former are responsible for feed production, which is bought by the latter, with prices adjusted and compensated by government agencies so as to assure equitable returns to both.

10. *Adaptational drift.* This consists of a movement or vector of decisions and adjustments in a certain direction due to the preservation of cultural style and the sanctioning of decisions by traditional precedent, usually for reasons related to social stratification. Other adaptational processes also become significant in "drift," such as the "vicious circle" of increasing efficiency in production, which demands ever-greater production at lower costs, until resources are depleted or abused.[14] The striking thing about adaptational drift is that it is frequently accompanied by an aura of rationality. While a degree of awareness of contradiction usually exists, it is surrounded with rationalizations; essentially, drift is a prolongation of the *status quo* disguised as planning.

11. *Rationalized approval.* This process frequently operates when power investments make it advisable to confirm a certain vector of adaptational decisions, or unforeseen consequences, by the *post hoc* discovery of positive sanctions. This sanctioning process is an adjustmental device in an attempt to convey the impression that "it was planned all along"—i.e., that the situation is under control or is self-regulating. The adaptational process is thus itself transformed into a value.

12. *Action constraint.* This refers to the effect of increasing the number of variables in a situation—a consequence of strategy design—and, by so doing, limiting or controlling future decisions and changes. This may be another way of referring to drift, but in "constraint" one is concerned with the tension produced by a contradiction between the desire to alter the pattern and the impossibility of doing so due to the binding power of decisions produced by a very heavy investment.

THE ALLOCATION OF RESOURCES

The basic meanings of policy in the context of cultural ecology concern the way resources are allocated to the converters of energy, and the regulations governing their use. The process of allocation is intimately related to the adaptive behavior and institutional patterns of the society: these will include subsistence systems, but also particular styles of tenure, legal norms, and patterns of interindividual responsibility and assistance. The fact that the latter can vary within given types of subsistence or economic production means that one cannot always expect similarities among groups with similar subsistence types. Where many of the conditions to which people respond emanate from sources outside the immediate community or region, the adaptive patterns may have even less to do with the particular economic or technological features distinctive of the local scene.

In my research on a Canadian agricultural community, I was concerned with the way resources were allocated in order to take into account both these local and external conditions (Bennett, 1967B). I was also concerned over the way the interplay between these local and external frames had shaped the internal system itself over a period of years. Historically, the people had settled the Western frontier with a package of institutions and adaptive responses shaped in a different milieu; one of considerable humidity and opportunity, and contrasting greatly with the aridity and privation of the West. Some of these responses were transferable—private land tenure was a notable one; others were not— wholly-owned riparian rights, for example, had to give way to the "prior appropriation" doctrine in a region of intermittent streams. In other words, the people came to the frontier with institutions already shaped by the external frames they contended with at the time we studied them; but, in addition, many of these had changed in response to the habitat and to the ways this habitat could be used in order to satisfy the continuing pressure exerted by the outside system. For example, bankers tried to maintain conservative credit policies of the Eastern industrial world, but the local people required much more liberal credit policies. In this kind of situation, various complex devices emerged by means of which the banks could be maneuvered into liberalizing their credit, or the local people could find new sources of credit. Government support programs for Western agriculture—developed and promoted, in all cases, by Western agrarian politicians—were another adaptive response.

If one views this process from a cultural anthropological standpoint, the point of departure lies in a description of the protocols for action— values, attitudes—characteristic of the local community at a given time. In our Canadian community, and elsewhere in rural North America generally, this system could be described as a synthesis of individualistic, egalitarian, and particularistic practices—what we have called an "IEP" social system (Bennett 1967B). It was individualistic in that the individual entrepreneur was supposed to obtain his resources and manage them on his own; it was egalitarian in that he was viewed as equal to his neighbors and equally capable; and it was particularistic insofar as the actual inequalities of access to resources and individual capabilities required adjustive actions to help people measure up or redress the inequalities to some degree. From the standpoint of the local system, then, the chief role of external resource inputs and aid was to assist the local individualistic-egalitarian pattern to survive, or at least to present a profile of reasonable consistency. Needless to say, the system worked imperfectly at best, and conformity to the ideal was often a matter mainly of simply denying the existence of exceptions.

But still, the local people did what they could to manipulate the external sources. These sources, government bureaus or private financial agencies like banks, operated on a different protocol: they were universalistic in that their regulations and benefices were equally applicable to everyone; and lawful, insofar as they were written down and sanctioned by the legislature and courts, and administered locally by bureaucratic offices and inspectors. These regulations were all of a type: no one had any right to obtain a resource if he did not live up to the specified conditions, and everyone had the same right to make application.

However, since the local people were concerned with redressing local inequalities, their conception of who should obtain a service or resource was often quite different from that of the agencies. The existence of this disparity would mean that pressures would be put on the agencies to supply the resources as exceptions to their rules—pressures that were often successful. Hence the resource allocation procedures of the agencies would depart in varying ways and degrees from the regulations. In any specific governing regime, the tendency would be toward an accumulation of such exceptions to the point where the agencies could be accused of favoritism, corruption, etc.—that is, their operations would begin to conform to the patterns of the IEP system.

We then investigated what this process meant for the physical resources of agriculture. Since the resources were, in general, for agriculture, specialized and refractory, like those of all cool, semi-arid climates, there existed a separate process of adaptation that developed through the years of settlement and somewhat independent of the resources allocation process. This adaptive process concerned itself with the ways of husbanding light soils, using scarce water, experimenting with the right crops, and so on, so that by the time of observation, the people had developed regimes that ameliorated most of the more serious blunders contributing to soil blowing, erosion, fertility exhaustion, and the like.

However, the one institution that did not change fundamentally during this period (1880–1965) was private ownership of land, and some degree of "ownership" of (or at least the right to take) water. It was this institution, in an exceedingly variable environment, that created the problem of allocation. Because no single acreage could be expected to have the same constituent resources, due to extreme variability, there was constant struggle for redressing imbalance between individual access. Here, the manipulations of the people, the agencies' own policies, and the covert particularistic exceptions tended to work in the direction of distributing resources more or less equally to the individual operators.

However, the individual operators were not equally endowed, nor did they have identical consumption needs and desires. Families differed in size, educational outlooks differed, skills differed. By tending to equalize access to resources, conservationist or sustained-yield treatment of the resources was *not* equalized. In fact, for a time it was worsened. "Good operators" were defined for a time as maximizers, and this often meant violation of the ecological or agronomic strategies mentioned previously—and *this* meant that some operators would over-produce and abuse their resources, while others would under-use, or under-produce from approximately the same resource base. In other words, the equalization of opportunity in an IEP system did not necessarily move in the direction of equalized environmental management.

But even here, there were continuing changes. In order to control this differentiation, the agencies began to institute programs of collective-use and cooperative resource allocation, such as community irrigation systems, community pastures, grazing cooperatives, and similar systems, which put the resource management in the hands of impartial experts and bureaucrats. These devices simultaneously protected the resources against abuse, and also continued to give (or even enhanced) equal access or at least access by impartially evaluated need. This system helped, but it gave rise to another round of adaptive problems. The people began their usual activity of persuading the agencies to grant exceptions: to permit more livestock in the pastures than were deemed good for the grass, or to permit people without the requisite need to rent irrigation plots. It was noted that the projects that did not give people something like title to ownership of the resource in question were more subject to abuse than those (like the grazing co-ops) where such title existed. Hence a new round of policy changes was in order—to shift collective-use resource schemes to local ownership and management. All of these were manifestations of the way policy changes in an interplay between local and external frames of resource allocation, and how adaptive solutions give rise to new problems.

While this brief outline of a process or system of resource allocation in a North American setting has "modern" and "market" dimensions, at the level of social interaction and decision making it has characteristics that echo those in such tribal cases as Melanesia and New Guinea, where tribal groups compete for land, seek to redress imbalances, move through cycles of abuse and recovery of resources, and become involved in internal-external relationships. The differences are of course obvious: the North American farmers do not resort to stylized warfare, nor do they engage in pig rituals to redress imbalances; and the tribals, at least in the aboriginal state, do not manipulate bureaus and banks (however, they are, to an increasing extent, doing this, and apparently just as cleverly and successfully as the Canadians). But the point is that we are dealing with processes that undercut subsistence and even technological levels, and it is this domain of cultural ecology that needs development so that policy-relevant findings can emerge.

THE PROBLEM OF REGULATION OF RESOURCE USE

Paul Ehrlich has noted that the idea of human control over Nature has been changing from its earlier notion of control for the means of freeing humans from the limitations of natural phenomena toward control for the purpose of permitting man to accomplish his ends and survive indefinitely. The former concept recognized no responsibility for Nature; the latter acknowledges its necessity; both views are anthropocentric, but one allows us to hope that environmental and social disruption can be controlled. Neither view allows us to find a solution to the ecological problem in a romantic return to tribal homeostasis.

Garrett Hardin extends the argument to include a recognition of the need for coercion to insure human observance of environmental integrity in his book on "new ethics for survival" (1972). Hardin develops his discussion around three basic concepts: freedom, responsibility, and control. The application of the concept of freedom leads to the "tragedy of the commons," or the tendency for individuals to encroach on the public domain, or simply to appropriate resources for their private benefit. Since humans seem to have a drive toward maximization of want satisfaction, the "freedom" to appropriate resources needs curtailment lest the supply be exhausted. As for responsibility, which as an attitude and behavior could control resource appropriation, Hardin states that it works well only when the decision maker and the one affected by the decision are one and the same person. Modern society has been moving rapidly toward a situation in which the two are always separated; thus, responsibility becomes "contrived"—it is really a license to exploit, not to control exploitation. Some sense of responsibility can be encouraged by exhortation, but this, Hardin feels, does not work either; it stimulates guilt feelings and provides opportunities for covert exploitation.

Coercion, then, is required in order to ensure a reasonable degree of conformity to a conservationist or sustained yield policy. The word "coercion" has acquired an unpleasant connotation in a society preoccupied with individualistic freedom, and yet no human society has ever been able to exist without it. Coercion is a "bad" thing when it is imposed on top of permissive arrangements, but, once institutionalized, resentment usually abates or disappears. The initially coerced conformity becomes an accepted routine of life; hence, human "adaptability" can facilitate the development of a system with greater respect for the environment along, of course, with the ability of humans to develop consensus.

Obviously, the real problem is just what is meant by "coercion" in any particular case, since it is difficult to generalize. A rationing system like that proposed by Walter Westman and R. M. Clifford (1973), in which the NRU—"natural resource unit"—is added to the present monetary system and can be expended for services with known impact on the environment, avoids the undesirable features of coercion and requires consensus rather than forced conformity. However, the initial stage of acceptance of such a scheme would meet with resistance, and it is clear that without actual shortages things would have to get much worse before effective control systems could be initiated. Material shortages and rationing may turn out to be the most effective means of control, but of course these generate requirements for bureaucratic institutions and control. There is generally no easy way.

In these remarks there are implications for the theory of conservatism and change in social behavior. Expansiveness, high wants, and destructive overgrowth are obvious causes of environmental disruption, but resistance to change in resource practices is equally evident and indicates that behavioral conservatism is equally at fault. Human capacities are at both ends of the change-conservatism continuum; both are involved in the environmental problem. The process involves an interplay between subsystems: once change begins in a subsystem, it can occur rapidly as consensus on the need or desirability of the change spreads through the group. If the changes spread to other subsystems, and become features of the exchange process between these groups, reform becomes very difficult. Accommodations are reinforced by social interests and bargaining; Nature becomes part of Society; and change in resource practices becomes equivalent to change in institutions and exchange systems. Hence "cleanup" becomes a more realistic (though inadequate) goal for environmental problems than genuine reform.

The issue of control keeps returning to the stubborn fact that it is easier to stimulate wants than to induce them to abate, especially when the mass culture has been constructed out of extensive promises. The "revolution of rising expectations" in the new nations following World War II, stimulated by foreign aid programs and improved communication networks, has had its consequences in population growth, unsettled social conditions, and mounting pressures on available resources in an effort to satisfy the awakened desires. As these conditions escalate, the possibility of control being exercised through consensus becomes less feasible, and coercive mechanisms involving the imposition of power without consensus tend to become more likely. The hesitance shown by the Soviet Union in liberating its consumer production indicates the fear of cycles of repressive control that might result from the stimulation of wants to the point where other priorities are threatened. Maoist China is an example of a system in which a population habituated to a modest scale of consumption was held there by efficient methods of building satisfaction consensus on other activities combined with strong authority and considerable use of power to control "deviance." It remains to be seen whether China can hold the line now that she is making an opening to the world.

Anthropologists, by virtue of their distinctive style of research, can shed light on another type of change process: *adaptive selection*. This involves the passage of time—perhaps a minimum of two human generations—and usually a good deal more, depending on many variables in the situation. Adaptive selection refers to the forging of a sustained-yield system, or something approximating it, through a series of experiments with natural resources plus the slow winnowing of particular behavioral styles suited to the emerging techniques—like the process of agricultural adaptation to the Great Plains alluded to in the previous section. The sustained-yield systems in tribal and peasant societies represent one instance of the process, although in no important case to my knowledge has an anthropologist studied these adaptive systems long enough to demonstrate how the system actually emerged—the single time-slice description must be used to infer the emergence over an unknown period of time.

Historical societies obviously offer better opportunities for the anthropological study of adaptive selection, since there is better data on the past, and often the cycles of experimentation and change leading to less abusive methods of resource exploitation are compressed into relatively short spans of time measured by a few human generations. In the Great Plains case mentioned earlier, about 70 years, or three or four generations were required to evolve a reasonably protective regime, although it was by no means finished. The evolution of constructive systems of use was helped by inputs of information from experimental stations and other sources and by the winnowing effect of market agricultural economy, which imposed severe cost restraints, thus favoring the more conservationist and efficient operators (Bennett, 1969, pp. 325-327).

At the local level, the process is an intricate combination of interlocking strategies in the agronomic, economic, and social systems of action. As noted earlier, land allocation for grazing purposes is controlled to a degree by external agencies that monitor the quality of operation and assign leases to the operators with the best performance in terms both of output and resource conservation. In addition, these allocation devices are under a certain amount of local control, and the community can arrange things so as to channel leases into especially desirable hands by manipulating the bureaus. There is also a tendency toward large-scale operation, which is generally more conservationist at the price of squeezing out the smaller, less efficient operators (a typical clash between ecological interests and human rights values—we shall see many more of these in the future). Maintenance of conservationist standards is also accomplished by local gossip and censoring techniques such as criticism of the neighbor who uses the wrong fallowing methods and permits his soil to blow and gully.

Over a period of three or four generations, the region tended to lose the more ambitious, aggressive "maximizers" who were inclined to seek quick profits by abusing their resources. This was accomplished in two ways: first, by out-migration by whole families of such persons, selling out to the more patient, averaging satisficers; and second, by a tendency for the more aggressive sons to leave the family at maturity and seek satisfaction in urban business and other occupations.

There is no doubt that such processes of adaptive selection occur, even in highly developed societies. However, external forces usually hold a whip hand. Fluctuations in the national economy exert increasing pressures on the "adapted" operators, who will continue to seek higher levels of living, and cycles of abuse of resources are likely to recur—as they have in the past. There is no certain guarantee of permanent sustained-yield systems in any human society. Because of this uncertainty in the situation, observation of adaptive processes must be continuous: anthropologists and resource specialists must develop monitoring research operations.

The unwillingness to pay the full costs of resource use—a process we mentioned earlier—is a cultural problem insofar as people are likely to put more emphasis on present gratifications than on future disasters, but it is also a consequence of the buffering effect of the large energy output in human ecology—that is, the amount of stored surplus energy in many societies (including hunting-gathering, on the basis of current research) may be great enough to carry a population at a survival-or-better level for some time while resources deteriorate. The inability of members of a society to comprehend the state of their resources of the future due to the abstruse nature of production and distribution technology results in indifference to potential ecological disaster.

Similarly, and typically, only a minority of members of the large modern populations are required to adopt particular strategic responses to environmental changes or problems. That is, the disaster contact front is usually small, not large as it is in a typical, small micronetwork society where experiences are shared by the majority. When it becomes necessary to shift behavior toward more environmentally protective patterns—for example, in attempts to encourage car pools to reduce air pollution by reducing the number of vehicles on the road—one confronts a mass of citizens who simply have experienced no undesirable consequences from the pollution. Again, the task is much easier if gasoline is in short supply, and sharing becomes a necessity. Smog disasters appear mainly to affect the aged, who are expected to die anyway; the younger person sees no need to change his ways.

Once more, then—the problem of control: how can people be induced to "adapt" when there are no immediate pressures, but when it is in their longer term interest to do so, or when their behavior endangers others? As we have already noted, the problem of human ecology concerns both flexibility and conservatism in social behavior. The sources of conservatism or inflexibility are sufficiently obvious: *one* is the relative ease with which humans can tolerate uncomfortable or dangerous situations, or the extent to which they can become accustomed to high risk. Rene Dubos calls this "adaptability," and notes that man's ability to tolerate underlies his acceptance of harmful or unhealthy institutions (1965, pp. 254–256). The *second* source of conservatism is the one discussed previously: the frequent narrowness of demographic contact with the ecologically problematic situation, and the consequent disinclination of large numbers of people to accept any change in routine. The *third* factor is the one of delayed costs and immediate benefits, and the disinclination of humans to forego these benefits, especially under a capitalist system, in favor of the putative future costs. The *fourth* source is "culture"—that is, the nature of the sanctions promoting traditional precedents in behavior and the amount of emotional investment in these precedents. Working together, the four sources of inflexibility configurate into institutions or bureaucratic assemblages of vested interests and established procedures for maintaining these interests, in which processes like drift, constraint, and rationalization become the rule. The greater the amount of energy transformed in our basic ecological equations, the more complex these institutions become, and hence the inflexibility—at least in many relevant ecological contexts—of behavior when there is no immediate present need or danger (or none that can be successfully communicated). In a high-energy society, this inflexibility will be most apparent in those very contexts where Nature is abused; least apparent in the sphere of everyday stylistic gratification. However, in the latter arise many of the constant pressures against resources, which are, in turn, manipulated by the guardians of the institutions.

In individualistic democratic systems of social order there is a reluctance to use force as the means of control, and various softer and persuasive measures are sought by the authority groups. Hence the current debate, in environmental science, over the carrot vs. stick measures, referred to in previous chapters. Incentive systems are sought to replace compulsion. These measures, however, beg the fundamental question: the establishment of consensus. Presumably, if persuasive incentives work, a consensus at the normative level is built automatically, but historical experience, especially in a socioeconomy with strong maximizing presses, does not give us much assurance that consensus will emerge without coercion. We are once again forced to contemplate the power of human wants in modern industrial society. There is really no way out: if sustained yield systems are necessary, and must be introduced relatively soon, they are going to have to be bought by drastic reconstruction of institutions and the redefinition of gratification; this process will be accompanied, in its earlier phases at least, by considerable social conflict. Shortages of raw materials will make the imposition of controls more palatable, but at the cost of big bureaucracy and big government. Nevertheless, there is a revolution hidden in ecology, and however optimistic we may be over man's ability to control his use of Earth, there is little room for pollyannas, at least among the serious students of the situation.

ADAPTATION AND MALADAPTATION

And so we come to the payoff issue: the standards required for policy-oriented cultural-ecological research. The question involves the normative meaning of "adaptation"; more specifically, the distinction between adaptation as a desired process and *mal*adaptation as an undesirable consequence. To avoid the latter, suitable choices must be made by the actors, and the question for the ecological scientist is whether, and how, he is to influence these decisions.

Throughout the book I have assumed that one major criterion for normative adaptation exists: *sustained yield* of resources. This is taken as axiomatic and no defense will be made of the proposition. Sustained yield is a condition that permits both human and environmental survival, although it is acknowledged that as an objective this may clash with a variety of other cultural values, and difficult choices will have to be made.

In Chapter 3, I discussed the relationship of adaptive-maladaptive criteria to the concepts of negative and positive feedback as developed by ecologists and systems analysts. It was pointed out that these latter neutral concepts constitute a different order of analysis, since they refer merely to conditions that sustain stability or help to retire energy (negative feedback); or to conditions that disrupt equilibrium and lead toward increasing organization and change (positive). Adaptive or maladaptive actions in humans systems can be found in both categories; that is, stability is not always the only objective in these systems: adaptations that fluctuate between overuse and underuse of resources are common, but can nevertheless permit sustained yield. Therefore, "homeostasis" is a more meaningful term when dealing with the human level than "steady state."

To begin, I shall list the criteria that are available for use in defining adaptive and maladaptive actions in human ecology:[15]

1. *The conditions of the natural (and social) environment, including biological species as well as inanimate species, before and subsequent to human actions.* Specific criteria will include sustained yield or some other standard, although sustained yield will predominate. Before any ecologically significant action is taken, the present environmental conditions will be investigated, possible future consequences assessed, cost-gain differentials and trade-off possibilities outlined. This procedure, however

ineffective it might be in particular applications, is actually followed today in benefit-cost accounting, and, to an increasing extent, environmental impact surveys are being legally required before major technological interventions will be permitted.[16]

For anthropologists, this means that a stronger effort must be made to incorporate studies of natural resources in field investigations. Such studies will be difficult to make in many parts of the world, due to remoteness, inconvenience, and lack of adequate baseline data. Easier are studies of the criteria for environmental quality and utility developed by the particular society (assuming continued anthropological specialization in the smaller social units). These local standards should be analyzed against the background of actual resource conditions and changes, along with the investigator's own set of standards, based on whatever scientific knowledge is available on the effects of given practices on resource abundance and quality.

2. The second set of criteria concern *the biological conditions of the human population*. Specifically, these refer to size, distribution, and the state of health of the population as these may be affected by particular actions. While there exist certain minimal standards for population and health based on reproductive continuity of the group, there is room for considerable movement, and choices must be made among the many shaded possibilities and alternatives.

As researchers, cultural ecologists can be perfectly free to accept or to devise particular standards of biological performance and health for the purposes of making assessments of the consequences of strategic action, or, if they wish, making positive recommendations based on explicit criteria.

3. The third set concern *states of being as defined by the human group as necessary to social continuity and peace of mind*. Here the problem is to compare the potential consequences of following particular preferences with the consequences of some other choice. This is, in fact, one distinctive responsibility of the cultural as opposed to the human ecologist. These preferred states of being may implement, or inhibit, sustained yield, human health and reproductive survival, beauty, or any other condition or criterion. Characteristically, as human society has become more complex, and economic growth has become a dominant feature, the number of conflicts between desired states of being has increased. Out of this situation competition for resources emerges, as well as human group conflict.

The role of cultural values in defining adaptive or maladaptive consequences should give us no particular difficulty once it is clearly understood that values and purposes are part of human ecology. The difficulties arise when we are required to make decisions on desirable courses of action, and our data or methods are found to be unequal to the task. This is why anthropologists should *initiate* research with comparison of alternative strategies and consequences as a major goal, and not relegate this sort of work to "applied anthropology"—that is, as a function of employment by a private or public organization, often with special interests.

With the increasing complexity and integration of world society, actions need to be assessed in terms of their consequences, and a choice made on the basis of a trade between one set of consequences and another: to an increasing extent, between desirability and survival. While trade-off thinking is a characteristic of all human action; it is particularly characteristic of the modern pluralistic situation.

The complexity of the situation means that an adaptive response from the standpoint of one of the three sets of criteria will be maladaptive from some other. We have referred to the situation typical of economic development: the adaptive responses from the standpoint of desired levels of living (criteria set 3), create pressures on the environment, yielding maladaptive effects in criteria sets 1 and/or 2—these are often delayed or cumulative. The current environmental movement seeks to make "sustained yield" (the accepted definition of adaptive strategy for criteria set 1) an adaptive response for the other categories as well. The difficulties of achieving this are manifold. The idealized vision is one of a controlled human population existing at a stable level of living, presumably more modest than current blue-sky aspirations, and utilizing resources in such a way as to permit continual supply and minimal interference with human and nonhuman species. As suggested in Chapter 5, this is, by and large, an abstract definition of ancient high civilizations (literate societies without powered technology). Clearly it is out of the question to ask the developed nations to return to this condition voluntarily, or the under-developed to cease their efforts at improvement, although the cumulative ecological damage—to the environment and to human life and health—might require this. It is therefore necessary to seek constructive change and, at the very least, to aim for a changing mix of abusive and controlled utilizations, with persistent attempts at control of resource use by responsible public authorities. Needless to say, international agreements are vital; the world resource balance will have to be kept by a series of agreements between consumers and producers, monitored by public, non-national bodies.[17]

NOTES

[1] I have not gone into detail on the problem of fertility control since this would involve us in demographic and biological issues beyond the scope of the book. The topic remains something of a mystery in spite of a certain amount of research and a good deal of observational data in ethnological monographs. Perhaps the most firmly established factor is the importance of postpartum sexual abstinence in reducing fertility (Nag, 1962, p. 142)—a practice that must be supported by rigorous reciprocal rules and sanctions. Additional possibly related factors found by Nag are the relatively high incidence of prolonged breast feeding, which reinforces postpartum abstinence (a practice typical of societies organized on primary-group principles), the extent of polygyny, the frequency of coitus generally, late age of women at marriage. Lindenbaum (1972) makes a case for the control of breeding in New Guinea by ritual means, via the concept of "polluting women," which limits sexual relations during the fertile years. She relates this specifically to groups where the "man-resource ratio is unusually high," offering an argument with some similarities to Rappaport's, although more specific. (For other reviews of fertility in anthropological contexts, see Polgar, 1968; Lee, 1972C; Spooner, 1972; Hawthorn 1970.)

[2] To some extent, the best cultural ecology monographs are concerned with strategies or resource use and production, and therefore do use an adaptational model. However, there is an important difference between the concept of strategy used in these studies and those outlined here. Most of the existing studies describe *techniques*—ways of doing something at the moment of observation or in the timeless "ethnographic present." There is relatively little data on the unfolding design, on change and variation due to adaptive choices and responses to altered circumstances. But this tendency is changing, as cultural ecologists become aware of the incorporation of local systems in larger ones and the existence of recurrent adaptive change processes. There is no doubt that, as anthropologists move toward serious ecological research on more complex systems, they begin to adopt an adaptational frame (compare Moerman's study [1968] of Thai agriculture, an incorporated system, with Waddell's study [1972] of a New Guinea tribal group, as yet relatively isolated—Moerman locates his study in the historical stream of Thai society; Waddell's is a timeless ethnographic presentation on the whole.)

[3] Hymes (1961) provides an approach that sees languages as instruments of adaptation to the environment, some more adaptive than others. R. L. Holloway, a physical anthropologist, has written one of the most useful commentaries on linguistic aspects of adaptational behavior (1969), and has been answered by M. Durbin (1971), a linguist. Holloway was concerned with the problem of the relationship of language to the making and use of stone tools, and Durbin points out that, contrary to Holloway's remarks, the linguistic and muscular behavior involved in tools illustrates the *lack* of "arbitrariness" in human thought processes—Holloway, following some of the linguists, considers arbitrariness to be a chief characteristic. This is an example of the need for some new thinking about language in an ecological context. In any case, and aside from Malinowski, we are largely dependent on the old distinction between *sign* and *symbol* (Langer, 1942); which, however crude it may be, does make a critical distinction between human and other animal behavior with ecological significance. For the basic discussion of emic and etic concepts, see Harris, 1964. The collection of readings on "communication and culture" edited by A. G. Smith (1966) contains many useful items on all these matters.

[4] The field of business management research uses adaptational approaches for the study of managerial decisions and behavior, which is appropriate considering the strong emphasis on

maximization and instrumental rationality in modern business (for a study, see Chandler, 1962).

[5]The terms, "adjustment" and "adaptation" have also been used by O. H. Mowrer in a different but related sense: "adaptation" referring to responses or actions of individuals that have survival value for the individuals and/or the group; and "adjustment" referring to behavior by the individual designed to reduce the particular tension or stimulation that triggered the behavior. These concepts have found their way into the social sciences in various forms, with "adaptation" often being reserved for social phenomena and functions, and "adjustment" being considered as a purely psychological function or process—as did Clyde Kluckhohn in his *Navajo Witchcraft* (1944). In any case, it is clear that in the original formulation, adjustive responses by individuals can be either adaptive or maladaptive for the group, as we indicate in this essay. Kluckhohn wrote a later paper (1949) in which he pointed out that adaptation and adjustment could not explain the whole of "cultural behavior" since they were instrumentally oriented; that is, they ignored the creative and expressive elements in behavior. This is a particularly sticky issue, and one's understanding of it depends on the definition of culture adhered to. If it is held that the sociocultural reality is divided into instrumental and expressive sectors, then the Kluckhohn self-critique holds. If, however, one approaches the problem of social behavior in terms of a theory like social exchange, or tension-reduction, then it can be held that *all* behavior is adjustive, and all behavior, including the expressive or creative, always will have some kind of adaptive or maladaptive function or effect.

[6]For a discussion of this feature of peasant culture, see Foster, 1965. His concept of "limited good," a version of zero-sum game behavior, is essentially high risk-avoidance, arising out of the knowledge that resources are finite or control over markets is minimal. We differ from Foster in putting stronger emphasis on the situational aspect of the attitude—as a response to objective conditions of management and deprivation, rather than as part of an ideal type of peasant culture (Bennett, 1966). That is, zero-sum game behavior is a strategic response to a particular configuration of gains and losses that will change as this configuration changes—always granting a certain amount of lag (i.e., the restraining power of cultural precedent, operating in the generational system of kinship and communication). Foster (1972) has recently taken account of the criticisms of his original paper, introducing a number of modifications of the concept. However, the zero-sum game attitude toward resources in peasant and tribal societies may well be related to the prevailing custom of collective ownership and use of resources. The community becomes the locus of all resources, and the diffusion of responsibility across the entire group leads to a philosophy of limits and conservation.

[7]The relevant distinctions between degrees and types of commitment to preconceived schemes or ideals, and the implications for outcomes, are treated by Boguslaw (1965). An exceedingly worthwhile project would be to apply Boguslaw's distinctions to existing anthropological data on decision-making and change in tribal societies. Following traditional ethnological concepts, tribal society would presumably be characterized by a greater adherence to Boguslaw's "formalistic design" procedures—but this typological categorization would obscure the very important sphere of nonprecedental decisions, or what Malinowski liked to refer to as the practical or "scientific" context of action.

[8]For another use of the concept of opportunity cost, in economic anthropology, see Mintz, 1964.

[9]The two classic sociological presentations are provided by Homans (1961) and Blau (1964): the latter is the more comprehensive. Uberoi's reanalysis of Malinowski's data on

economic and prestige exchanges in the *kula* ring (1962) is an example of the value of exchange theory in analyzing a social context where instrumental or cost considerations are uppermost in the behavior of the actors. Sahlins' paper (1965) on economic exchanges in tribal societies probably pioneered the application of exchange theory to tribal economics studies. Wilmsen (1972) provides a cross-disciplinary symposium on social exchange in archeological and ethnological contexts.

[10]Anthropologists have occasionally used games theory to analyze agricultural strategies and resource management in tribal-peasant societies (e.g., Davenport, 1960; Gould, 1963). The attempts have been interesting, but the many ambiguities in the technique need to be faced. For one, games theory is based on the notion of rational efficiency, a value that may or may not be followed in a particular activity, for good reasons. In the second place, to perform a games-theory analysis on a society where it is not immediately obvious that the strategy is being followed, or where (because of the unknowns in the situation) one cannot be certain if the actors have any awareness of minimax procedure, it is necessary to perform extensive research in advance in order to provide the raw data to test the games-theory rules against the reality of actual strategies. By the time these data are at hand, it is possible to determine whether or not, or to what degree, minimax strategies are being followed by methods less technical than the games-theory procedures. Moreover, since economic operators in such societies are usually not acquainted with the theory of games, their adherence to minimax strategies, when they do so adhere, is based on pragmatic grounds, not on the theory. One is inclined to wonder, therefore, if their reasons for following these strategies are more revealing than any games-theory analysis might be. Despite these complications, games theory, when used carefully, and purely as a tool or a check on conclusions, has utility and probably should be used more often.

[11]The best anthropological analysis of political behavior from a transactional or adaptive-strategic approach is found in Bailey's 1970 *Stratagems and Spoils* (1970). The analysis is particularly good in showing how tribal people engage in innovative and manipulative behavior of types identical to those in contemporary politics. The difference is not in the behavioral mechanisms; only in the nature and quantity of the resources and rewards. For a discussion and case study of the uses of "policy science" in ecological analysis, see Schachter, 1973—a study of enforcement of air pollution controls in U.S. society. For water policy, see White, 1969.

[12]For example, the value of fossil fuels used in farming is not added to the cost of producing the crops save at the artificially low rate charged the farmer for the converted oils. "Artificially low rate" implies, of course, that if we had to remain dependent on such fuels for the indefinite future, and their supply were steadily diminishing, their value would have to rise or a substitute would have to be found. Similarly, the external cost of the rapid and successful expansion of Neolithic-style farming in North Africa and the Near East was the loss of natural tree and shrub cover of most of the landscape—which it would now cost billions to replace. Mishan (1967) provides the pioneer analysis of these uncalculated costs of economic growth, and his 1970 book, *Technology and Growth*, is an updating. Hodson (1972) provides a more popular presentation. Starr (1969) considers the question of risks associated with supposed benefits from technological solutions to growth problems; Wagar (1970) opposes "quality of life" to economic growth, concluding that growth will inevitably slow down as values change toward the desirability of quality features such as cleaner air and water, more self-help, simpler pleasures. Standard of living in a growth-oriented economy is routinely calculated for public purposes as total goods produced divided by population, although to an increasing extent economists are subtracting losses from the

production numerator, measuring standard of living not only in terms of goods available for consumption but also goods *not* available, having been lost through failure to calculate costs of production. Rising prices, brought about through resource scarcities, would be an example. A further sophistication can be introduced if we also include quality of life, human experiences, time, various services, and enjoyments in the standard-of-living formula. Measured by these criteria, many observers hold that the standard of living has declined, although one recognizes a difficult problem of values in the inclusion of these "intangibles." L. A. Sagan (1972) has provided a pioneer analysis of the "human costs of nuclear power" in monetary terms: a first attempt to reduce some of the medical and biological consequences to concrete quantities. The objective is to determine whether the human costs of producing and utilizing nuclear energy are "equitably compensated for and represented in the price of such electricity." The findings are interesting: the major human costs turn out to be injuries incurred in the mining of uranium and other occupations in nuclear industry, costs that are not paid in full due to the inadequate insurance and compensation allowed the victims. On the other hand,

> the price of nuclear energy is maintained at an artificially high level by an over-protective governmental policy that restricts the public's exposure to radiation to a far greater extent than can be justified in terms of risk reduction or the costs of reducing other (that is, medical) exposures to radiation. (p. 493)

He acknowledges, of course, that other unpaid costs are in the sphere of environmental pollution although that issue is apparently on the way to some sort of solution—cooling schemes for thermal pollution, etc. The technical background issue in this whole complex problem of costs and benefits is the nature of mathematical devices used by economists to calculate the ratio of benefits to costs. Like everything else, these techniques have been influenced by the values inherent in economic growth philosophy, which define growth as a major and unchallenged good. Cost-benefit calculations have been extremely limited in the extent to which they have included "quality of life" and biological criteria, many of which cannot be easily quantified because they are not reducible, or easily reducible, to monetary standards. Economists are well aware of the problem, and the field of study is currently in ferment. (For a critical analysis of cost-benefit procedures in environmental contexts, see Davidson, 1967; Kneese, 1967; Krutilla 1973. See Wildavsky, 1970, for a more generalized treatment of the problem of values in economic-ecological analysis.) The interesting aspect of this problem is that in some other fields of economic evaluation, such as the assessment of the desirability of new types of taxation, a much wider conception of "benefits" or "costs" has been used for many years. Other new approaches are found in the "technology assessment" movement (Medford, 1973; Stober and Schumacher, 1973). The "policy sciences," an older approach, have more recently begun to handle environmental problems (Dror, 1971).

[13]Netting's study of the Kofyar (1968) contains some examples of the process. The section beginning on p. 77 describes variations in adaptive strategies according to altitude, topography, moisture and soil conditions, among the various groups inhabiting the subareas. His areal allocation diagram on p. 81 presents the end results of a progressive tendency toward specialization in a land tenure system lacking the constraints of rectilinear land surveying. The latter has been a serious cause of misuse of resources and an obstacle to adaptive specialization in all countries using this type of survey and tenure system. This is the case because land-use areas based on ownership conform to the tenure grid imposed by the survey, impeding the grouping of areas on the basis of particular specialized and linked

uses. However, attempts are being made to adapt to the tenure restrictions in the Western United States by working out cooperative relationships among specialized producers, especially where the natural course of land ownership patterns has been toward segregation by use (farmers on the terraces; ranchers on the rougher slopes leading up from the river valley).

[14]The killing of bison by Plains Indians toward the end of the aboriginal period in the 19th century represents something of the same: under White pressure, and in increasing panic over the impending loss of a traditional pattern of adaptation, the tribes slaughtered more and more bison, resulting, along with similar slaughter by White hunters, in the near-destruction of the species.

[15]Yehudi Cohen (in his essay, "Culture as Adaptation", in his textbook—1968) has provided a list of six adaptive devices used by human groups to achieve "freedom from their habitats" (p. 42). Aside from the fact that the whole idea of freedom from environmental limitations is pernicious and misleading, the six adaptive devices apply only to tribal societies and have no bearing on the problem of adaptation and maladaptation as we formulate it. The six are: (1) ability to subsist on essentially the same diet during the entire year, (2) ability to make substitutions in diet, (3) degree of reliance on domesticates, (4) knowledge about cause and effect in Nature, (5) the reduction of "fortuitousness" in social life resulting from control over Nature, (6) reduction of seasonal differences in cultural behavior. The real issue, of course, concerns the costs of obtaining these "freedoms."

[16]Hence the rapidly proliferating field of environmental law. Sax (1970) presents a useful summary of the litigation produced to date in the ecology movement, with incisive analyses of the strategies pursued and the conditions of success or failure of the court actions. The paper is especially good since it shows how legal manipulations take precedence over cultural and moral sanctions. Baldwin and Page (1970) provide the most authoritative collection of papers dealing with the more technical and philosophical aspects of environmental law. Caldwell (1970) presents a condensed, comprehensive survey of the need for criteria in all human activities dealing with environment, and Ridgeway (1970) provides useful discussions of politicolegal entanglements.

[17]Gropings toward this have already appeared; as this is being written, the idea of a comprehensive North American energy and natural resource control system has been broached by American government officials, but Canadian response has not been especially favorable. Laycock et al. (1972) present a symposium on the pros and cons, including a history of various negotiations on pollution control, water sharing plans, etc. Utton 1973 provides a study of Mexican-American relationships over pollution and resource control in the Rio Grande valley and elsewhere.

CHAPTER 10

Epilogue: Ecology, Culture, and Anthropology

Aside from the question of definition, there would seem to be three kinds of cultural ecology from the standpoint of subject matter: those dealing with nonagrarian and tribal-agrarian (isolated) systems, those with accessible agrarian systems, and those with industrial settings. Clearly the problems associated with industrial systems, and all the others, are very different: in the latter, the human actors must deal directly with natural substances, and cultural style is obviously bound up with the supply of these resources and the way they are used. In the cultural ecology of industrial systems, the majority of people supported by high technology have no direct involvement with natural substances, and their lives are not directly affected by resource-utilization patterns such as land tenure or the yearly round of agronomic activities. At the same time, these populations are part of the gross human ecological system because they consume the products of energy transformation and they man the engines that manufacture these products.

The problems susceptible of anthropological research in these two settings are very different. In the agricultural, the man-Nature contact zone is immediate and the anthropologist is required to spend time on the scene, observing manipulations of resources and how these affect social life. Much has already been accomplished along this line, but the work needs to be extended into closer studies of how the resources themselves are affected by these techniques and whether or not the social organization and economy can change to accommodate some alteration in the environment or in the economic conditions of agricultural production.

Thus, if the system has been relatively isolated from market influences, bureaus, taxation and absentee landlords, but is now exposed to these involvements, the anthropologist will need to study the operations of the market economy in detail, as well as the bureaucratic procedures that influence the locality. He will have to spend almost as much time in government offices, often far from his study site, as on the site itself. He will have to commute, if his subjects commute, to comprehend the different settings of their life activities.

If the anthropologist chooses to study the cultural ecology of industrial man, he will concern himself with questions of population, social class, power, bureaucratic organization, the basis of behavioral adaptation and change, the role of public opinion, and the nature of consumption wants and their satisfaction. Most of these are issues at considerable remove from the traditional topics of the discipline—still, "urban anthropology" as well as "economic anthropology" are vigorous subfields, and the tools for the study of urban cultural ecology may be found in them.

As I have said elsewhere, the anthropologist cannot do everything, and he will probably have to accept certain specialized functions in the larger research effort. A typical empirical research study of an ecological situation involving human intervention would require the following basic steps: (1) A definition of the existing physical and technical system into which change has been introduced: its properties, amount of balance between the parts, and its capacity for change and readjustment. (2) The existing strategies of action employed by the human actors in this system and how these vary by social strata. (3) The corpus of cultural precedents governing the strategy choices, and the degree of flexibility these may have in determining actions. (4) The nature of interventions or innovations in the system and (5) the way these are configured in systems of social class and political power. (6) Relations of all of the above with systems external to the immediate scene, and the attempts exercised by anyone at controlling or mitigating the consequences of the intervention. While the anthropologist can make some contribution to all of these general steps, he is probably best equipped to handle (3) and (5) on the basis of his present skills and knowledge. Even here, his professional preparation is probably more congenial to the study of cases of intervention in tribal and peasant societies.

The majority of cultural ecological studies published to date have been made in socially bounded human communities—at least defined as communities (tribes, hamlets, ethnic neighborhoods, villages) by the anthropologist. The exceptions are to be found in prehistory, where the lack of information on specific communities has led some archeologists to study the cultural ecology of larger units whose criteria are to be found in the material remains of patterns of resource development and use, which often cut across communities and cultures. As I have noted in other contexts, from an ecological point of view this is an advantage, not a defect, since cultural boundaries may be irrelevant for ecological or technological reasons. The impact of the Plains Indians on the biota and flora of the Great Plains transcended the ethnic divisions—here the recommendation of Vayda and Rappaport to study population units rather than cultures makes sense, if we define a population as a total human biomass subsisting on a total natural resource complex.

But the anthropologist remains interested in culture, and the question of whether resource-utilization systems can be synonymous with community cultures remains a genuine issue. This is the basic Stewardian problem: the extent to which cultural cores can be determinative of other institutions, or the extent to which cultural cores can themselves be shaped by these institutions. The technoeconomic-ecological systems complex can become part of the definition of distinctive cultures, or it can transcend cultural boundaries, permitting new definitions of boundedness. The corporation becomes more important than the "subsistence system."

Therefore, one of the important choices confronting anthropologists at this critical stage of their discipline concerns the level of generalization that is to characterize the field. The traditional ethnological approach has featured a low level and is largely descriptive, with generalizations appropriate to the specific case or to the relatively small number of cases in its class. The choice is apparent in this book: one could pitch generalization at the systemic level, including such crucial entities as the corporation and the state, or the anthropologist could study particular local cases of the relationship between behavior and environment—i.e., the familiar "micro" situations. Anthropologists as individuals will probably do either or both, depending on their proclivities. However, my prediction is that, for some time to come, the center of gravity in the field will rest with the latter type of research, and professionally the anthropologist will leave systems analysis on a large scale to other disciplines.

This is an important issue because very different kinds of generalizations are obtained from different levels of analysis. The significance of the ecological transition lies in the fact that it is characteristic of very large segments of population, society, and time: the human impact on the physical environment is viewed as exponential when the level of generalization is high. But, when ecological processes are viewed in the context of microsocial situations, limited in time, space, and population, the generalizations made at the higher levels may be reversed. Viewing single societies, one can perceive cases of ecological balance, homeostasis, or controlled impact. The anthropologist will have to develop a clear understanding of this difference in scope and significance of his work. It is not that the microsocial studies are unimportant; only that their generalizing power pertains to particular circumstances, and must not be taken as having universal applicability. This does not mean, however, that microlevel studies have no policy potential. In many ecological situations—e.g., in cases of fertilizer pollution—ameliorative programs must take into account microvariations in such things as physical drainage and human management strategies.

Thus, if interest shifts toward policy—what man does to Nature and himself in the process of using Nature—an additional requirement comes into view: representativeness. Intensive research on particular cultural-ecological systems prohibit large-scale study; the anthropologist therefore must choose his research sites with care, sampling larger universes in order to determine the effects. It is here that the concept of a *region* (Sauer, 1925; Spoehr, 1966) comes into view. Most cultural-ecological situations are larger than communities; they include a series of alternative resource systems with exchanges taking place between them: the classic case of Bantu farmers and pygmy hunters offering each other vegetable food and animal protein, or the many similar cases of symbiotic relationships in the Middle East between pastoral nomads and sedentary villagers, are the type cases in ethnology. To an increasing extent, cultural ecologists are turning to these regional complexes; as they do, the policy relevance of their work increases.

A region is therefore two things: (1) It is a geographical area in which a significant man-Nature interactive system is to be found. The criteria for defining this system include technology, level of wants and their satisfaction (economics), and the state of balance or imbalance of all these over a period of time. The system—or congeries of systems—may be characterizable as an ecosystem only if it satisfies the criteria of ecosystems as worked out by natural ecologists. If not, or if the period of time the system is under observation is brief, it is best not to use bioecological terminology, but simply to define it as a resource-utilization system, describing the effects as far as these can be determined during the period of study (e.g., Bose, 1971, for man-land ratios in tribal groups in India).

(2) A region is also a frame for multidisciplinary research: a demand for the integration of data from many realms of ecological reality and

therefore an opportunity for specialists, whether within anthropology or from anthropology and related fields, to work together on theoretical conceptions of human ecology as a synthesis. Only by such cooperative effort will a theoretical human ecology influenced by anthropological approaches have a chance of emergence; by the nature of ecology itself, this must be done in a reasonable complex existing system: a geographical region with diverse resources and human responses and varying problems of environmental concern.

If time depth is desired, there is an opportunity for collaboration between prehistorians and other social scientists. The recent work by archeologists and paleobotanists in the Mexican valleys, tracing the changes in human settlement and resource utilization, population increase and political hegemony, provides an excellent model. Not all parts of the earth are so neatly subdivided into valleys, with their continuity and development trajectories, but it remains true that such relatively clearly-bounded regions are common, and offer impressive possibilities for collaborative research.

Therefore, the boundaries of regions can be determined easily in some cases, with more difficulty in others. There will be two principal subsystemic sets of concern: human use of natural resources and transactions between humans—man's use of other men. The relationship between these subsystems will, in most cases, be a close one, and an understanding of the pattern of resource use will have to be preceded by a study of the adaptive social transactions. This is the heart of cultural ecology: the way man-man relations modify man-Nature relations in particular representative cases, and how the results affect the future of both.

Whatever the cultural ecologist chooses to do, he will need to understand that social and ecological phenomena are subsystemic parts of larger systems, and that an understanding of the ecological requires a knowledge of the social. This requirement has already been met in most of the contemporary studies of tribal and peasant agriculture; indeed, the delineation of relationships between social and natural systems is the chief accomplishment of these studies. A second requirement involves an appreciation of the social milieu as a resource: that men are part of the environment other men manipulate for gain or for satisfaction of their wants. This proposition, with its difficult methodological problems and disturbing value implications, has yet to become a part of cultural ecology, but it must do so if the cultural ecologist is to study contemporary societies at any level or type of development.

There is no question that the moral implications of a "social environment" requires constant attention, because the possibility of insensitivity to exploitative behavior on the part of the scientist who studies it is very great. The manipulation of other men has always produced rationalization and falsification of reality; it is not easy for the social scientist to maintain an objective viewpoint. The ideological traps in the idea are undoubtedly the major reason why it has proven so difficult to use it as the foundation of a general human ecological science.

If anthropologists are specialists in culture, they may find it possible to explore alternatives to the present destructive practices and values. The overriding problem of ecological reform is the need to provide psychologically gratifying and economically rewarding activities that substitute for those presently causing environmental degradation and pollution. At one level, this is a highly technical problem, requiring technological and industrial innovation, as in the case of the search for less harmful pesticides, automotive engines and fuels, or the manufacture of new or revived old products to replace those causing difficulties. Anthropologists can take a leaf from the "counter culture," which contains a number of desirable replacements: natural foods, simpler pleasures, the refocusing of social activities toward interhuman satisfactions and away from material accumulation. These emphases, however juvenile or disorganized they may appear at first sight, represent a genuine groping for a more humane approach to Nature, and to Man.

The burden of these remarks is simply that man's use of Nature is inextricably intertwined with man's use of Man, and that remedies for destructive use of the environment must be found within the social system itself. The need for radical reform of our present compartmentalized ecological control systems simply reflects the need for equally radical reorganization of human institutions. If, however, these institutions are arbitrary creations only to a limited extent (that is, if they are more or less inevitable due to the workings of the human mind), then the outlook is dim. On the basis of our present knowledge, it is impossible to answer this question; in any case, a negative answer simply cannot be seriously entertained if human survival and the quality of life is our goal. We must seek to do better; anthropologists can help by continuing and sharpening their inquiries into the social and cultural basis of man's relationship to the environment.

References

Abbott, Joan M. W.
  1970   "Cultural Anthropology and the Man-Environment Relationship: An Historical Discussion," *Kroeber Anthropological Society Papers,* 43: 10–31.
Abu-Lughod, Janet.
  1968   "The City is Dead—Long Live the City: Some Thoughts on Urbanity," in Sylvia Fleis Fava (ed.), *Urbanism in World Perspective: A Reader.* New York: Crowell.
Ackerman, E. A.
  1959   "Population and Natural Resources," in P. M. Hauser and O. D. Duncan (eds.), *The Study of Population.* Chicago: University of Chicago Press.
Ackoff, Russell L. and Emery, Fred E.
  1972   *On Purposeful Systems: An Interdisciplinary Analysis of Individual and Social Behavior as a System of Purposeful Events.* Chicago: Aldine-Atherton.
Adams, Richard N.
  1970   *Crucifixion by Power: Essays on Guatemalan National Social Structure.* Austin: University of Texas Press.
Adams, Robert McCormick.
  1962A   "Agriculture and Urban Life in Early Southwestern Iran," *Science,* 136: 109–122.
Adams, Robert McCormick.
  1962B   "A Synopsis of the Historical Demography and Ecology of the Diyala River Basin, Central Iraq," in Richard B. Woodbury (ed.), *Civilizations in Desert Lands.* University of Utah Anthropological Papers, Number 62. Salt Lake City: University of Utah Press, December 1962.
Adams, Robert McCormick.
  1965   *Land Behind Bagdad: A History of Settlement on the Diyala Plains.* Chicago: University of Chicago Press.
Alland, Alexander.
  1967   *Evolution and Human Behavior.* Garden City: Natural History Press.
Alland, Alexander.
  1970   *Adaptation in Cultural Evolution: An Approach to Medical Anthropology.* New York: Columbia University Press.

Alland, Alexander.
  1972   *The Human Imperative.* New York: Columbia University Press. Quotation used
          with permission.
Allred B. W. and Clements, E. S.
  1949   *Dynamics of Vegetation.* Selections from the writings of Frederic E. Clement,
          N. Y., Wilson.
American Anthropologist.
  1962   "Ecology and Anthropology: A Symposium," *American Anthropologist*, 64:
          15–59.
Anderson, A. H.
  1950   "Space as a Social Cost," *Journal of Farm Economics*, 32: 411–29.
Anderson, E. N., Jr.
  1969   "The Life and Culture of Ecotopia," in D. Hymes (ed.), *Reinventing Anthropol-
          ogy.* New York: Pantheon.
Anderson, Edgar.
  1956   "Man as a Maker of New Plants and Plant Communities," in W. L. Thomas (ed.),
          Man's Role in Changing the Face of the Earth. Chicago: University of Chicago
          Press.
Anderson, Walter (ed.).
  1970   *Politics and Environment.* Pacific Palisades, Calif.: Goodyear.
Appley, M. H. (ed.).
  1971   *Adaptation-Level Theory: A Symposium.* New York: Academic Press.
Arendt, Hannah.
  1958   *The Human Condition.* Chicago: University of Chicago Press.
Armillas, Pedro.
  1971   "Gardens on Swamps," *Science*, 174: 653–61.
Ashby, William R.
  1952–60   *Design for a Brain.* New York: Wiley.
Ashby, William R.
  1956   *An Introduction to Cybernetics.* New York: Wiley.
Ashley-Montagu, M. R. (ed.).
  1968A   *Culture: Man's Adaptive Dimension.* New York: Oxford University Press.
Ashley-Montagu, M. R.
  1968B   *Man and Aggression.* New York: Oxford University Press.
Ashley-Montague, M. R.
  1971   The New Litany of 'Innate Depravity,' or Original Sin Revisited," in Ronald
          Munson (ed.), *Man and Nature: Philosophical Issues in Biology.* New York:
          Delta.
Ayres, U. and Kneese, Allen V.
  1971   "Economic and Ecological Effects of a Stationary Economy," *Annual Review of
          Ecology and Systematics*, 2: 1–22.
Bailey, Alfred Goldsworthy.
  1937   *The Conflict of European and Eastern Algonkian Cultures, 1504–1700.* Saint
          John, New Brunswick: The New Brunswick Museum (The Tribune Press).
Bailey, F. G.
  1970   *Stratagems and Spoils: A Social Anthropology of Politics.* Oxford: Basil
          Blackwell.
Baker, Paul S. and Dutt, J. S.

1972   "Demographic Variables as Measures of Biological Adaptation: A Case Study of High Altitude Human Populations," in G. A. Harrison and J. A. Boyce, *The Structure of Human Populations*. Oxford: Clarendon Press.

Baker, Paul T. and Weiner, J. S. (eds.).
1966)   *The Biology of Human Adaptability*. Oxford: Clarendon Press.

Baker, Paul T. and Weiner, J. S.
1960   "Early Civilizations, Subsistence, and Environment," in C. H. Kraeling and R. McC. Adams (eds.), *City Invincible*. Chicago: University of Chicago Press. (Also published in Y. Cohen [ed.], *Man in Adaptation*. Chicago: Aldine, 1968.)

Baker, Paul T. and Weiner, J. S.
1972A   "Demography and the 'Urban Revolution' in Lowland Mesoamerica," in Brian Spooner (ed.), *Population Growth*. Cambridge: MIT Press.

Baker, Paul T. and Weiner, J. S.
1972B   "Patterns of Urbanization in Early Southern Mesopotamia," in Peter J. Ucko, Ruth Tringham, and G. W. Dimbleby (eds.), *Man, Settlement and Urbanism*. Cambridge: Schenkman.

Baldwin, Malcolm F. and Page, J. K., Jr. (eds.).
1970   *Law and the Environment: A Conference*. New York: A Conservation Foundation Publication.

Ballard, J. G.
1971   "Billenium," in *Chronopolis: The Science Fiction of J. G. Ballard*. Berkeley: Medallion Books, published in arrangement with J. P. Putnam's Sons.

Barker, Roger G.
1968   *Ecological Psychology: Concepts and Methods for Studying the Environment of Human Behavior*. Stanford: Stanford University Press.

Barker, Roger G. and Schoggen, Phil.
1973   *Qualities of Community Life*. New York: Jossey-Bass.

Barnes, J. A.
1954   "Class and Committees in a Norwegian Island Parish," *Human Relations*, 7: 39–58.

Barnett, H. G.
1953   *Innovation: The Basis of Cultural Change*. New York: McGraw-Hill.

Barnett, Harold J. and Chandler Morse.
1963   *Scarcity and Growth: The Economics of Natural Resource Availability*. Baltimore: Johns Hopkins University Press.

Barrows, Harlan H.
1923   "Geography as Human Ecology," *Annals of the Association of American Geographers*, 13: 1–14.

Barth, Frederik.
1950   "Ecologic Adaptation and Cultural Change in Archeology," *American Antiquity*, 15: 338–339.

Barth, Frederik.
1956   "Ecologic Relationships of Ethnic Groups in Swat, Northern Pakistan," *American Anthropologist*, 58: 1079–1089.

Barth, Frederik.
1967   "On the Study of Social Change," *American Anthropologist*, 69: 661–69.

Barth, Frederik (ed.).
1969   *Ethnic Groups and Boundaries*. London: Allen and Unwin.

Bartholomew, George A. and Birdsell, J. B.

1953   "Ecology and the Protohominids," *American Anthropologist*, 55: 481–98.

Basehart, Harry W.
1973   "Cultivation Intensity, Settlement Patterns, and Homestead Forms among the Matengo of Tanzania," *Ethnology*, 12(1): 57–74.

Bartlett, H. H.
1956   "Fire, Primitive Agriculture, and Grazing in the Tropics." In W. L. Thomas (ed.) *Man's Role in Changing The Face of the Earth*. Chicago: University of Chicago Press.

Bates, Marston.
1953   "Human Ecology," in A. L. Kroeber (ed.), *Anthropology Today*. Chicago: University of Chicago Press.

Bateson, Gregory.
1949   "Bali: The Value System of a Steady State," in M. Fortes (ed.), *Social Structure: Studies Presented to A. R. Radcliffe-Brown*. New York: Oxford University Press.

Bateson, Gregory.
1972   *Steps Toward An Ecology of Mind*. Collected Essays. London: Intertext. (U.S. edition by Chandler.)

Bayless, T. M. and Rozenzweig, N. S.
1967   "Implications of Lactase Deficiency and Milk Intolerance in White and Negro Populations," *Johns Hopkins Medical Journal*, 121: 54–64.

Beardsley, Richard K.
1964   "Ecological and Social Parallels between Rice-Growing Communities of Japan and Spain," in V. E. Garfield (ed.), *Symposium on Community Studies in Anthropology*. Seattle: University of Washington Press (American Ethnological Society).

Beardsley, Richard K., et al.
1962   "Functional and Evolutionary Implications of Community Patterning," in Philip L. Wagner and Marvin W. Mikesell (eds.), *Readings in Cultural Geography*. Chicago: University of Chicago Press. (Also published in *Memoirs of the Society for American Archaeology*, 9: 129–57. 1956.

Befu, Harumi.
1971   *Japan: An Anthropological Introduction*. San Francisco: Chandler.

Bell, E. H.
1942   *The Culture of a Contemporary Rural Community: Sublette, Kansas*. Rural Life Studies, No. 2. Washington, D.C.: Bureau of Agricultural Economics, U.S.D.A.

Bellah, Robert N.
1957   *Tokugawa Religion: The Values of Pre-Industrial Japan*. Glencoe: Free Press.

Belshaw, Cyril.
1970   *The Conditions of Social Performance*. London: Routledge & Kegan Paul.

Bennett, James P., Resh, H. M., and Runeckles, V. C.
1974   "Apparent Stimulations of Plant Growth by Air Pollutants," *Canadian Journal of Botany*, 52: 35–41.

Bennett, John W.
1944A   "The Development of Ethnological Theory as Illustrated by Studies of the Plains Sun Dance," *American Anthropologist*, 46: 162–81.

Bennett, John W.
1944B   "The Interaction of Culture and Environment in the Smaller Societies," *American Anthropologist*, 46: 461–78.

Bennett, John W.
   1946   "An Interpretation of the Scope and Implications of Social Scientific Research in Human Subsistence." *American Anthropologist*, 48: 553–73.
Bennett, John W.
   1963   "Social Patterns of Forest Exploitation," in J. W. Bennett and I. Ishino, *Paternalism in the Japanese Economy*. Minneapolis: University of Minnesota Press.
Bennett, John W.
   1966   "Further Remarks on Foster's 'Image of Limited Good,'" *American Anthropologist*, 68: 206–210.
Bennett, John W.
   1967A   "Japanese Economic Growth: Background for Social Change," in R. P. Dore (ed.), *Aspects of Social Change in Modern Japan*. Princeton, N.J.: Princeton University Press.
Bennett, John W.
   1967B   "Microcosm-Macrocosm Relationships in North American Agrarian Society," *American Anthropologist*, 69: 441–54. (Revised version published in M. Micklin, *Population, Environment, and Social Organization*. Hinsdale, Ill.: Dryden Press, 1973.)
Bennett, John W.
   1967C   *Hutterian Brethren: The Agricultural Economy and Social Organization of a Communal People*. Stanford: Stanford University Press.
Bennett, John W.
   1967D   "On the Cultural Ecology of Indian Cattle," *Current Anthropology*, 8: 251–52.
Bennett, John W.
   1968   "Reciprocal Economic Exchanges among North American Agricultural Operators," *Southwestern Journal of Anthropology*, 24: 276–309.
Bennett, John W.
   1969   *Northern Plainsmen: Adaptive Strategy and Agrarian Life*. Chicago: Aldine.
Bennett, John W.
   1970   "The Significance of the Concept of Adaptation for Contemporary Sociocultural Anthropology," Tokyo: VIII Congress of Anthropological and Ethnological Sciences, Symposium VII, pp. 237–41.
Bennett, John W.
   1973   "Ecosystemic Effects of Extensive Agriculture," in *Annual Review of Anthropology*, Vol. II. Palo Alto: Annual Reviews.
Bennett, John W.
   1974   "Anthropological Contributions to the Cultural Ecology and Management of Water Resources," in D. James (ed.), *Man and Water*. Lexington, Ky: Center for Developmental Change and University of Kentucky Press.
Bennett, John W. and Kohl, Seena B.
   Forth-   *Generations of Jasper: Society and Ecology in the Canadian West.*
   coming
Bennett, John W. and Levine, Solomon B.
   1975   "Industrialization and Social Deprivation: Welfare, Environment, and the Post-Industrial Society in Japan." In Hugh Patrick (ed.), *Japanese Industrialization and its Social Consequences*. Berkeley: University of California Press.
Bennett, John W., Smith, Harley L., and Passin, Herbert.
   1942   "Food and Culture in Southern Illinois," *American Sociological Review*, 7: 645–60.

Benson, L.
1960   *Turner and Beard—American Historical Writing Reconsidered*. New York: Free Press.
Berlyne, D. E.
1968   "The Construction and Selection of Environments," in D. C. Glass (ed.), *Environmental Influences*. New York: Rockefeller University Press and Russell Sage Foundation.
Bernard, Claude.
1927   *An Introduction to the Study of Experimental Medicine*, with an Introduction by L. J. Henderson. New York: Schuman. (Originally published in French in 1855.)
Berrien, F. Kenneth.
1968   *General and Social Systems*. New Brunswick: Rutgers University Press.
von Bertalanffy, L.
1950   "An Outline of General Systems Theory," *British Journal of Philosophical Science*, I: 134–65.
Bertram, Colin.
1959   *Adam's Brood: Hopes and Fears of a Biologist*. London: Peter Davies.
Binford, L. R.
1968   "Post-Pleistocene Adaptations," in L. R. and S. R. Binford (eds.), *New Perspectives in Archeology*. Chicago: Aldine.
Birdsell, Joseph B.
1958   "On Population Structure in Generalized Hunting and Gathering Populations," *Evolution*, 12: 189–205.
Birdsell, Joseph B.
1963   "Some Environmental and Cultural Factors Influencing the Structuring of Australian Aboriginal Populations," *American Naturalist*, Vol. 87 (Supplement): 171–207.
Birdsell, Joseph B.
1973   "A Basic Demographic Unit," *Current Anthropology*, 14: 337–56.
Black, John.
1970   *The Dominion of Man: The Search for Ecological Responsibility*. Chicago: Aldine.
Blanton, Richard E.
1972   "Prehispanic Adaptation in the Ixtapalapa Region, Mexico," *Science*, 175: 1317–26.
Blau, Peter M.
1964   *Exchange and Power in Social Life*. New York: Wiley.
Blau, Peter M.
1970   "A Formal Theory of Differentiation in Organizations," *American Sociological Review*, 35: 201–218.
Boas, Franz.
1888   *The Central Eskimo*. Sixth Annual Report of the Bureau of American Ethnology, 1883–1885. Washington, D.C.
Boas, Franz.
1896   "The Limitations of the Comparative Method on Anthropology," *Science* (new series), 4: 901–908.
Boffey, Philip M.
1970   "Energy Crisis: Environmental Issue Exacerbates Power Supply Problem," *Science*, 168: 1554–59.

Boguslaw, Robert.
1965   *The New Utopians: A Study of System Design and Social Change.* Englewood Cliffs: Prentice-Hall.
Boorman, Scott A.
1972   "Analogues in the Social Sciences," Part II of a joint review of R. H. MacArthur, *Geographical Ecology.* (New York: Harper & Row) in *Science,* 178: 391–93.
Bose, Nirmal K.
1971   "Land-man Ratio in Tribal Areas," *Man in India,* 51: 267–73.
Boserup, Ester.
1965   *The Conditions of Agricultural Growth: The Economics of Agrarian Change Under Population Pressure.* Chicago: Aldine.
Boughey, Arthur S.
1971   *Man and the Environment.* New York: Macmillan.
Boulding, Kenneth E.
1956A   *The Image: Knowledge in Life and Society.* Ann Arbor: University of Michigan Press.
Boulding, Kenneth E.
1956B   "Toward a General Theory of Growth," *General Systems Yearbook,* I: 66–75.
Boulding, Kenneth E.
1962   "Where Are We Going if Anywhere? A Look at Post-Civilization," *Human Organization,* 21: 162–67.
Boulding, Kenneth E.
1966   "The Economics of the Coming Spaceship Earth" in *Environmental Quality in a Growing Economy.* Baltimore: Johns Hopkins Press.
Box, Thadis W.
1971   "Nomadism and Land Use in Somalia," *Economic Development and Cultural Change,* 19: 222–28.
Boyden, S. V.
1970   *The Impact of Civilisation on the Biology of Man.* Toronto: University of Toronto Press.
Braidwood, Robert J. and Reed, C.
1957   "The Achievement and Early Consequences of Food Production," *Cold Spring Harbor Symposia on Quantitative Biology,* 22: 19–31.
Braidwood, Robert J. and Willey, G. (eds.).
1962   *Courses Toward Urban Life.* Viking Fund Publications in Anthropology, No. 32. New York: Wenner-Gren Foundation.
Branch, E. Douglas.
1963   *The Hunting of the Buffalo.* Lincoln, Neb: University of Nebraska Press (Bison Book).
Breed, Warren.
1971   *The Self-Guiding Society.* New York: Free Press.
Bresler, Jack B.
1966   *Human Ecology: Collected Readings.* Reading, Mass.: Addison-Wesley.
Bresler, Jack B.
1968   *Environments of Man.* Reading, Mass.: Addison-Wesley.
Bronowski, J.
1971   *The Identity of Man.* Garden City: Natural History Press.
Bronson, Bennett.

1972   "Farm Labor and the Evolution of Food Production," in Brian Spooner (ed.), *Population Growth.* Cambridge: MIT Press.

Brothwell, Don R.
1972   "The Question of Pollution in Earlier and Less Developed Societies," in Peter R. Cox and John Peel (eds.), *Population and Pollution.* New York: Academic Press.

Brown, Harrison.
1969   *The Challenge of Man's Future.* New York: Compass Books, Viking Press.

Brown, Lester R. and Finsterbusch, G. W.
1972   *Man and His Environment—Food.* New York: Harper & Row.

Buckley, Walter.
1967   *Sociology and Modern Systems Theory.* Englewood Cliffs: Prentice-Hall.

Bunzel, Ruth.
1938   "The Economic Organization of Primitive Peoples" in F. Boas et al., *General Anthropology.* Boston and N.Y.: Heath.

Burch, William R., Jr.
1971   *Daydreams and Nightmares: A Sociological Essay on the American Environment.* New York: Harper & Row.

Burling, Robbins.
1962   "Maximization Theories and the Study of Economic Anthropology," *American Anthropologist,* 64: 802–821.

Burton, I. and Kates, R. W.
1964   "The Perception of Natural Hazards in Resource Management," *Natural Resources Journal,* 3: 412–41.

Byers, Douglas S.
1967   *Environment and Subsistence. The Prehistory of the Tehuacan Valley,* Vol. 1. Austin: University of Texas Press.

Calder, Nigel.
1971   *Technopolis.* New York: Simon & Schuster.

Caldwell, Lynton K.
1970   *Environment: A Challenge to Modern Society.* Garden City: Natural History Press.

Callan, Hilary.
1970   *Ethology and Society.* Oxford: Clarendon Press.

Campbell, Donald T.
1965   "Variation and Selective Retention in Sociocultural Evolution," in H. R. Barringer et al. (eds), *Social Change in Developing Areas.* Cambridge: Schenkman.

Canfield, Robert L.
1973A   *Faction and Conversion in a Plural Society: Religious Alignments in the Hindu Kush.* Anthropological Papers. Museum of Anthropology, University of Michigan, No. 50.

Canfield, Robert L.
1973B   "The Ecology of Rural Ethnic Groups and the Spacial Dimensions of Power." *American Anthropologist,* 75: 1511–1528.

Cannon, Walter B.
1939   *The Wisdom of the Body.* New York: Norton.

Carneiro, Robert L.
1956   "Slash and Burn Agriculture: a Closer Look at Its Implications for Settlement Patterns," in A. F. C. Wallace (ed.), *Men and Cultures.* Philadelphia: University of Pensylvania Press.

Carneiro, Robert L.
1967   "On the Relationship Between Size of Population and Complexity of Social Organization," *Southwestern Journal of Anthropology*, 23 (3): 234–43.
Carneiro, Robert L.
1972   "From Autonomous Villages to the State, A Numerical Evaluation" in Brian Spooner (ed.), *Population Growth: Anthropological Implications*. Cambridge: MIT Press.
Carneiro, Robert L. and Hilse, Daisy F.
1966   "On Determining the Probable Rate of Population Growth during the Neolithic," *American Anthropologist*, 68: 177–81.
Carpenter, Richard A.
1970   "Information for Decisions in Environmental Policy," *Science*, 168: 1316–22.
Caudill, William and Scarr, Harry A.
1962   "Japanese Value Orientations and Culture Change," *Ethnology*, 1: 53–91.
Chagnon, Napoleon A.
1972   "Tribal Social Organization and Genetic Microdifferentiation," in G. A. Harrison and J. A. Boyce, *The Structure of Human Populations*. Oxford: Clarendon Press.
Chandler, Alfred D., Jr.
1962   *Strategy and Structure: Chapters in the History of American Industrial Enterprises*. Boston: MIT Press.
Chapple, Eliot D.
1970   *Culture and Biological Man: Explorations in Behavioral Anthropology*. New York: Holt, Rinehart and Winston.
Chapple, Eliot D. and Coon, Carleton S.
1942   *Principles of Anthropology*. Part II: Environment and Technology. New York: Holt.
Chartrand, Robert Lee.
1970   *Systems Technology Applied to Social and Community Problems*. New York: Spartan Books.
Childe, V. Gordon.
1936   *Man Makes Himself*. London: Watts.
Childe, V. Gordon.
1942   *What Happened in History*. London: Penguin Books.
Chisholm, G. G.
1913   "Is the Increasing Control of Man over Nature Making Him Independent of Geographical Conditions?" *Journal of Geography*, 12: 97–99.
Chorley, Richard J. and Haggett, P. (eds.).
1967   *Models in Geography*. London: Methuen.
Christian, John J.
1963   "The Pathology of Overpopulation," *Military Medicine*, 128: 571–603.
Chung, Roy.
1970   "Space-Time Diffusion of the Transition Model: The Twentieth Century Patterns" in George J. Demko, Harold M. Rose, and George A. Schnell (eds.), *Population Geography: A Reader*. New York: McGraw-Hill.
Clark, Grahame.
1952   *Prehistoric Europe: The Economic Basis*. London: Methuen, 1952. (Also Stanford: Stanford University Press, 1952.)

Clark, J. G. D.
1945   "Farmers and Forests in Neolithic Europe," *Antiquity*, 19: 57–71.
Clark, J. G. D.
1954   *Excavations at Star Carr*. Cambridge: Cambridge University Press.
Clarke, William C.
1966   "From Extensive to Intensive Shifting Cultivation," *Ethnology*, 5: 347–59.
Clements, Frederick E.
1916   *Plant Succession*. Washington, D.C.: Carnegie Institute.
Clements, Frederick E. and Chaney, R. W.
1936   *Environment and Life in the Great Plains*. Washington, D.C.: Carnegie Institute.
Coale, A. J.
1970   "Man and His Environment," *Science*, 170: 132–36.
Coe, Michael D. and Flannery, K. V.
1964   "Microenvironments and Mesoamerican Prehistory." *Science*, 143: 650–654.
Cohen, Percy S.
1967   "Economic Analysis and Economic Man," in R. Firth (ed.), *Themes in Economic Anthropology*. London: Tavistock.
Cohen, Yehudi A. (ed.).
1968–70   *Man in Adaptation*. 3 vols. Chicago: Aldine.
Cohen, Yehudi A.
1968   "Culture as Adaptation" in Y. Cohen (ed.), *Man in Adaptation: The Cultural Present* (Vol. 2). Chicago: Aldine.
Cole, H. S. D., Freeman, C., Jahoda, M., and Pavitt, K. L. R.
1973   *Models of Doom: A Critique of the Limits to Growth*. New York: Universe Books.
Cole, Lamont C.
1964   "The Impending Emergence of Biological Thought," *Bioscience*, 14: 30–32.
Collins, P. W.
1970   "The Logic of Functional Analysis" in *Anthropology*. Columbia University, Department of Philosophy, Dissertation (microfilm).
Colson, Elizabeth.
1971   *The Social Consequences of Resettlement*. Kariba Studies, Vol. 4. Manchester University Press.
Commoner, Barry.
1966   *Science and Survival*. New York: Viking Press.
Commoner, Barry.
1968   "Nature Unbalanced: How Man Interferes with the Nitrogen Cycle," *Scientist and Citizen*, 10: 9–13.
Commoner, Barry.
1971   *The Closing Circle*. New York: Knopf.
Commoner, Barry.
1972   "Summary of the Conference: On the Meaning of Ecological Failures in International Development," in M. Taghi Farvar and John P. Milton (eds.), *The Careless Technology*. Garden City: Natural History Press.
Conklin, Harold C.
1954   "An Ethnoecological Approach to Shifting Agriculture," *Transactions of the New York Academy of Sciences*, 17: 133–42.

Conklin, Harold C.
1957   *Hanunoo Agriculture.* FAO Forestry Development Paper, No. 12. Roome, FAO, United Nations.
Conklin, Harold C.
1963   *The Study of Shifting Cultivation.* Studies and Monographs, No. 6. Washington, D.C.: Union Panamericana.
Cook, Scott.
1966   "The Obsolete 'Anti-market' Mentality: A Critique of the Substantive Approach to Economic Anthropology," *American Anthropologist,* 68: 323–45.
Cook, Sherburne F.
1941   *The Mechanism and Extent of Dietary Adaptation Among Certain Groups of California and Nevada Indians.* Ibero-Americana, No. 18. Berkeley: University of California Press.
Cook, Sherburne F.
1943   *The Conflict Between the California Indian and White Civilization.* Ibero-Americana, Nos. 21–22. Berkeley: University of California Press.
Cook, Sherburne F.
1946   "Human Sacrifice and Warfare as Factors in the Demography of Pre-Colonial Mexico," *Human Biology,* 18: 81–102.
Corning, Peter A.
1974   "An Evolutionary Paradigm for the Study of Human Aggression." Paper presented to the Conference on War: Its Causes and Correlates, 9th International Congress of Anthropological Sciences. To be published by Mouton, 1974.
Cottrell, Leonard.
1955   *Energy and Society: The Relations of Energy, Social Change, and Economic Development.* New York: McGraw-Hill.
Covich, Alan.
1972   "Ecological Economics of Seed Consumption by *Peromyscus*: A Graphical Model of Resource Substitution," in E. S. Deevey (ed.), *Growth by Intussusception: Ecological Essays in Honor of G. Evelyn Hutchinson.* Hamden, Conn.: Archon Books.
Cowgill, Donald O.
1962–63   "Transition Theory as General Population Theory," *Social Forces,* 41: 270–74.
Cox, Peter R. and Peel, John (eds.).
1972   *Population and Pollution.* Proceedings of the Eighth Annual Symposium of the Eugenics Society, London, September 1971. New York: Academic Press.
Craik, Kenneth H.
1972   "An Ecological Perspective on Environmental Decision-Making," *Human Ecology,* 1: 69–80.
Cravioto, Joaquin.
1968   "Nutritional Deficiencies and Mental Performance in Childhood," in D. C. Glass (ed.), *Environmental Influences.* New York: Rockefeller University Press and Russell Sage Foundation.
Crosby, Alfred W., Jr.
1972   *The Columbian Exchange: Biological and Cultural Consequences of 1492.* Westport, Conn.: Greenwood Press.
Crowe, Beryl L.
1969   "The Tragedy of the Commons Revisited," *Science,* 166: 1103–1107.

Crutchfield, James A. and Pontecorvo, G.
    1969   *The Pacific Salmon Fisheries: A Study of Irrational Conservation.* Baltimore:
            Johns Hopkins Press.
Curry, Leslie.
    1952   "Climate and Economic Life: A New Approach with Examples from the United
            States," *The Geographical Review*, 42: 367–83.
Cussler, Margaret T. and DeGive, M. L.
    1942   "The Effect of Human Relations on Food Habits in the Rural Southeast,"
            Applied Anthropology, 1: 13–18.
Dales, George F.
    1966   "The Decline of the Harappans," *Scientific American*, 214: 92–101.
Dalton, George.
    1961   "Economic Theory and Primitive Society," *American Anthropologist*, 63: 1–25.
Damas, David (ed.).
    1969   *Contributions to Anthropology: Ecological Essays.* Bulletin 230; Anthropologi-
            cal Series, No. 86. Ottawa: National Museums of Canada.
Damas, David.
    1972   "Central Eskimo Systems of Food Sharing," *Ethnology*, 11: 220–40.
Darling, F. Fraser.
    1955–56   "The Ecology of Man," *American Scholar*, 25: 38–46.
Darling, F. Fraser,
    1964   "The Unity of Ecology." *Annual Report of the Smithsonian Institution*,
            Washington, D.C.: Smithsonian Institution Press, pp. 461–476.
Darling, F. Fraser.
    1970   "A Wider Environment of Ecology and Conservation" in Roger Revelle and
            Hans H. Landsberg (eds.), *America's Changing Environment.* Boston: Beacon
            Press.
Darling, F. Fraser.
    1972   "Intensification of Animal Productivity," Section IV in M. Taghi Farvar and
            John P. Milton (eds.), *The Careless Technology.* Garden City: Natural History
            Press.
Dasmann, Raymond.
    1966   "Man in North America," in F. Darling and J. Milton (eds.), *Future Environments
            of North America.* Garden City: Natural History Press.
Davenport, William.
    1960   *Jamaican Fishing: A Games Theory Analysis.* Yale University Publications in
            Anthropology, No. 59. New Haven: Yale University Press.
Davidson, Paul.
    1967   "The Valuation of Public Goods," in M. E. Garnsey and J. R. Hibbs (eds.), *Social
            Sciences and the Environment.* Boulder: University of Colorado Press.
Davis, A. E. and Bolin, T.
    1967   "Lactose Intolerance in Asians," *Nature*, 216: 1244–45.
Davis, Kingsley.
    1967   "Population Policy: Will Current Programs Succeed?" *Science*, 158: 730–40.
Day, Gordon M.
    1953   "The Indian as an Ecological Factor in the Northeastern Forest," *Ecology*, 34:
            329–34.
Deevey, Edward S.
    1960   "The Human Population," *Scientific American*, 203: 194–205.

De Vos, George.
    1966   "Conflict, Dominance and Exploitation in Human Systems of Segregation: Some
            Perspectives from the Study of Personality in Culture," in A. V. S. de Reuck and
            J. Knight (eds.), *Ciba Foundation Symposium on Conflict in Society.* London:
            J. and A. Churchill.
Dickins, Dorothy.
    1943   "Food Preparation of Owner and Cropper Farm Families in the Shortleaf Pine
            Area of Mississippi," *Social Forces,* 22: 56–63.
Dimbleby, G. W.
    1972   "The Impact of Early Man on His Environment," in Peter R. Cox and John Peel
            (eds.), *Population and Pollution.* New York: Academic Press.
Dixon, D. M.
    1972   "Population, Pollution and Health in Ancient Egypt," in Peter R. Cox and John
            Peel (eds.), *Population and Pollution.* New York: Academic Press.
Dixon, R. B.
    1928   *The Building of Cultures.* New York: Scribners.
Dore, R. P.
    1967   *Aspects of Social Change in Modern Japan.* Princeton, N.J.: Princeton Univer-
            sity Press.
Douglas, Mary.
    1966   *Purity and Danger: A Comparative Study of Concepts of Pollution and Taboo.*
            London: Routledge.
Douglas, Mary.
    1968   "Pollution," *International Encyclopedia of the Social Sciences,* pp. 336–342.
            New York: Macmillan.
Douglas, Mary.
    1970   "Environments at Risk," *Time Literary Supplement,* October 30, 1970, pp.
            1273–1275.
Douglas, Mary.
    1972   "Symbolic Orders in the Use of Domestic Space," in Peter J. Ucko, Ruth
            Tringham, and G. W. Dimbleby (eds.), *Man, Settlement and Urbanism.* Cam-
            bridge: Schenkman.
Downs, J. F.
    1960   "Domestication: An Examination of the Changing Relationships between Man
            and Animals," *Kroeber Anthropological Society Papers,* No. 22. Berkeley,
            California.
Downs, Roger M. and Stea, Davis.
    1973   *Cognitive Mapping and Spatial Behavior.* Chicago: Aldine.
Doxiadis, C. A.
    1967   "Man's Movement and His City," *Science,* 162: 326–34.
Doxiadis, C. A.
    1970   "Ekistics, the Science of Human Settlements," *Science,* 170: 393–404.
Dror, Yehezkel.
    1971   *Design for Policy Sciences.* New York: American Elsevier.
Drucker, Philip and Heizer, R. G.
    1960   "A Study of the Milpa System of La Venta Island and Its Archeological
            Implications," *Southwestern Journal of Anthropology,* 16: 36–45.
DuBois, Cora.

1941   "Food and Hunger in Alors," in L. Spier (ed.), *Language, Culture and Personality*. Essays in Honor of Edward Sapir. Menasha, Wis.

Dubos, Rene.
1959   *The Mirage of Health*. New York: Harper and Brothers.

Dubos, Rene.
1965   *Man Adapting*. New Haven: Yale University Press.

Dubos, Rene.
1969   *A Theology of the Earth*. A lecture delivered at the Smithsonian Institution. Washington, D. C.: Smithsonian Institution.

Dumond, D. E.
1961   "Swidden Agriculture and the Rise of Maya Civilization," *Southwestern Journal of Anthropology*, 17: 301–16.

Dumond, D. E.
1965   "Population Growth and Cultural Change," *Southwestern Journal of Anthropology*, 21: 302–24.

Duncan, Craig.
1962   "Resource Utilization and the Conservation Concept," *Economic Geography*, 38: 113–21.

Duncan, Otis Dudley.
1961   "From Social System to Ecosystem" *Sociological Inquiry*, 31: 140–49.

Durbin, Marshall.
1971   "More on Culture as a Human Domain," *Current Anthropology*, 12: 397–400.

Dyson-Hudson, R. and N.
1969   "Subsistence Herding in Uganda," *Scientific American*, 220: 76–89.

Edel, Matthew.
1969   "Economic Analysis in an Anthropological Setting: Some Methodological Considerations," *American Anthropologist*, 71: 421–33.

Edelman, Maurice.
1964   *The Symbolic Basis of Politics*. Urbana-Champaign: University of Illinois Press.

Edgerton, Robert B.
1971   *The Individual in Cultural Adaptation: A Study of Four East African Peoples*. Berkeley: University of California Press.

Edwards, R. D. and Williams, T. D.
1956   *The Great Famine: Studies in Irish History 1845–52*. London: Brown and Nolan.

Ehrlich, Paul R. and Ehrlich, Anne H.
1972   *Population Resources, Environment: Issues in Human Ecology*. Revised edition. San Francisco: Freeman.

Ehrlich, Paul R. and Holdren, J. P.
1971   "Impact of Population Growth," *Science*, 171: 1212–17.

Eichenwald, H. F. and Fry, P. C.
1969   "Nutrition and Learning," *Science*, 163: 644–48.

Eisenbud, M.
1970   "Environmental Protection in the City of New York," *Science*, 170: 706–12.

Emery, F. E. and Trist, E. L.
1973   *Towards a Social Ecology*. New York: Plenum.

Environment Magazine.
Published by the Committee for Environmental Information, St. Louis. (Best semi-technical source for current reports and studies of pollution problems.)

Environment Magazine.
1972   "Review: The Closing Circle." (Debate between B. Commoner and P. Ehrlich.)
Vol. 14, No. 2.

Epstein, T. S.
1962   *Economic Development and Social Change in South India.* Manchester: Manchester University Press.

Erasmus, Charles J.
1961   *Man Takes Control: Cultural Development and American Aid.* New York: Bobbs-Merrill.

Evanari, M. et al.
(1961   "Ancient Agriculture in the Negev," *Science,* 133: 979–96.

Ewald, William R. (ed.).
1967–68   *Environment for Man: Environment and Change: Environment and Policy.* 3 vols. Bloomington: Indiana University Press.

Ewers, John C.
1955   *The Horse in Blackfoot Indian Culture, with Comparative Material from Other Western Tribes.* Smithsonian Institution, Bureau of American Ethnology, Bulletin No. 159. Washington, D.C.: Smithsonian Institution Press.

Faris, James C.
1974   "Social Evolution, Population, and Production." Paper prepared for 9th International Congress of Anthropological Sciences, Chicago, 1973. To be published by Mouton, 1974.

Farvar, Boyouk.
1972   "Biological Disorders in the Genito-Urinary System Following the Introduction of New Technologies and Lifeways in the Less Developed Countries" in M. Taghi Farvar and John P. Milton (eds.), *The Careless Technology.* Garden City: Natural History Press.

Farvar, M. Taghi and Milton, John P. (eds.).
1972   *The Careless Technology: Ecology and International Development.* Garden City City: Natural History Press.

Ferdon, Edwin N., Jr.
1959   "Agricultural Potential and the Development of Cultures," *Southwestern Journal of Anthropology,* 15: 1–19.

Firey, Walter.
1957   "Patterns of Choice and the Conservation of Resources," *Rural Sociology,* 22: 113–22.

Firey, Walter.
1959   *Men, Mind and Land.* Glencoe: Free Press.

Firth, Raymond.
1954   "Social Organization and Social Change," *Journal of the Royal Anthropological Institute,* 84: 1–20.

Firth, Raymond.
1955   "Some Principles of Social Organization," *Journal of the Royal Anthropological Institute,* 85: 1–17.

Fitzhugh, William W.
1972   *Environmental Archeology and Cultural Systems in Hamilton Inlet, Labrador.* Smithsonian Contributions to Anthropology, Number 16. Washington, D.C.: Smithsonian Institution Press.

Flannery, Kent V.
  1965   "Ecology of Early Food Production in Mesopotamia," *Science*, 147: 1247–56.
Flannery, Kent V.
  1968   "Archeological Systems Theory and Early Meso-America," in B. J. Meggers
          (ed.), *Anthropological Archeology in the Americas*. Washington, D.C.: An-
          thropological Society of Washington.
Flannery, Kent V.
  1969   "Origins and Ecological Effects of Early Domestication in Iran and the Near
          East," in P. J. Ucko and G. W. Dimbleby (eds.), *The Domestication and
          Exploitation of Plants and Animals*. Chicago: Aldine.
Flannery, Kent V.
  1972A   "Evolutionary Trends in Social Exchange and Interaction," in Edwin N.
          Wilmsen (ed.), *Social Exchange and Interaction*. Museum of Anthropology,
          Anthropological Papers, No. 46. Ann Arbor: The University of Michigan
          Press.
Flannery, Kent V.
  1972B   "The Origins of the Village as a Settlement Type in Mesoamerica and the Near
          East: A Comparative Study," in Peter J. Ucko, Ruth Tringham, and G. W.
          Dimbleby (eds.), *Man, Settlement and Urbanism*. Cambridge: Schenkman.
Flannery, Kent V. and Coe, M. D.
  1968   "Social and Economic Systems in Formative Meso-America," in S. R. and L. R.
          Binford (eds.), *New Perpsectives in Archeology*. Chicago: Aldine.
Flannery, Kent V. et al.
  1967   "Farming Systems and Political Growth in Ancient Oaxaca," *Science*, 158:
          445–54.
Foa, Uriel G.
  1971   "Interpersonal and Economic Resources," *Science*, 171: 345–51.
Forde, C. Darryl.
  1934   *Habitat, Economy, and Society*. New York: Harcourt Brace (Second ed., 1937).
Forge, Anthony.
  1972   "Normative Factors in the Settlement Size of Neolothic Cultivators (New
          Guinea)," in Peter J. Ucko, Ruth Tringham, and G. W. Dimbleby (eds.), *Man,
          Settlement and Urbanism*. Cambridge: Schenkman.
Forrester, Jay W.
  1971   *World Dynamics*. Cambridge: Wright-Allen Press.
Fosberg, F. R.
  1963   *Man's Place in the Island Ecosystem*. Honolulu: University of Hawaii Press.
Foster, George M.
  1965   "Peasant Society and the Image of Limited Good," *American Anthropologist*,
          67: 293–315.
Foster, George M.
  1972   "A Second Look at Limited Good," *Anthropological Quarterly*, 45: 57–64.
Fowler, Melvin L.
  1971   "The Origin of Plant Cultivation in the Central Mississippi Valley: A
          Hypothesis," in S. Struever (ed.), *Prehistoric Agriculture*. Garden City: Natural
          History Press.
Frake, Charles O.
  1962   "Cultural Ecology and Ethnography," *American Anthropologist*, 64: 53–59.

Frankenberg, Ronald.
1966   "British Community Studies: Problems of Synthesis," in Michael Banton (ed.), *The Social Anthropology of Complex Societies*. New York: Praeger.
Frederiksen, Harald.
1969   "Feedbacks in Economic and Demographic Transition," *Science*, 166: 837–847.
Freeman, T. W.
1956   *Pre-Famine Ireland: A Study in Historical Geography*. Manchester: Manchester University Press.
Freilich, Morris.
1963   "The Natural Experiment: Ecology and Culture," *Southwestern Journal of Anthropology*, 19: 21–39.
Freilich, Morris.
1967   "Ecology and Culture: Environmental Determinism and the Ecological Approach in Anthropology," *Anthropological Quarterly*, 40: 26–43.
Fried, Morton H.
1952   "Land Tenure, Geography and Ecology in the Contact of Cultures," *American Journal of Economics and Sociology*, 9: 391–412.
Galle, O. R., Gove, W. R. and McPherson, J. M.
1972   "Population Density and Pathology: What Are the Relations for Man?" *Science*, 176: 23–30.
Garment, Leonard.
1970   *Toward Balanced Growth: Quantity with Quality*. Washington, D.C.: National Goals Research Staff. U.S. Government Printing Office.
Garner, B.
1967   "Models of Urban Geography and Settlement Location," in Richard J. Shorley and Peter Haggett (eds.), *Models in Geography*. London: Methuen.
Geertz, Clifford.
1963   *Agricultural Involution: The Processes of Ecological Change in Indonesia*. Berkeley: University of California Press.
Geertz, Clifford.
1963   "Two Types of Ecosystems," Chapter 2 in Geertz, *Agricultural Involution*. Berkeley: University of California Press.
Geertz, Clifford.
1965   *The Social History of an Indonesian Town*. Cambridge: MIT Press.
Gerlach, Luther P.
1969   "Participatory Ecology: An Embryonic Social Movement to Improve the Quality of Man's Environment." Mimeographed, Department of Anthropology, University of Minesota.
Gerlach, Luther P.
1971   "Movements of Revolutionary Change: Some Structural Characteristics," *American Behavioral Scientist*, 14: 812–35.
Gibbs, Jack P.
1958   "Urbanization and Natural Resources: A Study in Organizational Ecology," *American Sociological Review*, 23: 266–77.
Gibbs, Jack P.
1964   "Human Ecology and Rational Economic Behavior: Agricultural Practices as a Case in Point," *Rural Sociology*, 29: 138–41.
Glacken, Clarence J.
1966   "Reflections on the Man-Nature Theme as a Subject for Study," in F. Darling

and J. Milton (eds.), *Future Environments of North America.* Garden City: Natural History Press.

Gluckman, Max.
1945   "How the Bemba Make Their Living: An Appreciation of Richards' *Land, Labor and Diet in Northern Rhodesia,*" *Journal of the Rhodes-Livingstone Institute,* June 1945, 55–75.

Goffman, Erving.
1969   *Strategic Interaction.* Philadelphia: University of Pennsylvania Press.

Goldman, M. I.
1970   "The Convergence of Environmental Disruption," *Science,* 170: 37–42.

Goldman, Marshall I.
1972   *The Spoils of Progress: Environmental Pollution in the Soviet Union.* Boston: MIT Press.

Goldschmidt, Walter.
1947   *As You Sow.* New York: Harcourt, Brace.

Goldschmidt, Walter.
1959   *Man's Way.* New York: Holt, Rinehart and Winston.

Gottman, Jean.
1961   *Megalopolis.* New York: 20th Century Fund.

Gould, Peter R.
1963   "Man Against his Environment: A Game Theoretic Framework," *Annals of the Association of American Geographers,* 53: 290–97.

Gould, Richard A. and D. and C. Fowler.
1972   "Diggers and Doggers: Parallel Failures in Economic Acculturation," *Southwestern Journal of Anthropology,* 28: 265–81.

Green, Donald E.
1973   *Land of the Underground Rain: Irrigation on the Texas High Plains, 1910–1970.* Austin: University of Texas Press.

Groslier, Bernard Philippe.
1966   *Indochina.* New York: World.

Gross, D. and Underwood, B.
1971   "Technological Change and Caloric Costs: Sisal Agriculture in Northeastern Brazil," *American Anthropologist,* 73: 725–40.

Gross, Neal.
1948   "Cultural Variables in Rural Communities," *American Journal of Sociology,* 54: 344–50.

Gruber, Jacob W.
1971   "Ethnographic Salvage and the Shaping of Anthropology," *American Anthropologist,* 72: 1289–99.

Hall, A. D. and Fagen, R. E.
1956   "Definition of a system." *General Systems Yearbook,* 1: 18–28.

Hall, Edward T.
1966   *The Hidden Dimension.* New York: Doubleday.

Hall, Gus.
1972   *Ecology: Can We Survive under Capitalism?* New York. International Publishers Associates.

Hallowell, A. Irving.
1945   "Sociopsychological Aspects of Acculturation" in R. Linton (ed.), *The Science of Man in the World Crisis.* N.Y.: Columbia University Press.

Hallowell, A. Irving.
1960   "Self Society, and Culture in Phylogenetic Perspective" in S. Tax (ed.), *The Evolution of Man*. Chicago: University of Chicago Press.
Halprin, Lawrence.
1970   *The RSVP Cycles: Creative Processes in the Human Environment*. New York: Braziller.
Hardesty, Donald L.
1972   "The Human Ecological Niche," *American Anthropologist*, 74: 458–66.
Hardin, Garrett.
1963   "The Cybernetics of Competition: A Biologist's View of Society," *Perspectives in Biology and Medicine*, 7: 58–84.
Hardin, Garrett.
1968   "The Tragedy of the Commons," *Science*, 162: 1243–48.
Hardin, Garrett.
1972   *Exploring New Ethics for Survival: The Voyage of The Spaceship Beagle*. New York: Viking Press.
Hare, Kenneth.
1970   "How Shall We Treat Environment?" *Science*, 167: 352–55.
Harner, Michael J.
1970   "Population Pressure and the Social Evolution of Agriculturalists," *Southwestern Journal of Anthropology*, 26: 67–86.
Harrell, R. F., Woodyard, E., and Gates, A. J.
1955   *Effects of Nutrition on the Intelligence of Offspring*. New York: Columbia University Teachers' College.
Harris, David R.
1966   "Agricultural Systems, Ecosystems and the Origins of Agriculture" in P. J. Ucko and G. W. Dimbleby (eds.), *The Domestication and Exploitation of Plants and Animals*. Chicago: Aldine.
Harris, David R.
1972A   "The Origins of Agriculture in the Tropics," *American Scientist*, 60: 180–93.
Harris, David R.
1972B   "Swidden Systems and Settlement" in Peter J. Ucko, Ruth Tringham, and G. W. Dimbleby (eds.), *Man, Settlement and Urbanism*. Cambridge: Schenkman.
Harris, Marvin.
1960   "Adaptation in Biological and Cultural Science," *Transactions of the New York Academy of Sciences*, Ser. II, Vol. 23, No. 1, pp. 59–65.
Harris, Marvin.
1964   *The Nature of Cultural Things*. New York: Random House.
Harris, Marvin.
1966   "The Cultural Ecology of India's Sacred Cattle," *Current Anthropology*, 7: 51–66.
Harris, Marvin.
1968   *The Rise of Anthropological Theory*. New York: Crowell.
Hawley, Amos H.
1950   *Human Ecology: A Theory of Community Structure*. New York: Ronald Press.
Hawley, Amos H. (ed.)
1968   *Roderick D. McKenzie on Human Ecology*. Chicago: University of Chicago Press.

Hawley, Amos H.
   1973   "Ecology and Population," *Science*, 179: 1196–1201.
Hawthorn, Geoffrey.
   1970   *The Sociology of Fertility*. London: Collier-Macmillan.
Heizer, Robert F.
   1960   "Agriculture and the Theocratic State in Lowland Southeastern Mexico,"
           American Antiquity, 26: 215–22.
Helbaek, Hans.
   1969   "Appendix I," in Frank Hole et al., *Prehistory and Human Ecology of the Deh
           Luran Plain*. Memoirs of the Museum of Anthropology, No. 1. Ann Arbor:
           University of Michigan Press.
Helfrich, Harold W., Jr.
   1970   *Agenda for Survival*. New Haven: Yale University Press.
Helm, J.
   1962   "The Ecological Approach in Anthropology," *American Journal of Sociology*,
           67: 630–39.
Helms, Mary W.
   1969   "The Cultural Ecology of a Colonial Tribe," *Ethnology*, 8: 76–84.
Henderson, L. J.
   1913–58   *The Fitness of the Environment*. New York: Macmillan, 1913. (Revised
              edition, Boston: Beacon Press, 1958.)
Henderson, L. J.
   1970   *On the Social System*. Edited by B. Barber. Chicago: University of Chicago
           Press.
Heston, Alan.
   1971   "An Approach to the Sacred Cow of India," *Current Anthropology*, 12: 191–210.
Hillery, George, A., Jr.
   1966   "Navajos and Eastern Kentuckians: A Comparative Study of the Cultural
           Consequences of the Demographic Transition," *American Anthropologist*, 68:
           52–70.
Hoagland, Hudson.
   1963   "Cybernetics of Population Control," in R. O. Greep (ed.), *Human Fertility and
           Population Problems*. Boston: Schenkman.
Hodgen, Margaret T.
   1964   *Early Anthropology in the Sixteenth and Seventeenth Centuries*. Philadelphia:
           University of Pennsylvania Press.
Hodson, H. V.
   1972   *The Diseconomics of Growth*. New York: Ballantine Books.
Hole, Frank, Flannery, K., and Nealy, J. A.
   1969   *Prehistory and Human Ecology of the Deh Luran Plain*. Memoirs of the Museum
           of Anthropology. No. 1. Ann Arbor: University of Michigan Press.
Holling, Crawford S.
   1969   "Stability in Ecological and Social Systems," in *Diversity and Stability in
           Ecological Systems*. Report of Symposium held May 26–28, 1969. Upton, N.Y.:
           Brookhaven National Laboratory, Biology Department.
Holling, Crawford S.
   1973   "Resilience and Stability of Ecological Systems," *Annual Review of Ecology and
           Systematics*, 4: 1–23.

Holloway, Ralph L.
1969   "Culture: A Human Domain," *Current Anthropology*, 10: 395–412.
Holmberg, Allan R.
1950   *Nomads of the Long Bow*. Smithsonian Institution, Institute of Social Anthropology, Publication, No. 10. Washington, D.C.: Smithsonian Institution Press.
Homans, George C.
1961   *Social Behavior: Its Elementary Forms*. New York: Harcourt Brace and World.
Hornstein, H. A. et al. (eds.).
1971   *Social Intervention*. (Reader on strategies for changing social systems.) New York: Free Press.
Hunter, John M.
1967   "The Social Roots of Dispersed Settlement in Northern Ghana," *Annals of the Association of American Geographers*, 57.
Huntington, Charles C. and Carlson, Fred. A.
1933   *The Geographic Basis of Society*. New York: Prentice-Hall.
Hutchinson, G. Evelyn.
1973   "Eutrophication," *American Scientist*, 61: 269–79.
Huth, Hans.
1957   *Nature and the American: Three Centuries of Changing Attitudes*. Berkeley: University of California Press.
Hyams, E.
1965   *Soil and Civilization*. London: Tames and Hudson.
Hymes, Dell H.
1961   "Functions of Speech: An Evolutionary Approach," in F. C. Gruber (ed.), *Anthropology and Education*. Philadelphia: University of Pennsylvania Press.
Iversen, J.
1949   "The Influence of Prehistoric Man on Vegetation," *Danmarks Geologiske Undersogelse*, 3.6: 5–25.
Jacobsen, Thorkild and Adams, Robert McCormick.
1968   "Salt and Silt in Ancient Mesopotamian Agriculture," *Science*, 128: 1251–58.
Janzen, D. H.
1973   "Tropical Agroecosystems," *Science*, 182: 1212–18.
Johnson, Allen W.
1972   "Individuality and Experimentation in Traditional Agriculture," *Human Ecology*, 1: 149–59.
Johnson, Gregory A.
1972   "A Test of the Utility of Central Place Theory in Archaeology," in Peter J. Ucko, Ruth Tringham, and G. W. Dimbleby (eds.), *Man, Settlement and Urbanism*. Cambridge: Schenkman.
Johnson, Hildegard Binder.
1957   "Rational and Ecological Aspects of the Quarter Section," *The Geographical Review*, 47: 330–48.
Jones, E. R.
Forth-   "Economic Options in Highland Europe: 1550–1850," Ms, Northwestern
coming   University.
Kalmus, H.
1966   "Control Hierarchies," in H. Kalmus (ed.), *Regulation and Control of Living Systems*. New York: Wiley.

Kaplan, David.
1968   "The Formal-Substantive Controversy in Economic Anthropology: Reflections on its Wider Implications," *Southwestern Journal of Anthropology*, 24: 228–51.
Kates, Robert W.
1962   *Hazard and Choice Perception in Flood Plain Management*. Department of Geography Research, Paper No. 78. Chicago: University of Chicago Press.
Kates, Robert W. et al.
1973   "Human Impact of the Managua Earthquake," *Science*, 182: 981–89.
Keef, P. A. M. et al.
1965   "A Neolithic Site on Iping Common, Sussex," *Proceedings of the Prehistoric Society*, Vol. 31.
Klausner, Samuel Z.
1971   *On Man in His Environment*. New York: Jossey-Bass.
Kluckhohn, Clyde.
1944   *Navajo Witchcraft*. Papers on the Peabody Museum of American Archeology and Ethnology, Vol. 22, No. 2.
Kluckhohn, Clyde.
1949   "The Limitations of Adaptation and Adjustment as Concepts for Understanding Cultural Behavior," in J. Romano (ed.), *Adaptation*. Ithaca: Cornell University Press.
Kluckhohn, Florence R. and Strodtbeck, Fred L.
1961   *Variations in Value Orientations*. Evanston, Ill. and Elmsford, N.Y.: Peterson.
Kneese, Allen V.
1967   "Economics and the Quality of the Environment: Some Empirical Experiences," in M. E. Garnsey and J. R. Hibbs (eds.), *Social Sciences and the Environment*. Boulder: University of Colorado Press.
Knight, Rolf.
1965   "A Re-examination of Hunting, Trapping, and Territoriality among the Northeastern Algonkian Indians," in Anthony Leeds and Andrew P. Vayda (eds.), *Man, Culture, and Animals*. Publication No. 78, Washington, D.C.: American Association for the Advancement of Science.
Knight, Rolf.
1974   Review of "Bruce Cox (ed.) *Cultural Ecology: Readings on the Canadian Indians and Eskimos*." *Reviews in Anthropology* 1, No. 3, 349–359.
Koestler, Arthur.
1969   "Man: One of Evolution's Mistakes?" *The New York Times Magazine*, October 19, 1969, pp. 28 ff.
Kottak, Conrad P.
1972   "Ecological Variables in the Origin and Evolution of African States: The Buganda Example," *Comparative Studies in Society and History*, 14: 351–80.
Kraenzel, Carl F.
1967   "Deficit-Creating Influences for Role Performance and Status Acquisition in Sparsely Populated Regions of the United States," in C. C. Zimmerman and S. Russell, *Symposium on the Great Plains of North America*. Fargo: North Dakota State University.
Krantz, G. S.
1970   "Human Activities and Megafaunal Extinctions," *American Scientist*, 58: 164–70.

Kristof, Ladis K. D.
  1959   "The Nature of Frontiers and Boundaries," *Annals of the Association of American Geographers*, 49: 269–82.
Kroeber, A. L.
  1917   "The Superorganic," *American Anthropologist*, 19: 163–213.
Kroeber, A. L.
  1939   *Cultural and Natural Areas of Native North America*. University of California Publications in American Archeology and Ethnology, Vol. 38. Berkeley: University of California Press.
Krutilla, John V.
  1970   "Some Environmental Effects of Economic Development," in Roger Revelle and Hans H. Landsberg (eds.), *America's Changing Environment*. Boston: Beacon Press.
Krutilla, John V. (ed.).
  1973   *Natural Environments: Studies in Theoretical and Applied Analysis*. Baltimore: Resources for the Future and the Johns Hopkins University Press.
Kunstadter, Peter.
  1972A   "Spirits of Change Capture the Karen," *National Geographic*, 141: 267–84.
Kunstadter, Peter.
  1972B   "Demography, Ecology, Social Structure, and Settlement Patterns," in G. A. Harrison and J. A. Boyce, *The Structure of Human Populations*. Oxford: Clarendon Press.
Kushner, Gilbert.
  1970   "A Consideration of Some Processual Designs for Archeology as Anthropology," *American Antiquity*, 35: 125–32.
Ladurie, I. Le Roy
  1971   *Times of Feast, Times of Famine: A History of Climate Science the Year 1000*. Garden City: Doubleday.
Landsberg, H. E.
  1970   "Man-Made Climatic Changes," *Science*, 170: 1265–74.
Langer, Suzanne.
  1942   *Philosophy in a New Key: A Study in the Symbolism of Reason, Rite, and Art*. Cambridge: Harvard University Press.
Lansing, John B., Marans, Robert W., and Zehner, Robert B.
  1970   *Planned Residential Environments*. Ann Arbor: Institute for Social Research, Publications Division.
Lasswell, Harold D.
  1971   *A Pre-View of Policy Sciences*. New York: Elsevier.
Lattimore, Owen.
  1951   *Inner Asian Frontiers of China*. New York: American Geographical Society.
Lattimore, Owen.
  1962   *Studies in Frontier History*. New York: Oxford University Press.
Laughlin, William S.
  1972   "Ecology and Population Structure in the Arctic," in G. A. Harrison and J. A. Boyce, *The Structure of Human Populations*. Oxford: Clarendon Press.
Lave, Lester B. and Seskin, E. P.
  1970   "Air Pollution and Human Health," *Science*, 169: 723–33.
Laycock, Arleigh H. et al.
  1972   "The Environment," (symposium). *Association for Canadian Studies in the U.S.*,

Newsletter. Johns Hopkins School of Advanced International Studies, Vol. 2, No. 1, May 1972.

Leach, Edmund R.
1954–64   *Political Systems of Highland Burma.* London: London School of Economics. (Also published in paperback by Beacon Press, 1964.)

Leach, Edmund R.
1959   "Hydraulic Society in Ceylon," *Past and Present,* No. 15, pp. 2–26.

Leach, Edmund R.
1972   "Anthropological Aspects: Conclusion," in Peter R. Cox and John Peel (eds.), *Population and Pollution.* London: Academic Press.

Lee, Everett S.
1966   "A Theory of Migration," *Demography,* 3: 47–57.

Lee, Norman and Saunders, P. J. W.
1972   "Pollution as a Function of Affluence and Population," in Peter R. Cox and John Peel (eds.), *Population and Pollution.* New York: Academic Press.

Lee, Richard B.
1969   "!Kung Bushman Subsistence: An Input-Output Analysis," in D. Damas (ed.), *Contributions to Anthropology: Ecological Essays.* Bulletin 230, Anthropological Series, No. 86. Ottawa: National Museums of Canada. (Also published in A. Vayda [ed.], *Environment and Cultural Behavior.* New York: Natural History Press, 1969.)

Lee, Richard B.
1972A   "The Intensification of Social Life among the !Kung Bushmen," in Brian Spooner (ed.), *Population Growth.* Cambridge: MIT Press.

Lee, Richard B.
1972B   "Work Effort, Group Structure and Land-Use in Contemporary Hunter-Gatherers," in Peter J. Ucko, Ruth Tringham, and G. W. Dimbleby (eds.), *Man, Settlement and Urbanism.* London: Duckworth, Ltd.

Lee, Richard B.
1972C   "Population Growth and the Beginnings of Sedentary Life among the !Kung Bushmen," in Brian Spooner (ed.), *Population Growth.* Cambridge: MIT Press.

Lee, Richard B. and DeVore, Irven.
1968   *Man the Hunter.* Chicago: Aldine.

Leeds, Anthony and Vayda, Andrew P. (eds.).
1965   *Man, Culture, and Animals: The Role of Animals in Human Ecological Adjustments.* American Association for the Advancement of Science, Publication No. 78. Washington, D.C.: American Association for the Advancement of Science.

Leeds, Anthony
1969   "Ecological Determinants of Chieftainship among the Yaruro Indians of Venezuela." In Andrew P. Vayda (ed.), *Environment and Cultural Behavior.* New York: Natural History Press.

Leighly, J. (ed.).
1966   *Land and Life: A Selection from the Writings of Carl Ortwin Sauer.* Berkeley: University of California Press.

Leiss, William.
1972   *The Domination of Nature.* New York: Braziller.

Lindenbaum, Shirley.
1972   "Sorcerers, Ghosts, and Polluting Women: An Analysis of Religious Belief and Population Control," *Ethnology,* 11: 241–53.

Linton, Ralph.
1936   *The Study of Man*. New York: Appleton-Century.
Linton, Ralph (ed.).
1940   *Acculturation in Seven American Indian Tribes*. New York: Appleton-Century.
Litton, R. Burton, Jr.
1970   "Landscape and Aesthetic Quality," in Roger Revelle and Hans H. Landsberg (eds.), *America's Changing Environment*. Boston: Beacon Press.
Livingstone, Frank B.
1958   "Anthropological Implications of Sickle Cell Gene Distribution in West Africa," *American Anthropologist*, 60: 533–59.
Livingstone, Frank B.
1971   "Malaria and Human Polymorphisms," *Annual Review of Genetics*, 5: 33–64.
Lowenthal, D. and Prince, H. C.
1964   "The English Landscape," *The Geographical Review*, 54: 309–46.
Lowie, Robert H.
1937   *The History of Ethnological Theory*. New York: Farrar and Rinehart.
Lowie, Robert H. (ed.).
1938   "Subsistence," in F. Boas et al., *General Anthropology*. Boston & New York: Heath.
Luscher, Charles W.
1970   "Attitudes Toward Conservation in the Soviet Union," *The Living Wilderness*, 34: 13–19.
MacArthur, Robert H.
1972   *Geographical Ecology*. New York: Harper & Row.
MacKay, Donald M.
1961   "Informational Analysis of Questions and Commands," in C. Cherry (ed.), *Information Theory*. London: Butterworth.
MacNeish, Richard S.
1967   "A Summary of the Subsistence," in Douglas S. Byers (general editor), *Environment and Subsistence. The Prehistory of the Tehuacan Valley*, Vol. 1. Austin: University of Texas Press.
MacNeish, Richard S.
1972   "The Evolution of Community Patterns in the Tehuacan Valley of Mexico and Speculations about the Cultural Processes," in Peter J. Ucko, Ruth Tringham, and G. W. Dimbleby (eds.), *Man, Settlement and Urbanism*. Cambridge: Schenkman.
MacNeish, Richard S.
1973   "The Scheduling Factor in the Development of Effective Food Production in the Tehuacan Valley," in Donald W. Lathrap and Jody Douglas (eds.), *Variation in Anthropology: Essays in Honor of John C. McGregor*. Urbana: Illinois Archeological Survey.
Mair, Charles.
1890   *The American Bison—Its Habits, Method of Capture and Economic Use in the Northwest, with Reference to its Threatened Extinction and Possible Preservation*. Ottawa: Royal Society of Canada.
Malinowski, Bronislaw.
1935   "An Ethnographic Theory of Language," in *Carol Gardens and Their Magic*. Vol. II. London: Allen and Unwin.
Mangelsdorf, Paul C., MacNeish, R. S., and Galinet, W. C.
1964–70   "Domestication of Corn," *Science*, Vol. 143, pp. 538–45. (Reprinted in

S. Struever [ed.], *Prehistoric Agriculture*. Garden City: Natural History Press, 1971.)

Mangelsdorf, Paul C.
1974   *Corn:* Its Origin, Evolution, and Improvement. Cambridge: Belknap Press of Harvard University Press.

Manners, Gerald.
1964   *The Geography of Energy*. London: Hutchinson.

Mansfield, Edwin et al.
1971   *Research and Innovation in the Modern Corporation*. New York: Norton.

Margalef, Ramón.
1968   *Perspectives in Ecological Theory*. Chicago: University of Chicago Press.

Marsh, G. P.
1864   *Man and Nature: Or, Physical Geography as Modified by Human Action*. New York: Scribner.

Martin, Paul S.
1973   "The Discovery of America," *Science*, 179: 969–74.

Maruyama, Magaroh.
1963   "The Second Cybernetics: Deviation-amplifying Mutual Causal Processes," *American Scientist*, 51: 164–79.

Marx, L.
1970   "American Institutions and Ecological Ideals," *Science*, 170: 945–52.

Mason, O. T.
1895   "Influence of Environment upon Human Industries or Arts," *Smithsonian Institution Annual Reports*, pp. 639–65. Washington, D.C.: Smithsonian Institution Press.

Mauss, Marcel.
1954   *The Gift: Forms and Functions of Exchange in Archaic Societies*. Translated by Ian Cunnison. London: Cohen and West.

Maxwell, H.
1910   "The Use and Abuse of Forests by the Virginia Indians," *William and Mary College Historical Magazine*, 19: 86–104.

May, Jacques M. and McClellan, Donna L. (eds.).
1972   *The Ecology of Malnutrition in Seven Countries of Southern Africa and in Portuguese Guinea*. New York: Hafner.

Mayr, Otto.
1971   "Adam Smith and the Concept of the Feedback System: Economic Thought and Technology in 18th Century Britain," *Technology and Culture*, 12: 1–22.

Mazess, Richard B.
1973   "Adaptation: A Conceptual Framework," IXth International Congress of Anthropological and Ethnological Sciences. To be published in 1974.

McClelland, C. A.
1965   "System Theory and Human Conflict," in E. B. McNeil (ed.), *The Nature of Human Conflict*. Englewood Cliffs: Prentice-Hall.

McCracken, Robert D.
1971   "Lactase Deficiency: An Example of Dietary Evolution," *Current Anthropology*, 12: 479–518.

McCullough, John M.
1973   "Human Ecology, Heat Adaptation, and Belief Systems: The Hot-Cold Syndrome of Yucatan," *Journal of Anthropological Research*, 29: 32–36.

McHale, Thomas R.
  1962   "Econological Analysis and Differential Growth Rates," *Human Organization*, 21: 30–35.
McHarg, Ian.
  1970   *Design with Nature*. Garden City: Natural History Press.
McKenzie, R. D.
  1928   "Ecological Succession in the Puget Sound Region," *Publication of the American Sociological Society*, 23: 60–80.
McKinley, Daniel.
  1964   "The New Mythology of 'Man in Nature,'" *Perspectives in Biology and Medicine*, 8: 93–105.
McNaughton, S. J. and Wolf, L. L.
  1970   "Dominance and Niche in Ecological Systems," *Science*, 167: 131–39.
Mead, George H.
  1934   *Mind, Self, and Society*. Chicago: University of Chicago Press.
Mead, Margaret (ed.).
  1943   *The Problem of Changing Food Habits*. Bulletin 108. Washington, D.C.: Committee on Food Habits, National Research Council.
Mead, Margaret (ed.).
  1945   *Manual for the Study of Food Habits*. Bulletin 111. Washington, D.C.: Committee on Food Habits, National Research Council.
Mead, Margaret (ed.).
  1955   *Cultural Patterns and Technical Change*. A Manual Prepared by the World Federation for Mental Health: UNESCO. New York: Mentor Books, 1955. (Also published by IJsel Press, Deventer, Holland, 1943.)
Meadows, D. H. et al.
  1972   *The Limits to Growth: A Report on the Club of Rome's Project on the Predicament of Mankind*. New York: Potomac Associates and Universe Books.
Medawar, P. B.
  1960   *The Future of Man*. New York: Basic Books.
Medford, Derek.
  1973   *Environmental Harassment or Technology Assessment?* New York: American Elsevier.
Meggers, Betty J.
  1954   "Environmental Limitations on the Development of Culture," *American Anthropologist*, 56: 801–24.
Merriman, R. O.
  1926   *The Bison and the Fur Trade*. Bulletin of the Departments of History and Political Science in Queen's University, No. 53. Kingston, Ontario: Queen's University.
Mesarovic, Mihajlo D. and Reisman, Arnold (eds.).
  1973   *Systems Approach and the City*. New York: American Elsevier.
Micklin, Michael.
  1973   *Population, Environment, and Social Organization: Current Issues in Human Ecology*. Hinsdale: Dryden Press.
Mikesell, M.
  1967   "Geographical Perspectives in Anthropology," *Annals of the Association of American Geographers*, 57: 617–34.

Millon, Rene.
1962   "Variations in Social Responses to the Practice of Irrigation Agriculture," in Richard B. Woodbury (ed.), *Civilizations in Desert Lands*. University of Utah Anthropological Papers, Number 62. Salt Lake City: University of Utah Press, December 1962.

Miner, Horace.
1955   "The Folk-Urban Continuum," in Paul F. Lazarsfeld and Morris Rosenberg (eds.), *The Language of Social Research*. Glencoe: Free Press.

Mintz, Sydney.
1964   "The Employment of Capital by Market Women in Haiti," in R. Firth and B. S. Yamey (eds.), *Capital, Credit and Saving in Peasant Societies*. Chicago: Aldine.

Mishan, E. J.
1967   *The Costs of Economic Growth*. London: Staples Press.

Mishan, E. J.
1970   *Technology and Growth: The Price We Pay*. New York: Praeger.

Moerman, Michael.
1968   *Agricultural Change and Peasant Choice in a Thai Village*. Berkeley: University of California Press.

Moncrief, L. W.
1970   "The Cultural Basis for Our Environmental Crisis," *Science*, 170: 508–12.

Montgomery, Edward.
1972   "Stratification and Nutrition in a Population in Southern India." Ph.D. dissertation, Columbia University, New York.

Montgomery, Edward, Bennett, John W., and Scudder, Thayer.
1973   "The Impact of Human Activities on the Physical and Social Environments: New Directions in Anthropological Ecology," *Annual Review of Anthropology*, II.

Moran, Emilio.
1973   "Energy Flow Analysis and the Study of *Manihot esculenta Crantz*". *Acta Amazonica*, 3: 29–39.

Mowat, Farley.
1959   *The Desperate People*. London: M. Joseph.

Mulvaney, P. J. and Golson, J. (eds.).
1972   *Aboriginal Man and Environment in Australia*. Canberra: Australian National University.

Munson, Ronald (ed.).
1971   *Man and Nature: Philosophical Issues in Biology*. New York: Delta.

Murphey, Rhoads.
1951   "Decline of North Africa Since the Roman Occupation: Climatic or Human?" *Annals of the Association of American Geographers*, 41: 116–32.

Murphey, Rhoads.
1957   "The Ruin of Ancient Ceylon." *Journal of Asian Studies*, 16: 181–200.

Murphy, Robert F. and Steward, Julian H.
1956   "Tappers and Trappers: Parallel Process in Acculturation," *Economic Development and Cultural Change*, 4: 335–55.

Nadel, S. F.
1951   *Foundations of Social Anthropology*. Glencoe: Free Press.

Nag, Moni.
1962   *Factors Affecting Human Fertility in Non-Industrial Societies: A Cross-Cultural Study*. New Haven: Yale University Publications in Anthropology.
Nagel, Ernest and Tustin, Arnold.
1955   "Feedback: The Principle of Control," Part I of *Automatic Control*. Scientific American Book, New York: Simon and Schuster.
National Research Council.
1970   *Resources and Man*. Committee on Resources and Man, National Academy of Sciences. San Francisco: Freeman.
Neitschmann, Bernard Q.
1973   *Between Land and Water: The Subsistence Ecology of the Miskito Indians*. New York: Seminar Press.
Netting, Robert McC.
1968   *Hill Farmers of Nigeria: The Cultural Ecology of the Kofyar of the Jos Plateau*. Seattle: University of Washington Press.
Netting, Robert McC.
1969   "Ecosystems in Process: A Comparative Study of Change in Two West African Societies," in D. Damas (ed.), *Contributions to Anthropology: Ecological Essays*. Bulletin 230; Anthropological Series, No. 86. Ottawa: National Museums of Canada.
Netting, Robert McC.
1972   *The Ecological Approach in Cultural Study*. McCaleb Module. Reading, Mass.: Addison-Wesley.
Neuhaus, Richard.
1971   *In Defense of People: Ecology and the Seduction of Radicalism*. New York: Macmillan.
Newcomer, Peter J.
1972   "The Nuer and Dinka: an Essay on Origins and Environmental Determinism". *MAN*. N.S. 7: 5–11.
Newman, James L.
1970   *The Ecological Basis for Subsistence Change among the Sandawe of Tanzania*. Washington, D.C.: National Academy of Sciences.
Newman, Marshall T.
1962   "Ecology and Nutritional Stress in Man," *American Anthropologist*, 64: 22–33.
Niehoff, Arthur H.
1966   *A Casebook of Social Change*. Chicago: Aldine.
Niering, W. A. and Goodwin, R. H.
1962   "Ecological Studies in the Connecticut Arboretum Natural Area: 1. Introduction and Survey of Vegetation Types." *Ecology*, 43: 41–54.
Nisbet, Robert A.
1969   *Social Change and History: Aspects of the Western Theory of Development*. New York: Oxford University Press.
Northrop, F. S. C.
1946   *The Meeting of the East and West*. New York: Macmillan.
Nurge, Ethel and Ng, W. K.
1974   "Human Ecology and the Physician," *Journal of the Kansas Medical Society*, 75: 77–81.
O'Connor, David.

1972   "The Geography of Settlement in Ancient Egypt," in Peter J. Ucko, Ruth Tringham, and G. W. Dimbleby (eds.), *Man, Settlement and Urbanism.* Cambridge: Schenkman.

Odend'hal, S.
1972   "Energetics of Indian Cattle in Their Environment," *Human Ecology,* I: 3–22.

Odum, Eugene P.
1953;   *Fundamentals of Ecology.* Philadelphia: Saunders, 1953.
1971   (3d ed., 1971.)

Odum, Eugene P.
1969   "The Strategy of Ecosystem Development," *Science,* 164: 262–70.

Odum, Howard T.
1971   *Environment, Power, and Society.* New York: Wiley.

Ogburn, William F.
1956   "Technology as Environment," *Sociology and Social Research,* 41: 3–9.

Oliver, Symmes C.
1962   *Ecology and Cultural Continuity as Contributing Factors in the Social Organization of the Plains Indians.* University of California Publications in American Archaeology and Ethnology, Vol. 48, No. 1. Berkeley: University of California Press.

Orleans, L. A. and Suttmeier, R. P.
1970   "The Mao Ethic and Environmental Quality," *Science,* 170: 1173–76.

Parrack, Dwain W.
1969   "An Approach to the Bioenergetics of West Bengal," in A. Vayda (ed.), *Environment and Cultural Behavior.* New York: Natural History Press.

Parsons, Talcott.
1951   *The Social System.* Glencoe: Free Press.

Patterson, Robert W.
1970   "The Art of the Impossible," in Roger Revelle and Hans H. Landsberg (eds.), *America's Changing Environment.* Boston: Beacon Press.

Patterson, Thomas C.
1971   "The Emergence of Food Production in Central Peru," in S. Struever (ed.), *Prehistoric Agriculture.* Garden City: Natural History Press.

Paulik, Gerald J.
1971   "Anchovies, Birds, and Fishermen in the Peru Current," in W. W. Murdoch (ed.), *Environment: Resources, Pollution and Society.* Stamford, Conn.: Sinauer.

Piddocke, Stuart.
1965   "The Potlatch System of the Southern Kwakiutl: A New Perspective," *Southwestern Journal of Anthropology,* 21: 244–64.

Pirages, Dennis and Ehrlich, Paul R.
1974   *Ark II: Social Response to Environmental Imperatives.* San Francisco: Freeman.

Pitt-Rivers, Julian (ed.).
1963   *Mediterranean Countrymen: Essays in the Social Anthropology of the Mediterranean.* Paris and The Hague: Mouton.

Pitts, James N. and Metcalf, R. L. (eds.).
1969   *Advances in Environmental Sciences.* New York: Wiley-Interscience.

Polanyi, Karl, Arensberg, C., and Pearson, H. W. (eds.).
1957   *Trade and Market in the Early Empires.* Glencoe: Free Press.

Polgar, Steven.
   1968   "Cultural Aspects of Natality Regulation Techniques," *Proceedings of the 8th International Congress of Anthropological and Ethnological Sciences*, Vol. 3, pp. 232–34.
Polgar, Steven (ed.).
   1971   *Culture and Population: A Collection of Current Studies.* Carolina Population Center, University of North Carolina, Monograph 9. Chapel Hill: University of North Carolina Press.
Polgar, Steven (ed.).
   1972   "Anthropology and Population Problems," (symposium), *Current Anthropology*, 13: 203–78.
Porter, Philip W.
   1965   "Environmental Potentials and Economic Opportunities—A Background for Cultural Adaptation," *American Anthropologist*, 67: 409–20.
Powell, J. H.
   1949   *Bring Out Your Dead.* Philadelphia: University of Pennsylvania Press.
Price, Edward T.
   1955   "Values and Concepts in Conservation," *Annals of the Association of American Geographers*, 45: 64–84.
Pryde, Philip R.
   1970   "Victors Are Not Judged," *Environment*, 12: 30–39.
Pryde, Philip R.
   1972   *Conservation in the Soviet Union.* New York: Cambridge University Press.
Raikes, Robert.
   1967   *Water, Weather and Prehistory.* London: Baker.
Rapoport, Anatol.
   1968   "Systems Analysis," *International Encyclopedia of the Social Sciences*, pp. 452–458. New York: Macmillan.
Rappaport, Roy A.
   1965   "Nature, Culture and Ecological Anthropology," in Harry L. Shapiro (ed.), *Man, Culture and Society.* New York: Oxford University Press.
Rappaport, Roy A.
   1967A   "Ritual Regulation of Environmental Relations among a New Guinea People," *Ethnology*, 6: 17–30.
Rappaport, Roy A.
   1967B   *Pigs for the Ancestors: Ritual in the Ecology of a New Guinea People.* New Haven: Yale University Press.
Rappaport, Roy A.
   1971A   "Ritual, Sanctity, and Cybernetics," *American Anthropologist*, 73: 73–76.
Rappaport, Roy A.
   1971B   "The Flow of Energy in an Agricultural Society," *Scientific American*, 224: 116–33.
Rappaport, Roy A.
   1971C   "The Sacred in Human Evolution," *Annual Review of Ecology and Systematics*, 2: 23–44.
Ravenstein, E. G.
   1885   "The Laws of Migration," *Journal of Royal Statistical Society*, 48: 167–227; also 52: 241–301 (1889).

Redfield, Robert.
   1941   *The Folk Culture of Yucatan.* Chicago: University of Chicago Press.
Redfield, Robert (ed.).
   1942   *Levels of Integration in Biological and Social Systems.* Lancaster, Pa.: Jacques
           Cattell Press.
Redfield, Robert.
   1953   *The Primitive World and Its Transformations.* Ithaca: Cornell University Press.
Redfield, Robert.
   1955   *The Little Community.* Chicago: University of Chicago Press.
Reed, Charles R.
   1969   "The Pattern of Animal Domestication in the Prehistoric Near East." In P. J.
           Ucko and G. W. Dimbleby (eds) *The Domestication and Exploitation of Plants
           and Animals.* Chicago: Aldine.
Revelle, Roger and Landsberg, Hans H. (eds.).
   1970A   *America's Changing Environment.* Boston: Beacon Press.
Revelle, Roger.
   1970B   "Ecology as an Ethical Science." Section I in Roger Revelle and Hans H.
           Landsberg (eds.), *America's Changing Environment.* Boston: Beacon Press.
Reynolds, Earle L.
   1960   "Irradiation and Human Evolution," *Human Biology,* 32: 89–108.
Richards, A.
   1939   *Land, Labor, and Diet in Northern Rhodesia.* London: Oxford University Press.
           For the International Institute of African Languages and Cultures.
Ridgeway, James.
   1971   *The Politics of Ecology.* New York: Dutton.
Ridker, Ronald G.
   1972   "Population and Pollution in the United States," *Science,* 176: 1085–90.
Riegel, K. W.
   1973   "Light Pollution," *Science,* 179: 1285–90.
Ripley, S. Dillon and Buechner, Helmut K.
   1970   "Ecosystem Science as a Point of Synthesis," in Roger Revelle and Hans H.
           Landsberg (eds.), *America's Changing Environment.* Boston: Beacon Press.
Robinson, Herbert W. (ed.).
   1971   *Cybernetics, Artificial Intelligence, and Ecology.* 4th Annual Symposium of the
           American Society for Cybernetics. New York: Spartan Books.
Roe, F. G.
   1951   *The North American Buffalo.* Ontario: University of Toronto Press.
Ruesch, J. and Bateson, G.
   1951   *Communication: The Social Matrix of Psychiatry.* New York: Norton.
Russell, W. M. S.
   1967   *Man, Nature and History.* London: Aldus Books.
Saarinen, Thomas F.
   1966   *Perception of the Drought Hazard on the Great Plains.* Chicago: University of
           Chicago Press.
Saarinen, Thomas F.
   1969   *Perception of Environment.* Commission on College Geography, Association of
           American Geographers, Resource Paper, No. 5. Washington, D.C.: Association
           of American Geographers.

Sagan, L. A.
1972   "Human Costs of Nuclear Power," *Science,* 177: 487–93.
Sahlins, Marshall D.
1957   "Land Use and the Extended Family in Moala, Fiji," *American Anthropologist,* 59: 449–62.
Sahlins, Marshall D.
1958   *Social Stratification in Polynesia.* Seattle: University of Washington Press.
Sahlins, Marshall D.
1961   "The Segmentary Lineage: An Organization of Predatory Expansion," *American Anthropologist,* 63: 322–45.
Sahlins, Marshall D.
1962   *Moala: Culture and Nature on a Fijian Island.* Ann Arbor: University of Michigan Press.
Sahlins, Marshall D.
1964   "Culture and Environment: The Study of Cultural Ecology," in S. Tax (ed.), *Horizons of Anthropology.* Chicago: Aldine.
Sahlins, Marshall D.
1965   "Exchange-Value and the Diplomacy of Primitive Trade" in June Helm (ed.), Paul Bohannan and Marshall D. Sahlins (co-eds.), *Essays in Economic Anthropology.* American Ethnological Society. Seattle: University of Washington Press.
Sahlins, Marshall D.
1972   *Stone Age Economics: Production, Exchange, and Politics in Small Tribal Societies.* Chicago: Aldine-Atherton.
Sahlins, Marshall D. and Service, Elman R.
1960   *Evolution and Culture.* Ann Arbor: University of Michigan Press.
Sanders, William T.
1962   "Cultural Ecology of Nuclear Mesoamerica," *American Anthropologist,* 64: 34–44.
Sanders, William T.
1965   *The Cultural Ecology of the Teotihuacan Valley.* Preliminary Report on the Results of the Teotihuacan Valley Project. Philadelphia: Pennsylvania State University.
Sanders, William T.
1968   "Hydraulic Agriculture, Economic Symbiosis, and the Evolution of States in Central Mexico," in B. J. Meggers (ed.), *Anthropological Archeology in the Americas.* Washington, D.C.: Anthropological Society of Washington.
Sanders, William T.
1972   "Population, Agricultural History, and Societal Evolution in Mesopotamia," in Brian Spooner (ed.), *Population Growth.* Cambridge: MIT Press.
Sapir, E.
1914   *Time Perspective in Aboriginal American Culture.* Ottawa: Canadian Department of Mines.
Satin, Maurice S.
1969   "An Empirical Test of the Descriptive Validity of the Theory of Demographic Transition on 53-Nation Sample." *Sociological Quarterly,* 10: 190–203.
Sauer, Carl O.
1925   *The Morphology of Landscape.* University of California Publications in Geography, 2: 11: 19–54.

Sauer, Carl O.
  1965   *Land and Life: A Selection from the Writings of Carl Ortwin Sauer.* (Edited by J. Leighly) Berkeley: University of California Press.
Sax, Joseph L.
  1970   "The Search for Environmental Quality: the Role of the Courts," in H. W. Helfrich (ed.), *The Environmental Crisis.* New Haven: Yale University Press.
Sax, Joseph L.
  1971   *Defending the Environment: A Strategy for Citizen Action.* East Setauket, N.Y.: Environmental Defense Fund.
Schachter, Esther R.
  1973   *Enforcing Air Pollution Controls.* New York: Center for Policy Research.
Schneider, Harold K.
  1974   *Economic Man: The Anthropology of Economics.* New York: Free Press.
Schultz, Vincent and Whicker, F. Ward (compilers).
  1972   *Ecological Aspects of the Nuclear Age.* Springfield, Va.: Office of Information Services, U.S. Atomic Energy Commission.
Schuphan, W.
  1972   "Nitrate Problems and Nitrite Hazards as Influenced by Ecological Conditions and by Fertilization of Plants" in M. Taghi Farvar and John P. Milton (eds.), *The Careless Technology.* Garden City: Natural History Press.
Schwartz, S. I. and Foin, T. C.
  1972   "A Critical Review of the Social Systems Models of Jay Forrester," *Human Ecology*, I: 161–73.
Science.
  Published by the American Association for the Advancement of Science. (Best single source for technical reports on current environmental science.)
Scientific American.
  1971   Vol. 228, No. 3, September. Special issue on energy.
Scudder, Thayer.
  1952   *The Ecology of the Gwenbe Tonga.* Manchester: Manchester University Press, On behalf of the Rhodes-Livingstone Institute, Rhodesia. "Kariba Studies, No. 2."
Scudder, Thayer.
  1968   "Social Anthropology, Man-Made Lakes and Population Dislocation in Africa," *Anthropological Quarterly*, 41: 168–76.
Scudder, Thayer.
  1972A   "Ecological Bottlenecks and the Development of the Kariba Lake Basin," in M. Taghi Farvar and John P. Milton (eds.), *The Careless Technology.* Garden City: Natural History Press.
Scudder, Thayer (Chairman).
  1972B   "Irrigation and Water Development." Section II in M. Taghi Farvar and John P. Milton (eds.), *The Careless Technology.* Garden City: Natural History Press.
Scudder, Thayer.
  1973   "The Human Ecology of Big Projects: River Basin Development and Resettlement," in E. Montgomery, J. W. Bennett, and T. Scudder, "The Impact of Human Activities on the Physical and Social Environment," *Annual Review of Anthropology*, II.
Sears, Paul B.
  1954   "Human Ecology: A Problem in Synthesis," *Science*, 120: 959–63.

Sears, Paul B.
   1972   "The Processes of Environmental Change by Man," in R. L. Smith (ed.), *The Ecology of Man: An Ecosystem Approach*. New York: Harper & Row.
Selby, Henry A.
   1972   "Social Organization," in B. Siegel and A. Beals (eds.), *Biennial Review of Anthropology, 1971*. Stanford; Stanford University Press.
Semple, Ellen C.
   1911   *Influences of Geographic Environment, on the Basis of Ratzel's System of Anthropogeography*. New York: Holt.
Shack, W.
   1971   "Hunger, Anxiety and Ritual: Felt Deprivation and Spirit Possession among the Gurage of Ethiopa," *Man*, 6: 30–43.
Shea, Mary B. and Emmons, Mary E.
   1972   "Anthropology and Social Problems: Population, Environment, Education." *Current Anthropology*, 13: 279–83.
Shephard, Paul and McKinley, D.
   1969   *The Subversive Science: Essays Toward an Ecology of Man*. New York: Houghton-Mifflin.
Shephard, Paul.
   1969   "Introduction: Ecology and Man—a Vewpoint" in Paul Shephard and Daniel McKinley (eds.), *The Subversive Science*. Boston: Houghton-Mifflin.
Sills, David L.
   1975   "The Environmental Movement and its Critics." *Human Ecology*, 3: 1–41.
Simmons, I. G.
   1969   "Evidence for Vegetation Changes Associated with Mesolithic Man in Britain." in P. J. Ucko and G. W. Dimbleby (eds.), *The Domestication and Exploitation of Plants and Animals*. Chicago: Aldine.
Sims, J. H. and Baumann, D. D.
   1972   "The Tornado Threat: Coping Styles of the North and South," *Science*, 176: 1386–92.
Skinner, B. F.
   1938   *The Behavior of Organisms*. New York: Appleton-Century-Crofts.
Skinner, B. F.
   1971   *Beyond Freedom and Dignity*. New York: Knopf.
Smith, Alfred G.
   1966   *Communication and Culture*. New York: Holt, Rinehart and Winston.
Smith, Frank E.
   1966   *Politics of Conservation*. New York: Pantheon Books.
Smith, Guy-Harold (ed.).
   1965   *Conservation of Natural Resources*. New York: Wiley.
Smith, Philip E. L.
   1972A   *The Consequences of Food Production*. An Addison-Wesley Module in Anthropology, No. 31. Reading, Mass.: Addison-Wesley.
Smith, Philip E. L.
   1972B   "Land-Use, Settlement Patterns and Subsistence Agriculture: A Demographic Perspective," in Peter J. Ucko, Ruth Tringham, and G. W. Dimbleby (eds.), *Man, Settlement and Urbanism*. Cambridge: Schenkman.
Smith, Philip E. L. and Young, T. Cuyler, Jr.

1972   "The Evolution of Early Agriculture and Culture in Greater Mesopotamia: A Trial Model," in Brian Spooner (ed.), *Population Growth*. Cambridge: MIT Press.

Smith, Robert Leo.
1972   *The Ecology of Man: An Ecosystem Approach*. New York: Harper & Row.

Soleri, Paolo.
1971   *Arcology: The City in the Image of Man*. Cambridge: MIT Press.

Solow, R. M.
1971   "The Economist's Approach to Pollution and Its Control," *Science*, 173: 498–503.

Speck, Frank G.
1935   *Naskapi: The Savage Hunters of the Labrador Peninsula*. Norman: University of Oklahoma Press.

Spicer, Edward H.
1952   *Human Problems in Technological Change: A Casebook*. New York: Russell Sage Foundation.

Spoehr, Alexander.
1956   "Cultural Differences in the Interpretation of Natural Resources," in W. L. Thomas (ed.), *Man's Role in Changing the Face of the Earth*. Chicago: University of Chicago Press.

Spoehr, Alexander.
1966   "The Part and the Whole: Reflections on the Study of a Region," *American Anthropologist*, 68: 629–40.

Spooner, Brian.
1970   "Towards a Generative Model of Nomadism." Paper Presented at the American Anthropological Association annual meeting, San Diego.

Spooner, Brian (ed.).
1972   *Population Growth: Anthropological Implications*. Cambridge: MIT Press.

Spooner, Brian.
1972   "The Iranian Deserts," in Brian Spooner (ed.), *Population Growth*. Cambridge: MIT Press.

Spooner, Brian.
1973   *The Cultural Ecology of Pastoral Nomads*. An Addison-Wesley Module in Anthropology, No. 45. Reading, Mass.: Addison-Wesley.

Stagner, Ross.
1951   "Homeostasis as a Unifying Concept in Personality Theory," in Carrol C. Pratt (ed.), *Psychological Review*, 58: 5–17.

Starr, Chauncey.
1969   "Social Benefit vs. Technological Risk," *Science*, 165: 1232–38.

Starr, Chauncey and Rudman, Richard.
1973   "Parameters of Technological Growth," *Science*, 182: 358–64.

Stein, Maurice R.
1960   *The Eclipse of Community*. New York: Harper & Row.

Steward, Julian H.
1936   "The Economic and Social Basis of Primitive Bands," in *Essays in Honor of A. L. Kroeber*. Berkeley: University of California Press.

Steward, Julian H.
1937   "Ecological Aspects of Southwestern Society," *Anthropos*, 32.

Steward, Julian H.
1938   *Basin-Plateau Sociopolitical Groups.* Bulletin 120. Washington, D.C.: Bureau of American Ethnology.
Steward, Julian H. (ed.).
1955A   *Irrigation Civilizations: A Comparative Study: A Symposium on Method and Result in Cross-Cultural Regularities.* Social Science Monographs, 1. Washington, D.C.: Pan American Union.
Steward, Julian H.
1955B   "Multilinear Evolution: Evolution and Process" in J. Steward, *The Theory of Culture Change.* Urbana: University of Illinois Press.
Steward, Julian H.
1955C   "The Concept and Method of Cultural Ecology" in J. Steward, *The Theory of Culture Change.* Urbana: University of Illinois Press.
Steward, Julian H.
1955D   "Levels of Sociocultural Integration: An Operational Concept" in J. Steward, *The Theory of Cultural Change.* Urbana: University of Illinois Press.
Steward, Julian H.
1955E   "Analysis of Complex Contemporary Societies: Culture Patterns of Puerto Rico" in J. Steward, *The Theory of Culture Change.* Urbana: University of Illinois Press.
Steward, Julian H.
1955F   "Culture Area and Culture Type in Aboriginal America: Methodological Considerations" in J. Steward, *The Theory of Culture Change.* Urbana: University of Illinois Press.
Steward, Julian H. et al.
1956   *The People of Puerto Rico.* Champaign, Ill.: University of Illinois Press.
Stober, Gerhard J. and Schumacher, Dieter (eds.).
1973   *Technology Assessment and Quality of Life.* New York: American Elsevier.
Stocking, George W., Jr.
1968   *Race, Culture, and Evolution: Essays in the History of Anthropology.* New York: Free Press; Collier-Macmillan.
Stoddart, D. R.
1965   "Geography and the Ecological Approach: Ecosystem as a Geographic Principle and Method," *Geography,* 50: 243–51.
Stoddart, D. R.
1967   "Organism and Ecosystem as Geographical Models," in R. J. Chorley and P. Hackett (eds.), *Models in Geography.* London: Methuen.
Stolnitz, George.
1964   "The Demographic Transition," in Ronald Freedman (ed.), *Population and the Vital Revolution.* Garden City: Anchor Books.
Stoltzfus, Victor.
1973   "Amish Agriculture: Adaptive Strategies for Economic Survival of Community Life," *Rural Sociology,* 38: 196–206.
Stott, D. H.
1962   "Cultural and Natural Checks on Population Growth," in M. F. Ashley-Montagu (ed.), *Culture and Evolution of Man.* New York: Oxford University Press, 1962. (Also reprinted in A. Vayda [ed.], *Environment and Cultural Behavior.* New York: Natural History Press, 1969.)
Strett, J. M.

1969   "An Evaluation of the Concept of Carrying Capacity," *The Professional Geographer*, 21: 104–107.

Strong, Anna Louise.
1970   "Crisis Mentality and the Deteriorating Environment," in Roger Revelle and Hans H. Landsberg (eds.), *America's Changing Environment*. Boston: Beacon Press.

Struever, Stuart.
1968   "Problems, Methods and Organization: A Disparity in the Growth of Archeology," in B. J. Meggers (ed.), *Anthropological Archeology in the Americas*. Washington, D.C.: Anthropological Society of Washington.

Struever, Stuart (ed.).
1971   *Prehistoric Agriculture*. Garden City: Natural History Press.

Suzuki, Tatsuzo.
1970   "A Study of the Japanese National Character—Part IV," *Annals of the Institute of Statistical Mathematics*, Supplement 6. (Tokyo).

Sweet, Louise E.
1965   "Camel Pastoralism in North Arabia and the Minimal Camping Unit," in Anthony Leeds and Andrew P. Vayda (eds.), *Man, Culture and Animals*. Washington, D.C.: American Association for the Advancement of Science.

Swenson, G. W., Jr. and Cochran, W. W.
1973   "Radio Noise from Towns," *Science*, 181: 543–44.

Tansley, A. G.
1935   "The Use and Abuse of Vegetational Concepts and Terms," *Ecology*, 16: 284–307.

Technology Review.
1971   Three-part series on energy production and environment. Vol. 74 (Nos. 1, 2, 3). Cambridge: MIT.

Theodorson, George A. (ed.).
1961   *Studies in Human Ecology*. New York: Row, Peterson.

Thomas, Dorothy Swaine.
1938   "Research Memorandum on Migration Differentials," *Social Science Research Council*, Bulletin 43.

Thomas, Franklin.
1925   *The Environmental Basis of Society: A Study in the History of Sociological Theory*. New York: Century. (Also reprinted by Johnson, 1965.)

Thomas, William L., Jr.
1956   "Introductory" in William L. Thomas, Jr. (ed.), *Man's Role in Changing the Face of the Earth*. Chicago: University of Chicago Press.

Thomas, William L., Jr.
1956   *Man's Role in Changing the Face of the Earth*. Chicago: University of Chicago Press.

Thomlinson, Ralph.
1965   *Population Dynamics*. New York: Random House.

Thompson, L.
1949   "The Relations of Men, Animals and Plants in an Island Community (Fiji)," *American Anthropologist*, 51: 253–67.

Thompson, Warren S.
1929   "Population," *American Journal of Sociology*, 34: 959–75.

Tooker, Elizabeth (ed.).
1967   *Iroquois Culture, History and Prehistory: Proceedings of the 1965 Conference on Iroquois Research.* Rochester, N.Y.: State Museum.
Trigger, Bruce.
1972   "Determinants of Urban Growth in Pre-Industrial Societies" in Peter J. Ucko, Ruth Tringham, and G. W. Dimbleby (eds.), *Man, Settlement and Urbanism.* Cambridge: Schenkman.
Tringham, Ruth.
1973   *Ecology and Agricultural Settlements: An Ethnographic and Archeological Perspective.* Andover: Warner Modular Publication.
Tubbs, Colin R.
1969   *The New Forest: An Ecological History.* London: David and Charles-Newton Abbott.
Turnbull, Colin M.
1972   "Demography of Small-Scale Societies," in G. A. Harrison and J. A. Boyce, *The Structure of Human Populations.* Oxford: Clarendon Press.
Uberoi, J. P. Singh.
1962   *Politics of the Kula Ring: An Analysis of the Findings of Bronislaw Malinowski.* Manchester: Manchester University Press.
Ucko, P. J. and Dimbleby, G. W. (eds.).
1969   *The Domestication and Exploitation of Plants and Animals.* Chicago: Aldine.
Ucko, Peter J., Tringham, Ruth, and Dimbleby, G. W. (eds.)
1972   *Man, Settlement and Urbanism.* Cambridge: Schenkman.
Ulrich, Rudolph.
1953   "Relative Costs and Benefits of Land Reclamation in the Humid Southeast and the Semiarid West," *Journal of Farm Economics,* 35: 62–73.
Utton, Albert E. (ed.).
1973   *Pollution and International Boundaries: United States-Mexican Environmental Problems.* Albuquerque, University of New Mexico Press.
Van Dyne, George M. (ed.).
1969   *The Ecosystem Concept in Natural Resource Management.* New York: Academic Press.
Vayda, Andrew P.
1960   *Maori Warfare.* Polynesian Society Maori Monographs, No. 2. Wellington: Polynesian Society.
Vayda, Andrew P.
1961   "Expansion and Warfare among Swidden Agriculturalists," *American Anthropologist,* 63: 346–58.
Vayda, Andrew P.
1967   "Research on the Functions of Primitive War," *Peace Research Society (International) Papers,* 7: 133–38.
Vayda, Andrew P.
1969A   "An Ecological Approach in Cultural Anthropology," *Bucknell Review,* 17.
Vayda, Andrew P. (ed.).
1969B   *Environment and Cultural Behavior.* New York: Natural History Press.
Vayda, Andrew P.
1970   "Maoris and Muskets in New Zealand: Disruption of a War System," *Political Science Quarterly,* 85: 560–84.

Vayda, Andrew P.
1971   "Phases of the Process of War and Peace among the Marings of New Guinea," *Oceania*, 42: 1–24.
Vayda, Andrew P., Leeds, A., and Smith, D. B.
1961   "The Place of Pigs in Melanesian Subsistence," in V. Garfield (ed.), *Proceedings of the 1961 Annual Spring Meeting of the American Ethnological Society*. Seattle: University of Washington Press.
Vayda, Andrew P. and Rappaport, R. A.
1968   "Ecology: Cultural and Non-Cultural," in J. Clifton (ed.), *Introduction to Cultural Anthropology*. Boston: Houghton Mifflin.
Vernadsky, W. I.
1945   "The Noosphere," *American Scientist*, 33: 1–4.
Vidich, A. J. and Bensman, J.
1958   *Small Town in a Mass Society*. Princeton: Princeton University Press.
Waddell, Eric.
1972   *The Mound Builders: Agricultural Practices, Environment, and Society in the Central Highlands of New Guinea*. Seattle: University of Washington Press (American Ethnological Society).
Wagar, J. Alan.
1970   "Growth versus the Quality of Life," *Science*, 168: 1179–84.
Wagner, Philip L.
1960   *The Human Use of the Earth*. Glencoe: Free Press.
Wagner, Philip L. and Mikesell, Marvin W.
1962   *Readings in Cultural Geography*. Chicago: University of Chicago Press.
Wagner, Richard H.
1971   *Environment and Man*. New York: Norton.
Ward, James and Weiss, Brian.
1973   *The Turtle People*. (Ethnographic film.) Los Angeles: B and C Films.
Watanabe, M.
1974   "The Conception of Nature in Japanese Culture," *Science*, 183: 279–81.
Waterbolk, H. T.
1962   "The Lower Rhine Basin," in R. J. Braidwood and G. Willey (eds.), *Courses Toward Urban Life*. Viking Fund Publications in Anthropology, No. 32. New York: Wenner-Gren Foundation.
Watson, O. Michael.
1972   *Symbolic and Expressive Uses of Space: An Introduction to Proxemic Behavior*. An Addison-Wesley Module in Anthropology, No. 20. Reading, Mass.: Addison-Wesley.
Watson, Patty Jo, LeBlanc, Steven A., and Redman, Charles L.
1971   *Explanation in Archeology*. New York: Columbia University Press.
Watson, R. A. and Watson, P. J.
1969   *Man and Nature: An Anthropological Essay in Human Ecology*. New York: Harcourt, Brace and World.
Watters, R. F.
1971   *Shifting Cultivation in Latin America*. Rome: Food and Agriculture Organization of the United Nations.
Webb, W.
1931   *The Great Plains*. New York: Ginn.

Wedel, Waldo R.
1941   "Environment and Native Subsistence Economies in the Central Great Plains," in *Smithsonian Miscellaneous Collections*, Vol. 101, No. 3. Washington, D.C.: U.S. Government Printing Office.
Wedel, Waldo R.
1960   "The Central North American Grassland: Man-Made or Natural," in *Studies in Human Ecology*. Washington, D.C.: Pan American Union.
Weinberg, Alvin M. and Hammond, R. P.
1970   "Limits to the Use of Energy," *American Scientist*, 58: 412–18.
Weiner, Joseph S.
1972   "Tropical Ecology and Population Structure," in G. A. Harrison and J. A. Boyce, *The Structure of Human Populations*. Oxford: Clarendon Press.
Weisberg, Barry.
1972   *Beyond Repair: The Ecology of Capitalism*. Boston: Beacon Press.
Weisenfeld, Stephen L.
1967   "Sickle Cell Trait in Human Biological and Cultural Evolution," *Science*, 157: 1134–40.
Wells, P. V.
1969   "Postglacial Vegetational History of the Great Plains," *Science*, 167: 1574–81.
West, James (Carl Withers).
1945   *Plainville, U.S.A.* New York: Columbia University Press.
Westman, Walter E. and Clifford, R. M.
1973   "Environmental Impact: Controlling the Overall Level," *Science*, 181: 819–25.
White, Gilbert F.
1966   "Formation and Role of Public Attitudes," in H. Jarrett (ed.), *Environmental Quality in a Growing Economy*. Baltimore: Johns Hopkins Press for Resources for the Future.
White, Gilbert F.
1969   *Strategies of American Water Management*. Ann Arbor: University of Michigan Press.
White, Leslie A.
1948   "Man's Control over Civilization: An Anthropocentric Illusion," *Scientific Monthly*, 66: 235–47.
White, Leslie A.
1954   "The Energy Theory of Cultural Development," in K. M. Kapadia (ed.), *Professor Ghurye Felicitation Volume*. New Delhi.
White, Leslie A.
1959A   "Energy and Tools" in L. A. White, *The Evolution of Culture*. New York: McGraw-Hill.
White, Leslie A.
1959B   "Man and Culture" in L. A. White, *The Evolution of Culture*. New York: McGraw-Hill.
White, Lynn.
1967   "The Historical Roots of our Ecologic Crisis," *Science*, 155: 1203–1207.
Whitehead, Alfred North.
1951   *The Aims of Education*. New York: The New American Library.
Whitten, Norman.
1969   "Strategies of Adaptive Mobility in the Colombian-Ecuadorian Littoral," *American Anthropologist*, 71: 238–42.

Whitten, Norman and Whitten, Dorothea S.
  1972   "Social Strategies and Social Relationships," in Bernard Siegel (ed.), *Annual Review of Anthropology*, Vol. 1. Palo Alto: Annual Reviews.
Whitten, Norman and Wolfe, Alvin A.
  1972   "Network Analysis" in J. Honigmann (ed.), *Handbook of Social and Cultural Anthropology*. Chicago: Rand McNally.
Wiener, Norbert.
  1949   *Cybernetics, or Control and Communication in the Animals and the Machine.* Cambridge: Technology Press of MIT.
  Wiener, Norbert.
  1950   *The Human Use of Human Beings: Cybernetics and Society.* Boston: Houghton Mifflin. (2nd ed., Garden City: Doubleday, 1954.)
Wiens, John A. (ed.).
  1972   *Ecosystem Structure and Function.* Proceedings of the 31st Annual Biology Colloquium, Corvallis, Oregon, April 1970. Corvallis: Oregon State University Press.
Wildavsky, Aaron.
  1970   "Aesthetic Power, or the Triumph of the Sensitive Minority over the Vulgar Mass: A Political Analysis of the New Economics," in Roger Revelle and Hans H. Landsberg (eds.), *America's Changing Environment.* Boston: Beacon Press.
Wilkes, H. Garrison.
  1972   "Maize and its Wild Relatives." *Science*, 177: 1071–77.
Willhelm, Sidney M.
  1962   *Urban Zoning and Land-Use Theory.* Glencoe: Free Press.
Wilmsen, Edwin N.
  1972   "The Study of Exchange as Social Interaction" in Edwin N. Wilmsen (ed.), *Social Exchange and Interaction.* Museum of Anthropology, Anthropological Papers, No. 46. Ann Arbor: University of Michigan Press.
Wilson, Monica.
  1971   *Religion and the Transformation of Society: A Study in Social Change in Africa.* New York: Cambridge University Press.
Wissler, Clark.
  1926   *The Relation of Nature to Man in Aboriginal America.* New York: Oxford University Press.
Wissler, Clark.
  1936   *Population Changes among the Northern Plains Indians.* Yale University Publications in Anthropology, No. 1. New Haven: Yale University Press.
Wittfogel, Karl.
  1957   *Oriental Despotism: A Comparative Study of Total Power.* New Haven: Yale University Press.
Wohlwill, Joachim F. and Carson, Daniel H.
  1972   *Environment and the Social Sciences.* Washington, D.C.: American Psychological Association.
Wolf, E. R.
  1956   "Aspects of Group Relations in a Complex Society: Mexico," *American Anthropologist*, 58: 1065–1078.
Woodburn, James.
  1972   "Ecology, Nomadic Movement and the Composition of the Local Group among Hunters and Gatherers: An East African Example and Its Implications," in Peter

J. Ucko, Ruth Tringham, and G. W. Dimbleby (eds.), *Man, Settlement and Urbanism*. Cambridge: Schenkman.

Woodbury, Richard B. (ed.).
1962   *Civilizations in Desert Lands*. University of Utah Anthropological Papers, Number 62. Salt Lake City: University of Utah Press, December 1962.

Woodham-Smith, Cecil.
1962   *The Great Hunger*. New York: Harper & Row.

Woodwell, G. M.
1970   "Effects of Pollution on the Structure and Physiology of Ecosystems," *Science*, 168: 429–33.

Wynne-Edwards, V. C.
1962   *Animal Dispersion in Relation to Social Behavior*. New York: Hafner.

Yengoyan, Aram A.
1966   "Ecological Analysis and Agriculture," *Comparative Studies in Society and History*, 9: 105–17.

Yi-Fu Tuan.
1970   "Our Treatment of the Environment in Ideal and Actuality," *American Scientist*, 58: 244–49.

Zelinsky, Wilbur.
1973   *The Hypothesis of the Mobility Transition*. Andover: A Warner Modular Publication. (Reprinted from *The Geographical Review* 61, 1971.)

Zimmerman, Carle C.
1967   "The Great Plains as a Region," in Carle C. Zimmerman and Seth Russell (eds.), *Symposium on the Great Plains of North America*. Fargo, North Dakota: North Dakota State University Press.

Zipf, G. K.
1949   *Human Behaviour and the Principle of Least Effort: An Introduction to Human Ecology*. Cambridge: Addison-Wesley.

Zubrow, Ezra B. W.
1971   "Carrying Capacity and Dynamic Equilibrium in the Prehistoric Southwest," *American Antiquity*, 36: 125–26.

Index